NAVY GRAY

D0904316

MAXINE TURNER

NAVY GRAY

Engineering the Confederate Navy on the Chattahoochee and Apalachicola Rivers

MERCER UNIVERSITY PRESS
1979   1999
TWENTY YEARS OF PUBLISHING EXCELLENCE

ISBN 0-86554-642-8
MUP/P190

© 1999 Mercer University Press
6316 Peake Road
Macon, Georgia 31210-3960
All rights reserved

Original © 1988 by
The University of Alabama Press
Tuscaloosa, Alabama 35487
Second printing 1989.

This edition uses the original designed text by the University of Alabama Press
and is used with permission.

∞The paper used in this publication meets the minimum requirements of American
National Standard for Information Sciences—Permanence of Paper for Printed
Library Materials, ANSI Z39.48-1984.

Library of Congress Cataloging-in-Publication Data

Turner, Maxine Thompson. Navy gray.
"Sponsored by the Historic Chattahoochee Commission
and the James W. Woodruff, Jr. Confederate Naval Museum."
Bibliography; includes index.
1. Confederate States of America. Navy—History.
2. United States—History—Civil War, 1861-1865—Naval operations.
3. Chattahoochee River—History. 4. Apalachicola River (Fla)—History.
I. Historic Chattahoochee Commission. II. James W. Woodruff, Jr. Confederate
Museum. III. Title.
E596.T87   973.7'57   86-16047
ISBN 0-86554-642-8

FOR MY FATHER

Mack Thompson Turner

C O N T E N T S

PART FOUR
Last Stronghold of the Confederacy

Author's Note: The new subtitle *Engineering the Confederate Navy on the Chattahoochee and Apalachicola Rivers* reflects the presence of "the hidden *e*" in *Navy Gray*. My technical communication students and engineering colleagues at Georgia Tech introduced me to the hidden *e* as a way to explain the prevalence of engineering in our culture.

When the cruel necessities of war introduced the Industrial Revolution to the South, the Confederate Navy became noted for technical innovations. When the Union Blockade visited deprivation upon civilians, what money could no longer buy, mother wit earned by hard labor. Even if engineering is a contemporary word, innovation and mother wit are not anachronisms.

The fires that destroyed Columbus industries in 1865 still smoldered as citizens negotiated with their conquerors to rebuild; slaves who had worked building Confederate ships, returned to work as skilled freedmen earning good wages.

Thus the hidden *e*, while not universally perceived even today, left a permanent mark along the rivers of Navy Gray.

PREFACE

Navy Gray is a story that has developed within a community. Quite apart from the history it relates, the book has a history of its own.

Before the Historic Chattahoochee Commission approved the writing of the book in 1982, the history of the Confederate Navy on the Chattahoochee and Apalachicola rivers had already taken many forms. Steamboat captains told the history as a part of river lore as their craft steered clear of the wreck of the gunboat *Chattahoochee* at Race Pass; the burned-out hulk of the ironclad *Jackson* gave its name to Gunboat Pass on the Chattahoochee River. In Columbus, Georgia, the Columbus Iron Works continued to operate on the site of the Columbus Naval Iron Works, which had supplied machinery for a good portion of the Confederacy's ships. Many local historians dredged up bits and pieces of the naval history of the Chattahoochee country. Most people who live along the rivers have always known something of Civil War history there. *Navy Gray* draws many fragments of history together to create a story.

Douglas Clare Purcell, Executive Director of the Historic Chattahoochee Commission, convened a meeting in Columbus in 1982 to plan a new history. Those present represented a confluence of historical interests and personal involvements with the project.

Columbus historian Joseph M. Mahan was present, as he had been at meetings during the late 1950s and early 1960s when plans were made to salvage the *Chattahoochee* and *Jackson*. He had worked with a group of volunteer divers and boat owners to bring off the feat of raising the vessels and towing them to Columbus for display. The Army Corps of Engineers contributed to the effort, the state of Georgia voted funds, and local families like the Woodruffs shared in the project. At the time of the Civil War centennial, local interest and individual effort had played a major part in one of the earliest efforts to salvage a sunken Confederate vessel.

Janice Biggers of the Historic Columbus Foundation was also present at the 1982 meeting. She represented a large group of Columbusites who had seen Civil War–era houses in the historic district reclaimed. Both the Historic Columbus Foundation and the Columbus Consolidated Government had seen the Columbus Iron Works Convention and Trade

Center become an attraction to tourism and to industries surveying the area.

William N. Still, Jr., came to the meeting from the riverbank adjacent to the iron works, for underwater archaeologists from Eastern Carolina University were in Columbus that week to survey the river opposite where the *Jackson* had been constructed. When Still began his scholarship on the Confederate Navy in the late 1950s, he called on Miss Joan Warner, granddaughter of the commander of the Naval Iron Works, to gather the fragmentary sources that existed locally at that stage of this history.

Florence Foy Strang, of the Historic Chattahoochee Commission's Publications Committee, brought to bear her experience from other projects in hearing the group discuss the proposed book. Funded by Georgia and Alabama, the HCC has as one of its major tasks supporting publication of histories of the eighteen Georgia and Alabama counties in the Chattahoochee country. Books that she and Purcell helped to plan and publish were to contribute to this story.

By October 1982, A. Robert Holcombe had devoted eight years of his career to being Curator of the James W. Woodruff, Jr., Confederate Naval Museum in Columbus. He had overseen the technical work of preserving the gunboats and of identifying and displaying relics from the vessels. Even more important for the *Navy Gray* project, he had worked to make the museum a clearinghouse of information about the Confederate Navy. Still had contributed many of his research notes from Civil War manuscript collections, as had Steve Wise and Ralph Donnelly. Mahan and another local historian, John Lupold, had deposited their collections of notes and papers with the museum as well.

Other acquisitions included Lt. Augustus McLaughlin's log from the Confederate Navy Yard, Warner's mechanical drawings, and family memorabilia contributed by Miss Warner. As Columbus had been a center for Confederate naval construction, Holcombe worked to make the museum a center for preserving its navy history.

Most significant to the *Navy Gray* project was Holcombe's work of searching government collections and various naval history collections throughout the country. By 1982, this research had yielded many hundreds of vouchers that formed a detailed record of the Confederate Navy's activities in Columbus: acquisition and allocation of equipment and materials, travel, labor, transportation, and the like. A major contribution was locating Warner's letter book, which a Union naval lieutenant had carried to Buffalo, New York, following the war.

Purcell invited me to the meeting in my accustomed role as writer for a community project that had engaged my interests since 1955. My task was to take the consensus of the meeting and compose a book based on the museum's collection. In contrast to my first scholarly writing, when I had concentrated upon reading the basic chronology of this history into the record, I was given three specific tasks: to expand an earlier scholarly work on the topic, to use the museum's collection of sources, and to write a book for the general reader that would reflect larger aims of the Historic Chattahoochee Commission and the museum in their service to the community.

At that point in the evolution of *Navy Gray,* the subject of the project had already engaged me in writing of several different forms: an undergraduate paper at Huntingdon College in 1956; a master's thesis at Auburn in 1961; an expansion of that work for the *Alabama Historical Quarterly* in 1975; feature articles for the *Columbus Ledger-Enquirer* in 1975 and 1977; and even a poem in the *Humanities in the South* in 1979. I had researched the topic in the National Archives, the Library of Congress, the Maryland Historical Society, at local libraries in Columbus and Selma, and at the University of California at Berkeley. The Society for Technical Communication had credited my *AHQ* article in voting me senior member in 1980. Much of the material for *Navy Gray* would be new, but I had already spent much of my career with the topic.

In addition to general familiarity with the topic, I found three areas of experience exerting a very strong influence upon how I approached my assignment. Graduate study and many years of teaching literature influenced me to write *Navy Gray* as a narrative, rather than as formal historical exposition. I believe, quite simply, in the power of the story, not only to tell us what happened but to help us experience and understand history. Happening as it did in an age of diary keeping and letter writing, the Civil War produced many vignettes. And, like so many other Southerners, I first heard of the Civil War through stories of family members. Thus I have tried to draw this history to human scale, using not only the personal writings of the major characters but also characters and incidents from local histories and personal reminiscences of the Chattahoochee country. Whatever the range and sweep of major historical events, and whatever the larger issues of politics and economics, the Civil War carries in my imagination a terrible immediacy on a human and individual level.

In the 1975 *AHQ* article, I compared the tension and lack of action in naval operations along the rivers to "a cold war." Retracing my reading of the sources, particularly those related to the Union blockade of Apalachicola, suggested an even more contemporary parallel with Vietnam. Hence I use a number of words associated with that era: noncombatant, defense perimeter, search and destroy. These are meant to be descriptive terms, but they are also designed to trigger the reader's sense of men confronting national policy, local politics, tropical heat and disease, and faulty equipment—when what they had set out to do was fight and win a war.

A contemporary point of view also governs my treatment of the sources on the Confederate Navy Yard and the Columbus Naval Iron Works. Chapters 6, 7, and 8 of the book are based almost entirely upon hundreds of vouchers and one-sentence or one-paragraph business and technical letters. I brought to the processing of those sources several years of work as a teacher and consultant in technical writing, and I had already read and marked thousands of such documents in my daily work.

In one way, the mass of technical data created a rather uneventful history, especially as Civil War history. In another sense, engineers at any given time must command a massive amount of detail, even for a relatively small project. A shipment that is delayed for a day points up the critical interaction of various economic, technical, and human factors in any large project. If the price of copper rises fifteen cents per pound in any year, that is a noteworthy event to a project manager who oversees a budget. If such data constitute much of Chapters 6 and 7, such matters were nevertheless the daily concerns of the Confederate Navy in Columbus.

A forced march through the technical detail of constructing the *Jackson* and facilities to manufacture marine machinery can render a sense of the heroic efforts Warner and McLaughlin put forth. Certainly the record of their work resists any except the most practical workaday interpretation. Given my well nigh reverential respect for engineers, I regard that as a virtue of their story.

In such matters, then, as employing a narrative form, using a contemporary vocabulary, and filtering research sources through my own experience of working with engineers, I have claimed *Navy Gray* as my story to tell. At the same time, I have kept in mind the initial assignment to expand an earlier work; the new source material has changed no major conclusion in that work even if we know more of the details. Holcombe's work in collecting additional sources has made the critical difference in producing a new dimension in that history. And my imagination has returned again and again to the elusive "general reader" discussed in October 1982. If reading Civil War history can be a means for readers to escape day-to-day routine, *Navy Gray* more nearly shows that daily dramas of train schedules and cash flow problems are not limited to our day and time.

This history of *Navy Gray* cannot cite every individual contribution to a project that has continued now for more than thirty years. I must acknowledge, however, that Dean Les A. Karlovitz and Dr. A. D. Van Nostrand of Georgia Tech introduced me to a new dimension of this project—funding for research.

Finally, I would observe that my work here has not been that of a scholar who is isolated and apart from the community; rather, my writing has been the exercise of but one skill among many skills necessary to locate and salvage the gunboats, preserve them, display and explain relics, publicize the museum, solicit support from local government, and maintain funding sources to operate the museum. My assigned task has been to tell a story that speaks for the work of many people. The work of research and preservation continues. *Navy Gray* creates a fixed point, or an established event, in the history of a community's interest in its past. The project continues and remains focused on the future.

Author's Note: The future is now for Columbus's Civil War Naval Museum. By the time this edition of Navy Gray is released in early 1999, work will be underway to construct a state of the art museum fronting the Chattahoochee river just south of the museum's current site.

Friends of the Naval Museum led by Tom Gates have brought the project through the planning stage where new staff member Bruce Smith will continue the fund raising and construction phases. The museum will exhibit the past in the most futuristic ways.

PROLOGUE

The reader who enters the Civil War—whether through fiction or scholarly history—is engaged by a familiar, often-told story. The story always begins with the same issues: the bitter sectional and economic rivalries, the slavery question, the issue of the nature of union under the Constitution. No matter the variations of point of view and technique, historians must always allow for those constants.

The story of the Confederate Navy has been less often told than the spectacular history of the armies, but many of the familiar elements are there: the exuberant hopes of the Confederacy, the risks in spite of very long odds against success, the basic deficits in resources becoming desperate needs, and the dogged, exhausted persistence in the face of certain defeat.

If the naval heroes of the Civil War are not the towering figures of Grant and Lee, Sherman and Johnston, or Jackson, Sheridan, and Stuart, the history of the navies is no less a part of that story. The story is epic in its importance to a nation and a people. It is tragic by the definition of classical tragedy: "to reenact the thing lamented." And the Civil War touches the ancient human impulse to tell stories of "old, unhappy far-off things and battles long ago."

New strategies and developing technology, however, introduce new elements into this story of the Civil War. The Union Navy steamed in to blockade the small west Florida port of Apalachicola—but the officers and men were defeated at every turn by a national policy and a local tangle of political, economic, and social issues. Southern officers resigned their Union Navy commissions to fight for principle—and soon found themselves enmeshed in construction schedules and bureaucratic delays. All too often, naval officers on both sides found themselves engaged in what is now termed "modern warfare."

In this story of the Civil War, the phrase "arms and the man" begins to take on the contemporary ring of man and machine, and man within and against the system.

The Apalachicola–Chattahoochee River System

CHAPTER 1

History and the Rivers
The Confluence of Currents

Rivers dominate the geography of the South. From the James and the Rappahannock in Virginia, down the Atlantic coast past the Neuse, the Pee Dee, the Savannah, and around Florida past the St. Johns and the Hillsboro and farther past the Alabama, to the Mississippi and the Rio Grande—major features of Southern geography are these rivers and their ports: Newport News and Portsmouth, Wilmington, Charleston, Savannah, Jacksonville, Tampa, Mobile, New Orleans, Galveston.

For veterans of twentieth-century wars, these cities have been ports of call and ports of embarkation. For vacationers, an even longer list of names has peacetime associations: Santee, Pamlico, Murill's Inlet, Hilton Head, Darien, Fernandina. And, along the Gulf coast, Cedar Key, Sea Horse Key, Port St. Joe, Santa Rosa, Dauphin Island, Ship Island.

Ruins of a fortification and a historical marker, or a remembered history lesson here and there, recall such names as sites of Civil War action: the battle of the ironclads at Hampton Roads, the blockade runners that slipped out of Wilmington or in under the signal light of Fort Sumter, the ironclad *Savannah* and Admiral Farragut's words at Mobile Bay, "Damn the torpedos. Full speed ahead!"

Civil War history recalls, in turn, the economic significance of ports and shipping to the Old South. As the major agricultural area of the United States, the states that became the Confederacy were closely linked to the world market for raw materials and agricultural products. Those products were shipped out of Southern ports; then manufactured goods, household goods, luxury items, and industrial raw materials were shipped back.

The rivers, which had been the pathways of settlers moving inland, became avenues of commercial and economic development long before the advent of railroads. Rivers gave whole areas along the Atlantic coast

Lower Chattahoochee and Apalachicola river system in 1861
Drawn by Robert Holcombe, Curator, James W. Woodruff, Jr., Confederate
Naval Museum, Columbus, Ga.

the name "tidewater." Inland, the first settlements and then important towns grew up around portage points. This development was especially true where the fall line separated piedmont and coastal plain at Columbia, South Carolina; Augusta, Macon, and Columbus, Georgia; Montgomery, Alabama; and Meridian, Mississippi. At Columbus, where the Chattahoochee falls are the southernmost in the United States, water power supplied much of the drive for economic power.

The economics of Southern rivers became politics in a lengthy battle over the disruption of trade during the War of 1812; the conflict of economic interests continued through controversies over protective tariffs in the 1820s and 1830s. The issue of the slave trade, of slavery in new states and territories, and of the place of slavery in the Southern economy further enflamed the North-South conflict to the point of secession and Civil War.

Lincoln's proclamation of a blockade of Southern ports in April 1861 cast the economic significance of commerce in a new light; war translated economic importance into strategic significance. In economic terms, the Union blockade became a major component in an economic war against the Confederacy's ability to wage war. If the blockade could seal off ports and rivers, the Union could cut off the vital flow of agricultural products to Europe and the return of manufactured goods.

In a naval and military sense, the ports and rivers that had opened the South to commerce now opened it to attack. The rivers cut into the South like the spokes of a giant wheel, not only along the coast, but inland along the Tennessee River system as well. Any navigable system of tributaries cut deeply inward toward the most significant military objectives. Today, strategists might account little importance to the Apalachicola in Florida, the Chattahoochee in Georgia, the Tombigbee in Alabama, or the Yazoo and Arkansas off the Mississippi; yet operations on such rivers during the Civil War called forth great ingenuity from the Confederates and created serious concerns for the Union Navy.

The Apalachicola–Chattahoochee river system was a significant economic and strategic area in 1861. Cutting southward through northwest Florida, west Georgia, and east Alabama, this system was one spoke in the wheel described by Southern rivers. Columbus at the head of navigation was the hub; Apalachicola, just more than three hundred miles to the south, was the port at the end of the spoke; and St. Vincent's, St. George's, and Dog islands rimmed the coast just beyond the port. On June 11, 1861, two months after the blockade proclamation, the Union steamer *Montgomery* stood outside West Pass between St. George's and St. Vincent's islands, and a cutter crossed the shallow bar to the town wharf. The Union naval commander who read the blockade proclamation translated the economic importance of the river system into the strategy of war.[1]

When the Apalachicola–Chattahoochee river system became an area of strategic interest to the Union in 1861, it had already caused economic rivalry and military conflict. Hardly more than thirty years had passed since the end of the Indian wars opened that territory to extensive settlement. Acts of the Georgia and Florida legislatures in 1828 had designated Columbus and Apalachicola as trading centers at both extremes of the river system. At the time of the Civil War, fresh evidence still remained of the actions that had displaced the Indians to open the area for sustained and systematic development by white settlers. Eighteenth-century struggles of the British, French, and Spanish had occurred in the area; and seventeenth-century missionaries and the sixteenth-century explorer Hernando DeSoto had visited the area.[2]

In the 1820s, the Chattahoochee River formed the western boundary of the frontier. A circuit rider writing of the trading post at Columbus described Indians across the river engaged in a spirited ball game like lacrosse. The choice of some early settlers like Dr. S. M. Ingersoll to cross the river to what is now Russell County, Alabama, was a move to a raw frontier.[3] In 1861, much evidence remained of the Indian influence and of the military actions that had displaced it.

Fort Mitchell south of Columbus was a remnant of the Indian wars. Confederate soldiers inducted and shipped out from that site walked over pottery fragments and Fourth Infantry Regiment buttons from 1825.[4] The same was true at Fort Gadsden where the Confederates placed a battery near Apalachicola. Maj. Gen. Andrew Jackson had called for a report on its fortification and the defense of the surrounding coast in 1818; Capt. James Gadsden's reply included many features cited by Confederate engineers in the 1860s and concluded on an especially important point about fortifying Apalachicola: "as giving security to an extensive and rich back country the valuable qualities of the soil of which will at no distant period invite populous settlement."[5] A widow's walk atop one of the oldest houses in Apalachicola served a dual purpose that embodied the area's history: to look out to sea, reflecting the area's commercial future, and to watch up the river for any remnants of attacking Indians.[6]

Thus Confederate fortifications and batteries were at first constructed upon an earlier stratum of the military history of the area.
Officers at the time remembered Andrew Jackson and spoke of "our last
war with Great Britain" (1812) much as people in the 1980s speak of
World War I.[7] As a small boy living near Mobile, Stephen R. Mallory had
seen Jackson and his men ride by.[8] Noting the graves of some of Andrew
Jackson's soldiers at Chattahoochee, Florida, at the confluence of the
Chattahoochee and Flint rivers, Confederate Lt. George W. Gift referred to events of recent history as one might view World War II relics
in the 1980s.[9] Less than twenty years before, troops from Columbus had
shipped out of Apalachicola for Texas and the Mexican War.[10]

Despite the history of earlier wars, the only military installation along
the rivers was the U.S. Arsenal at Chattahoochee, Florida. Constructed between 1832 and 1840 during the Indian wars, the arsenal had
passed in and out of use as an obscure post in the 1840s and 1850s. Its
military presence served mainly as a point of contrast to the predominant economic interests flowing past it to Apalachicola, Albany, or Columbus.

The Flow of Commerce: Apalachicola

As Union naval strategists began laying plans to carry out Lincoln's
blockade policy in 1861, they were aware of the economic importance of
the area depicted on their maps of Georgia and Alabama and illustrated
in the coast survey of west Florida. They might have divided their
objective into three parts: the commercial importance of Apalachicola
and its link to the sea; the industrial importance of Columbus, Georgia,
and its rail connections to the northern Confederacy; and the agricultural importance of lands that lay along the rivers between those two
points.

A coast survey of west Florida showed numerous creeks and inlets
from Tampa to Mobile. To the west of Apalachicola, Santa Rosa Island
formed a narrow barrier opposite Pensacola. Sixty miles to the east, St.
Mark's stood at the mouth of the St. Mark's River and was linked by
eighteen miles of railroad to the state capital at Tallahassee. Union
planners could see four islands creating a semicircle to enclose Apalachicola Bay.

A large river, a roadstead sheltered by islands, and four entryways into the bay appear on a chart as ideal features for shipping and commerce. Looking further to the soundings data changes that picture, even today. Steering toward Apalachicola reveals very shallow water in much of the bay, sandbars, and a constant shifting of sand spits and islets. Near the city itself, the Apalachicola River carries silt and debris in a steady stream. Union seamen quickly learned in 1861 that Apalachicola was best approached with caution.

From the 1830s, seagoing vessels had overcome such obstacles in maintaining regular schedules from Apalachicola to Key West and Havana, to New York, and to English and European ports. Very large vessels were a rarity, but schooners, barks, and brigs functioned well in the approaches to the port.[11] Lighters transferred cargo from heavy-draft vessels at East Pass for the remaining twelve miles to the wharves.[12] A thriving coastal trade also carried cargo and passengers from Apalachicola to Pensacola, Mobile, and New Orleans. Experienced coastal and harbor pilots could steer such shallow-draft vessels with sufficient ease to maintain regular contacts along the Gulf coast.

This commercial activity made Apalachicola especially important within the overall blockade strategy once the Civil War began. At a time when Tampa's population was 885, Apalachicola was one of only nine Florida towns with a population of more than 1,000.[13] The 1860 census bears out the importance of the rivers and sea in Apalachicola's growth. Such occupations as engineer, steamboat clerk, steamboat master, stevedore, lightman, tide gauger, and pilot predominate. Such jobs in the port had drawn most of its population from elsewhere: England, Ireland, Scotland, Germany, Denmark, and, among the oystermen and fishermen, Italy, Sicily, and Portugal.[14]

Seasonal commerce gave Apalachicola an unstable population, for many who did business there had their primary residences elsewhere. Cotton brokers, corn merchants, and agents might spend only the fall and winter months in Apalachicola. Places north on the river or north as far as New York and New Jersey were their permanent homes. During the trading season, the five hotels of the town became centers of the affluent life they lived. Steamers shipped in fine wines, and there was wild game on the hotel menus, as well as Apalachicola oysters.

The economic activity rose and fell with the river, however. As reported in the Apalachicola newspaper in November 1844: "The river is riz—the boat bells are ringing, ships are loading, draymen swearing, negroes singing, clerks marking, captains busy, merchants selling, packages rolling, boxes rumbling, wares rumbling, and everybody appears to be up to his eyes in business."[15]

In contrast, the summer months of the growing season and low water on the rivers were a time when the commercial population sought other, cooler climates. As an Apalachicola editor described the change: "We are at length reduced to our summer population and in place of the business crowd, and the noise and bustle that surrounded us a few weeks ago we scarcely see a lounger on our streets, and all is comparatively quiet."[16]

The blockade would make that scene, and worse, a condition of life in the port for the duration of the war.

The Flow of Industry: Columbus

As important as Apalachicola was to Union strategists, the port owed its existence to agricultural and industrial products shipped downriver and cargoes shipped north along the river system. Columbus, Georgia, was both the head of navigation and the economic headwaters of the entire area. In 1860, it was already a nucleus for the industrial center it was to become during the Civil War. Called "the Lowell of the South" because of its mills, it was, next to Richmond, the most industrialized city of the Confederacy.

The cotton industry drew population into Columbus when people from the surrounding rural counties of Georgia and Alabama left the farm to work long hours for small wages in the cotton and woolen mills.[17] In turn, machinists and engineers were drawn to these industries from more industrialized areas: Maryland, New Jersey, New York, Connecticut, and England. Half, or more, of such workers listed in the 1850 census were born outside the South.[18]

Because rivers provided the chief means of transportation for cotton and finished cotton goods, a thriving industry grew up around the construction, maintenance, and operation of steamboats. William R. Brown's Columbus Iron Works constructed engines and boilers and supplied fittings for river steamers. Charles Blain, who arrived from Delaware via Apalachicola in 1834, became first a carpenter and finally a boat captain by 1860. Samuel J. Whiteside and Harry Hall emigrated from New York to the steamboat industry in Columbus. Birthplaces of other Columbus residents show many ports of call: ports along the northern coast of the United States, inland ports along the rivers of Ohio and Pennsylvania, and distant points like Liverpool and Calcutta. These manpower resources were noted by the Union, but they stood even higher on Confederate inventories as the Civil War began.

Opposite Columbus was Girard, Alabama, a short drive across the Chattahoochee on the bridge that was constructed in 1832 by John Godwin and his slave, Horace King. As its modern counterpart Phenix City was to do, Girard supplied workers to Columbus mills. Still sparsely populated because of more recent Indian settlement and ownership, surrounding Russell County had rich timber resources that were to become essential to Confederate naval construction.[19]

The Columbus city directory of 1859–60 shows a prosperous and varied economy. The eight cotton brokers and six banking agents are measures of the importance of commerce. A more pervasive commercial influence is shown in the advertisements of various merchants: Havana cigars at Jose Mir and Company, canes with sterling or ivory heads at Thomas S. Spear's jewelry store, "New York and Philadelphia celebrated Trotting Buggies" at H. C. McKee's Carriage Repository, fine china and glassware at Cowdery and Company, stereoscopes and views and "pictures of all styles on exhibition" at G. J. Williams's "Gallery." William H. Phelps advertised "foreign and domestic fruits"; sardines, lobsters, salmon; and "ICE always on hand (in season)." Thomas Kenny's Marble and Granite Works offered fine Italian marble, the Smith and Daniel Shoe Emporium stocked French calfskin, Barringer and Morton Steam Manufactory could fit wooden sashes with French or German plate glass, and W. K. Harris's novelty works offered furniture in mahogany and rosewood.

Items more necessary for life and the conduct of business were also shipped to Columbus. A. C. Saunders and Company advertised "Negro Brogans" to supply laborers with the heavy shoes they needed for outdoor work. "TO COUNTRY MERCHANTS," the ad read, "we offer goods at New York prices and by giving us a call you can save 15 to 20 percent." Across the page is an ad for machine belting from Sherman and Company; just above that is D. B. Thompson's ad for pumps, patterns, lead and iron pipe. John J. McKendree offered bagging, rope, and twine; druggists and chemists Acree and Iverson advertised themselves as dealers in "foreign and domestic drugs, medicines, chemicals, acids."

As the blockade closed in on the Southern coast, all such items would be transferred to the growing list of scarcities. Even those who responded to the ads for insurance with companies in Hartford, New Haven, and New York would find themselves caught short by the changes brought on by the war.

Druggists Urquhart and Chapman played upon the growing war sentiments with an ad that announced

WAR! WAR!
is declared against
PAINS OF ANY KIND
By Dr. A. W. Allen's
SOUTHERN LINIMENT
And every Southerner will be satisfied by using
ONE DOLLAR'S WORTH
that they have no further use for Northern liniments.

Also for sale in Bainbridge by D. J. Dickinson and Company and E. R. Peabody and Company, the liniment was said to cure "Rheumatisms, Neuralgia, Strains, Burns, Bruises, Fresh Cuts, Pains in the Back or Limbs, Colic in Man or Beast, and Blind Staggers in Horses."[20]

Whether or not readers of the Columbus city directory laid in a large supply as Dr. Allen advised, the hardships of war would bring on all such frailties of human and horse flesh.

Currents of Custom and Circumstance: Life Along the Rivers

As Union blockading vessels kept their stations off Apalachicola for four years, they tried to piece together a coherent picture of life beyond the port and northward along the rivers. Lacking the tools of census records and commercial directories, they engaged in what naval officers of today would call "intelligence gathering." A Confederate deserter might come aboard a Union ship and give an inventory of troop strength at the Chattahoochee Arsenal or at Fort Gadsden. An industrial worker might return from Columbus to his home in Apalachicola with intelligence about industrial output at the Confederate Navy Yard or the Columbus Naval Iron Works. Escaped slaves, or "contrabands" as they were called, supplied a picture of life in a rich economic area the Union planned to shut down as a part of its strategy. The people of Apalachicola came and went freely from the blockading vessels; and, from time to time, the Union officers were able to ship on board a much-prized pilot who knew the treacherous waters on their station.

Cruising or riding at anchor outside Apalachicola Bay in their heavy-draft vessels, the blockaders were unable to steer their heavy ships into the bay and up the rivers. For any craft, river travel was hazardous at any season. A steamer that drew five or six feet was in peril of low water during the summer months; snags might rip the hull or a craft might founder helplessly on a sandbar. High water was as great a peril as low when driftwood and debris churned along the river current with the boats.[21]

Just north of Apalachicola, the Apalachicola River was navigable near the coast. Before a boat reached Chattahoochee, Florida, however, there was a series of bends for several miles called the Narrows. At Chattahoochee where the Flint River branched north to Bainbridge and Albany, Georgia, travel became even more perilous; the Flint was more winding, the channel narrower, and the water levels even less reliable than they were on the Chattahoochee. Steamers like the *Munnerlyn* had to be specially designed for the Flint; another steamer was much prized for its ability to carry a thousand bales of cotton in four feet of water. Sometimes, crude rafts called "boxes" were used to float cotton downriver to Apalachicola.[22] Union captains gathered such data and despaired.

Along the Chattahoochee River north of Chattahoochee, Florida, steamers met with continued perils in high water or low; in the still relatively undeveloped area of steam technology, there were the added risks of fires and boiler explosions. But the commercial investors of the area factored in those risks. If the river was too high to pass under a bridge, a captain and pilot might steer around it through flooded fields. If the river might rise and flood stores of cotton awaiting shipment, multistory warehouses were built so that the cotton could be moved to higher floors. Passengers took their chances in such a transportation system—to the considerable consternation of an English governess who found herself pushed, part lifted, and part dragged up the muddy river-bank to dry land in Eufaula, Alabama.[23]

The Union blockaders heard stories of river travel; and officers eager for action kept up a steady flow of reports about how they might set out from Apalachicola, ascend the rivers, and capture Columbus. But for those who lived north of the port, neither the blockade nor the necessity to run it introduced the first risks into the river system. Vagaries of tide, weather, and water levels had always been constants along the commercial wharves of Apalachicola and at the plantation landings where people listened for the steamboat whistle. The blockade became but one more risk in a system where men already took long chances.

The Union officers readily understood such strategic factors as the commercial importance of Apalachicola and the industrial importance of Columbus. Numbers of vessels clearing the port, numbers of steamers making the voyage from Columbus with numbers of bales of cotton or finished goods from its factories—these were quantifiable measures of life along the rivers. Beyond that, the Union knew that the entire economy depended upon the plantation system to produce such wealth. They knew that the system rested upon the peculiar institution of slavery, and they knew that was wrong. What they could not factor into the economic and strategic assessments of the blockade was how tenaciously the people in the plantation system would endure a blockade of the port and the rivers.

Somewhere to the north along vast, seemingly unpopulated stretches of the rivers rested the heart of the system. The plantation was the basic economic component: geographically isolated, self-sufficient, but bound economically to the geography of river and sea.

In 1860, the plantations were neither industries nor an extensive labor pool for industries, but their operation had always required a whole range of skilled workers. They would become another part of the labor pool for Confederate industry in Columbus. Where land transportation was by horse, mule, or ox, a whole cluster of skills collected around the maintenance of that kind of transportation: husbandry of the animals themselves; tanners, saddlers, and harness makers; blacksmiths to keep the horses and mules shod; wagon makers and wheelwrights; wagoners, draymen, and livery stable operators.

On a plantation, mechanics were needed to construct cotton gins, gristmills, cane mills, and sawing operations and to keep them in operation. Coopers supplied barrels for meal and flour, syrup, and turpentine. Well diggers and pump makers also had specialized skills.

The Union officers who destroyed salt-making operations on the Gulf Coast and a twentieth-century historian who wrote about them marveled that they might damage utensils and turn their howitzers on a large iron vat one week only to see the saltworks back in operation the next.[24]

Neither the records nor the commentary fully account for the necessities of plantation life when people with multiple skills had to exercise constant effort to keep common farm implements in operation. It was a rare plantation that did not have a forge, nor was basic skill limited to blacksmiths by trade. Cast-iron kitchen implements and vessels, wash pots, scalding vats for slaughtered animals in meat processing, syrup pans for making syrup and sugar—a whole array of such containers had to be kept in good repair on a working plantation. So also with knives and scissors (likely to be among the most carefully kept of all implements), hoes and rakes, scythes, plows, and all such implements in this *omnia opera* of tasks that made a sparse population "men of all work."

Taken together, the skills necessary to run a self-contained economic unit kept the plantations isolated. As the Civil War began, the available resources of skilled labor in the river system were a mere handful compared to an industrial center like Columbus or to an industrialized Northern city. But these skills in wartime were sufficient to aid the Confederates along the river and, perhaps more important, to sustain the population through four years of the Union blockade.

Many in the population were, after all, but a generation away from the most primitive frontier conditions. Small farmers still lived on the edge of survival. If children needed clothing, cotton was planted, picked, carded, spun, woven into cloth, cut, and sewn by hand. If there was food, the general population cleared new ground, planted a garden, and harvested and then preserved the food. If there was sugar and flour—and if the hens laid—there were cakes. If not, there were not. If a family needed a house, the community gathered to cut and trim the trees, roll the logs until they were free of bark, notch and peg the logs, and in a sustained and Herculean labor, erect a house.[25]

Such inventories and stories the romances often omit, but the people who lived on the land along the rivers were called "hard timey" people, lower-class whites who lived by the natural law of "root hog or die poor." The coming of war was but another increment of difficulty in a life that was already a battle to survive and prosper. Men fit for that life were fit for the work of hoisting heavy timbers and even heavier cannon onto gunboats.

Reflecting more traditional concepts of antebellum life, contemporary accounts of life along the river, as well as later reminiscences, rival the romantic fictions of the Civil War.

In Eufaula, banker John McNabb epitomized what wealth along the river could create. He and his family traveled abroad each year. At home, they rode in a silver-mounted closed carriage, they wore Irish linen, Scottish tweeds and shawls, and drank Chinese tea—all imported.[26] Shipping along the river from Apalachicola gave access to more elegant accoutrements from Europe and England: brass fittings, chandeliers, and door hardware. As one family found in the 1960s when they began the tedious work of paint stripping on a family home in Eufaula, lock plates were sterling silver. During the war, many metal fittings from such homes found their way to foundries to aid the cause of preserving that way of life.

A similar pattern of life was repeated at other plantations along the Chattahoochee River in Georgia. Before the blockade had worked its effects upon plantation life, Confederate Navy Lt. George Gift was invited into the life of "The Pines" from his duty station at Saffold in Early County, Georgia. He writes of arriving on horseback at dusk, of being ushered to a room where a body servant prepared his bath and laid out fresh linen and his uniform. Downstairs, candles and an open fire illuminated a large room with French windows opening onto a verandah. There were comfortable chairs, tables for reading by lamplight, a secretary for writing, a piano piled high with music. At a dinner table laid with the finest silver, china, and crystal, he was stimulated by the cross fire of conversation among Shackelford family members and their guests from Virginia and Charleston. Although he was a naval officer who had, by then, a far-reaching experience of the world, life on the river left him thoroughly impressed.[27]

The Shackelfords of "The Pines" on the Chattahoochee and the Munnerlyns of "The Refuge" on the Flint River figure prominently in this story of the navies along the river. If the antebellum South prided itself upon its culture and society, and if "way of life" became a code phrase for an economy based upon slavery, then these wealthy and influential families embody both the ideals and the underlying political and economic interests associated with the Civil War.

The Munnerlyns lived on the Flint River near Bainbridge, across the triangle created by the path of the Chattahoochee and Flint rivers through southwest Georgia. When Gift visited the Munnerlyns' "The Refuge," he noted the lovely mansion set in an English garden on a plantation covering thousands of acres. The house was presided over by the elder Shackelford sister, Eugenia, of whom it was written that "Mrs. Munnerlyn is a rare person; highly cultivated, with a grace and manner peculiarly her own—her intimates call her 'the Empress.'"[28]

Such monied and powerful families very often maintained homes in more than one location or held extensive land holdings elsewhere. Governor John Milton of Florida was said to have owned 14,000 acres near his Sylvania plantation and thousands more in Georgia and Texas.[29] The Saffold family was another example, particularly a son-in-law, David S. Johnston, the wartime entrepreneur who built the gunboat *Chattahoochee*. He had lived his early life in Madison, Georgia, a cultural center of the times. To the advantages of birth and education he added the advantage of marrying well, for Anne Saffold was a woman of similar background. As was characteristic of a man of his time and place, he had diversified financial interests in farms and timberland throughout the region.[30]

The same was true of Howell Cobb, who would become a Confederate Army general and commander of the area drained by the lower Flint and Chattahoochee rivers. Cobb's wartime letters from his son refer to farming interests in Sumter, Worth, Bibb, and Baldwin counties. To manage such extensive holdings, the younger Cobb refers to work that required moving herds of fattening hogs from one plantation to the other, thousands of bushels of corn, tens of thousands of pounds of fodder, and the transportation of slaves from one point to another—along with providing adequate clothing for this work force and even dealing with an outbreak of measles.[31] Such families were likened to seasonal birds who wintered along the Chattahoochee and Flint rivers and along Spring Creek during hog-killing and cotton-shipping season. Once hot weather brought fever and summer chills, they were off once more to cooler climates.

Remembering his days as an overseer in Early County before the war, W. H. Andrews wrote to the *Early County News* in 1916: "There was a friendly rivalry among the overseers to see who could have the best regulated farms and produce the most corn and cotton to the acre. To a man who loved farming it was a treat to ride over one of those plantations during the growing season and especially in July, when the corn and cotton had matured."[32]

But there was a darker underside to that life. Andrews speaks off-handedly of patrols to hunt escaped slaves. Citing his reason and sense of fairness as an overseer, he remarks that he would never allow a black foreman to flog a hoehand or a plowhand—"except in my presence." To geographic isolation, and the insular quality of money and power, was added an ideological isolation from how the rest of the country held different values and lived different lives.

In rural Barbour County, John Horry Dent owned and managed—and kept meticulous records of—a large plantation, practicing agribusiness nineteenth-century style. The business of such men was business; when the Civil War came, it was speeches and political theory, but it was business as well.[33]

If the size of plantations served to separate one small community from another, river travel served to create ties between them. The families were close-knit despite the distances. The ritual of the visit bound such families together socially and in times of trouble and sorrow; sometimes out of the visits grew romances and marriages that bound their interests even more closely. From the visit, when it was not unusual for someone to pack a trunk and spend a month with a cousin across state, grew more extended travels.

These customs seemed remarkable to Catherine Hopley, an English governess employed to teach Florida Governor Milton's ten children. As she labored to establish some kind of order in their daily activities, the dark-eyed young ladies were operating in another system entirely.

> Such were my pupils in Florida; not only the Governor's daughters, but sundry cousins who dropped in . . . in the course of the next month, to join the others in their studies.
>
> [As] two or three vanished, . . . two or three more appeared; the carriage was going and returning continually, bringing and fetching young ladies; and though no one thought it necessary to tell me what was going on, I found that they were exchanging visits with other young ladies in the neighbourhood; going to stay for a day and a night, and bringing home friends who in their turn spent a day and a night, and again carried off another pair of black eyes.[34]

The way of life maintained along the rivers especially influenced education. Until after the Civil War, the area bordering the Chattahoochee knew no widespread establishment of tax-supported schools for the upper classes. The river separated the school-age population on the plantations; for the lower classes agriculture left little time for schooling.[35]

Most larger plantations had tutors or governesses, both because of the affluence of the families and because of the great distances children would have had to travel to centralized schools. Sometimes a family would send a child to a relative's home where there was a tutor or, in the case of eleven-year-old Charles Munnerlyn, where he could be taught by his older Shackelford aunts at "The Pines": "We all have commenced our studies to day & have fixed up stairs for a schoolroom. Aunt Georgia heard our History lesson & Aunt Hannah attended to our writing lesson. I am going to try & be a good boy & behave my self well, & study hard."[36]

Among the general population, children typically were occupied with chopping and hoeing cotton in the spring and early summer and picking cotton and pulling corn in the fall. This schedule left only the winter months when whites were free to attend school. Slaves were, of course, denied education by custom and law.

In a society strictly divided between the leisure class and a laboring class, there was no lack of leisure activities. There was horse racing, boating on the river, picnics—and always, the visit.

While the leisured and educated class set great value upon the ability to afford such activities, an equal or greater value was placed upon the skills that made education and culture available. A man like Johnston might have held a law degree, but his ability to organize a work force and construct a gunboat—when he'd never seen a boat built before—lent him stature. A man like McNabb might have flaunted his wealth, but under wartime conditions he had the savvy to slip through the blockade to preserve it. Dent might practice sketches in his journal and reflect upon his reading, but he also had the practical grasp of economics and agriculture to salvage his holdings from the Civil War. These planters may have seemed isolated and inbred, living in the closed and harmonious system of their own way of life; but their fortunes rose and fell on a world commodities market for cotton, and Northern industry supplied the machine components of their agribusiness. They had both the financial means and the financial reasons to seek stronger and more efficient transportation ties to a larger world beyond the rivers.

Railroads: The New Tributaries

The blockade and wartime conditions to come would threaten life along the rivers. Blockade the port, restrict river travel, and much of the familiar, privileged life of the Shackelfords, Munnerlyns, Saffolds,

Dents, Cobbs, and Johnstons of the South was choked off as well. But before 1860, contemporary accounts bespeak a population that could be, and was, mobile enough to maintain contacts far beyond the seemingly isolated towns and plantations along the Chattahoochee River.

Money derived from land and slave labor gave planters control over their lives and fortunes. Their lives were subject to the forces of nature—summer drought and low water that hampered travel on the river, floods in the winter and early spring—but they were nevertheless men who mastered their environment. Their fortunes enabled them to move easily beyond the isolation of their plantation homes. Rail travel could extend the ritual of the visit to even more distant family connections and to even more interesting sights.

Detailed travel accounts are contained in John Horry Dent's journals as a record of times, distances, and modes of travel whereby members of the affluent class were carried on business or by personal concerns throughout the South and along the East Coast. A journey that Dent made to Vermont required him to leave his home near Eufaula, Alabama, on a Thursday evening. He arrived in Columbus by 9 o'clock the next morning and, setting out on a journey Confederate Navy men would make countless times, departed by train for Macon at 4:15, arrived there at 9 P.M., changed to a train for Savannah at 9:30, and arrived there the following morning at 7:30.

Following another series of steamer, ferry, omnibus, and train connections, Dent arrived in Vermont—after a week in transit in more modern accommodations and at greater speed than travel by carriage would have made possible. After what most contemporary travelers would consider an ordeal, Dent remarks only, "Left [the Richmond depot] immediately for [his wife's] Fathers residence, where I needed rest and repose after so long and tiresome a journey." On his return to Alabama, Dent experienced an even longer series of detours and delays. Stopping over in New York, he "went out to the Navy Yard" August 27 to see the steam frigate *Niagara* under construction.[37] In May 1861, the vessel would become flagship to the squadron that established the blockade of the river which flowed near Dent's plantation.[38] During the war, it was the railroad that would rescue the area from complete isolation imposed by the blockade.

Perhaps that is one of the reasons that the new power of railroad technology interested men like Dent. More rapid, less subject to the ebb and flow of river and tide, the railroad could be directed by capital in a more direct line to the destination of their money crop and their own travel.

A line that a group of Russell County entrepreneurs planned as early as the 1840s would link the easternmost town in Alabama to its large port on the Gulf of Mexico. During the 1840s and mid-1850s, S. M. Ingersoll, John Godwin, and Robert S. Hardaway were among the group who moved construction in that direction. Antoinette Hague, a governess en route west from Girard to Hurtville, described the land along the Mobile and Girard: "tall, long-leaved pines and funereal cypress-trees rising here and there on either side" and "the dark green gloom of almost unbroken forests" before "the train gathered itself up in the village of Hurtville."[39]

The men who conceived the railroad's importance did not always look further to a single coordinated system of rail transportation. Montgomery and Atlanta were linked by rail, but the gauge changed at West Point, Georgia, where one company's line ended and another's began. A line that terminated at Macon or Augusta made transfer to another line's depot necessary as travelers continued on their journey. Albany investors, hoping to overcome the vagaries of river travel to Apalachicola along the Flint River, began in the 1820s to lay one line after another. One reached north as far as Americus, another reached Macon, a third stretched almost as far as Brunswick, a fourth almost to the Florida state line, and still another to a dead end at Fort Gaines on the Chattahoochee.[40]

Despite the lack of coordination within the rail system, the railroads served the immediate needs of the area. The new technology was forward looking and a source of great civic pride as well. Combined with river ports at Columbus, Montgomery, Macon, and Augusta, this system sufficed before the war. But this loose confederation of local lines would become badly overtaxed by the war.

New Currents Along the Rivers: Secession and Civil War

For the men who had shaped plantations and riverboats and factories and railroads, it must have been difficult to conceive that the wealth the land produced could be shut down, the river closed off, factories converted to war production, and the railroad converted to an essential component of military rather than economic strategy. As national politics and economics advanced them toward war, they had already won too much to consider the possibility of defeat.

In 1860, as was the custom in an affluent, closely knit planter class, visits and parties made Christmas a joyous time. To the visits and caroling and egg nog parties that year was added the secession party. South Carolina had seceded on December 19; on Christmas Eve came a call for delegates to be elected to the Alabama secession convention set to meet January 7. Anticipation set people to singing "We Conquer or Die." John Horry Dent wrote of escorting his Vermont and abolitionist wife to a secession party in Eufaula at the home of Lewis Lewellen Cato, a radical secessionist.[41] Another Eufaula diarist, Mrs. G. H. Rhodes, recorded the celebration that secession news evoked:

> There was never such a time in Eufaula as that night, a gala night, with the booming of cannon in our ears. Flags were floating in the breeze in all directions and everybody prepared for the great illumination. The most gloriously magnificent sight I ever beheld. Almost every home appeared as if studded with diamonds in a glorious sunlight, so brilliant were the bonfires. Each of the military companies were out.[42]

As Christmas passed and the South rang out the old year, events continued to move swiftly: Alabama and Florida seceded on January 10, Georgia on January 19; on February 4 the Confederacy adopted a constitution. On February 9, Jefferson Davis was elected Confederate president; February 12 the Eufaula Rifles left; February 18 Davis was inaugurated. By April the blockade was proclaimed; by April 12 the firing on Fort Sumter brought war.

An incident that occurred early in the new year in Chattahoochee, Florida, might have gone unnoticed among the speech making, flag waving, and reading of dispatches from Montgomery and Charleston. Secessionist tensions of 1860 had led Florida Senators David L. Yulee and Stephen R. Mallory to inquire of Acting Secretary of War Joseph Holt about Florida ordnance stores and installations. The senators wrote on January 2; Holt had a report dated January 3 from his captain in charge of ordnance, but his January 9 reply withheld the intelligence requested: "the interests of the service forbid that the information you ask should be made public."[43]

Holt's evasive maneuver turned out to be three days too late, for Yulee and Florida Governor M. S. Perry had already ordered action. Yulee wrote Joseph Finegan at Tallahassee: "The arsenal at Chattahoochee should be looked to, and that at once, to prevent removal of arms." About the same time, Governor Perry ordered the Quincy militia to seize the Chattahoochee Arsenal.[44]

At 7 A.M., January 6, 1861, the Florida militiamen entered the arsenal held by U.S. Ordnance Sgt. Edwin Powell and a force of two men. Sergeant Powell at first stood his ground, telegraphing the ordnance chief: "The arsenal has been taken possession of by the state this morning, 7 o'clock. I have refused keys of magazine and armory. Answer, with instructions." Newspapers quoted Powell's statement to Colonel Duryea: "If I had had a force equal or even one-half the strength of yours, I'll be damned if you would have ever entered that gate. You see I have but three men."[45]

Later in the day, Powell renewed his plea to the ordnance chief, enclosing at this writing a copy of the January 6 order headed STATE OF FLORIDA, EXECUTIVE CHAMBER, signed by the governor of Florida, and forwarded to the Florida secretary of state. Still later on January 6, Powell wrote from Quincy, several miles inland from his post, reporting his surrender and adding: "I would be pleased to receive advice as to what disposition I shall make of myself and men."[46]

The seizure of the Chattahoochee Arsenal was a minor incident recorded in a series of minor dispatches that must be sought out in the Rebellion Records. The arsenal had never been a point of strategic importance; during the Civil War, it did not become particularly useful or important to action along the rivers flowing past it.

The January 6 incident was, however, the first military action of the Civil War in the Apalachicola–Chattahoochee river system. From that date, the list of stops on a steamboat schedule became an inventory of strategic sites. Along the Apalachicola toward the Gulf, the deep creeks that entered the river became anchorages for blockade runners taking on stores of cotton. Iola and Ricko's Bluff had been busy landings; the latter was to become a supply depot and fortified garrison. The treacherous winding course of the Apalachicola at the Narrows became the site of an obstruction to block attacks from the Gulf. Alum Bluff was a site where Columbus residents wanted to sink an obstruction.

Northward from Chattahoochee along the river, cotton bales on the plantation landings became spoils of war to be protected from the Union blockade as well as a commodity to smuggle out through the port of Apalachicola. Columbus was to become a major Confederate industrial complex. And near Saffold Landing, "Navy Yard Landing" was soon to become the next item on an inventory of strategic points along the river.

The Twelve Days of Christmas—December 25, 1860, with its secession parties, through January 6, 1861, with the minor incident of the fall of the Chattahoochee Arsenal—began a series of events that was to change life along the rivers in ways the beneficiaries of that life could not possibly have imagined.

Warships on the Gulf
and Rivers

CHAPTER 2

Such Ability as You May Have at Hand

Blockade and Defense of Apalachicola, 1861–1862

Union blockading vessel R. R. Cuyler
Peabody Museum, Salem, Mass.

As a blockade of Southern ports and rivers became central to Union strategy, Confederate response took two forms in the Apalachicola-Chattahoochee area: defending the coast and the interior and running or raising the blockade off Apalachicola.

Land defense and naval offense would seem to lend themselves to a neat distinction between army and navy operations. Developments in the Confederacy early in 1861 showed no such pattern, however. The times were too much in transition to make possible a timely, systematic defense of the geographic area and the economic system. A government that might have deployed an army to defend the land and a navy to control the seas was itself in the process of being formed. At the same time defenses were being planned around Pensacola and Apalachicola, the army was being organized, staffed, and supplied. The Confederate States Navy hardly existed at all; six months of the war passed before the gunboat *Chattahoochee* was even in negotiation with contractors.

Army operations in the river system during the first year of the Confederacy defended both land and water. Political as much as military, the operations can be best characterized perhaps as a barrage of letters—from local militiamen and government officials, from military officers of varying rank and unit, and from the concerned governor-elect, John Milton of Florida.

A delegate to the Alabama State Convention, H. E. Owens, sent to Secretary of War Leroy Pope Walker a summary of a letter from Gen. A. C. Gordon of Henry County on the lower Chattahoochee; it serves as a summary of conditions an army and navy would have to address:

> Nothing doing at Apalachicola. No cotton is selling, nor can shipments be made from that port. Unless some of our companies are sent to Apalachicola it will be burned up and our cotton taken if war should be declared. There is now over one million (value) of cotton at Apalachicola at ten cents. Call the attention of our President to the situation of our people in that particular. No forts or guns at that place to defend it. Two companies of volunteers are there without balls or powder. Something should be done, and that very soon, for the protection of that place and property. Alabama will suffer more than Florida will if that place should fall into the hands of an enemy.[1]

He ended on a strong economic note: "A large portion of the people of Southeastern Alabama ship their cotton to that port for market, and apprehend danger to their interests there."

On the day prior to that March 8 letter, Gen. Braxton Bragg had been appointed commander of forces in the Pensacola area. A week later Acting Adj. Gen. George Deas was writing to Bragg about requisitions for troops, how to form regiments from the various Confederate states, and about specific requisitions for artillery and munitions.

For all his dispatch in soliciting requisitions, Deas had few supplies and no trained supply officers to fill the requests. Instead, he advised

Bragg: "It will be necessary for you to rely upon such ability as you may have at hand."[2]

"To rely upon such ability as you may have at hand" was an approach that Lt. Col. D. P. Holland was already having to learn at Apalachicola; he wrote Secretary of the Navy Stephen R. Mallory on the same day that, except for four volunteer companies, "The port of Apalachicola is without any means of defense."[3]

Through the spring and summer of 1861, citizens in Apalachicola gave their best efforts to defense, more concerned with their immediate physical safety and with the security of their town than with the economic concerns of the cotton planters inland.

In June they appealed to the Florida government for two 32-pound cannons; later they sent a messenger to Richmond to procure more guns.[4] The military officers assigned to help organize the volunteer companies and to fortify St. Vincent's Island wrote letters: a request for ten teams of horses to work on fortifications, requisitions for wheelbarrows by the thousands, four 32-pounders on barbette carriages, two 24-pounders on seige carriages, two more 24-pounders on seige or field carriages, and at least a thousand friction primers. Governor-elect John Milton forwarded one lieutenant's letter to Secretary of War Walker with an added request for a good artillerist who could also drill the troops.[5]

Walker's letter of reply came within two weeks, but not with the results Milton needed. Florida's requisitions were answered with the appointment of a military commander, Brig. Gen. John Breckinridge Grayson.[6]

A Mexican War veteran and old friend of Milton's, Grayson was variously described as "in a dying condition," "nearly spent with consumption," "in such an enfeebled state of health and constitution as almost to forbid hope of amendment." He was, in short, without "the physical strength to discharge necessary duties in Florida."[7] Even if Grayson had been physically healthy, his energies might well have been dissipated in a confused, inefficient management system.

Both the government in Montgomery and the letter writers in Florida suffered confusion about the authorization of Confederate, state, and local military authorities; the division of the area into military commands; and an effective deployment of forces. There was confusion about whether Grayson's command extended to include Apalachicola or whether the port fell within the jurisdiction of General Bragg at Pensacola. Whether D. P. Holland as lieutenant colonel and Charles F. Hopkins as major at Apalachicola were under state command as reserves in Florida or under the War Department of the Confederacy was another question of order. Yet another question arose over dispersing of a thousand troops into nine or ten companies to defend Apalachicola, St. Mark's, Cedar Keys, and Tampa.[8]

A scattershot pattern characterized the flow of communications about such matters. The 1861 letters contained in the Rebellion Records for both the armies and the navies are variously directed to high officials of the Confederate government: from an army lieutenant colonel to the secretary of the navy; from an army general through a relatively minor state official to the secretary of war; and from a governor-elect to the secretary of the navy requesting that a state regiment be transferred to a nearby army command in exchange for another, better-trained regiment.[9]

No doubt one reason for the delays in establishing adequate coastal defenses was that distinctions between Confederate and states' jurisdiction, chains of command, and an orderly flow of men and supplies had not yet been established, nor were there effective lines of communication for making requests. In addition to the absence of an established chain of command and means to organize and supply a military force, Confederates were faced with the dichotomy of answering a naval threat through military means. As Gen. Robert E. Lee made a survey of defenses in east Florida near Fernandina, he viewed the general confusion and expressed the hope that the Union "would be polite enough" to allow Confederates time to get organized before they attacked.[10]

The Union Navy was struggling with many similar problems of disorganization and unpreparedness. If the Florida Confederates were coordinating the triple burdens of organizing a government, organizing an army, and fighting a war, the Union Navy had undertaken a task unprecedented in the history of warfare. Blockades had existed before, of course; but even with the disruption of shipping during the War of 1812, a fleet of seven hundred British vessels had not completely closed a single U.S. port.[11]

With only forty-two ships in commission, the Union now undertook a blockade of 3,549 miles of Confederate coast from Virginia to the Rio Grande, a distance greater than the Atlantic coast of all Europe.[12] After the war, a veteran of the blockading fleet was to call the effort "the very apotheosis of cheek."[13] Cheek was to suffice, and had to, for another four score years elapsed before World War II brought forth the Shortest Path Method for mobilizing a navy.

The navy secretary's first rough estimate was that the blockade would require thirty sailing ships and only one in Apalachicola waters would suffice; the Union blockading fleet was finally to include six hundred ships. But the beginnings were based on the principle the Confederates also lived by: "to rely upon such ability as you may have at hand."

One place to begin was in repairing and fitting out twenty-eight older war ships that were not in mothballs but lying dismantled at various shipyards. Merchant vessels were purchased and converted to armed vessels. Tugboats and river steamers were also put into service; some, like the *Somerset* and *Fort Henry*, would serve out the war in the East Gulf Blockading Squadron.

Shipyards to do the work of fitting out a navy were too few; skilled workmen were so few that many naval officers had to train and then work with unskilled workers. More than three hundred experienced officers resigned from the "Old Navy" to join the Confederate Navy; to man what ships they could mobilize, the Union had just more than two hundred seamen available for service at Northern ports. Merchant sailors were available, along with the merchant ships, but their experience did not include training to handle heavy guns at sea.[14]

Not out of politeness, then, as General Lee had joked, but because of delays and deficits in manpower and supplies, the Union Navy did not appear off Apalachicola until two months after the war began.

Under orders from Flag Officer William Mervine of the newly organized Gulf Blockading Squadron, the USS *Montgomery* arrived off Apalachicola about noon on June 11, 1861. The 787-ton screw steamer had a complement of sixty-six men and five guns under the command of Cdr. T. Darrah Shaw.

Despite the traffic into and out of the port of Apalachicola, west Florida was almost literally uncharted waters in 1860. The eighteenth edition of Edward W. Blunt's *American Coast Pilot* in 1857 did not contain complete information about the area. Much of the region was unsurveyed and such statements as "this bay has not been surveyed" and "we imagine that there is five feet of water in this bay" provided scant information for inexperienced sailors.[15]

Having no chart to direct his ship, Shaw steered a very careful entry through West Pass with frequent soundings, for removing bouys and dismantling lighthouses had been the Confederates' first defense measures against the blockade. The vessel almost ran aground before coming into position to command the entrance to the port.[16]

Shaw's first mission was to announce the blockade. He had with him Mervine's announcement that an effective blockade of the port of Apalachicola, Florida, had been established and would be rigidly enforced and maintained against all vessels (public armed vessels of foreign powers alone excepted) attempting to enter or depart from the port.[17] To Mervine's statement Shaw added the condition that no coasting vessels would be allowed into Apalachicola; foreign and neutral vessels would be allowed ten days, or until June 21, to clear the port.[18]

Late on the afternoon of the *Montgomery*'s arrival, a pilot boat under a flag of truce approached the ship. When the three civilians asked Shaw about his mission at Apalachicola, he asked that they deliver the blockade proclamation to the mayor, the postmaster, the collector of customs, and the commercial reading rooms.[19]

Shaw's first duty was to comply with international law by making formal proclamation and publication of the blockade. This "paper blockade" provided due notice to neutral vessels that the port of Apalachicola, and other Southern ports, were under blockade. Although suspect ships were subject to boarding and search, each neutral was entitled both to a general diplomatic notice and to one direct warning before becoming liable for capture for violating the blockade.[20] Thus the blockade that Shaw proclaimed allowed a grace period following the formal proclamation.[21]

The really critical factor in the blockade was the point of international law that "Blockades to be binding must be effectual."[22] This second part of Shaw's mission, actually blockading Apalachicola, was not so easily dispatched. In his first report to Mervine he pointed out the difficulties of the *Montgomery*'s position. He cited the impossibility of preventing steamers from slipping unseen through the shoal water to the east and west of the *Montgomery*'s station at the main entrance to the port. He further pointed out that most of the traffic at Apalachicola was made up of light-draft steamers, and he requested that a lighter vessel be sent to aid his ship.[23]

This request for light-draft vessels that could maneuver in the shallow coastal waters was the first canon of a litany that continued throughout the war, not only from Apalachicola but all along the Gulf coast. A class of vessel scarcely existed, however, that contained all the necessary specifications for blockade duty on the Gulf; so Horatio L. Wait wrote:

They must be heavy enough to contend with the Rebel rams, or they would be driven away from the principal ports. They must be light enough to chase and capture the swift blockade-runners. They must be deep enough in the water to ride out in safety the violent winter gales, and they must be of such light draught as to be able to go near enough to the shallow inlets at night to blockade them efficiently.[24]

Although Apalachicola was the first blockaded port in Florida, hundreds of other harbors and inlets remained open. Thus Shaw's request for added strength off Apalachicola brought no immediate response.

The arrival of the Union Navy immediately succeeded, however, in setting up a counterforce to the Confederate Army defenses on shore. Fears expressed for Apalachicola in the spring of 1861 became, by late summer, urgent calls to respond to an immediate threat. For the remainder of 1861, the Union Navy and Confederate Army sparred with each other—and overreacted.

The Confederates continued their efforts to reinforce their hold upon Apalachicola. With the help of citizens of Apalachicola they were erecting batteries named Fort Mallory on St. Vincent's Island. The lieutenant commanding the project sent an August 10 request to Governor John Milton of Florida for additional guns and cited the "exceedingly small supply of ammunition."[25]

After receiving the report, Governor Milton went to inspect the fortifications on St. Vincent's. He wrote to the secretary of war on August 16, asking that an artillery officer be sent to aid the force at Apalachicola. The governor concluded his request: "Of all places in this State Apalachicola is most important to the commercial interests of Georgia, Alabama, and Florida, and at present it is in a condition almost defenseless. Now is the time to prepare for its defense. A few weeks hence may be too late."[26] The governor's message had not reached the secretary of war before the blockade off Apalachicola was strengthened.

The impetus that later sent the USS *R. R. Cuyler* to Apalachicola may have been touched off in the city itself. On July 30 a citizen of Lansingburgh, New York, wrote a letter to the secretary of state that was first sent to Gideon Welles in the Department of the Navy and then forwarded to Flag Officer Mervine on August 5. The information contained in this circuitously routed message came from a woman in Apalachicola who had written to her uncle in Lansingburgh. She told him that the blockade was a farce: only one small vessel guarded four passages from Apalachicola to the Gulf, making it rather easy for vessels to escape to sea. The woman's directions to her uncle that he reply to her letter through a firm in New York City indicated to the Union that there was still communication by sea with Apalachicola.[27]

Whether or not the department acted on the strength of this intelligence is not stated, but it was exactly two weeks after Welles sent his message to Mervine that the *Cuyler* joined the *Montgomery* off Apalachicola. The addition of the *Cuyler*, a 1,200-ton screw steamer with 111 men and ten guns, tripled the number of men and guns stationed at Apalachicola. Moreover, the *Cuyler* was one of the two fastest ships in the Union fleet, capable of fourteen knots in smooth water.[28]

Within ten days, her captain had action to report at his new station. On the night of August 26, five boats from the *Cuyler* and the *Montgomery* were sent on a reconnaissance mission toward a large ship at anchor in Apalachicola Bay. The Union force discovered the ship *Finland* and the schooner *New Plan* and were able to capture the two vessels without opposition. Because the *New Plan*'s papers were in order, the schooner was released after the crew took the oath of allegiance to the United States.

The *Finland*, however, was thought a lawful prize and the Union seamen began efforts to remove their prize from the bay. They found the sails and spars housed and spent all night bending sails and sending spars aloft. At dawn they began, against unfavorable winds and tides, to attempt towing their prize to the Union blockading station at East Pass. Nightfall found the *Finland* grounded on St. Vincent's Bar, four miles from the Union anchorage, and forty men were left behind to free the ship.[29]

Efforts to tow the *Finland* from the bar lasted all night. At dawn a steamer with a large schooner in tow appeared heading into Apalachicola and steered directly toward the Union prize. Unable to free the *Finland* from the bar and unable to call upon the *Cuyler* or *Montgomery* for defense, the seamen had to fire the *Finland* and take to their boats.[30] So precarious was the position of the Union seamen that they were routed by nine men from the Apalachicola Guards who came upon the scene in the schooner towed by the steamer. That detachment boarded the burning *Finland* and recovered the lifeboats and a few useful articles that could be salvaged.

Though the shots from the Apalachicola riflemen had caused no injury, Lt. Francis B. Ellison recorded an injury to their pride that the Union inability to enter the bay allowed the "rebels to make this demonstration with impunity."[31] Ellison also deplored the loss of the *Finland* as a prize, for he had planned to send her to New York for adjudication.

The Union force was hampered by the lack of vessels and equipment suitable for operation in the shallow water of the area. These circumstances served to dim the accomplishment of the blockading force in capturing its first prize vessel. Had the Union ships been able to enter the bay, they could have protected the prize with their batteries against the threat of the steamer and schooner. Had they had kedge anchors and hausers they might have been able to operate more effectively. Ellison added that with a steamer or gunboat of twelve-foot draft or less, their force could have captured the two Confederate vessels easily.

The critical deficiency in equipment was of more than technical concern to Ellison, for a "lawful prize" also meant a considerable increment to the pay of officers and crew. As a paymaster who served off Charleston expressed it, "As I looked upon the trim, clean model of my ship, visions of unlimited prize money rose before me." Finding his ship also unsuited for blockading service, he later noted, "I never realized before the agony of being in a slow ship."[32] Ellison was, therefore, something more than dutiful in wanting the most effective craft possible for Apalachicola service.

The Confederates who had trained their rifles on the Union ships almost immediately turned their attention back to their government. Ten days after the *Finland* incident, Confederate Secretary of the Navy Mallory forwarded to Secretary of War Walker a dispatch from the garrison on St. Vincent's. The series of letters that sent guns to Apalachicola shows that the department bureaucracy was well underway after six months of operation; five letters routed through nine officials in the navy, army, Florida militia, and private sector accomplished the shipment in a mere ten days.[33]

These efforts to supply defenses failed to satisfy the citizens of Apalachicola, however, and they wrote to the secretary of war on October 1, listing their grievances. They pointed out that they had bought guns, sent requests to Richmond for attention to their needs, helped construct fortifications on St. Vincent's, and had organized themselves into volunteer companies. When the department had sent men and guns to their aid, the colonel in command had removed the battery from the city to St. Vincent's Island, thus leaving the city itself with only one artillery company and two companies of undrilled infantry.

The forces stationed at Apalachicola to defend the citizens and allay their fears were doubtless intent upon discharging their duties well. If the Union ships were unsuited for service under prevailing conditions, however, Confederate soldiers were equally unsuited for serving to defend against them. They suffered deficits not only in equipment but also in organization, leadership, and training. One guard force near Apalachicola showed how they hadn't quite got the knack of soldiering. Fearing that their presence would draw fire from the blockading vessels upon their homes, they evacuated the town by river, poling a flatboat. Once in midchannel, they could not touch bottom with their poles and thus were carried away on the current into the hands of the Yankees. The entire guard force was lost in broad daylight without a shot fired.[34]

Governor Milton complained of others who had rather romantic notions of military service. When the state most needed a defense force of infantry and light artillery, authority was granted to an attorney to raise a cavalry regiment, an action that touched off a surge of popularity for "riding into service." As he wrote to President Davis about the inappropriateness of cavalry for any engagements likely to be fought in Florida, the relative expense of mobilizing cavalry, and the drain of horses from agriculture, Milton expressed his utter exasperation that "Almost every man that has a pony wishes to mount him at the expense of the Confederate Government."[35]

For early volunteers sent to Florida, soldiering was a difficult and unfamiliar way of life, as William Miller's letter of April 23, 1861, expresses:

> Florida, I think, is a poor place. It is very cold at night and awful hot in the day. My ears have been pealing off for several days, occasioned by the hot sun. Tell all the family to write to me. They must not expect me to answer every letter. Our regiment is kept working hard all the time. We have to do guard duty, picket guard, work on the sand batteries, pull powder on the railroad (such as it is, the sand in some cases being a foot above the iron on the track), guard the redoubt, where they keep the powder, and do mule duty and anything they (the young, sap-head officers of the regiment) say do. In addition, we have to drill at 8 o'clock and at 3:30 o'clock

and have a dress parade at 6 o'clock every day. I don't mind the fighting part of the business, but I hate the menial work.[36]

To the general lack of experience and training was added a belief that soldiers had rights: to elect their own officers, to serve in a location of their choosing, and to be given thirty-day furloughs. These unseasoned, often unrealistic troops also had very real concerns about those left behind at home. Letters of the time express the men's dreadful home-sickness on the one hand and the wives' critical need for their farm labor and protection on the other. One letter sent to Pensacola pleads with an absent husband, "I have got no corn nor no meel, nor any way of giting of hit. . . . I want you to send sum corn soon or fetch hit." The postscript suggests special pleading: "Let your Captain reade this."[37]

While the men suffered some deprivation, and certainly worried about their families, military life in the Apalachicola garrison was not unremitting hardship by any means. Writing many years after the war, S. P. Richardson, who had served the Confederacy officially as an army major and unofficially as a chaplain, wrote that there were about 1,200 men at Apalachicola at the end of 1861. According to his account, they did not feel extreme pressure from the Union blockade. In fact, he describes an approach to military life that seems somewhat casual. He had been urged by the men of his congregation to enter the army as a chaplain, whereupon he jestingly told them that he would go only if they elected him major so that he could "command them and preach too." To his astonishment "they met and elected me major, and I had to go; for here came my commission, and with it orders to Apalachicola."

Richardson describes the following incident of a rather unbuttoned garrison:

> The general and all the field officers but myself drank. We had fine bands and they frequently serenaded us. . . . One day the Lieuten-ant Colonel came to me and said that I loved music and that the band had to be treated. I told him that I would not treat my father if he were to rise from the dead; but to show him that it was not money but principle with me, I said that if he would serenade me as a Christian I would treat them as Christian.

A band came with a singer to Richardson's quarters one evening and played "Before Jehovah's awful throne, ye nations bow with sacred joy," and he afterward treated them with oysters. Richardson gave only passing mention to the garrison's military duties, concluding "we finally had to abandon the place."[38]

Little wonder, then, that residents of Apalachicola were left, after nine months of Confederate defense, with a "deep sense of insecurity, and anxiety for the safety and protection of their families and property."[39]

The Union force was, in fact, greatly overestimated in their fears, for the blockading ships continued to labor under the disadvantages of operations in the shallow coastal waters. The commander of the *Cuyler* was especially disturbed by his inability to engage shallow-draft vessels that passed near his position. His ship was suited to apprehending a blockade runner at sea, but it could not engage vessels on the coast and in the bay. He asked that his superior consider "the size and draft of water of his ship, without a launch or boats sufficiently large to carry out an anchor, without even a kedge on board, or any of the ordinary means and appliances for getting the ship off, in the event of grounding."[40] Within a month the flag officer of the Gulf Blockading Squadron took action to remedy the situation by sending the *Marion* to relieve the *Cuyler*. A month later the *Hatteras* was sent to relieve the *Montgomery*.

This new combination of vessels for the Apalachicola blockade was more suited to the area of operations. The *Hatteras*, commanded by Cdr. George F. Emmons, was an 1,100-ton side-wheel steamer with a complement of 101 men and five guns. The *Marion*, commanded by Lt. George W. Doty, was a 566-ton sloop carrying 80 men and fourteen guns. Besides being more maneuverable in Apalachicola waters, the two vessels increased Union firepower by four guns.

While the *Marion* and the *Hatteras* reported no captures during their first weeks of duty, the blockade at Apalachicola nevertheless became increasingly more effective. Of five schooners that cleared the port in late November, only one, the *W. P. Benson*, returned safely—and it was captured on its second run out. The *W. A. Rain* was taken with a cargo of cotton on the outward voyage. The *Onward*, *Franklin*, and *Phoenix* were able to clear the port with cargoes of cotton and turpentine, but they were all captured on their return voyages.[41] A report of the harbor collector concerning these captures was sufficient to set off a rapid exchange of telegrams among Governor Milton, Secretary Mallory, and Secretary of War Judah P. Benjamin.

On November 25, 1861, Milton, signing himself "Governor and Commander in Chief," ordered Col. R. F. Floyd at Apalachicola to allow no vessel with cotton to leave the port. He gave orders to sink any vessels attempting to do so and to imprison any person attempting to ship cotton. Floyd reported two days later that he had ordered three hundred bales of cotton back up the river and that he had forbidden shipment of turpentine as well. On November 29, Milton wired Mallory for an opinion regarding the shipment of turpentine. His brief answer was, "I know of no objections to the departure of the vessels." Mallory had evidently asked the opinion of Benjamin on the matter, for he telegraphed Milton the same day (November 30) and again on December 5 to say that there was no law or reason to prevent vessels from running the blockade with cotton "unless there is reason to believe the cotton is really intended for the enemy under the guise of neutral."[42]

Apart from such official statements, and on a practical and operational level, coastal shipping along the Gulf continued during the first year of the war much as it had during peacetime. The official relationship of neutrals to the Union blockade and the Confederate Cause was still being sorted out. The status of blockade runners—privateers, common pirates, or active supporters of the Confederate government—presented another tangle of issues. While diplomats like British Foreign Minister Lord Lyons and officials like Milton and Benjamin exchanged substantive communiqués on a broad range of topics related to the blockade, men and their ships went about their business very much as usual. Throughout 1861, mail boats regularly left New Orleans for Mobile, and vessels coming into and out of New Orleans were duly recorded in the *Daily Picayune* with their dates of intended departure. Many took the Union blockading effort lightly. About the time that the *Montgomery* arrived at Apalachicola in early June, the *Picayune* published this statement about traffic from New Orleans: "Surely if women and children are willing to run the gauntlet (if there is any to run), the Company [which was suspending mail service] should be willing to take the same risk. There cannot be much risk when the enemy's steamers can be seen with the naked eye at a distance of at least ten miles, and with a glass twice as far."[43]

At Apalachicola, the presence of the two blockaders no doubt caused ships' captains to exercise greater than usual caution, but during 1861 the Union had been able to station only a small fleet along the 1,300 miles of Florida coast. Total captures for 1861 show that seven Union ships captured nine ships with the blockade, with a total prize money recorded of about $4,900.[44] To place that sum in context, a British Foreign

Office official estimated that ships under the British flag in New Orleans harbor as the blockade was implemented in June carried cargoes with an aggregate value of "not less than £1,000,000 sterling."[45] A really effective blockade of the Gulf coast would have required a vessel at every port, pass, and inlet, with combined capabilities of sail and steam, strength and swiftness, and ordnance with skill to use it.

Lacking those necessary capabilities, the Union blockaders off Apalachicola were as watchful as they could be while waiting for a stronger force better suited for that station. From a strictly military standpoint, the blockaders were in no great peril. Conditions in the Confederacy, not Union naval action, had already done the work of driving the defense perimeter off the barrier islands and into the town of Apalachicola. By December 1861, Union reconnaissance found defenses on St. George's and St. Vincent's islands abandoned to the elements of tide and sand or destroyed by other Union search parties. There was little of official interest left to report from Apalachicola by the end of 1861.

In the early months of 1862, the sparring match between Union Navy and Confederate Army first slowed and then the advantage began to shift to the Union side. The Confederates began their retreat both from Apalachicola and from their earlier policy for its defense.

Recognizing the importance of Apalachicola as an entrance to a significant economic area, the Confederate government responded to civilian fears and pressures. But the response had been in the most conventional terms: enemy ships were and would be off the coast threatening an attack; therefore, the outermost perimeter (the barrier islands) and the land approaches to the town should be fortified. Both plans were standard, textbook answers to the strategic problem at Apalachicola.

In actual practice, the Confederate military and governmental officials found themselves with few guns, little ammunition, not enough troops to man fortifications, and not enough experienced officers to make any strategy effective.

Like their counterparts in the Confederacy, Union officials and policy makers had set about formulating their own plans for war. Blockading the Southern coastline was to be the cornerstone of that policy. Despite the scale of this blockade, to blockade a port was a standard, conventional method of operations called for by the Southern economic situation: the port of Apalachicola was the entrance to an important economic area; therefore, ships were stationed to blockade the port.

Despite the overall significance of the blockade in Civil War history, in actual practice that policy foundered upon specific conditions of operation at Apalachicola. Moreover, the blockade's success in broad general terms does not account for the severe hardships imposed upon individual sailors stationed aboard the blockading vessels.

Another element that must be factored into any view of the Apalachicola blockade is the demographics of the 1860 census; powerful commodities merchants made the port wealthy and important, but only during cotton season. The Civil War ended "the season" on cotton and left the port to its permanent population of clerks, lighters, stevedores, fishermen, oystermen, and their families. If the port was closed for planters upriver, new markets had opened in a wartime economy. Columbus mills needed cotton, and Confederate armies in Virginia and Tennessee needed all the foodstuffs the area could produce. As for blockade runners, they could more profitably unload cargo at a port like Charleston or Wilmington. Running into Apalachicola meant shifting cargo to river steamers for a long, perilous shipment to Columbus.

Declining commercial importance of Apalachicola itself meant declining strategic importance. The sparsely settled west coast of Florida also became a very low priority item for already taxed Confederate resources. In the spring of 1862, the Tennessee River to the north cut through a far more strategically important area than west Florida, and troops were needed for duties other than guarding Apalachicola. Great plans for Fort Mallory on St. Vincent's Island yielded to other, more important plans at Fort Henry and Fort Donelson in Tennessee.

Having established that their heavy-draft ships were not fully effective in Apalachicola Bay, the blockading officers yielded in early 1862 to conditions at their duty station. If they could not steam into the bay in their large ships, they could send reconnaissance expeditions in smaller boats. If they could not attack Apalachicola directly, they could keep a close watch on operations in and around the port city. If they could not navigate the Apalachicola River north of the port, at least they could collect as much intelligence as possible about Confederate operations.

With virtually no blockade runners leaving port—and with a naval threat that was, at best, remote—the Union ships lay at anchor under conditions of general inaction, and the blockading crews sought ways to occupy their time as they settled down to service there. Small sloops or steamers occasionally drew a round from the *Sagamore*'s Parrott gun, but her heavy draft made her men and guns not much use for operations in Apalachicola Bay. A report of seeing a light on shore, sending in a shell, and being answered with three rifle shots reads almost like an account of restless boys "pinging" with their .22s.

The crews often went exploring on the nearby islands. On St. Vincent's in early January 1862 they found the abandoned fort. As described in the journal of Walter K. Schofield, an assistant surgeon on the *Sagamore*, the fortification was "made in the sand supported by wooden fence inside where several guns might have been placed—also several remains of barracks that had been burned, probably when the enemy retreated." He wrote how he warily explored a house on the island "all deserted apparently in great haste, water remaining in pans—went up stairs in right hand chamber & sought for books papers tools & whatever of value—Medical stores in reception room on right side of the house—trophies of saws nails cooking utensils & mirror—Wrung a hen's neck and brought her away from the henpen—The rooster escaped into the woods in the rear it being dusk— . . . [Found] Letter of Captain of Fourth Regiment of Volunteers of Florida."[46]

The lighthouse on St. George's Island was also of interest to the Union sailors. They found the lens and lamp taken away and several of the sixteen large plate-glass lights smashed. The keeper's house on poles and the lighthouse entrance four feet above ground level gave them an indication of tide levels. And the young surgeon Schofield was interested to find beneath the house a "human skeleton nearly perfect."

As sailors familiarized themselves with the area they were blockading, reconnoitering often doubled as foraging expeditions. Accounts of wild hogs and cattle on St. Vincent's made their way into official reports, but the surgeon's diary also catalogs deer, wild turkey, and at least one bear on St. George's. A return expedition to the deserted house resulted in the destruction of a capsized boat and confiscation of "five or six bushels of good sweet potatoes," and "three fowls, one for Cap & other two for ward room." On an expedition up Crooked River a small force "Captured one hive of honey and the bees also."[47]

The now famous oyster beds near Apalachicola soon gained fame among the blockading vessels, making it, if not a desirable station, at least a less undesirable one along a nearly deserted coastline. The *Sagamore* sent out a launch in late January and collected, by Schofield's report, "10 or 15 bushels in three hours."

As the blockaders became more familiar with the area and somewhat reassured that no strong Confederate force would attack, the crews set up the lighthouse and keeper's house "for a smoking and lounging saloon—Expedients of unemployed minds and bodies to kill time." On a Thursday in early June, just a year after Union vessels implemented the blockade, the diarist recorded the day's activities: "Left the inner anchorage at daylight. Rusticating at Light House and in the Light keeper's house—Written account of the Crooked River affair to Jennie—Caught only a hundred mullet."[48]

The "Crooked River affair" recounted in a letter home was an exceptional bit of action in the usually dull blockade duty. A reconnaissance party had been en route up Crooked River. When a crewman on the river fired at a duck, that evoked answering fire from a Confederate ambush. The Rebels flung curses as well, as the Union men dived out of their cutter and used its sides as a shield. The *Sagamore* fired several volleys of shot and shell into the position and then turned her guns upon a sail that appeared at the mouth of the river. The approaching ship turned out to be a sloop manned by two Italians who had recently visited the ship; they were not on the attack but were ferrying a wounded gunnersmate back to ship.

A number of elements combine in that incident to describe the nature of the Union presence off Apalachicola during 1861 and early 1862. An expedition in a cutter, which doubled as a hunting expedition, drew fire from unfriendly forces; but the only vessel that appeared was manned by civilians befriending a wounded crewman.

Both official correspondence and recorded daily activities on the blockade reflect that mixture of friend and foe and the constant contact between occupying force with noncombatants.

Very frequently, "contrabands," or fleeing slaves, made their way to the blockade, as did Italian, Portuguese, and Irish refugees from the mainland. The log of the *Somerset* records instances of families hailing the blockader from small boats containing what they were able to salvage of their household goods—and of their expectation that they and all their possessions would be taken aboard.

While most communications of the Union officers are notably free of political opinion, Lt. George E. Welch's report of a contraband slave coming aboard the *Amanda* illustrates the slavery issue that most often went unspoken: one contraband was received "having on his leg shackle bars weighing 15 pounds, a charge of unextracted buckshot in the back of his neck gangrened and festering and his flesh torn from his body by dogs."[49]

These refugees were a continuing concern to the blockaders. Some were transported to safety at Key West early in the war; others were housed in tents or in the lighthouse and dwelling on St. George's later in 1862.

A troublesome factor in all such dealings was the lack of clear distinction between friendly and unfriendly noncombatants. Some inhabitants of Apalachicola readily took an oath of allegiance to the Union. Welch described others as "guarded in their sentiments." Some came aboard a blockader with a sick woman or child in search of a doctor or asking safe conduct to travel in search of a doctor. Very often the officers were able to gather intelligence about military fortifications on shore and upriver; sometimes the Tallahassee newspaper came to hand, and once a Tuscaloosa, Alabama, paper reported an action near the blockading station.

As the blockaders interacted more and more with the residents of Apalachicola, they gained a better personal sense of the population. The recorded instances of civilians coming aboard ship in search of their escaped slaves is evidence that the people on shore had no great fear of the men of the fleet. This kind of interaction is well summarized in the journal entry: "Mrs. King came on board after one of her slaves but did not get him. Professes to be union now but threatened to boil the Yankees in the salt kettle a few days ago."[50]

Threats from other Apalachicolans were not shrugged off. Lieutenant Welch of the *Amanda* wrote to a Mr. Harvey in Apalachicola: "I put that rascal John Miller in double irons because after taking his salt kettles he having the range of the ship he snatched a pistol from the belt of the lookout man on the forecastle and expressed the amiable wish that the Ram would come down and blow us the hell out of the water."[51]

The nature of the blockade off Apalachicola is perhaps best summarized by what contemporary military history has brought to the word *presence;* that is, the Union ships were there, but they were not in such force nor active in such a way as to pose a real and present danger to the inhabitants of Apalachicola. The interaction of the Union Navy with the people and the coastal area made their presence more political than military in nature. This was especially true in that local coastal shipping and river traffic had not been disrupted by the naval presence during the early part of the war.

These conditions did not mean that the war had not changed life in Apalachicola. But if the populace suffered, they suffered more from the neglect of their military and governmental officials than from the naval exertions of the enemy. Early in 1862, the Florida legislature voted away its authority over the state militia and placed it under the jurisdiction of and at the disposal of the Confederate government. Governor Milton could no longer write to the commander at Apalachicola, and sign himself "Governor *and Commander in Chief.*"

The Union officers were not unaware of these changes in the Confederacy. Apalachicola had been the first port blockaded along the Gulf, but New Orleans and Mobile soon displaced its importance. The blockade was maintained, but the officers who took up their duties there knew they had not been sent into the thick of action. Instead, they settled into a largely administrative routine.

One matter of administration the officers attended well was sending a steady stream of reports to the squadron commanders. As each new ship arrived for duty, an officer wrote a lengthy intelligence report; December and January throughout the war usually showed their renewed resolve to take the situation in hand at Apalachicola.

In early January 1862, the commander of the *Sagamore* reported action that, while not spectacular, indicated a growing aggressiveness on the part of the Union. A part of the *Sagamore*'s crew of seventy-eight landed on St. Vincent's and, finding the batteries dismantled, destroyed the barracks and other buildings the Confederates had constructed there.[52] On February 7, another boat expedition landed on the coast near Apalachicola and destroyed two small and two large sloops that had been hauled ashore for repairs.[53]

Lt. George W. Doty of the *Marion* made reports of a different nature during February. He supplied Flag Officer Mervine with intelligence concerning the traffic in Apalachicola Bay and in the Apalachicola River. From refugees he learned something of military and commercial conditions within the city of Apalachicola.

According to Doty's report, Confederate harbor operations consisted of patrols made by several small, unarmed sloops. These carried crews of about ten men who reported blockade conditions to larger vessels anchored up the Apalachicola River. Several schooners were rumored to be anchored some five or six miles above the city in the Jackson River. The schooner *Kate L. Bruce* lay at anchor in Apalachicola five months after she had run in a cargo of fruit from Havana. Three of the eight river steamers in the waters lay at Apalachicola in order to tow schooners to the outlets to the Gulf. The steamer *Wave* was reported to have left for Scaffold, Georgia, to be converted into a gunboat.

Doty learned that means of evading the blockade and supplying Apalachicola had been developed. Vessels landed cargo at Bear Creek off St. Andrew's Bay and transported it overland to Ochese, Florida, twelve miles south of Chattahoochee. River steamers then transported supplies some ninety miles downriver to Apalachicola. Coffee was transported in this way in late January and cotton was sent from Apalachicola to load the vessel for the return voyage.

The report went on to describe military conditions in Apalachicola as very poor. The military post consisted of about 450 soldiers, mostly citizens of Apalachicola who were armed with flintlock muskets and shotguns. Because of the scarcity of arms, one company was reportedly unarmed. Other defenses consisted of twelve light cannons mounted upon earthworks that had been erected 150 yards from shore. They extended for 500 yards from southwest to northeast before the town.

Doty also noted that the city of Apalachicola had begun to feel the restrictions of the blockade. Most of the stores had been closed and many of the citizens had moved inland. Even though coffee had been landed at St. Andrew's, the Apalachicola price was seventy-five cents per pound. Salt, which was produced at extensive saltworks on Cape San Blas, sold for five dollars per half bushel.[54]

A clear Union advantage began to emerge from reports submitted by Cdr. H. S. Stellwagen of the *Mercedita*, a steamer with nine guns and 135 men that replaced the *Marion* on March 12. He made additions to the intelligence that Doty had collected, giving an indication that Apalachicola was still dominated by secessionist sentiment. He gathered information about fortifications and naval construction up the river as well.

From civilians who had contact with the blockade, Stellwagen received reports that Apalachicola had been evacuated on March 14, two days after his arrival. He sent a boat expedition to confirm the information and found "not a soldier, a cannon, or apparently any weapon or war" left there. The civilian population had been ordered away by Governor Milton. Stellwagen included the refugees' description of the operation:

> The exodus of the poor frightened women and children is represented by the negroes as heart rending. Taken away at the shortest notice, in a storm, thrown ashore on the low bluffs many miles up the river, with their house hold goods, furniture, and everything

they could snatch up in their flight, and left all night in a deluge of rain, the river rising and threatening to carry them away, with scarcely any shelter for the weak and sick, there most of them laid in the mud, almost perishing with cold, until the latter part of the next day, when they were taken away by rafts and flats over the deluged country.[55]

Left in the town were a group of 500 to 600 people, among them members of about a dozen white families, a few slaves, and some Spanish fishermen.

This first-hand report gave data upon which the blockaders could act. In part to press a military advantage by occupying the abandoned town and partly as a mission to save the civilians, the blockaders decided to take Apalachicola. Achieving either advantage would resolve the impasse of being not fully able to blockade the port and not fully in control of the port city. Control of the town would place control of the bay and nearby river passages in Union hands and help to sort out political allegiances among its residents. It would also resolve the tension of being no more than a presence just off shore.

Stellwagen sent a boat from the *Mercedita* to request that the city be surrendered without opposition and thus be spared naval bombardment. The Union seamen found in the town no one in authority to make the surrender or ask for terms. Nevertheless, the secessionists left at Apalachicola still had means at their disposal to prevent the surrender of the city. They threatened to starve any who expressed Union sentiments. They further threatened to burn the entire town should any of the citizens hold conference with members of the blockading force. Because the *Mercedita* could not anchor near the city, the commander had no means of preventing the secessionists from carrying out their threats at night. Stellwagen therefore delayed pressing his advantage for a few days.[56]

On March 30, Stellwagen began planning a show of military force at Apalachicola. He sent a gig from his anchorage in the Gulf to the *Sagamore*, which was stationed at East pass thirty miles away, and asked that she join the *Mercedita*. The next day both ships began preparing their small boats for the expedition. Six of the boats, one of them armed with a howitzer, were to set out at night past the town and up the river, followed at daylight by two gigs.

The boats left the Union steamers at nine o'clock on the night of April

2, but the strong current and darkness forced them to anchor until daybreak. Soon after first light they captured the *Octavia*, a blockade runner anchored at Apalachicola. Three of the boats remained there while the other three pulled upriver. Seven miles upstream they captured the schooner *New Island* at anchor in a small creek. After towing their prize into midstream, the expedition continued up the river where they were able to take the schooner *Floyd*, two pilot boats, and the schooner *Rose*, which was laden with cotton. They then set about towing their prizes to Apalachicola, meeting no opposition during the entire operation.

Although the Union boat expedition had been able to move at will in Apalachicola Bay and in the river near the city, they faced the old problem of freeing their prizes from the harbor. Only the *Rose* and the *Octavia* were cleared. When the *New Island* and the two pilot boats grounded in seven feet of water, Stellwagen ordered them burned.[57]

Having gained his military objective, Stellwagen then set about gaining the political objective of placing Apalachicola under Union control. Late in the afternoon of April 3, he gathered his entire force to proceed to the landing of Apalachicola. There he was met by most of the residents, with whom he conducted, according to his own account, a very effective interview. He began by saying: "My countrymen, for even you who are engaged in this unholy, unnatural war against our Government are my fellow-countrymen, we come not to injure the defenseless, or women and children; I like the people of the South, I hate secession and rebellion, which have brought such calamities and misery upon all parts of our late happy land." The citizens answered: "We have had no part in it," or "The innocent must suffer with the guilty."[58]

Stellwagen then told the people that he had brought his force as proof that the blockading crew had ample means to use force against them. Knowing of their distress, however, he had decided to treat the city mercifully, offering safety to all who would take the oath of allegiance to the United States. Leaving all the fishing and oyster boats unharmed, he promised that they could fish and oyster in the bay safely as long as there was no firing upon Union vessels, no aid for blockade runners, nor any harboring of soldiers in the town. Any of these violations would bring severe punishment.

Continuing in his talk with the group, Stellwagen pointed to the Confederate sand batteries and said: "See what protectors your soldiers are; look at the fort built in the midst of your houses, so that a few shells even from boat guns at them would be sure to burn your town. (Laughter and cries, 'Oh, they're no great soldiers; there's no engineers amongst them!')" He then announced the Union successes at Fort Henry, Tennessee; Fort Donelson, Tennessee; Columbus, Kentucky; and Nashville, Tennessee. He concluded by telling the people of Apalachicola that he did not require their help if it would endanger them. But he again reminded them that actions against his vessels would result in severe retaliation.[59]

Stellwagen knew at that time that Confederate efforts for the war in his area of command had been increased. Refugees had informed him of the small garrison stationed on Ricko's Bluff, fifty-seven miles north of Apalachicola, and of a larger force at Johnston's Landing, thirty-three miles up the Chattahoochee River from Chattahoochee, Florida. Recurrent reports of Confederate naval construction at Saffold held great significance for the blockade officers. Reports varied from counts of one gunboat underway at Saffold to several. Rumors began in late 1862 of an ironclad under construction in Columbus. Then another refugee reported not one, but two ironclads. The constant in this variety of intelligence reports was Union interest in Confederate naval construction.

In time, Confederate naval officers at Saffold would speak in personal terms of their Union counterparts on the Gulf. George W. Gift had served with Stellwagen in the Old Navy. Catesby ap R. Jones had an advantage of victories over George Morris from his days at Drewrys Bluff. Whether the Union officers also longed to try themselves in combat to determine the better man is not known. What they did write expressed a desire to break a stalemate—of Union ships too heavy to enter the rivers and Confederate ships too heavy to get out and engage the blockaders in combat. If Confederate men-of-war were to appear on Apalachicola Bay, that was a threat to the Union worth noting. To inactive men at anchor in the shallow coastal waters off Apalachicola, it was almost a welcomed threat.

A *Steam Ship* and *No Boat*
The Gunboat *Chattahoochee*

Lt. Augustus McLaughlin, C.S.N.
James W. Woodruff, Jr., Confederate Naval Museum, Columbus, Ga.

Union blockading officers need not have felt undue concern about their position off Apalachicola—whatever intelligence reports they received. It was true that policy was taking shape that would result in a Confederate Navy, and plans were laid early in the war to construct ships and machinery on the Chattahoochee. In addition, naval officers already experienced in the Union service were united in the opinion that the Confederacy should and could develop an effective naval force. As the blockaders were charged with laying down a "paper blockade," however, the Confederacy they feared lacked even a "paper navy."

Secretary of the Navy Stephen R. Mallory took office with a short list of two former U.S. shipyards and two hundred former Union naval officers to man fifteen guns on a miscellaneous collection of ten ships.[1] More significantly, Mallory was without an administrative structure needed to build, arm, man, launch, and operate a navy.

The former Florida senator's work on the U.S. Naval Affairs Committee had given him an idea of what his navy needed. He had advocated more federal funds to develop the port of Apalachicola and had been instrumental in having a marine hospital established there. Evidence of Senator Mallory's efforts diminished and then disappeared quite rapidly as the Civil War began. Records of the marine hospital were closed out by the summer of 1861 and the entries that recorded shipping into and out of the port finally ceased as blockade running replaced commerce.[2]

Secretary Mallory assumed a far more powerful and complex role in government, for he was, according to *DeBow's Review*, "better acquainted with naval matters than any man in the Confederacy."[3] Politically, he had to lobby for a navy in a Confederate Congress more favorable to building an army. Financially, he had to lobby for appropriations needed to convert existing vessels of war and merchant vessels, to purchase vessels in England and France, and to design and build vessels in the Confederacy.

The South possessed three basic components for mounting a large-scale construction effort: facilities, materials, and labor. However, a shipbuilding industry for peacetime river and coastal shipping had to be reorganized for war. An abundance of iron and coal deposits and vast timber resources were of little use unless they could be readily fabricated as machinery, forges, and ships' hulls. A labor force was present in the Confederacy as the war began, but many foreign shipwrights emigrated and native Southerners were all too often conscripted for army service.[4]

As Mallory soon learned, any ship the Confederacy actually launched had first to navigate the heavy seas of congressional approval for funding, strategic and technical planning, contract negotiations, site plan-

*Stephen R. Mallory, Confederate Secretary of the Navy. As a U.S. Senator
from Florida, Mallory had served on the Naval Affairs Committee, where
he had access to British and French reports on experiments with ironclads
and newer naval technology.* Debow's Review *considered Mallory "better
acquainted with naval matters than any man in the Confederacy."
Certainly he understood the enormity of the Confederacy's task of building
a navy and a navy department simultaneously.*
Francis Trevelyan Miller, ed., Photographic History of the Civil War in Ten
Volumes. *New York: The Review of Reviews Co., 1911.*

ning, personnel, materials acquisition and allocation, and every last detail down to a purchase order for twine and a pay voucher for a sail maker—if either could be located.

As he summed up the task before him: "The Union have a constructed navy, we have a navy to construct."[5] And he might have added this: if possessing the basic components of a system was an asset, shaping the parts into an effective, productive whole was quite another matter.

As the blockade policy was laid down along the Gulf coast, Union intelligence reports were accurate at least that Confederate policy was being implemented on the Chattahoochee. Columbus industries were being adapted to naval construction—though not to the production of two ironclads very early in 1862. A wooden gunboat was being constructed at Saffold in Early County—but its arrival at Apalachicola to run or raise the blockade was unlikely for a ship without decks or engines in early 1862. And if reports seemed contradictory—that the army and citizenry were obstructing the Apalachicola River even as the Confederate Navy was building warships to descend it—such reports were nevertheless true.

In fact, Confederate policy and planning had coordinated sufficiently by the fall of 1861 to begin a construction project on the Chattahoochee. On October 2, Lt. Augustus McLaughlin was ordered off the Apalachicola batteries to select a place in Columbus, Chattahoochee, or Apalachicola for constructing a steam gunboat.[6]

By October 19, McLaughlin had negotiated a contract with David S. Johnston at Saffold, a steamboat landing some 175 miles south of Columbus and 140 miles north of the port of Apalachicola. Witnessing the contract, and no doubt participating in the negotiations, was Chief Eng. James H. Warner. He had resigned the Old Navy in July and was then transferred south from the Gosport Navy Yard. His specific duty was to report to McLaughlin and begin "preparing the details and drawings for the engines and etc. of a steam Gun Boat" to be built at Columbus.[7]

For the duration of the war, these two officers would work together on the gunboat *Chattahoochee* project and at the Confederate Navy Yard and Columbus Naval Iron Works in Columbus, Georgia. In these very early stages, it was likely that McLaughlin was an officer in the right place (convenient to Columbus) at the right time (a point when policy translated to orders). Born in Baltimore, he had received his Annapolis appointment from Arkansas; he had been dismissed from the academy for drunkenness, was reinstated, and then served with the Union Navy in the Mexican War and most recently on supply ships. Whatever the problem in the court-martial proceedings of his midshipman days, the Confederate Navy offered him a new career. He was to become the steady, administrative presence who kept the whole Columbus operation on course.[8]

Warner was no doubt specifically intended for one of the few industrial centers of the Confederacy so that his experience and design skills could be put to maximum effective use. Born in Virginia and brought up in Ohio, he had amassed considerable experience both in riverboat design and as a chief engineer in the Union Navy. Columbus was to become both his duty post, where he superintended operations for constructing and overhauling ships and engines, and his base of operations for superintending projects throughout the Confederacy. By late 1864, engines from the Columbus Naval Iron Works would power a large percentage of the Confederate Navy.[9]

For the gunboat project, the two officers selected a site and negotiated a contract that fully accorded with a naval policy still in its formative stages. The industrial capabilities of Columbus steamboat works nicely balanced out the boat yard on the Chattahoochee. Near Johnston's timber holdings were steam sawmills that could turn out about five thousand board feet a day. Even before McLaughlin had contracted with Johnston, his wife had written an Alabama cousin on October 4, "Col. J. is very busy sawing for the Government. I have never seen him so busy."[10] Johnston also had a corps of ninety slaves who would serve as laborers on the project.[11] Carpenters, blacksmiths, and any others with mechanical skills were recruited from the area nearby; once conscription laws went into effect, the promise of exemption from military duty would be an added incentive.

By mid-December, Mrs. Johnston was writing Martha Fort Fannin, "You would not know the landing if you were first out there and not told where you were."[12] As had happened during the Indian wars, and as was to happen at nearby Camp Rucker and the Bainbridge Army Air Station in World War II, a wartime project was changing the face of the land. The construction was also different from the peacetime task of keeping riverboats afloat. Mrs. Johnston referred to the *Chattahoochee* as "The Boat" or "Our Boat" with the qualification, "Lieut. McGlocklin says it is a *steam Ship* and *no Boat*." The "very handsome *Ship*" that so interested Mrs. Johnston was a class of wooden gunboat that Navy Secretary Mallory had described as "Small propeller ships, with great speed, lightly armed with [rifled] guns . . . the light artillery and rifles of the deep, a most destructive element in naval warfare."[13]

Under the prevailing policy, Johnston would enjoy almost complete autonomy in fulfilling his contract with the navy while McLaughlin and Warner were at work elsewhere. Johnston was to be paid $47,500 in six installments as each of six stages of construction was completed. Under terms of the contract, however, each payment was reduced by 20 percent to about $6,300; only when the gunboat was completed would Johnston receive the balance of $9,500.[14]

Model of the C.S.S. Chattahoochee *on display at the*
James W. Woodruff, Jr., Confederate Naval Museum.
James W. Woodruff, Jr., Confederate Naval Museum, Columbus, Ga.

Specifications calling for 130-foot length, 30-foot beam, and 10-foot depth of hold made the *Chattahoochee* slightly shorter and wider than the standard riverboat. By comparison, a standard 140-foot riverboat had a 23-foot beam and 4-foot depth; it was expected to carry its own weight in cargo and draw fourteen inches empty and thirty inches loaded. The rule of thumb for such construction called for length just greater than six times the width and a depth of 1 foot for every 33 feet in length.[15]

Construction according to those specifications would have suited the *Chattahoochee* for maneuvering on the inland river, but the ship had a multipurpose design. The hold had to accommodate steam engines that propelled twin screws, not the more familiar paddle wheel of river craft.

The four broadside batteries had to be allowed sufficient width for the eleven-man gun crews to tend muzzle-loading cannon, and for the recoil of the gun on its carriage as it fired. Laden with a heavy battery and fitted with sail for the open sea, the ship needed a deeper keel for stability. The masts were so designed that they could be housed, or lowered into the hold, to present a blockade runner's low profile.[16] The stone color first applied to the ship also indicated the intention to employ her in running the blockade.[17]

Whatever the other specifications, ships or boats in Apalachicola Bay or on the Apalachicola and Chattahoochee rivers succeeded or failed according to depth of draft compared to the water level in the rivers. With a pilot, a ship could cross the bar into Apalachicola Bay drawing twelve feet; an eight-foot draft would take a ship into the channel near the wharf; but six feet, and preferably four, were most desirable for making a safe trip to Columbus. The pilot aboard the *Chattahoochee* pronounced the final word on all plans: he could clear the Apalachicola Bar with a six-and-a-half-foot draft, no more.[18] The Union blockading officers were, of course, already living by those data—and filling their dispatches with requests for light-draft vessels—by the time the *Chattahoochee*'s keel was laid. In time, Confederate communications would continually speculate upon and fret over the ship's draft, the water level, possible draft when fully laden, possible water level at certain seasons, and so on.

Quite aside from where she was constructed and what she must draw to navigate there, the *Chattahoochee* was designed according to an overall policy for river defense. She was but one of eight such vessels to be constructed in Savannah, in Charleston, and in Elizabeth City and Washington, North Carolina. The policy of dealing with private contractors meant that there was no standard design—a factor that was to plague the engineers who had to construct machinery and armaments. Local availability of material and navigation conditions also influenced design. The *Chattahoochee* was somewhat larger than the 106- to 112-foot gunboat designed by Matthew Fontaine Maury, and smaller than the 150- to 198-foot vessels constructed at Pensacola, Jacksonville, Mobile, and Mars Bluff, South Carolina.[19]

If the *Chattahoochee* was to be built of raw timber, at a place remote from the sea on a river difficult to navigate, it was but one project in a massive construction effort proceeding on all fronts. Confederate agents were in England and France in search of warships to purchase or to commission for construction; officers like Maury were lobbying for a much smaller, less expensive gunboat; others were pressing for the secretary's choice of a few good ironclads that might overwhelm numbers with invulnerability and firepower.[20] Mallory's reports to the Confederate Congress for 1861 and 1862 reflect the level of activity and the growing level of expenditures for creating a navy.

In carrying out the narrow range of their duties within the navy's plans, McLaughlin and Warner closed their deal with Johnston and went about other duties while he was responsible for constructing the gunboat.

During the 120 days scheduled for the *Chattahoochee* project, McLaughlin traveled from Columbus to Apalachicola, a distance of about three hundred miles, with periodic stops at Johnston's Navy Yard at Saffold. When he was not traveling the river on the steamboats *Jackson* or *Uchee*, he was busy communicating by telegraph: to Apalachicola on October 24, 26, 28, and 30; to Richmond on November 3 and 4; and twice to Apalachicola on November 8.[21]

Warner, meantime, was traveling to various construction sites to consult with other officers on plans, drawings, and the condition of machinery for vessels. He had hardly been ordered to Columbus on October 21 when he received an October 31 order from Secretary Mallory to prepare drawings for the *Chattahoochee*'s engines, to report to Flag Officer Josiah Tattnall in Savannah about the *Fingal*'s engines, return to Columbus to superintend engine construction, and also write regular progress reports.[22] On December 17, Warner was ordered to Jacksonville from Columbus to consult with construction officers there.

Columbus was, at that stage of the war, a convenient base of operations for McLaughlin and Warner. The Quartermaster Department had the major responsibility for utilizing Columbus industrial production for the Confederacy, and also pressed into army service the small fleet of river steamers on the Chattahoochee, Flint, and Apalachicola rivers. In time, their trips south with cotton reversed direction as they transported loads of corn and fodder to Columbus for the Confederate armies. The Columbus Iron Works where William R. Brown had constructed and maintained riverboats began operations under an Ordnance Department contract. Until early 1862, army Capt. F. C. Humphries had the administrative duties Warner would later assume. Until the spring of 1862, McLaughlin and Warner supervised construction for the *Chattahoochee* and oversaw iron works operations while being on call for work at other sites.

Orders and travel vouchers show Warner traveling west from Columbus to New Orleans, Pensacola, Mobile, and Selma. Projects at Savannah and Charleston sent him east, sometimes via Atlanta to consult on facilities there. And he was subject to orders from Richmond like Commodore Tattnall's March 9, 1862, telegram: "Proceed without delay to Richmond to report to the Secretary of the Navy."[23]

Records for the second quarter of 1862 give some idea of Warner's demanding schedule. In Savannah to work on the *Fingal*, he received an April 5 letter from Duncan N. Ingraham in Charleston: "I wish you to return here as early as you possibly can after examining the Fingal." He had no sooner arrived in Charleston when he received a telegram from the commander of the Savannah station, Thomas Brent: "Sir, come on here by tomorrow morning's train, you are wanted in relation to the *Fingal*." On April 21, Warner returned to Columbus via Atlanta, having logged 639 miles in seventeen days.[24]

Warner was at work at the Columbus Iron Works for a month before he traveled 175 miles on May 21 and 22 while on a trip to Saffold for work on the *Chattahoochee*. Two weeks later he traveled 291 miles to Savannah. From June 15 to June 20 he traveled 212 miles to arrange engines, boilers, and propellers for the ironclad being built in Selma.[25]

McLaughlin's work at the navy yard did not require him to travel as extensively, but he sometimes fared little better in his own schedule. On March 3, 1862, he was ordered to Pensacola, a distance of 260 miles via Montgomery. On March 13 he was ordered to Richmond to confer about the battery for the *Chattahoochee*. He had scarcely returned when he received a telegram ordering him to Pensacola to assist Thomas Brent with the removal of naval stores. Then the first week of April found him ordered back to Richmond and from there to Charleston and Savannah to confer with Warner about purchasing a steamer.[26]

If civilian businessman John Horry Dent had endured delays and primitive travel conditions before the war, the overburdened transportation system of the Confederacy made travel more taxing for men like Warner and McLaughlin. When McLaughlin requested reimbursement for his April return from Richmond, he noted: "I reached Columbus, Geo. via Macon, Atlanta, West Point, Opelika—the road direct from Macon to Columbus not being used in consequence of heavy damage from a freshet—and have calculated mileage accordingly." On another occasion, travel by train and riverboat to Apalachicola took him first northeast about eighty miles to Fort Valley, then southwest about eighty miles to Albany, and from there southwest through Bainbridge, and finally south to Apalachicola.[27]

If Warner and McLaughlin were working and traveling at the maximum rate through 1861 and early 1862, the Confederate Navy as a whole was laying down and launching vessels along the shortest path possible to break the blockade, defend the interior, and open the South once more to river and ocean commerce. While Warner and McLaughlin crisscrossed the Confederacy by rail and steamer, D. S. Johnston was left to fulfill his contract with little official assistance or interference.

February 17, 1862, marked the 120-day completion schedule for the *Chattahoochee*, but it receives no mention in correspondence or financial records. On March 5, Mrs. D. S. Johnston wrote again to her Alabama cousin about the gunboat: "She is all ready to plank up and in one month more will be ready for the water." She also noted the high waters of the winter and spring months: "You never saw such as river as we had. Our Boat was nearly covered with water for several days. We were very fearful she would not stand, but not one block or timber moved." Thus the ever-changing conditions of weather and water level on the river might have delayed the work, as it was to plague construction efforts at Columbus later on. She expressed a feeling that was doubtless shared by her husband and the construction officers as the schedule lagged behind: "I hear nothing but war and Gun Boats until I am mighty nervous."[28]

Johnston was suffering the labor shortages so characteristic of all Confederate naval construction, and on March 4 he advertised in the *Columbus Daily Sun:*

HANDS WANTED

AT THE

C. S. NAVY YARD

LOCATED ON THE

CHATTAHOOCHEE RIVER

AT SAFFOLD, EARLY COUNTY, GEORGIA

TO BUILD GUNBOATS

Twenty ships' carpenters, joiners, caulkers, and hands accustomed to ship and steamboat work are wanted at the Confederate States Navy Yard to work on gunboats . . . as several gunboats are under contract steady employment and good wages. All hands employed

at the Confederate States Navy Yard are exempt from military duty and anyone in the Army can be furloughed to work there.
D. S. Johns[t]on[29]

Delays seem not to have deterred the Confederate Navy from planning further projects with Johnston. His wife noted in early March that he had contracted to build two more gunboats, and on March 25 McLaughlin signed a contract with Mrs. Johnston's father, William O. Saffold, and her brother, Adam G. Saffold, for two gunboats to be constructed at Saffold and delivered July 1, 1862, for $50,000.[30] Also on March 25, McLaughlin paid $5 to Columbus attorney Wiley Williams for drawing up a contract with the Columbus Iron Works, most probably for engines and boilers for the craft.

The first measurable sign of progress on the *Chattahoochee* also occurred on March 25 with McLaughlin's check to Johnston for $21,333.33. Because the contract of October 1861 called for an 80 percent payment once each one-sixth part of the labor and materials had been completed, this sum represents three one-sixth payments of $6,333.33 each plus a partial payment of $2,333.34. At about 45 percent of the projected total cost, the sum McLaughlin tendered also becomes a measure of the delay. The next payment of $10,333.33 was recorded nearly two months later on May 20, three days after McLaughlin paid Thomas Berry of Columbus $1,700.00 for engine boilers.[31]

As had occurred in March, operations were catching up on the delays of work in progress on the one hand while introducing new work into the system on the other. On May 23, McLaughlin paid $12,000 for the *Kate L. Bruce*, a schooner that had run into Apalachicola from Havana with a cargo of fruit in 1861.[32] Trapped there by the blockade, she was put up for sale.[33] Adding still another dimension to construction under his supervision, McLaughlin decided to convert this commercial vessel for war.

Once boilers were purchased for the *Chattahoochee*, Warner made trips from Columbus to become more active on site at Saffold. Carpentry got underway on the *Kate L. Bruce*, and the ship doubled as a barracks for workmen sent to Saffold in June. McLaughlin also began to make orders for materials paid for from a *Chattahoochee* project account. A payment for oil and oil cans and one for making scuppers to drain the ship's decks are among the endless details McLaughlin handled during the gunboat's construction.[34]

Confidence in Johnston's ability to meet his contractual obligations evidently began to erode, for McLaughlin asked in June that a steamboat captain stop at the Navy Yard Landing to consult with the master carpenter about Johnston's progress. There was the suggestion that the civilian contractor was more interested in building his facility for long-term personal gain than for completing the wartime project.[35] Whether or not there was profiteering, McLaughlin's records show his greatly increased level of direct involvement in the project beginning in June and July. His August 12 voucher for $6,333.33 was the last lump-sum payment to Johnston.

Thereafter, smaller payments were accompanied by detailed lists of materials and labor. With the final $1,139.85 payment Johnston received on January 19, 1863, his total receipts fell short of the agreed-upon $47,500.00 by $13,833.34. Once McLaughlin instituted closer accounting methods, Johnston received only an additional $1,588.12 for labor (including as little as $1.50½ for one day's slave labor and as much as $2.00 to install a door lock), $256.15 for materials (including 40¢ for sixteen 1.5-inch screws), and $3.00 for one and a half days' use of one of Johnston's tools.[36] Total labor, materials, and tool rental reduced the difference in payment to $11,985.07.

As was hinted in various correspondence, Johnston might have enriched himself as a civilian contractor, placing his major expenditure in his boat yard. If so, McLaughlin was able to step in to save the project budget. The vouchers show that his steady, meticulous accounting reserved enough from the $47,500 allocation to cover the $12,000 cost of the *Kate L. Bruce*. On June 30, McLaughlin closed out his special account on the gunboat and placed surplus funds in a general account.[37]

By mid-July, McLaughlin was ordering rubber packing and copper piping, more than a ton of iron, and three hundred pounds of material for shafting. The latter was directed to Warner for his work on machinery. Work was also in progress on making the ship habitable for a crew: installing stove pipes, a galley stove, boilers with cocks for the stove, oven pans, and three water closets. Two Columbus coppersmiths, William Fee and Martin Costa, were employed by the firm of D. B. Thompson to do this work. Through August, inventory for the ship continued to develop: twelve mess kettles; twelve mess pans; twenty-five each of pans, spoons, and sailor pots; seventy-five cups; and seventy-five pans. Inflated currency had not yet caught up with the project, for a box to pack that order of $115.13 cost $1.00 from McLaughlin's project

Lt. Catesby ap R. Jones, C.S.N. Before commanding the Chattahoochee, *Jones had already distinguished himself as executive officer of the* Virginia *in her battle with the* Monitor. *His association with Columbus operations continued throughout the war as the Selma Naval Iron Works under his command supplied rifled cannon for Confederate ships. Jones was sometimes called "little ap" because of the prefix to his middle name meaning "son of." His sons, Catesby ap Catesby and Roger ap Catesby, continued that usage well into the twentieth century.*
James W. Woodruff, Jr., Confederate Naval Museum, Columbus, Ga.

account; drayage to the wharf for shipment downriver was $1.50. As he continued to fit out the galley, McLaughlin ordered such items as wood buckets, dippers, lanterns, lamps, a large knife, and a shovel and tongs.[38]

As plans took shape to fit the *Chattahoochee* for her crew, the next components to add were the batteries and other details to make her an effective warship. The original plan had been to deliver the completed ship to the navy and then undertake adaptation for combat. By late July, Johnston's work was already five months in arrears and his work was soon to be phased out entirely. Lt. Catesby ap R. Jones was assigned to the gunboat to begin the work of making her a fighting ship.

The Ship Becomes a Man-of-War

In its wealth of experienced officers, the Confederate Navy was seldom more fortunate than in Jones. Like so many of his fellow officers, he was already an experienced Union officer when the Civil War began. The previous March he had gained a place in history as the executive officer of the *Virginia* in its battle with the *Monitor* at Hampton Roads. No doubt the Navy Department's first choice for him was command of the ironclad to be built at Columbus. A wooden gunboat, reached by more than thirty-six hours' travel to an isolated station, would have to serve until the Confederates could float a larger navy.[39]

Men who had served on the *Virginia* came with Jones to Saffold: Hardin Beverly Littlepage, Henry H. Marmaduke (who had commanded one of the ironclad's batteries), and Charles King Mallory, Jr., a Hampton, Virginia, midshipman (the gallant "Young Mallory" who had been the first to board the US *Congress* after the *Virginia*'s attack forced her surrender). William Conway Whittle, son of the commander of the New Orleans station, was another officer who came aboard. His family rather anxiously noted "little William's" assignment more than one hundred miles from Columbus in "a dreadful climate."[40] He wrote to James M. Whittle that he was serving on a badly constructed steamboat, and this news was passed on in a letter to Lewis N. Whittle in a family's effort to keep track of their sons at war.[41]

Two others to arrive at Saffold in September 1862 were Asst. Engrs. Henry Fagan and John Horry Dent, Jr. Both had served on the *McRae* and the *Louisiana* in New Orleans before being captured at the fall of

Lt. William C. Whittle, C.S.N. This photograph—sent to his mother—illustrates the comment that the Chattahoochee's *officers were "sons of the old aristocracy." Whittle, who shared the feeling among the officers of isolation and inactivity, sought a transfer to a more exciting post and succeeded in getting an appointment abroad. He later served on the C.S.S. Shenandoah.*
Bill Turner, Clinton, Md.

Forts Jackson and St. Philip on April 28, 1862. After being imprisoned at Fort Warren, they were exchanged August 5 and arrived in Saffold scarcely a month later. At least young Horry was nearer his home in Barbour County, but his father fretted over his health much as the Whittles exchanged anxious notes about "little William."

Soon after his arrival, Horry wrote his father a list of officers that included Mdn. W. J. Craig, Gunner John A. Lovett, and Chief Engr. J. W. Tynan. He was suitably awed by their commander: "Capt. Jones . . . is said to stand second to none in the Navy. Officers [at Saffold] say there is no man in the Navy who can excel him scientifically with the exception of Maury. . . . He is quite reserved and they say he is very strict on a ship."[42]

Volunteers who transferred from the *Virginia* were Coxswain John Rosler, Boatswain's Mates William Young and James C. Cronin, Capt. Top George May, and Seamen John Perry, John Dunlop, John Joliff, A. W. Tembler, Pat Martin, and Thomas Sanders.[43] Lt. George W. Gift, who had served with Jones in the Pacific Fleet, also joined this company of officers.

Something of an adventurer, Gift had left the navy to speculate in the boom times of California in the 1850s. He had edited a newspaper, held various posts in state government, and made a marriage that was rumored to have ended in divorce. At news of the secession, he had traveled overland from California with Albert Sidney Johnston to join the new navy. His part in the career of the *Arkansas* on the Mississippi quickly established his career and Adm. Franklin Buchanan later praised him as a competent officer.

Gift characterized the *Chattahoochee*'s officers as "sons of the old aristocracy, who are carrying on the traditions creditably."[44] That such a company was assigned to Saffold is both a positive measure of the importance of having a vessel in that area and an indication that there were not enough Confederate ships afloat to utilize the advantage of an experienced officer corps.

Letters that these men mailed from the *Chattahoochee* went to major Confederate figures: Robert Dabney Minor, chief of Ordnance and Hydrography; John Mercer Brooke, ordnance expert and designer of the Brooke rifled cannon; Secretary Mallory; Capt. Duncan N. Ingraham of the Charleston Squadron. The letters expressed the officers' concern at being out of the mainstream of naval strategy and politics and concern about who would receive votes of thanks from the Congress, who ranked well on the promotions list, and what Congress, senior officers, and policy makers actually *ought* to do to win the naval war. The length and frequency of letters, and inquiries about not receiving replies, also bespeak a duty station where there was no fighting action but one mail call per week and ample time both for sea stories and for scuttlebutt about what was happening elsewhere—and what could happen if the *Chattahoochee* ever got afloat and free of Apalachicola Bay. The letters were also filled with the practical human concerns of keeping healthy, well clothed, and supplied with equipment.

William Whittle was soon writing his friend Robert D. Minor in Richmond with an offer to have a pair of shoes made by a local cobbler. The price was only $6.50, though the leather was not well tanned. By the time Whittle had sent the shoes to Richmond (first by boat to Columbus and then by rail express) the price had escalated to $8.00.[45] Such personal channels of supply would become quite familiar to the Confederate Navy.

Horry Dent kept up a running commentary to his father as Chattahoochee steamboats carried his weekly letters home to Eufaula. No stranger to the area or to the vagaries of navigation on the river, his comments about construction and hopes for the gunboat offer a wry and realistic counterpoint to the rather grandiose dreams of officers like Gift. While the others were caught up in the romance of sail on deck, Horry was in the hold below grappling with the practicalities of defective cylinder heads and the sound of boiler rivets giving way.

Until the *Chattahoochee* was fitted out for the crew in early December, the officers were housed at the Johnstons' home. Horry reported they fared "elegantly, [and] have as elegant table as one would wish."[46] Johnston was also very kind to nurse Horry through one of his first bouts of chills and fever. As work continued more and more under Jones's supervision, Johnston set about fulfilling his contract to build two additional boats. His entrepreneurship much impressed Horry, who had been brought up in a world that valued the shrewd business sense of an Ingersoll, a McNabb, a Howell Cobb, or his own father. His estimate of Johnston was doubtless of particular interest to John Horry, Sr.: "He is the most energetic man I ever saw. He is a Lawyer by profession. Married a Miss Saffold with this immense fortune. He has another plantation near Madison, Ga. so he has just taken these contracts to occupy himself. He never saw a boat built before."[47] The boat was a measure of Johnston's wealth and skill, but such a man also prided himself on providing an ample table, leaving the "elegance" to his wife.

For most of the officers, an interesting feature of the duty station at Saffold was the social matrix of the nearby plantations—not only Mrs. Johnston's home but "The Pines" with the Shackelford sisters and "The Refuge" where the older Shackelford sister presided over Col. Charles J. Munnerlyn's mansion. Mrs. Johnston was described as being "very understanding" of the young officers' need for the company of young ladies. Her understanding of her role as the contractor's helpmeet included taking responsibility to see that the officers and gentlemen were well fed and well entertained.

The ritual of the visit from plantation to plantation was expanded to include the officers from the *Chattahoochee* once they took up residence on board. The officers would spruce up their quarters with bouquets of flowers and the ladies would bring pound cake, strawberries, and cream for an on-board tea.[48] Four damask cushions that appear unaccountably in financial records can be explained perhaps as accoutrements of such occasions.[49]

Horry Dent gave no reports of such invitations; instead, he wrote warmly of business counsels with Johnston. Perhaps he left the taking of tea to the Virginia gentlemen—or perhaps the caste system on ship extended to shore. Three weeks after his arrival, he wrote bitterly to his father: "I will never stay in the Navy when the War closes as an Engineers berth is one of the most contemptible for an Officer. It does very well in Port where you rig yourself and go ashore. But when in motion then comes the tug of war. Smut, grease and filth of all kind you are then covered with to keep things in working order."[50] At that point he was determined "to see the old tub through," but he soon wrote of plans to transfer or resign.

As the officers were generally accepted into the plantation society of Early County, deep ties of affection developed, adding to the general hopes for the gunboat's success. George Gift and Ellen Shackelford fell in love, though her father opposed her marriage to someone who was unknown to the family and the area.[51] Thus a dimension of romance was added to the story—and a dimension of daily details from his letters about what life was like for these sons of the aristocracy.

As the officers continued to settle into their new duty station, work on the *Chattahoochee* continued. Throughout August and September, a steady stream of orders continued for chairs, hammocks, tables, a looking glass, and items like door butts for finishing work on the interior. Sail twine, one hundred yards of canvas, and pay for sail makers meant that the "Boat" was rapidly becoming a ship. An order for two steering wheels, one of them brass-mounted, was an indication that it would indeed be handsome.[52]

Horry persisted in calling the ship a "Boat" and he did not consider it "handsome" at all. While he at first thought her a "credit to the Chattahoochee [River]" and "a better Boat than is given credit for," he began to find Johnston's work a disappointment. The shallow-draft construction dictated by conditions on the river would, he thought, become a marked disadvantage at sea: "She will be a perfect old tub." His assessment of the engines was also a mixture of positive and negative. He found the plan "excellent" but the work "very indifferently finished." He took care to describe for his father the low-pressure horizontal direct-acting engines with a twenty-two inch stroke and a twenty-eight-inch cylinder driving two six-foot propellers.[53] These were a technical novelty on an inland river where engines with a much longer stroke drove paddle wheels; the new engines had to generate sufficient RPMs to whirl propellers. Converting from paddle wheel to screw required the Columbus Iron Works to retool machinery, retrain workers, and redesign engines intended for civilian river steamers. Once complete, the engines were fitted into a very small space in the vessel's shallow hold. Once the boilers were fired and the steam engines were at work, Horry was to find that the economical design created very uncomfortable work conditions. But before the engines could raise steam and heat up the engine room, months of work were required along with materials in very short supply.

Continuing work on the ship's machinery and metal fittings called for lead pipe, copper tubing and coppersmiths, tin and a tinner to work it, large orders for lead and boiler iron, and many days' labor at $3 to $5 for skilled workers. River steamers were kept busy on trips to and from Columbus with workers and supplies.[54] While Horry reported to his father from time to time that the engines "progressed finely," he had little praise for the engine fabricators in Columbus: "Seems everything they send down have to have some alterations," he wrote September 7; and on September 14: "We could complete the engines very soon if we had the work down from Columbus. They seem to take their time up there."[55]

As he and his mates Fagan and Tynan made headway, the navy was making headway in administrative procedures. Word came down from

Richmond that all three would have to pass a qualifying exam to be engineers. Horry was first reassigned in September to Columbus for instruction in the work he was already performing in Saffold, and then he was ordered to Savannah in November to appear before the examining board. Tynan was directed to Mobile in December to appear before the same board for the same purpose, and his absence delayed their work further.

In Columbus, McLaughlin was engineering matters of procurement, labor, and budget. His vouchers give a good idea of the relative cost of labor and materials for this work. Making sails first required constructing ten sail-makers' benches at $2.50 each. Labor to construct the sail room was $350.00, for the rigging loft $130.00. The Columbus Factory and other individual contractors supplied yards of duck and canvas and pounds of sail twine. Charles W. Godwin of Columbus was paid $4.25 per day for forty-six of the sixty-one days' work required for sail making. To McLaughlin's dismay, James Dempsey worked well as a sail maker and then returned to Apalachicola beyond the reach of Confederate naval authority. In all, sails as a component of the vessel cost about $1,000.00.

Vouchers also show that costs for copper fittings on the ship were considerably higher. Thomas Costa and William Fee spent 114 man-days between August 1862 and March 1863 on this work, at a cost of $4.00 to $6.00 per day, or $541.00. Items made of copper are among the most expensive on the materials list: $4.50 for a copper box, $28.75 for a copper tank, $1.00 for a copper flange, and $7.00 for a copper scoop funnel. By the pound, the price of copper ranged from $1.50 to $2.50 during the months Fee and Costa worked. By comparison, steel was $1.00 per pound, lead was 30 to 50¢, and iron about 12½¢ in cruder forms or 35¢ for railroad iron. Two-inch screws were $1.50 per gross; copper nuts $2.50 per pound.[56]

During the first two years, prices for "strategic metals" for the *Chattahoochee* did not constitute a great percentage of the total project cost, even when a single item was relatively expensive. Later on during the Civil War, such materials could scarcely be had at any price. The blockade worked to close off supplies, and a characteristic of the Southern economy worked another disadvantage. The Confederacy had raw materials but insufficient means to see a resource like copper sent from ore through smelting to pig copper to boiler tubing for a gunboat.[57]

As labor continued on the gunboat's machinery, guns for the battery began to arrive by rail in Columbus for transport to Saffold by steamboat. On August 13, the first two guns came in; on August 15, two gun carriages arrived. Through September, Jones began his most important work of getting the batteries in place.[58]

A conventional feature of the ship's ordnance was the four 32-pounders mounted broadside on trucks. This 6.4-inch smoothbore cannon took its name from the 32-pound shot it fired. An elevation of five degrees and a point-blank range of 313 yards gave the cannon standard firepower for naval vessels of the time, though the broadside mounting limited their maneuverability.[59]

The most powerful gun on board was a nine-inch Dahlgren mounted forward on a pivot. John A. Dahlgren, a contemporary and former colleague of the *Chattahoochee*'s officers in the Union Navy, had distinguished himself in designing this cannon. Cast with a preponderance of weight toward the rear, in a shape like an elongated blunderbuss, this design allowed the firing of heavier charges and shot because the heavy distribution of metal could withstand the force of detonation. Capt. Henry Wise of the U.S. Naval Ordnance Bureau said that the weighted design was "the very best form in which a gun can be made to attain the greatest strength." Adm. Samuel F. DuPont said there was "relatively none better," and U.S. ships were armed with Dahlgrens.[60] To mount this gun, Jones made a large order of iron from the Mobile and Girard Railroad and orders for twenty-four-pound sledge hammers, spikes, and augers. The next task was to lay a rail track on the deck to guide the gun carriage in an arc around its center point.[61]

The 32-pound rifled cannon, while not as powerful, was the state-of-the-art component in the battery. Matthew Fontaine Maury, in urging the use of the rifled cannon on a pivot, had praised its range and effectiveness. The tendency of a spinning projectile to ricochet on water raised questions about the rifle's effectiveness for naval warfare, but its ability to fire shots that would pierce armor overrode all other factors. Within the next two years, John Mercer Brooke in the Bureau of Ordnance and Hydrography and Jones at the Selma Naval Iron Works would rival their former colleague Dahlgren by turning out the finest rifles used in the Civil War.[62] Here the Confederacy's new navy worked to Brooke's advantage, for the Old Navy was committed to Dahlgren's design.

Even if the ordnance was state of the art, the Confederate Navy had to recruit its sailors from a rural, agricultural population; Horry said they were "mostly Backwoods Floridians."[63] Recruiting and training a large, well-drilled crew to man batteries presented a formidable task. The Dahlgren and the rifle each required a crew of seventeen; the broadside pieces required a minimum of eleven each. To supply the guns, ten men were required as runners, for the magazine, the passage, and scuttles; the shell room required six. By comparison, only six of the crew manned the wheel, con, signals, lead, and pumps.[64] Having the batteries on the open deck gave crews more room to maneuver. This placement especially relieved gun crews, for hits amidship could throw shattered wood inward with a shrapnel effect.

Preliminary tests of the nine-inch Dahlgren on October 3 showed the deck bearing the recoil well even though the gundeck was unshored. To witness the novelty of heavy cannonades on the Chattahoochee River, Jones invited Mrs. Johnston, Mrs. Shackelford, and all five Shackelford daughters—"the Batch of Shackelfords," Horry called them. They were overawed by the display of firepower, and the inexperienced crew suffered "as much consternation as the People in the Neighborhood," according to Horry.[65]

Even as Jones received the guns and began to mount them and to train gunners, he had concerns about obtaining ammunition. Lt. David P. McCorkle at the Atlanta Naval Ordnance Works had been able to supply gun carriages but not ammunition. Jones then wrote his friend Minor in Richmond to search sources in Richmond and Charlotte.

Even if the guns had been in place and the *Chattahoochee* had been ready to sail at full steam, Jones also needed coal. As he waited for a thousand tons that were on order, the fifty tons on hand had been "several times under water . . . coated with river mud." Jones asked that Minor inquire about it and "if necessary see the Secy." "We want everything for her and have nothing, and can't get anything . . ." was Jones's summation of his work.[66]

As Jones busied, and worried, himself with arming the gunboat, William Whittle expressed his concern about the climate and the health of the crew. His first clue to the fever-ridden conditions at Saffold had come at his arrival; he asked when his baggage would be unloaded and was answered, "In a couple of shakes." The problem with men disabled with chills and fever became more and more serious in the later summer. In late September he reported that three officers and twenty-two men were hospitalized in Columbus; by mid-October he reported that they had only two of thirty-eight men able to work on the gunboat, both of them convalescent.[67]

River steamers regularly carried men to hospital in Columbus; then most of the crew were sent upriver in late September to await cold weather and better conditions. Horry's letters to his father were full of references to his own health and others': "I never saw men so afraid of chills. They think down here is the sickliest place on earth." He invited his friend Fagan to recuperate at the Dent plantation, while he struggled to keep healthy in Saffold. After only a month on duty at Saffold, he began to write of going home to Barbour County himself to recover. Then he considered resigning the navy altogether.[68] After two months on duty, he wrote on November 7 a clear description of what he and his mates were suffering:

> I am now in bed with a severe fever. Actually the first day I reached this place I was attacked with cool sensations. An ache in the lower part of my back and all my joints the same way affected. I did not give up the 1st two days. They were good symptoms. And the 5th, 6th, & 7th seized on to me in good earnest. I have now had three good shakes. I am scarcely able to write this letter but as the Boat goes up tonight I will attempt to scribble a few lines to you.[69]

Health conditions, of course, affected availability of labor on the ship. Then the concern became whether men could be retained at the station at all. By November 29, Horry reported to his father:

> This morning I was taken about 10 o'clock with one of the severest chills I ever felt. It was followed by a dreadful fever which has stuck to me throughout the day and [is] on me yet, but not so severe. I have never had an attack weaken me so. I could scarcely move about. And with any exertion it makes me dreadfully sick at my stomach. We have now about 40 or 50 invalids [from a complement of 100]. I succeeded in getting the Captains to forward my resignation but I am afraid it is uncertain whether Mallory will accept it. I hope he will as I never saw such a country in my life. Always sick. And it is one of the most uncomfortable affairs I ever saw (the ship). . . . I never saw a set of Officers so sick of a Boat in my life.[70]

Once Horry's health improved during the winter, he wrote on February 11: "It is a settled case with me. Capt. Jones today made me give him a certificate that I had recovered from chills and now enjoying good health."[71] He and his father had begun discussing parental efforts to arrange a transfer.

Much in need of a system to maintain a crew at full strength, McLaughlin ordered from the pharmacy of Urquhart and Chapman an ounce of quinine at twenty-five dollars.[72] Whittle noted the need for whiskey as a stimulant and for medicinal purposes; Peruvian bark, a source of quinine, was soaked in whiskey to make it serve both purposes. Although Jones had duly requisitioned a barrel of whiskey from Montgomery, Whittle's request to expedite the order went to Minor in the Bureau of Ordnance and Hydrography in Richmond with the request that Cdr. French Forest in the Office of Orders and Detail give orders to the naval storekeeper at Montgomery that a second barrel of whiskey be sent.

The senior officers worked to have a ship's surgeon assigned. Dr. Marcellus Ford came aboard in early October but could hardly effect a cure where other medical officers—Union as well as Confederate— were failing. The supply system, too, was insufficient for their needs.

They found the process ponderous and slow in responding to their requests. Minor was asked to see Secretary Mallory himself about locating two midshipmen. Even the request for a gunner's quadrant was channeled along a personal route from the gunboat direct to the highest levels of Confederate government administration. And the request for a paymaster was directed to Minor from Whittle within this context: "We ought to have a paymaster. I would write Uncle A[rthur] about it but do not think it necessary as you will mention it. Give my love to him."[73]

D. S. Johnston was, of course, responsible for the design and construction of the ship, but this system also began to malfunction. As navy man Jones set to work with the planter-entrepreneur, trouble soon followed. Johnston evidently considered the younger Dent a neighbor and known quantity and so confided his difficulties. He had contracted only to build the *Chattahoochee*'s hull and had fulfilled that contract by June 1. When Jones arrived, he called for a series of alterations and the addition of masts—a redesign that cost weeks of time to dismantle part of Johnston's finished work. Horry wrote his father that, by his own legal interpretation of the case, "Col. Johnston could relieve himself of his contract if he wished."[74]

Navy yard vouchers show that Johnston's crews performed extensive alterations through September—and billed the navy for work above and beyond the original contract. The ship's galley was relocated and a sail loft and rigging room constructed. Smaller parts like quoins and marlin spikes also had to be fabricated. Payment for this work was not settled until December 3, after the navy had pulled out of Saffold to concentrate its work in Columbus.

Jones and Whittle also disagreed about the overall design. Whittle wanted the ship bark rigged, but Jones's preference for a three-masted schooner prevailed. Either way, the work of installing the masts was slow. By September 14, one mast was in, another ready for installation, and a third in preparation. That job was completed by October 3, but the work of rigging was also a lengthy process. McLaughlin reported on June 30 that sail maker Charles Godwin had evidently returned to his home at Apalachicola; Horry noted that the work was much delayed for lack of experienced sailors. Not until the gunboat was commissioned January 1 were the sails fully rigged.

Concerns continued that the ship would be too slow. Whittle first estimated a six-foot draft, but he did not account for the weight the *Chattahoochee* would have to carry. Even only partially loaded with coal, shells, and supplies, the ship drew seven feet three inches. From his station in the engine room, Horry later noted that the ship drew seven and a half feet with an eight-day supply of thirty tons of coal and would probably draw nine feet with a full supply of eighty tons.[75] The critical factor added to those data was "too much to cross the [Apalachicola] bar."[76]

Toward the end of November 1862, the navy revoked its contract with Johnston altogether. Plans had been made to construct "an immense Iron Clad boat" in Columbus under McLaughlin and Warner. "So this will be the end of the Navy Yard," Horry wrote his father. By the first week of December, Johnston was "winding up his business," as all his workers transferred to Columbus.[77] His operation had fallen victim to a policy change that consolidated construction under the navy's control at Columbus. In personal terms, Johnston may have fallen victim to himself.

In a letter to H. B. Littlepage in Savannah, Jones expressed his anger at Johnston: "the longer he lives, the greater rascal he becomes."[78] Just how much a rascal, George Gift reported in a confidential note to Ellen Shackelford in Saffold: "the *gallant Colonel* lost $800 playing faro on his last trip to Columbus; got exceedingly drunk and did many other things not very profitable to his reputation or his finances."[79]

Jones also gave vent to his disappointment: "adieu to our hopes of prizes &c. We are condemned to remain in the muddy waters of the Apalachicola."[80] How different from the high deeds they had performed at Hampton Roads and how different the prospects of Littlepage on the *Atlanta* at Savannah.

Adieu to Our Hopes of Prizes

Not just a rascally civilian contractor and the technical inadequacies of his ship, but civilian and military politics were also restricting Jones's career on the *Chattahoochee*. As work had continued through 1862 to ready the craft for action, anxiety continued to build along the Chattahoochee River; land fortifications and batteries were inadequate to defend the area from Union attack and yet the gunboat designed to break the blockade fell many months behind schedule. To obstruct the river seemed the best plan.

As their ship went into commission on January 1, 1863, Jones and his fellow officers found themselves in competition with the Confederate Army, not the Union Navy. Their duty was to defend the river; more and more it seemed that fulfilling that duty excluded their naval ambitions.

Immediate needs for defense thus overrode long-range plans of action. At the time the Union had gained control of the port of Apalachicola, the river northward was defended only by a battery of ten guns at Ricko's Bluff, fifty miles north of the city, or about half the distance to Chattahoochee, Florida. This was obviously inadequate protection for an area where, according to a report by Gen. Joseph Finegan, eighty thousand bales of cotton were stored in April 1862.[81]

Concern spread northward, where the Columbus City Council addressed the problem, citing the "notoriously inefficient character" of river defense. The council commissioned Alfred Iverson to confer with the Secretary of War George W. Randolph about providing adequate defenses.[82]

Early in May, Randolph ordered Gen. John C. Pemberton to assign a competent engineer to survey the Apalachicola and determine the most advantageous place for sinking an obstruction. As had been the case with Mallory's policy regarding the construction of gunboats, Randolph's statement of river defense policy was followed by difficulty in execution.

Pemberton's first difficulty was that he had no engineer to make a survey of the river. He went himself, however, to make observations of the Apalachicola and to make a report to Insp. Gen. Samuel Cooper.

Based on his observations, he recommended Fort Gadsden, at a point twenty miles north of Apalachicola, as a possible site.[83] Later in May, William R. Boggs was assigned the survey duties. He began his expedition at Columbus and continued downriver to Fort Gadsden by river steamer.

Boggs was displeased with conditions at the Chattahoochee Arsenal, finding no guard stationed at the arsenal landing to guard supplies. Conditions farther down the Chattahoochee at Ricko's Bluff were no better:

> The guns were on top of a bluff at least three hundred feet above the river, with a range of only half a mile. The most of the cotton was some twenty miles down the river. Near it was a small battery of field artillery, behind an epaulment, supported by a battalion of infantry. Owing to a deep creek coming in to a very short range in their rear, the position was untenable. Below this point the Federals were in full possession.[84]

The presence of the blockaders did not prevent Boggs from continuing his trip as far as Apalachicola. The owner of the steamboat had been a resident of Apalachicola and so they pulled into the wharf of the deserted town almost casually.

Soldiers, who at first kept out of sight, fell to work loading the steamer with castings, machinery, and other much-needed items that the blockade of Apalachicola had cut off. A Union steamer was in sight down the bay—and Lieutenant Welch's diary mentions such Confederate engineering activity[85]—yet Boggs and his men arrived and left unchallenged.

Upriver from the port, Boggs discovered refugees along Owl Creek. One man had simply moved his entire household and all his slaves to a settlement of cabins they constructed in a clearing. A fisherman and his family had settled in a tent made of sail to wait out the war. They were all startled at the smoke and sound of a steamer on the creek, fearing that the Union blockaders had come; otherwise, they were living a relatively comfortable life in an area Boggs described as "exceedingly beautiful."[86]

In reporting to Pemberton about his excursion, Boggs agreed that Fort Gadsden offered a good position for the obstruction. He observed that it was elevated above the river with good roads to the sea and a long, straight road in front of the position. The swampy areas on either side of the river would offer an obstacle to a land attack. The river at that point was of average width and depth; therefore, Boggs suggested that cribs like those used at Savannah be sunk there.

Fort Gadsden was actually the most southerly point on the Apalachicola where an obstruction was practical, for below that point the river widened considerably. It presented the disadvantage of being an unhealthy location for quartering troops. Despite this observation, Boggs asked Pemberton to supply Fort Gadsden with two eight-inch columbiads with carriages, platforms, and other implements.

The second site that Boggs suggested for sinking an obstruction was called the Narrows. This is a five-mile stretch of the Apalachicola River lying fifty-five miles below Chattahoochee and thirty-six miles above Apalachicola. From a generally southerly course, the river bends and flows due east for nearly a mile before it curves back to flow due west for another mile. From there, it takes a sharp southeast–north northwest turn and flows south in a straight course for a mile before entering two more miles of short, abrupt bends. The disadvantage of this area was that it offered no position to command an obstruction with a land battery.

Having completed his survey, Boggs began his efforts to gather men and supplies to carry out his plans. He requested one hundred hands supplied with rations and tents from the Confederate quartermaster at Columbus. Getting no encouragement from the quartermaster, he then appealed to the mayors of Columbus and Eufaula. From them he learned that workmen could not be obtained until crops had been harvested. Even an advertisement offering one dollar per diem wage, lodging, rations, and medical care did not bring response to Boggs's efforts.

Boggs received no more aid from Pemberton than he had received from the army or local governments. The general informed him that no guns could be spared for fortifications and that there would be no tents for a working force until winter. Pemberton promised Boggs $15,000 as soon as it could be made available, but he added that the department at the time was without funds. After making a report of his difficulties to the Department of Engineers, Boggs resigned on June 4.[87]

Like a conscientious engineer, Boggs had made a thorough survey that translated into technical and quantitative terms the problems, needs, and anxieties of a civilian and nontechnical group; and he had made his recommendations for action and requests for funding. While his memoirs give a terse, unadorned account, his letters to various military, government, and civilian groups are models of political and social skill. Expressions of appreciation are exchanged, complimentary flourishes abound, and every correspondent has the "honor to remain" every other correspondent's "humble and obedient servant." But none of the exchanges served to produce results based on Boggs's recommendations. The placing of obstructions was thus delayed until very late in 1862.

Citizens near Saffold in Early County, who were much concerned about the delays both in constructing the *Chattahoochee* and in obstructing the river, wrote to the secretary of war in October asking that something be done about river defense. They pointed out the strategic importance of Columbus's position near the West Point Railroad and the value of one hundred thousand bales of cotton stored in the river valley.[88] They could also see for themselves that the gunboat at D. S. Johnston's place was not yet able either to raise the blockade or defend against attacks on the river.

On November 5, 1862, the Columbus City Council took up the issue anew by adopting a resolution to allocate $3,000 for obstructing the river.[89] The mayor, Dr. James F. Bozeman, wrote a letter to Randolph expressing the council's concern for the safety of the Apalachicola-Chattahoochee area. Bozeman also set about winning the navy's support for plans to obstruct the river, probably at the Narrows. He issued Jones an invitation "to come up at the Earliest day practicable, that we who are interested in a common object may confer together, and cooperate understandingly to the desired end." He ended with a courteous flourish; "Desiring the early pleasure of meeting with you here I remain, with high respect Yr. obt. Svt."[90] Randolph tried to assure Bozeman that the Chattahoochee would be defended, but on November 22 the Columbus council announced plans to sink an obstruction in the Apalachicola River at Alum Bluff twenty-two miles below Chattahoochee, Florida. As local government preempted the national government, Governor Milton of Florida raised immediate objections to the council's actions.[91]

An effort was made to untangle the local, state, and national plans. In November the governors of Georgia, Alabama, and Florida appealed to Jefferson Davis. Soon afterward, the Middle Florida Military District was created. Extending from the Suwannee River to the Choctawhatchee River, the principal area within the district was the Apalachicola River. The renewed efforts to defend the Apalachicola began under the command of a new officer, Gen. Howell Cobb, and under the direction of a new engineer, Capt. Theodore Moreno. The two men met in Columbus where they formulated plans for the defense of the district. The first concern was to obstruct the Apalachicola and the second was to defend the land approach to Tallahassee from St. Mark's, Florida.[92]

By the end of December, Jones had done the duty of an officer and a gentleman by acknowledging the plans to obstruct his passage to sea and by offering his cooperation to the army. Cobb's response, as Bozeman's had, reflects a sensitivity to the *Chattahoochee*'s situation: "I am gratified to know that I shall have your cooperation in the defence of the river, whilst I regret on your account that you cannot have a larger and more congenial field of operations."[93] To further assuage Jones's disappointment, Cobb placed the steamer *Munnerlyn* at his disposal and offered to visit Jones at Chattahoochee "at any time you will designate." Despite the understanding expressed, the army nevertheless had its own mission to dispatch.

Moreno received suggestions for obstructing the river from Maj. A. L. Rives, assistant chief engineer of the Confederate Engineers. Rives recommended, as Boggs had, that a complex of cribs be used. This design involved two parallel rows of square cribs placed twelve feet apart across the current and built up to the low-water mark of the river. The two rows were thirty feet apart in a staggered arrangement. Rives suggested that rafts be attached to the cribs to rise and fall with the river and thus secure the obstruction even at high water.[94]

The plan that Moreno devised incorporated part of Rives's proposal. The rafts were supplied from Columbus, but Moreno altered the plan by sinking the rafts in the channel and adding a large chain to catch debris floating downriver. In directing river defenses, Moreno chose Rock Bluff, a point thirteen miles south of Chattahoochee, as the site of the second obstruction.[95]

Fortifying the obstructions at the Narrows and Rock Bluff posed the next problem in river defense. As Boggs had pointed out in his first survey of the river, any advantages of the Narrows were counterbalanced by the fact that constructing batteries there would be difficult. Nevertheless, Cobb planned to place his best and heaviest guns there. He ordered three 32-pounders placed in one battery and planned another of the same strength. At Rock Bluff 18- and 24-pounders from Alum Bluff were mounted on wooden frames that had been built in Columbus. Concerning these defense measures, Cobb wrote to the commander of the District of South Carolina, Georgia, and Florida, Gen. P. G. T. Beauregard: "These obstructions constitute the main defense of the river. If the enemy breaks there, there is little hope of successful resistance above."[96]

Until the completion of the batteries, measures were taken to defend the force at work upon them. From the fewer than 1,000 troops in the District of Middle Florida, Cobb ordered more than 100 sharpshooters to lookout posts below the obstructions. The army tried to impress slaves to strengthen the lookout system, but terrified farm laborers used this duty as a means of escape.[97] Some escaped to the Union blockaders, and others traveled by foot along the river back to their homes.

By the end of 1862, work had gone on for nearly a year. Correspondence and on-site visits had involved General Pemberton himself; engineers Boggs and Moreno; the governors of Georgia, Alabama, and Florida; and sundry mayors, councilmen, and anxious citizens. To add a final safeguard to the defense system, the gunboat *Chattahoochee* was called into service to aid in protecting the defense works. Because the machinery on the vessel had not been completed, it was to be towed down the river. The battery on the gunboat could be put to use while work continued on installing the machinery.[98]

When Moreno visited Saffold during his survey of the river in November, he informed Jones that piles had been sunk into the riverbed at the Narrows and barges would be moored to them. Horry Dent observed from a distance Jones "speaking spiritedly" to Moreno, and he judged then "the Chattahoochee's fate is sealed."[99] He also wrote his father in early January that Johnston, who had lost his work for the navy, had begun sawing lumber for Moreno's fortifications at Fort Gaines. Nor did Horry share his mates' disappointment that the *Chattahoochee*'s reputation would suffer if the obstructions blockaded her: "Capt. [Jones] is still under the impression that he is going to sea. Notwithstanding the clamor of the people along the river. He knows as any sensible man ought to know if the Yankees can come up the River, the Chattahoochee will be no impediment to them."[100]

While navy Lieutenant Jones was every bit the cooperative officer to army General Cobb in their correspondence about the obstructions, in private he expressed himself more freely. In a January 2 letter to H. B. Littlepage at Savannah, he told how he objected to placing the obstruction and had appealed to Secretary Mallory that a passage be left to allow the *Chattahoochee* free access to sea. Neither his objection nor his proposed compromise held. For the time being, the obstruction did not hold, either, for strong river currents in the winter months delayed the project.

Laying Here in the River

Unusually high water in December swept away bridges upstream and carried the obstruction with it. The high water raised hopes that the *Chattahoochee* would get to sea after all. The masts and rigging were almost complete but the work went slowly for lack of experienced sailors. The engines were only awaiting Tynan's return from his qualifying exam in Mobile. In continued efforts to shape up the crew, Jones ordered the conscripts into Confederate gray uniforms so that they would "look a little more sailorlike." In Horry's view, it was a losing battle: "I never saw such a ragged and worthless set of men in my life. They are the very scourings of Florida." He was soon in trouble about his own dress, however. First the tailor to whom he'd paid $125 delayed delivery of his uniform; and then Jones refused to permit him on deck during quarters without regulation dress.[101] Almost every letter to his father asked that the uniform be hurried along on a river steamer.

The officers were hopeful about the ship's sailing capabilities, but Horry wrote to his father: "that is more speculation though, most of the officers are inexperienced being young, they have no idea of staying in the river, but the McRea crew was equally sanguinary or more so. And all their hopes exploded."[102] Horry was still exploring options for transfer.

In January the *Chattahoochee* received orders to steam downriver to guard the flood-torn obstructions until they could be completed and fortified. The orders raised hopes that she could get out to sea. Just as it seemed that the ship could clear the obstructions—and the political pressures and interservice rivalries that placed them—that hope was deferred when the engines malfunctioned.[103]

The engineers had begun trials of the machinery during the first week of January. A porous casting created too much play in the cylinder heads; and rather than being recast, the cylinders were patched. As the steam gauge began to rise toward thirty pounds, boiler rivets began to pop loose when the gauge reached twenty-one pounds. Tynan made a trip down from the Iron Works in Columbus with brackets to brace the boilers more securely. Laboring below deck, Dent and Fagan found their engine room "a perfect oven with scarcely any ventilation. Boilers and engines on the same deck. Consequently we will have to bear all the heat thrown out of three furnaces." For all the mechanical skills he was acquiring with state-of-the-art propulsion systems, Horry found that there was "no honor to be attached to such a ship as an Engineer."[104]

Once the boilers were bracketed, then a small hole developed and steam began to escape from the cylinder used to discharge condensed steam. Horry had "no serious apprehension of its doing any damage but I suppose it will [be] fixed to be on the safe side." Struggles with the machinery continued until, on the evening before the gunboat was to cast off for Chattahoochee, Florida, the air pump gear proved faulty and the steamer *Uchee* had to be sent upriver to tow the gunboat. By that time, Horry was thoroughly disgusted with his naval career: "I have heard nothing of my resignation. I wish it had been accepted as this boat in my opinion is one of the grandest failures of the war."[105]

By 5 A.M. on the day of their departure, the crew was on deck preparing the ship to cast away by 8:15. Within two hours the gunboat ran aground while negotiating a short bend in the river. The rudder was smashed, the stern post was sprung, and she began to leak badly. Pumps on board were able to remove enough water to keep the ship afloat and, after a long delay, this maiden voyage of the *Chattahoochee* down the Chattahoochee River was resumed.

At one point when towing proved infeasible, the ship was "dropped" downstream by the current while men on shore manned lines to keep her in the channel. When the ship tied up at 8 P.M., the crew members were exhausted and the officers hoarse from shouting orders during that fifteen-hour day. After getting on deck at 5 A.M. the next day, they started with the sun and arrived in Chattahoochee at 10:30 A.M.— almost twenty hours to traverse a distance of just more than thirty miles.

Commenting on this trip, George Gift wrote to Ellen Shackelford of "The Pines" that the engine failure would mean "We are doomed to abide at Chattahoochee six weeks to two months." To Miles Collier he wrote that the ship was "in a splendid condition for service, a strong leak and no engines. I wish the confounded vessel in Jerico. If our engines had been successful and no accident had occurred, we would have had conversation with the blockaders off Apalachicola before today."[106] Even the more ambitious and dashing officers were beginning to adopt Horry

Dent's view: "So the fate of the *Chattahoochee* has been decided on and the officers and crew will share the same ignominious fate. Laying here in the river to be prostrated by chills and fever in the Spring and Summer."[107]

After just more than fifteen months of effort, the gunboat contracted for completion in 120 days had beome little more than a floating battery. Her officers with their experience in the Union Navy and with their past action on the *Virginia* and *Arkansas* were ambitious to move elsewhere. Gift applied to the Charleston shipping firm of John Fraser and Company to serve as a mate on one of its commercial vessels.[108] Whittle arranged to transfer to the *Chicora* at Charleston, and Jones was to be transferred by early February to Gen. John Magruder's staff in Texas. Horry continued efforts to transfer.

Until such plans could advance their careers, they had little choice except to establish a shipboard routine on the *Chattahoochee*, drill the gun crews, and go about their duties as though the situation were more hopeful. Their most important duty was to work with the gun crews for forty-five minutes each morning until each of six crews was drilled. At 3:30 P.M. there was a half-hour drill and then fire quarters.[109] As the crews became more proficient, Gift wrote proudly to Ellen Shackelford of the drills: "We ran out loaded and fired three broadsides in forty seconds (the rifle in sixty-two seconds) the forward 32 pdr got through in thirty-five seconds. Six broadsides in eighty-three seconds, the forward thirty-two in seventy-seven. This cannot be excelled by any crews."[110]

Gift's description of plans for a photograph creates a kind of tableau of how the gunboat *Chattahoochee* looked during such a gun drill:

> One [pose] with the Crew exercising the guns at Quarters, with one gun at "serve vent and sponge," [prior to loading] another at "run-out" [or drawn by pulleys to the gunport] another at "point!", and the fourth at "ready-fire!" . . . in addition the shell whip will be supplying shells, the powder boys will be procuring powder, the landsman crying the soundings (he will hardly be *heard* in the picture) and the helmsmen in the act of "righting" the wheel at a "steady!" officers all in their proper places.[111]

Another letter of Gift's adds sound to the picture of a gun drill. Sitting below decks during an afternoon drill, he wrote: "All hands are at quarters, and the whole ship is alive and busy. 'Ready!' 'Point!' 'Run out!'

'Sponge!' 'Load with cartridge!' are being hastily said on deck; whilst around me the boxes are going to the magazine for a '6# charge' 'rifle charge' and '10# charge.'"[112]

These were hardly the smell of gunsmoke and the bloody decks of action many of the officers and crew had seen, but they remained eager to have that "conversation with" the blockaders. By the time Gift's courtship of Miss Shackelford had taken full sail in such descriptions, Horry Dent had arranged a transfer to the *Hampton* in the James River Squadron. His letters from the *Chattahoochee* to his father ceased after February 1863. But the tone of others' letters had, by that stage of the gunboat's career, begun to reflect his sustained criticism of the whole business.

During the day-to-day routine in tight quarters on a ship tied up at a remote river town, frustrations and disagreements arose. Gift was subjected to "bulkheading"; that is, some of the crew stood near his quarters when they knew he would be within earshot and loudly complained of one's preference to sleep in a hammock rather than a bunk and of the general displeasure that their servants had to stand nightwatch. Crew members were inspected and penalized if they did not keep themselves clean. Punishment for such small infractions in this nineteenth-century navy was physical: pacing the deck for three hours carrying a thirty-two-pound shot, being placed in irons in intervals of four hours over a period of days, or being triced (stretched) on a hammock hook.[113]

As Gift detailed in his letters to Ellen Shackelford, his duties on the *Chattahoochee* extended to other, less military areas. When the ship's mess fell into "a state of anarchy," it became Gift's duty to reorganize it. And given the shipboard fare, which often consisted mainly of sweet potatoes, six dozen hot rolls from the galley of the steamboat *Indian* was a welcomed treat.

The officers' influence included concern about the younger men's development. Mdn. Hamilton Golder's logbook record was checked for spelling: "receaved 2½ bushels of Char-cole"; the dropping on the trip downriver was "tedeous"; the "jurnals" were too small. Mdn. Mayo, who read Tennyson as the most popular poet of the day, was set to work learning the first five theorems of plane trigonometry to prepare for a promotion examination.[114]

Although smoking was later allowed in the wardroom, the vice of swearing was noted and discouraged. By precept Gift tried to "silence the Mids of their swearing proclivities" and by example began "fast curing myself of this foolish habit." Prayer was the order of the day at eight o'clock each morning, and their efforts "to be Christian" brought a complaint when the crew had to work repairing the ship on Sunday.[115]

Like some military officers before and after him, Gift expressed a feeling of awkwardness about conducting divine services. Whether the Book of Common Prayer service for shipboard was too complicated for an unlettered crew concerned him. He also puzzled over whether he should deliver a brief homily or simply read something like the Sermon on the Mount.[116]

When some crewmen died from the fever-ridden conditions of their service at Chattahoochee, Gift procured headboards to place over the graves and wrote of that sad duty:

> The burial of these men forcibly reminded me of the singular life poor sailors lead. Amongst the *seamen* of this ship there is not one in ten who has a single relative in the Confederacy; their shipmates of today are their only friends. If one dies we put him away according to Military form. Some poor sinner like myself reading the burial service; a head board marks his resting place for a few years and then all is oblivion.

Very much in the reflective manner of a Victorian gentleman in an era when people read Tennyson's *In Memoriam*, Gift continued his reverie about death:

> I wonder if in cold regions of the Rhine there are not mothers who often think of these wayward erratic creatures, and pray to God that *they* be shielded from harm and temptation. Do they have sisters whose petitions are ever being thrust before the almighty in favor of brothers whose thoughts are seldom turned homeward? Do they have sweethearts? I think not, or they'd scarcely stray so far away from the Fatherland.[117]

The situation of the *Chattahoochee* as a landlocked ship at Chattahoochee, Florida, evoked memories of former service. On a "cold wet and disagreeable" day in late January, Gift wrote: "The ship is our only world now; and it puts me very much in mind of being at sea; all that we lack is the creaking of spars and the rattle of cordage to make the thing real, with an occasional lurch and splash of *salt* water." Instead of the sound of a ship at sea, there were more frequently the sounds of a damaged ship being kept afloat: "Oh! those horrible pumps, how dolefully they sound in the mid-watch, rattle, rattle chuck, chuck at least one third of the time."[118]

As the pumps did their work, carpenters from Johnston's Navy Yard were at work repairing the vessel. Within a week after the ship ran aground in the river, Johnston filled a larger order for lumber and other materials to construct a coffer box; this would create a kind of dry dock to repair the leaks. The steamer *William H. Young* delivered fifteen pounds of wrought spikes to Chattahoochee, fifty pounds of putty were ordered, and the payroll list of carpenters, painters, and coppersmiths resumed in late January and early February. Thus major work began to repair the gunboat before vouchers for finishing work for it had been cleared from November and December of the previous year.

Johnston provided a total of 6,301 board feet of lumber to construct the coffer box. At a cost of $190.92, the order included 4,241 feet of two-inch boards, 1,800 feet of four-by-six-inch boards, 360 feet of six-by-six-inch boards, and other materials that no doubt had to be cut to order: 1,200 feet in lengths 4 inches by 10 inches by 45 feet, 625 feet of sill pieces in lengths 10 inches by 10 inches by 25 feet, and a Kelson piece measuring 10 inches by 12 inches by 62 feet. He also delivered an oak sternpost to replace the damaged part ($24.00) and an oak flitch beam to strengthen the structure with two beams bolted to an iron plate between them ($7.50).[119]

Using little more than the brute strength of manpower and horse-power, the workers had a slow and heavy job to construct the box. Then they had to position it under a ship tied up at a steamboat landing far removed from the construction yard at Saffold. At a cost of $935, carpenters spent 162 man-days on the project; caulking required 24 days, and painting the finished ship another 8 days. Linseed oil cost $670 for a forty-eight-gallon barrel, by far the most expensive item on the project. Labor at $5 per day and lumber at 10¢ per board foot seem drastically low by contemporary terms and in light of all that has been related about Civil War inflation. The linseed oil becomes an indicator of how one scarce item greatly inflated the cost of repairing and painting the *Chattahoochee*.

After their difficulties with Johnston as a navy contractor, he probably would not have been the first choice for such work. However, his location near the gunboat's remote station made him the only choice.

Gift's description of how the coffer box was made combines many of the flourishes of the style of the times with a very clear description of how this technical feat was brought off. He wrote to Ellen Shackelford:

> In the first place a heavy strong "box" was constructed on shore composed of timber and plank, almost as heavy as those of a ship; it was made 25 feet long, 30 feet wide and 9 feet deep; then by accurate measurements, the form of a cross section of the vessel was ascertained just forward of the cabin bulkhead (partition) in the Engine room. Then one end of the box is cut out to fit this cross-section. [Here there is a small illustration in the letter.] Now the "box" is launched, and enough weights put in to sink it 'til its top is just out of the water. (The Edges of the box that fit the form of the ship's bottom are "Cushioned," by nailing on a bag of canvas stuffed with Cotton.) The "box" is then hauled under the ship, the weights are taken out and it rises up, the cushion fitting tight. The pumps and buckets soon throw all the water out, and in a few hours you are astonished to see rudder propellors and keel all dry—in a "band box." The most interesting part of the matter is to see the exact nicety of the fit—as perfect as a neat glove on a handsome hand.[120]

Gift ended playfully, "This is more ship's carpentry than I intended to inflict on you, and more probably than you have read through." Even if the technical description was not of consuming interest to the lovely Miss Shackelford, she reported in a reply that her father was so interested in Gift's accounts of the *Chattahoochee* that he read the letters first and then passed them among family members. While this practice no doubt restricted the courtship, Gift's long journal letters helped to impress an older, disapproving father who would later become his father-in-law.

As repair work continued on the ship, the officers and men sought what recreation they could. Much time on board was spent reading whatever newspapers they could get and popular works of the day, such as the novels of Columbus author Augusta Evans Wilson. References to her weave in and out of accounts of social life; prior to the success of *St. Elmo*, another of her novels earned her the nickname "Beulah."

Men engaged in horseplay in the wardroom with Marmaduke and Ford practicing broadsword exercises across the reading table. And Ford suffered the ridicule of his mates for tearing up page after page of stationery attempting to write a letter to "his dulcina." To aid them in such exercises, the wardroom library contained an etiquette book, *The Habits of Good Society.*

At two miles' distance from the wharf, a small force of militia was stationed at the Chattahoochee Arsenal. Gift was rather derisive of "our *colonel* D. P. Holland" who had withdrawn northward from Apalachicola; but others evidently enjoyed the sessions when Holland spun yarns about Florida.[121] Life aboard ship also left the crew time to have the captain of the fore top tatoo them. Wyndam Mayo chose an eagle and Confederate shield around his neck, Henry Marmaduke made the more conservative choice of a coat of arms, and Daniel Trigg made the patriotic choice of *Sic Semper Tyrannis* for his forearm.[122]

The officers had to be vigilant to keep the area natives among the crew on board and on duty; sometimes their duties included searching out missing men. On one such occasion, Gift discovered a sailor camping in the woods with his wife. Just as the officer approached to take the man into custody, the sailor leaned languidly toward his wife and said, "Sugar, gimme a nother tater," to which she replied, "Ain't got nary nother." Before Gift could collect himself to be properly authoritarian, he had to "retire behind a tree and laugh immoderately."[123]

Curious residents of Chattahoochee came down to the wharf to inspect the gunboat. The men on board conducted their inspection in return, especially "Young Mallory." After his heroism on the *Virginia*, and in the far less dramatic service on an inland river, he was very much the pet of the crew and thus the subject of this story:

> Young Mr. Mallory discovered quite a good-looking *damsel* (as he supposed) standing on the wharf and looking wistfully aboard; so diminutive gallantry gave chase and was alongside the stranger, and politely enquired if she would go onboard. "Don't know Sir, I'm 'fraid *husband* wouldn't like it." He abandoned the prize forthwith.[124]

The acting bos'n had little better luck, for he returned with "a couple of horrible old female creatures; one wore 'specs' habitually." Gift reported to Ellen Shackelford this lack of social life along with the officers' plans to remedy the situation.[125]

The officers had few formal naval duties to perform and Jones was preparing to leave the ship for duty elsewhere. Thus in this inactive period, both Gift and Jones welcomed the request from General Beauregard for a report on the proper method of fighting turreted Union

Midshipman Charles King Mallory. "Young Mallory" was a great favorite among the Chattahoochee's *officers and men. The first to board the U.S.S.* Congress *after the* Virginia *had defeated her, he was transferred with Catesby ap R. Jones to the* Chattahoochee. *The account of his death following the boiler explosion on May 27, 1863, combined bravery and pathos. His family had his remains sent home to Virginia and interred at St. John's, Hampton.*
Virginia Historical Society, Richmond

ironclads like the *Monitor.* After spending a time together working on the report, the two officers turned their talk to the ladies of Columbus and their eagerness to have visitors.

In their travels through Columbus to Saffold and on visits there, officers like Jones and Gift had been welcomed into Columbus society. Those experiences put them on good terms with a number of families like the Howards, the Shorters, and the Hargraves. On a much deeper than social level, the officers of the *Chattahoochee* were indebted to Columbus women for nursing their sick crewmen in the hospital there.

As a way of showing their appreciation, they conceived a plan to have the Soldiers' Aid Society travel downriver by steamer to be received on the gunboat at Chattahoochee, Florida. Gift immediately wrote an invitation to Miss Lila Howard, "informing her of the intended fete," asking that she "invite all handsome and intelligent young ladies," and adding that the party should stop at Saffold to include the Misses Shackelford in their party.

The February 4 invitation was for at least two weeks later because workers were still busy repairing the ship. The delay also allowed time to make extensive plans: to have flags flying, banners on the masts, and crewmen cheering in the rigging as the steamboat arrived. To have a gunnery drill perhaps followed by a ball completed the plan.

Whittle, who was then convalescing in Columbus, was to hand deliver an invitation to the Soldiers' Aid Society. He failed in that duty; in the meantime, the city newspapers got wind of the plans and announced them before the ladies had received direct word from their would-be hosts. Miss Howard's reply to Gift refers to that lapse in a way that is archly satiric and graceful in its style:

> Excuse me if it appears officious, but I think there must be some mistake about the society receiving any invitation at the last meeting. I heard that the subject was mentioned but having only heard of it through the city papers—which were not invitation, but allusions to an invitation having been sent—they could take no action upon it. I was not present, Mrs. David Hudson is now acting President I think.
>
> I am sure a gentleman of your high and delicate sense of honor could not expect me to do otherwise than decline a pleasure, the acceptance of the invitation to which would so seriously compromise me as a patriot—being indebted to the doubt of my patriotism

for the invitation. Hoping that your first party may pass off as agreeably as we all wish, I am respectfully your Lila Howard.[126]

Whatever the cause, the planned visit of the Columbus ladies to Chattahoochee, Florida, did not occur. The officers and crew did have another occasion to display their skills and impress a group of ladies soon after their arrival there, however. When Jones went to Tallahassee to confer with Gen. Howell Cobb about the coordination of the *Chattahoochee* and the obstructions, Cobb returned with a group of staff officers to inspect the ship. They came on board to find a group of ten ladies—"nice country girls," Gift calls them—who had been invited aboard by a purser's clerk, Mr. Bones.

This impromptu meeting of officers and ladies became the audience for a gun drill. Gift's fondness for quoting the shouted commands gives immediacy to how the drill progressed from firing single guns to all the guns: "'Enemy close aboard, fire the broadsides rapidly,' then 'board away,' 'rally the foremast,' 'stand by to board on the port bow,' 'pikemen support boarders.'" Young Mallory, Marmaduke, and other veterans of the *Virginia-Monitor* fight had heard and followed such orders in actual combat. Here, the simulated action was conducted to impress any army general and his staff.

The drill continued: "'All guns shift positions.' That is the rifle came amid ships, and the 32 pdr shot at a ricochet, sent the shot skipping and bounding over the water up the river; throwing up beautiful jets at every point of contact along the water."[127] General Cobb was duly attentive to all that went on in the naval exercises, but Gift noted with amusement that the staff officer who served as chief of artillery found an acquaintance among the visiting ladies and so paid no attention whatever to the drills.

There were few such breaks in routine, and the isolation of the ship's station together with the lack of action still weighed heavily upon the officers. Jones was preparing to join General Magruder's staff in Texas or to command the Selma, Alabama, Naval Iron Works. Of these concerns Gift wrote: "I was proud of my men and longed to have them and their endeavors properly appreciated." As long as the obstructions remain unfinished, they still had hope that the *Chattachoochee* would leave the river. But continued work on the obstructions would frustrate those hopes.

By March 1, 1863, Capt. Theodore Moreno was able to report to

General Cobb that his mission to obstruct the river was accomplished by using a combination of a raft built in Columbus and a chain to catch driftwood. He reported to Cobb, "I walked this morning from one side of the river to the other without getting my feet wet so thick and compact is the tangled mass of logs, trees, timber and trash that is brought down by the freshet."[128]

To completely secure the obstruction, Moreno had needed a second chain, but procuring it required daring and ingenuity. Writing years after the war, he described how he and his men brought off the feat:

> Learning that a long and heavy chain was lying on the wharf in Apalachicola I took fifteen soldiers and passed quietly down the river at night. We approached the city, anticipating every moment an encounter from some Yankee boat. On two occasions distant lights on the water admonished us to approach cautiously, as we knew there were war vessels anchored in the harbor, ready at a moments notice to use their guns on a venturesome blockader who might try to pass by. But I secured my chain, and I will never forget the terrible clank it gave as it dropped on board, we listened breathlessly for a moment fearing we were discovered, but the enemy made no sign and we proceeded safely up the river with our prize. Fastening it at both ends to the bank, and adjusting it to the "Wave," a boat I had placed in position, I awaited the result of the next freshet.[129]

Once Moreno had obstructed the river, General Cobb evidently reassessed the decision not to allow an opening that would permit the *Chattahoochee* to descend the Apalachicola and go to sea.

In a March 13 letter to Cobb, Moreno cited the missed communication of an undelivered letter and then went on to say that removing the obstruction would be "a very difficult undertaking." He supported that opinion with a description of the status of the obstruction: "The banks on both sides are under water and no boat of any size can now approach it. There are at least 100 yards of entangled [drift] both ashore and below it; and I think it very necessary to the permanency of our obstructions."[130]

Hopes that the *Chattahoochee* could go downriver were thus entirely closed off. Catesby Jones had moved on to another assignment, and Lt. John Julius Guthrie had assumed command of the gunboat. Guthrie was a North Carolinian who, like so many of his fellow officers, had served in the U.S. Navy. Like young Dent and Fagan, he had served in the New

Lt. John Julius Guthrie, C.S.N., as a young naval cadet. Guthrie, as second commander of the Chattahoochee, *was not as warmly accepted or as admired as Catesby ap R. Jones. He served competently, however, and later saw more distinguished service on the staff of North Carolina Governor Zebulon Vance as captain of the blockade runner* Advance.
N.C. Division of Archives and History, Raleigh

Orleans action. A Roman Catholic and evidently a quietly devout man, he entered a volatile situation on the *Chattahoochee* as Jones made his exit.[131]

The heading on Guthrie's March 13 letter to Jones reflects his good humor at the unpleasant certainties of his own situation and the uncertainties of Jones's career:

C. S. Steamer "Chattahoochee"
Muddy River, Fla. March 13th, 1863

To
Lieut. C. ap. R. Jones CSN
Mobile, or elsewhere
Continent of America

Clearing up the business of assuming command, Guthrie reported and inquired about the paymaster's accounts and went on to comment both on the generally unpleasant conditions at Chattahoochee and the failure of the Columbus ladies to visit the ship.

Guthrie's main duty became the preparation of the *Chattahoochee* for a trial run along the Flint and Apalachicola rivers. An excursion up the Flint was planned for the last week of March, but pilot William B. Bilbro, a Columbus resident, was absent from the ship. Gift expressed the crew's disappointment: "I have a great desire to hurl some anathema at the innocent head of 'Old Bill.' . . . Is he not the cause of our being delayed from ascending the beautiful Flint and astonishing the natives with the display of our terrible engines of war?"[132]

Guthrie took a considerably more official tone in notifying General Cobb on March 30 that the gunboat was "sufficiently finished to make a trial trip" and needed to test the "efficiency and fitness for the defense of this river." He requested that Cobb come aboard to accompany him on the trial run and offered to set a convenient date for the general.[133]

Detach Me from This Vessel and Order Me to Sea

On April 7, the gunboat left Chattahoochee, Florida, to steam downriver to the obstructions.

Because of the disaster the *Chattahoochee* had suffered on the first trip from Saffold to Chattahoochee, Florida, Guthrie and Bilbro ordered a speed of about ten miles per hour. In a long account of the trip, Gift wrote Ellen Shackelford that they remained in "a state of continual alarm for fear of an accident." Doubtless this fear was not betrayed to the group of local ladies who welcomed the ship at Ochese. By the time the ship got as far downriver as Alum Bluff, it "steamed majestically past the batteries," without acknowledging the army officers there. Then for no one in particular and without a target in view, the gun crews were assembled to fire three rounds from the rifled cannon and six from two of the 32-pounders.

Finally, 424 days after the 1861 contract was signed, the gunboat *Chattahoochee* was underway as an armed, fully fitted-out ship of war. And the next day it steamed as far as the obstructions that blocked passage to the open sea.

To the officers on board, the obstructions made a far different impression than they had upon Captain Moreno who had designed them. Gift wrote to Ellen Shackelford about the battery at the obstruction: "I never have in my life seen so miserable a place, entirely surrounded on all sides by water, mud and swamp." Of the batteries he wrote: "miserable contrivances, poorly constructed and worse manned and armed." Of the troops there: "raw infantry troops." Of the officers: "very raw, green unsophisticated, who have no confidence in their position, their guns or themselves." And of the commander: "a cross eyed 2nd Lieutenant."

To demonstrate the gunboat's firepower as an addition to the batteries of 32- and 24-pounders, Guthrie ordered an artillery drill. By Gift's report, the gun crews acquitted themselves well. One shot from the rifle "was a 'palpable hit' exploding the percussion shell and throwing splinters several hundred feet into the air, damaging the mark so badly as to make it necessary to find a new tree." More important than the pyrotechnics of this target practice at trees was the successful trial of the ship itself, which "showed no signs of injury from the firing, everything resisting the repeated shocks in a very satisfactory manner."

Equally as important, Gift wrote of the crew: "I confess that I hardly believed it to be in the power of guns and men to hit such small marks as ours did repeatedly. Not a shot was fired . . . that would not have badly injured a ship."[134]

Guthrie's report to Catesby Jones is more in the businesslike tone of one officer writing to another, not of a gallant impressing a lady: "The engines did not brake down, nor did the steamer get on shore, butt up against any of the huge trees upon the margins of the Chat. or meet with any accident. We fired the guns upwards of twenty times striking a target about six hundred yards dist. four times fairly."[135] Both Gift and Guthrie added news of distant battles in the South in their letters about the trial trip. However well the ship, men, and guns tested out in the trials, they remained acutely aware of being on a landlocked ship in the warm, mosquito-breeding currents of a muddy river far isolated from the action.

The situation was beginning to wear more than thin with Lieutenant Gift, who referred contemptuously to "our peacock Captain" who spoke of "the efficiency of *his* crew—made so by Jones' precepts and my hard work—confound him!" Successful as it was, the gunnery practice was termed "this display of folly and expenditure of ammunition."[136]

Gift's temper continued to fray with the situation of the ship's inaction and with the officers on board. On May 8, he wrote to Ellen Shackelford from Chattahoochee a full account of a conflict with Asst. Paymaster Leslie E. Brooks. The very length and tedium of the six-page account give an immediate sense of a group of inactive fighting men turning inward upon the minutiae of their daily duties.

The point at issue was Gift's ordering Midshipman Trigg to accompany him on a trip up the Flint River on a social call to Ellen at the Munnerlyn plantation. Paymaster Brooks needed Trigg's services as clerk and so reported to Guthrie that Gift had gone "to gratify his own whims." First Gift copied the charges against him for Ellen to read and then let fly with: "In all my experience I have never seen anything so low, so vile and contemptable. That it is entirely beneath the notice of a gentleman I admit. But in spite of me I could not hold down my rising indignation. That the blackguard should dare to drag in matters sacred to every gentleman in an official report." Reaching an even more fevered pitch of anger, Gift mentioned his willingness to duel Brooks: "At that moment I would have given all I possess and my left arm to have throttled the viper. Night came and I carefully thought the matter over; I was satisfied that the scoundrel could not be driven to fight, although I had procured the services of a friend &c &c in case he should be goaded up to the mark." Gift ended his long recitation to Ellen by stating his decision to request a transfer from the *Chattahoochee*—to "commence vagabondizing," for assignment in Columbus, or "in procuring iron from one of the Florida roads."[137]

Other men serving in the area were not exempt from similar frustrations, as Capt. Theodore Moreno expressed in a letter to General Cobb on May 9. He cited the difficulty of keeping a work force together to haul provisions and shore up the batteries at the Narrows obstructions. Continuing the catalog of deficiencies, Moreno cited insufficient guards or guards absent from duty "after bed time" at various points along the river. An "old man named Austin" who had moved from Apalachicola to settle up the Flint River was "said to be very *friendly* with the Yankees" and had "sometimes threatened persons there with these particular friends should [Moreno] prevent his taking down provisions and not allow him to come up again." As a matter of evidently quite serious concern, Moreno reported further to General Cobb:

I desire to mention that the telegraph office at Chattahoochee does not furnish sealed dispatches. I have recd several recently—one from you this morning with reference to the Kate Bruce—of them forwarded to me *open*. Is there not a penalty attached to this? I spoke of it to the agent who says the Superintendent of the line does not furnish the envelopes. A word from you to this Supdt. would, I think, correct it. Though on this river now about six months I have never rec'd a dispatch in an envelope.[138]

Whether General Cobb turned his serious attention to Captain Moreno's complaint is not recorded, but a May 9 letter of Young Mallory to his father gives evidence of the growing strain upon junior officers as well:

Dear Father I wish you would write to the Secty of the Navy and ask him to detach me from this vessel and order me to sea as there are officers constantly going to Europe and I think that they will be in great way of going over shortly. My reasons for wanting to get off this vessel is because we can do nothing for the river is so securely obstructed that we cannot get over them and in a short time the river will be so low that we cannot get up or down and will have to lay stationary the entire summer and fall.[139]

Young Mallory's request for transfer brought no official action, but action at the remote duty station did begin to increase within days after his letter.

And All Their Hopes Exploded

Gift, in particular, had nurtured a high sense of drama about how a daring move might change things for the *Chattahoochee* and her inactive crew.

In his eagerness for action, he proposed a way to capture Apalachicola. With a crew of sixty from the *Chattahoochee*, he planned to go down the Apalachicola on the steamer *Swan* as far as Jackson River, six miles north of Apalachicola. He and his force would proceed from there to the outskirts of Apalachicola, sending three Apalachicolans from the crew into town as if on leave. Lt. George Morris of the *Port Royal* would be notified of their presence and come ashore in search of prisoners.

Morris customarily patrolled the city with a force of about sixty men. After placing his howitzer in position at the landing with a guard of ten or fifteen men, Morris then would set about searching the town. It was Gift's plan to attack and capture the guard left at the howitzer and take the remainder of the force as they returned to the landing. Dressed in the Union uniforms, the Confederates could then approach and capture the *Port Royal* unchallenged and engage the other blockaders in turn.[140] Gift was unable to carry out this plan, for two weeks later the *Chattahoochee* became involved in the most important operation of its career.

During the last week of May, Lieutenant Morris learned that the schooner *Fashion* was anchored up the Apalachicola. Cotton was being placed on board the vessel in preparation for running the blockade at Indian Pass. To prevent an escape, Morris ordered a boat expedition to ascend the river and capture the schooner by surprise. On the night of May 23, forty-one men under the command of Acting Master Edgar van Slyck left the *Port Royal* in three boats.

The Union seamen rowed up the Apalachicola under cover of darkness in a heavy rainstorm, passing Fort Gadsden at 2 A.M. By 10 A.M., they had rowed about forty-five miles without seeing any sign of the *Fashion*. Giving up the search, they were returning downriver when they sighted a barge near Scott Creek. Its presence made them suspect that a large vessel was being loaded nearby. The boats entered the creek, where one discharge of the howitzer brought the surrender of the *Fashion* without opposition. The Union seamen were able to tow their prize into the river and from there to Apalachicola and the blockading station.[141]

News of the capture of the *Fashion* caused great concern at Chattahoochee, Florida. Aboard the *Chattahoochee*, Lieutenant Guthrie decided to attempt crossing the obstructions to give aid to the *Fashion* and cast off from Chattahoochee on May 26, continuing twenty-eight miles downstream to Blountstown Bar.

Finding that the bar carried only seven and a half feet, Guthrie ordered an overnight wait, hoping that the river would rise. The river did not rise, and at ten o'clock the following morning the order was given to raise steam in preparation for returning to Chattahoochee. The order triggered an argument in the engine room over how much water the boilers contained. Chief Engineer Fagan heard the discussion from his bunk and hurried to the engine room. Curiosity had also drawn the pilot Bilbro, who started the donkey engine just as Fagan descended the engine room ladder. Water poured into the boilers and they exploded.

Pandemonium followed on the *Chattahoochee*. Those who had been scalded ran about the deck frantic with pain. Because the boilers of the ship were within three feet of the magazine, one of the gunners warned of an explosion, sending the crew into further panic and sending many of them over the sides into the river. Three drowned before Midshipman Craig could restrain those trying to abandon ship. Dr. Ford went about the deck trying to aid the injured and Lieutenant Guthrie came from his cabin to begin administering baptism to the dying.[142]

As the ship began to sink, Guthrie left off his attention to the wounded to give orders for flooding the magazine, saving what articles they could, and abandoning ship.

Then began a slow, rather confused process of attending the wounded, rescuing the survivors, and salvaging the very valuable guns from the wreck. The steamer *William H. Young* first reached the *Chattahoochee* around midnight May 27, about twelve hours after the accident. It transported Guthrie and six others seventeen miles upstream to Ochese. On the following morning it returned to take aboard the dead and injured, who were transported to Chattahoochee that afternoon. After another trip down the river, this time to salvage two of the guns, the *Young* set out for Columbus, a trip requiring three days.[143]

And thus began the process: first reports of *what* had happened, then questions about *how*, and the impact of *why* upon the principals who lived out this drama.

News of the disaster preceded the *Young* upriver. At Saffold, Ellen

Shackelford heard only of the explosion but received no word of her fiancé. How welcome, then, must have been this letter from Gift:

> Wreck of the C.S.S. "Chattahoochee"
> Blountstown, May 28th 1863
>
> The prayers of some righteous person have prevailed in my favor, as through the mercy of Almighty God I have been spared from one of the most terrible of deaths. On arriving at Chattahoochee last Tuesday Mr. Gibbs and myself found the ship gone down the river. We remained at Capt. Hill's quarters until this afternoon when we received the startling intelligence that the Chattahoochee had been blown up. We immediately proceeded down the river meeting the "Young" with the dead and wounded. Mr. Fagan Mr. Hodges & my asst Engineers Mr. Henderson and the Pilot were instantly killed, making five officers. My boy Bill Moore was also killed. Mr Mallory is badly scalded on the face hands & feet but the Doctor thinks there is hope. A number of men were scalded to death or drowned—in all 18. Guthrie was not hurt. From the position in which various parties were killed I am sure that had I been on board my duties would have called me to a fatal part of the ship, that is aft. The ship had sunk to her decks, her large supply of ammunition is all lost. I shall get her guns out as soon as possible. Thus ends this fated and useless craft. The sick & wounded will be sent to Columbus immediately. By remaining at Quincy I missed this dreadful scene. I need scarcely apologize for this hasty and badly written letter.
>
> I thank God for my preservation
> Geo. W. G.[144]

In Columbus, McLaughlin made speed to inform Catesby Jones of the accident. His staccato statements of what personal facts he could gather fill out the news account he sent with his letter.

> Columbus, Ga., June 1, 1863.
>
> My Dear Jones: I hasten to inform you of the sad accident which happened on board the *Chattahoochee* and as the quickest method I enclose the account furnished the newspaper by Gift, who, though not on board at the time, came up on the *Young* with the wounded. Young Mallory is badly hurt and his recovery considered doubtful. The statements as to how the accident occurred are very conflict-

ing. Some say that the steam gauge had been out of order the day previous. At the time of the explosion it was showing only 7 pounds of steam. Others say that pumping water in the boiler, the water at the time being low, was the cause. She was at anchor and only waiting for steam to be reported to get underway. Mr. Fagan at the time was sick, though had just gone into the engine room. He was the only one on board having any knowledge of the engines. The gunner is at the vessel with most of the crew. The medical officers have moved their efforts to Chattahoochee. Captain Guthrie is here. I will write you again soon.

Yours truly,

A. McLaughlin.

Commander C. ap R. Jones, C.S. Navy

McLaughlin enclosed newspaper clippings that were, in turn, printed in the Navy Official Records.

GUNBOAT CHATTAHOOCHEE DESTROYED—TERRIBLE LOSS OF LIFE.

Just as the steamer *Jackson* was pushing out from the wharf at Chattahoochee, Fla., a courier arrived from below with news that the boilers of the gunboat *Chattahoochee* had exploded, killing the pilot, William Bilbro, for a long series of years a pilot on the Chattahoochee River, and wounding nearly every officer on board. The *Jackson* could not remain to learn any further particulars; they have doubtless been received before this. The steamer *Munnerlyn* went down to the scene of disaster.

Since the above was put in type we have received, through the courtesy of Lieutenant G. W. Gift, the following list of persons killed by the explosion of the boiler of the *Chattahoochee* May 27, viz: Henry Fagan, second assistant engineer, of Key West, Fla.; Euclid P. Hodges, third assistant engineer of Maryland; Fred W. Arents, third assistant engineer, Richmond, Va.; Eugene Henderson, paymaster's clerk, Tuskegee, Ala.; William B. Bilbro, pilot, Columbus, Ga.; Joseph Hicks, first-class fireman, Georgia; Enoch C. Lanpher, second-class fireman, Columbus, Ga.; Edward Conn, coal heaver, Apalachicola, Fla.; Charles H. Berry, quartermaster, Tampa, Fla.; John Joliff, seaman, ———; Lewis C. Wild, landsman, Florida; John Spear, landsman, Florida; William Moore, landsman,

Florida; James Thomas, landsman, Florida; Charles Douglas, second-class fireman, residence unknown; James H. Jones, landsman, Florida.

MORTALLY WOUNDED.—M. Faircloth, landsman, Florida.

DANGEROUSLY WOUNDED.—Midshipman Charles K. Mallory, of Virginia, face, hands, and feet badly scalded; Cornelius Duffy, of Apalachicola, Fla., face and hands badly scalded.

SLIGHTLY WOUNDED.—Hamilton Golder, master's mate, Maryland, right arm scalded; Joseph Sia, Apalachicola, face burned; Midshipman W. J. Craig, Kentucky, foot slightly burned; Joseph E. Coles, coal heaver, Florida, foot burned.

The vessel was sunk below her decks. The wounded were brought up to the city last evening by the steamer *William H. Young*.[145]

By June 3, Gift was writing of Young Mallory's funeral the previous day at 11 A.M. and an evening funeral for another of the victims.

Despite the sorrowful time, Gift goes on in his letter to discuss prospects for transfer. His thoughts also turn rather quickly to an account of the previous evening's social activities. Miss Lila Howard had invited Gift to "dine and take tea." This opportunity he welcomed; what he had not anticipated was the expectation that he would also attend an amateur opera performance. With Miss Howard's brothers Robert and Jesse, Gift escorted "Miss Marshall" and "Miss Flournoy" while "Mr. Shorter" escorted "Miss Lila."

The selections from *Lucrezia Borgia*, *Norma*, and *Somnambula* were sung with accompaniment by the Columbus Orchestra and "sundry amateurs." Doubtless, Gift was not in a mood to be entertained, but he also expresses himself in terms of the most discriminating critic. He was, like the singers he critiqued, "as miserable as miserable could be."[146]

As the singers sang and as the assembled company enjoyed the beaux arts, life in Columbus went on and Young Mallory's descent into death went on in the way that a jumble of such events rushes along in wartime.

By June 15, McLaughlin was able to send Jones a full report. In it was mixed the administrative and technical concern about what actually happened, the pathos of what happened to crewmen—particularly Young Mallory—and the political concerns of who was responsible, who might have done differently or better, and what would happen next.

Naval Station, Columbus, Ga., June 15, 1863.

My Dear Jones: Your letter of the 8th has just reached me, enclosing a letter to Gift. As he has left here permanently with orders to Mobile, I have done as you directed, opened the document and forwarded the letters of recommendation, through Pembroke Jones, at Savannah, with a request that he will hand them to the men. I will go on to explain and endeavor to furnish you with all the information connected with the lamentable accident which happened to the ill-fated steamer. The accounts, such as we get, are most conflicting, but Gift having taken an active part in placing the information before the public, I think, has prevented the matter from being as freely discussed as would otherwise have been the case.

The only officers on board at the time were Guthrie, Midshipmen Craig, Mallory, and Gibbs, Golder, Dr. Ford, and the gunner, and the engineers, whose names have already appeared in print with the exception of Third Assistant Engineer Armand De Blanc, of New Orleans, who, not being on duty, escaped uninjured. The vessel had started for the obstructions, and had gone but 20 miles when it was found there was not sufficient water on the bar to admit of her crossing. The vessel was anchored. The next morning it was ascertained that the river had swollen, when orders were given to raise steam, and, as near as I can learn, they commenced firing up at or near 10 o'clock with wood. At 12 m., when the relief came down (which, by the way, accounts for the number of deaths), the steam gauge was showing 7 pounds of steam. It is now understood that it was out of order the day previous. A discussion now arose with regard to the quantity of water in the boiler. Mr. Fagan, the senior engineer, being at the time in his bunk with a chill, hearing the dispute, and fearing from the length of time since the fires had been started that something was wrong, hastened to the engine room and was descending the ladder when the explosion took place. Curiosity had taken the pilot to the engine room, and some think it was he who started the pump. The explosion was instantaneous with the starting of the pump. Guthrie, at the time was in his cabin. There is some difference of opinion about the time of his arrival on deck. Otherwise I do not hear of his name being mentioned, except by Dr. Ford, who speaks of his administering baptism to those who had been wounded and were about to die.

It being reported that an explosion of the magazine was imminent, caused a panic among the crew. Three, I believe, were drowned in trying to reach the shore. Among the number was a quartermaster by the name of Berry. No description, I am told, could possibly be given of the scene on the deck of the *Chattahoochee*, men running about frantic with pain, leaving the impression of their bleeding feet, and sometimes the entire flesh, the nails and all, remain behind them. The dead and wounded were taken on shore, where they remained until the next afternoon, most of the time a terrible storm raging. Finally they were taken on board the *Young* and reached Columbus on Sunday night, just five days after the accident. No attempt was made to dress the wounds until after their arrival here, which could not be avoided. Poor Mallory! I shall never forget his appearance. I would not have known him had he not spoken. His face, hands, and feet were scalded in the most terrible manner; he pleaded piteously to have his wounds attended to. I urged the doctor, who, by the way, was almost used up himself, to pay Mallory some attention. He then told me that he would have to wait for some assistance. He then said that Mallory could not live. You would have thought differently had you seen him. I could not make up my mind that he would die. When they first commenced to remove the cloths he was talking cheerfully, but the nervous system could not stand the shock. He commenced sinking and was a corpse, before they had gotten half through. Duffy, the fireman, expired on the next day. You would have been surprised to have seen the effect produced on Mr. Craig and Golder, who were only slightly injured, Mr. Craig in the foot, Mr. Golder side of face, arm and hand. They were so prostrated after their wounds were dressed that they were only roused by the use of stimulants. It seems almost useless to mention that they received all the attention that could possibly have been bestowed. The Home was literally besieged with ladies, and for one week the street in front of the Home was blocked up with vehicles of all descriptions. I really looked on with astonishment. The four worst cases were placed together in the room upstairs, directly in front of the steps. It was with the utmost difficulty that I could remain in the room sufficiently long to ascertain what was required and to see what service I could render, the atmosphere was so unpleasant, yet the ladies did not seem to notice it and remained at their post till the last.

Guthrie came up on the boat, bringing the guns, which, strange to say, he turned over to Major Humphreys [at the army arsenal], with a request that he would hold them subject alone to his order or that of the Secretary of the Navy. I immediately made a report of the affair. The Secretary, through the Office of Ordnance, replied promptly by telegraph, directing the guns and everything pertaining to them, as well as ship's stores be turned over to me. The matter caused considerable talk among the people in town. It was not understood why naval guns should not have been placed under the control of naval officers. It does appear to me that Guthrie's conduct throughout the whole affair has been most singular. He has given leave of absence to some of his crew to visit a place in possession of the enemy, and some 13 of his men left him at Chattahoochee with the intention of not returning. Among the number was a man by the name of Lee, whom you will no doubt recollect. After placing the guns in charge of Major Humphreys he took his family and started for Chattahoochee, where [he] remained four or five days, when he again embarked for Columbus, bringing the crew, minus the 13 mentioned above. At that time I had in my possession a telegram from Richmond to Guthrie, directing him to send the crew to Savannah. He remarked he would turn them over to me, and I might do what I pleased with them, but he thought I had better wait for further instructions. As Guthrie appeared to be laboring under some bodily infirmity, I gave the men quarters in my mold room and sent 40 of them the next day to Savannah. They arrived on the day the *Savannah* was put in commission. The men were all nicely dressed when they left here, and on their arrival at Savannah, being all straight and in good condition, were the cause of many remarks. It was certainly reflecting great credit to those who had organized and disciplined the crew. I felt proud of them. During their stay with me there was not one guilty of the slightest impropriety. Cronin, May, and Rosler expressed deep regret that they had not time to put a piece in the paper thanking the ladies for their many kindnesses, but said they would do so on their arrival at Savannah. The crew of the *Chattahoochee* will ever remember the latter and the paymaster. They would have been willing to have gone anywhere to have gotten rid of the vessel. Webb was exceedingly anxious to get hold of some of the men. He will have some of the landsmen; the remainder will remain on the *Savannah*. I ordered Dr. Jones and Midshipman Gibbs and Mr. Golder with the crew. They are now attached to the *Savannah*.

The 6.4-inch rifle belonging to the *Chattahoochee* I was directed to send to Charleston. It is to be double-banded and returned, to be used, I suppose, on the *Muscogee*. I am doing very well. The calkers have commenced to-day, and I am laying the spar deck. The engines are about being placed in position. I will keep you advised from time to time of the progress.

With kind regards to Simms, I remain, truly yours,

A. McLaughlin.[147]

As his report concludes, lost hope for the *Chattahoochee* is displaced by McLaughlin's hope for the *Muscogee*, an ironclad and super weapon that promised success where the conventional gunboat had failed.

As work on the ironclad continued, and as the Confederate effort was now centered at the northernmost point of the entire defense area, the gunboat *Chattahoochee* lay submerged at the scene of the accident.

To John Horry Dent, Sr., was left a personal matter in concluding the business of the *Chattahoochee*. Just before his death, Henry Fagan asked that his personal effects be given to his friend Horry's charge. Dent began on June 25 trying to trace the items through the naval bureaucracy. On July 18 he continued his search with a letter to Paymaster Leslie E. Brooks, and later he made an inventory of what he would send to Fagan's mother at Key West after the war:

Copy list of the effects of the late Henry Fagan CS Navy—received from Capt. John J. Guthrie Commanding C.S. Steamer Chattahoochee on 31 day July 1863—at Eufaula.

One full dress uniform coat

One full dress uniform waistcoat

One linnen sack coat

Two linnen waistcoat

13 shirt collars

One pillow slip

One good watch, maker E.S. Yates & Co., Liverpool no 18564

One small bundle containing two packages of letters official and
   correspondent

One tooth brush
One man's brush

John H. Dent[148]

By mid-August D. S. Johnston was back at work on the gunboat, this time with his blacksmiths, carpenters, and slave hands laboring ten days to raise the wreck for towing to Columbus for repairs. Expenses for the job came to $877.50, including $10.00 for "a boy" to dive into the wreck and close a valve, and another $120.00 for four gallons of whiskey "for the Hands" and the "Medical Dept."[149]

The ship had been a priority project in the earliest days of the war; it combined the best thinking of planners and policy makers in how it was designed, where it was built, and the mission it was meant to fulfill. The ship foundered in a system that did not function effectively to manage the detailed work of supervising a contractor, hiring skilled labor, procuring essential materials, and keeping labor and materials on course to a timely completion. The project was well within budget; it was so far off schedule that the river was obstructed before the ship could ever sail out to sea. The machinery and design for its placement were well conceived, but execution of the design at a naval iron works just getting organized was badly flawed. There was no shortage of experienced and daring officers to take the gunboat through the blockade to sea; but neither sailmakers, riggers, and firemen nor smartly uniformed and well-drilled gun crews were to be found in the backwoods of Georgia and Florida. When men were conscripted, they were difficult to train; if trained, they fell victim to the unhealthy climate. Even the highest morale of the officers broke under such conditions and they applied for transfer almost as quickly as they were assigned. Finally, an argument among the crew about the operation of the boilers quite literally exploded the whole project.

From the scene of the wreck, Gift wrote reflectively about Young Mallory: "Had he fell fighting the foe, I would not have minded it half so much."[150] So also with the ignominious fate of the CS *Chattahoochee*.

PART THREE

Effects of the Blockade

The Phantom Ram Which Comes —And Does Not Come

Life on the Blockade Station

Destruction of a Rebel Salt Factory
Harper's Weekly, *Nov. 15, 1862*

A storm broke over the Gulf and inland along the Apalachicola River soon after the boiler explosion aboard the gunboat *Chattahoochee*. On the river, the driving rain hampered salvage and rescue operations, leaving some of the injured crewmen to writhe in the mud along the bank. On the Gulf, the Union blockaders were having their own problems with the storm. Steamers could raise steam and thus hold reasonably steady in a gale, but in the engine room of the *Port Royal*, the men on duty still kept a close watch on their gauges. At thirty-five pounds of steam and wide open, the engines still could not maintain slack in anchor chains stretched as taut "as harpstrings."[1] As continual checks of the falling barometer showed no break in the weather, they could make out the nearby *Brockenborough* dragging backward toward St. Vincent's Island on her anchor chain.

At dawn on May 27 Union sailors were able to see the much smaller sailing bark *Amanda* run aground about 1,200 yards off Dog Island. The disaster had drawn beachcombers from Apalachicola "wading about among the breakers picking up fragments" of the wreck. In the midst of the disastrous scene, one sailor did not fail to note how the women "had no scruple to raise their dresses and wade out in full view of the ship's company."[2]

The official report of the wreck gave an inventory of salvaged guns, a kedge anchor, and waterlogged ordnance stores.[3] There was also the startling occurrence that Lt. George E. Welch of the *Amanda* destroyed his ship to prevent capture by Confederates in the area.[4] In the storm's aftermath, concern about Confederate operations upriver were displaced by more immediate duties.

Even so, news of the explosion aboard the *Chattahoochee* was not long in reaching the blockading vessels. On June 6, a boat from Apalachicola brought news of the disaster to the *Port Royal;* June 8 brought further confirmation when the *Chattahoochee*'s cook, J. C. Cook, came aboard and took the oath of allegiance.[5] Q.M. Elias Lee was shipped on the *Port Royal* as pilot.[6]

Implicit in Union Lt. George Morris's June report to Adm. Theodorus Bailey was news that he had bested his old rivals in the Confederate Navy without a confrontation: they had put their own gunboat out of commission.

That the *Chattahoochee* was no longer a threat to the blockade was of interest to the Union; the failure of its bid to raise the blockade came as no surprise. The steady stream of intelligence to Morris from travelers and deserters had not raised Union apprehension. William Martin came aboard Morris's ship in late April after a journey that took him from Tennessee, south through Atlanta, and down the Chattahoochee and Apalachicola just prior to the accident at Blountstown. He reported having gone aboard the *Chattahoochee* at Chattahoochee, Florida, about April 24. While Martin furnished a rather complete and accurate account of the gunboat's armament and machinery, he also passed along the intelligence that "The general belief of the people in that vicinity is that the *Chattahoochee* will never come down the river." He added that "one of her own crew made the same assertion."[7]

J. C. Cook added details of the explosion at Blountstown and of the rescue and salvage efforts; otherwise, he did little more than corroborate reports that the gunboat had indeed been destroyed. According to Morris's report, Elias Lee was more valuable as a pilot than as an informant because he was reputed to be among the best in the sound and along the coast. Certainly that practical need in the treacherous waters around Apalachicola overrode any suspicion Morris may have had about Lee's loyalty to the Union.[8]

Lt. Alexander F. Crossman of the USS *Somerset* off East Pass was also passing along reports of the Blountstown accident to the squadron commander. In a raid along Alligator Bay, he had flushed out two contrabands who gave news of the *Chattahoochee*. Useful intelligence to the Union was that attempts to salvage the gunboat had been abandoned; instead, efforts were being concentrated upriver at Columbus to complete an ironclad. As with Martin's earlier report about the conventional gunboat, however, reports discounted the threat of the ironclad. Data about the vessel's draft surfaced in the report: "7 or 8 feet." "If so," Crossman concluded, "she can not cross the bar off the town. . . . According to my notion, [the ironclad] will be of about as much service in getting down the river as the famed Chattahoochee itself." In fact, Crossman was more concerned about the health of his crew than the threat of Confederate attack, ending his letter with a request that the *Somerset* be drawn off the blockade station for a "short respite" at Key West. Implicit in that request is a strong statement about his estimate of the state of the Confederate threat in early June 1863.[9]

In the absence of any possible threat to the Union blockade, its officers stepped up their operations around Apalachicola within three weeks of the destruction of the *Chattahoochee*. Their immediate objective was the extensive series of saltworks in the Apalachicola area. The *Somerset* sent a force of sixty-five armed men and a work force armed with sledge hammers into the works at Alligator Bay just east of Dog Island.

With the steamer standing within range with its batteries, the armed men deployed along an inland perimeter to protect the work party. Seamen and engineers set about demolishing sixty-five salt kettles; then they scattered two hundred bushels of salt over the sand to prevent its recovery. Next the entire installation of thirty huts and houses, along with all the equipment for running the operation, was destroyed.

News that a cavalry force was en route from a post farther inland sent the Union force scattering for the boats to return to the *Somerset*. But the raid had produced a good day's effort for the blockaders. An unexpected trophy from the raid was a Savannah newspaper giving the blockaders their first news of the fall of Vicksburg more than two weeks before.[10] In his own report to Secretary of the Navy Gideon Welles, Admiral Bailey reported that "the work was handsomely accomplished."[11]

A raid on a salt-making operation, with more hard work wielding a sledge hammer than doing battle with the enemy, seems in some ways a very minor incident indeed. The blockaders were carrying out one of their primary missions, however: an economic war, and an attack upon the enemy's ability to wage war. If a skirmish in an economic war was not a raid upon a ship construction facility like the one at Saffold, to disrupt or destroy saltworks had gained equal importance in Union policy and strategy by 1863.

Much of the area's work force, many of them men from Saffold, had moved south to the Apalachicola Bay area to erect saltworks. Not only were they engaged in an essential and lucrative enterprise, but they could be exempted from conscription as well if they could produce twenty barrels of salt per day. They found that water from the bays and marshes around St. Andrew's Bay had a particularly high saline content. Years of drought just before the war had increased the potential yield of seventy-five gallons of salt for every one hundred gallons of water boiled to extract salt crystals.[12]

Applying many of the skills of plantation life, the salt makers built little settlements of houses, work sheds, and furnaces for boiling salt. The process was somewhat similar to making sugar from cane juice. The liquid was boiled in a large flat pan over a slow fire until, through constant stirring and evaporation, crystals formed. The much greater volume of saltwater and the much greater need for salt in volume made innovations off the sugar-making process necessary. Plantation sugar pans were insufficient, so steamboat boilers were cut in half. Metal harbor buoys became 150-gallon salt kettles once the retreating Confederates removed the navigational aids from coastal waters.

If large vessels were not available, other means were used to render the salt. Sometimes the brine was placed in a barrel and allowed to settle; at other times, thick brine was placed to drain in a sack or in a sieve to complete the extraction process.

In the larger government works, however, the process was much more sophisticated and the works much more extensive. They included kilns for brick making, furnaces, pumps and pipes or aqueducts for transferring brine, carpenter and blacksmith shops, and extensive warehousing facilities. Wagons and horses, mules, or oxen were necessary parts of the operation, for much of the salt from the Apalachicola area was carried overland to Saffold as a transfer point for shipment either up the Chattahoochee or inland for private or government use. A meat-packing installation at Albany, Georgia, on the Flint River created an especially critical need for salt.[13]

Throughout the summer and fall of 1863, the blockaders were kept busy in search-and-destroy missions against the saltworks. When Adm. James Lardner replaced Theodorus Bailey in command of the East Gulf Blockading Squadron, he continued the strategy. He was highly aware of the economic importance of salt to the whole chain of supply that ended in meat for the Confederate armies in Tennessee, Virginia, and elsewhere in the Confederacy.[14]

Sometimes the Confederates put up resistance to the Union raids, and sometimes either side took a few casualties in wounded. At times Confederate troops served as guards—either for saltworks or for fishermen who sun-dried their catch to supply the Confederate armies.[15] More often, however, the Confederates responded as a band of noncombatants, taking cover during raids and then coming out again to repair the damage and resume operations. Operations on both sides became a repetitive cycle of build and start up production, search and destroy, rebuild and resume production, search and destroy—and so on for the duration of the war.

Six months after one major raid, Acting Master W. R. Browne reported the destruction of 290 saltworks in the same general area. His raid took thirty-three covered wagons, twelve flatboats, two sloops of five tons each, six ox carts, 4,000 bushels of salt, 268 buildings, 105 iron boilers, and 529 iron kettles averaging 150 gallons each. Even when a crew took a howitzer ashore to blast a hole in a large kettle, the salt makers would somehow resume operations. After his massive assault on saltworks, Browne still estimated that an additional 100 facilities existed in the area.

When the blockaders went back to the St. Andrew's Bay installation six months after their June raid, they destroyed 4,000 bushels of salt, 1,000 kettles and boilers, and 700 buildings in 500 separate works. Estimated total loss was $6 million. The casualty figures in this kind of war were always economic. The loss of salt to the Confederates during peak demand in the meat-curing season was, of course, incalculable.[16]

Aside from their shore raids, the Union ships had to maintain the blockade. By mid-1863 their efforts had become far more effective. No doubt obstructions in the Apalachicola River also contributed to the diminished flow of traffic. Blockade runners were setting course for Florida ports, but records show that few were on course for Apalachicola. Only two were captured outward bound from Apalachicola, though four were taken in Apalachicola Sound during 1863 and another seven in the area around St. Joseph's Bay, St. Andrew's Bay, and the area between Apalachicola Bay and St. Mark's.[17]

The blockading crews had to remain constantly alert, however, in the event a blockader did try to enter or exit the port. Asst. Engr. Oscar D. Lewis recorded regular instances of "Sail 'O!" but the call was most often for the supply boat or a tender. The *Hendrick Hudson* stopped by the Apalachicola station with one hundred bales of cotton picked up after the *Cuyler* had engaged in an exciting chase of a blockade runner that jettisoned cargo to make her escape.[18] On one occasion the *Port Royal* gave chase to a strange sail that proved to be a supply ship bound for New Orleans, but the crew came away with some lemons for their trouble. In general, expeditions to move upriver to capture a blockade runner, as the *Fashion* had come under attack in May, were rare occurrences off Apalachicola by the midpoint of the war.

On another occasion, the *Somerset*'s crew was summoned to all hands on deck in the middle of the night; guns were trained on an unidentified object that turned out to be driftwood. As Lt. George E. Welch reported to Admiral Lardner, "It has had the effect to make our men 'toe the mark' as far as a vigilant lookout is concerned and the alarm (possibly a false one) may prove our salvation. . . . You may be assured that the boarding of this ship in small boats will be an exceedingly difficult operation."[19]

Lieutenant Crossman had begun the year with a proposal to mount an expedition up the Apalachicola-Chattahoochee to capture Columbus. From maps and intelligence reports he had traced rail lines and roads. He assessed the value of wild herds of cattle on St. Vincent's to supply an army of ten thousand. And he even suggested the assignment of "six or seven iron-plated river gunboats" to the proposed expedition. Six months later—with the gunboat *Chattahoochee* destroyed and the iron-clad *Jackson* no more than a strong potential threat—such effort hardly seemed advised, even if it had been a feasible plan. Instead, the Union force at Apalachicola was reduced by June 15. In March, a bark and four steamers (one-third of the steamers in the entire squadron) with 447 men and thirty-five guns had blockaded the port. By June the force was diminished to two steamers and a schooner with 225 men and twenty-three guns.[20]

As it had turned out, very little of their work involved giving chase to blockaders and taking prizes. They were serving what can only be termed "hardship duty." Apalachicola was a station where the block-aders seemed less and less likely to win either prize money or promotions. During January–April 1862, the most lucrative period for ships in immediate Apalachicola waters, total prize money from the *Lizzie Weston*, the *Octavia*, and the *Rose* was $84,751.07. The formula for dividing the prize sent 50 percent to the pension fund and 50 percent to be divided among the squadron commander, the commander of the blockader, the ship's officers, and the crew. A man's share was determined by his rank. The numbers of ships and men to share the few prizes, however, might reduce each sailor's share to a few dollars. The *Octavia* alone netted only $686.00 to the *Mercidita* and *Sagamore*. Unlike the whaler who returned home broke, these sailors could hardly lay claim to having "a devlish good sail."[21]

For the most part, the Union blockade maintained its presence in a way much different from the operations the first tentative shore parties carried out in the summer and fall of 1861. Even though the Union men had few or no armed confrontations, their dealings with noncombatants created a continual drain upon the blockaders' resources. After two years, Union and Confederate sympathies among the inhabitants of Apalachicola with whom the naval personnel had dealings had been largely identified. The wartime population of Apalachicola had also stabilized at about five hundred. After the initial reconnaissance on both sides, each group had settled into the basic work of surviving the war. The ships made some exceptions about transporting refugees. In one instance, a Mr. Morrison with his wife and two children were brought aboard the *Port Royal* as cabin passengers. Soon scheduled for rest and recreation at Key West, the ship was chosen so that these refugees from

Macon, Georgia, could make connections there for the Northern states. No doubt Mr. Morrison's having $70,000 in gold and silver coin helped his chances for getting passage.[22]

As ship's surgeon Schofield recorded in his diary, there were areas set aside on St. George's and St. Vincent's islands where the crew might "rusticate" in the lighthouse and fish or swim along the beach. More often than not, however, boredom and inactivity were major problems for Union crewmen. Asst. Engr. Oscar Lewis's diary records activities—and inactivity—on blockade duty:

> Wednesday, October 28 [1863]
> 4 A.M. Roze and went on duty in the Engine room until 8 A.M. and then took breakfast and penned theses few lines and spent the morning in steerage writing—Nothing occurred during the day to distract the monotony of the ceaseless tiresome life experienced here. Spent the day reading and sleeping.
> Thursday, October 29 [1863]
> 7:30 A.M. Roze and took breakfast and at 8 A.M. went on duty in the Engine room until 12 mer then took dinner and penned these few lines spent the afternoon reading and at 8 P.M. went on duty in the Engine room until 12 mid the weather was very thick and stormy and the old Pt Royal rolled and tossed fearfully her timbers groaning fearfully and making her leak badly—nothing occurred to change the usual monotony.[23]

Some officers passed the time reading. The fall and occupation of New Orleans had meant the breaking up of private libraries in the captured city and the transfer of books to used-book sellers. One officer on leave had a group of fifty contribute one dollar each to buy a ship's library of 150 volumes.[24] Younger men who had not yet passed qualifying examinations to become passed midshipmen spent time studying, as did the younger crew on the Confederate *Chattahoochee*. Lewis kept a careful account of his studies and also of many days spent reading novels like *The Count of Monte Cristo* or the works of Jean Jacques Rousseau.

Others who had had experience in the merchant service spun stories of whaling adventures and foreign ports of call. Elias Lee sat on deck the evening of July 17 telling of his adventures in the *Chattahoochee* explosion.[25] Talk might turn to issues of how effective various generals had been in the Civil War, of emancipation, the abolition of the spirit ration in the navy, whether the Confederacy would receive diplomatic recognition from France or Britain, and the like. There were also visits from ship to ship, to pass along mail, exchange supplies, or by special invitation. For Christmas 1862, the *Port Royal*'s crew entertained visitors from the *Somerset* with "theatricals."[26] Card playing often substituted for those more elevating activities. And out of boredom the crew bet upon almost everything; "raise the beef boat" was one popular form of gambling whereby bets were laid to see who could predict the next arrival of the supply steamer. Bets were also placed on who would receive the most mail when the steamer did arrive. One sailor described the arrival of the mail boat as "the most important event of our lives."[27]

Supply steamers were scheduled to visit every three weeks, but the more remote stations did not always receive regular service.[28] In January 1863, Lieutenant Welch reported the *Amanda* low on provisions and about to go on half rations if stores were not forthcoming. The ship's account was also depleted and the officers were running out of money to contract for game and fish off the islands.[29] Ships at times traded provisions with each other. After one such exchange, a disagreement arose when the commanders of the *J. S. Chambers* and *Roebuck* refused to repay the *Amanda*, charging that Welch had culled out his spoiled provisions for the exchange.[30]

The log of the *Somerset* gives an inventory of the stores the supply ships brought: one barrel pork, one barrel beef, two barrels flour, 840 pounds preserved meat, 175 pounds dried apples, 467 pounds sugar, 53 pounds tea, 400 pounds coffee, 96 pounds butter, 110 pounds DM vegetables, 72 gallons beans, 44 gallons molasses, 42 gallons vinegar; for the use of the crew: 351 pounds tobacco, 300 pounds soap, 10 pounds black thread, 5 pounds white thread, ninety-six handkerchiefs, 2,000 needles, twenty-eight thimbles, thirty-six jackknives, thirty-six scissors, twelve razors, ninety-six cases shaving soap, twenty-four fine combs, forty-eight coarse combs, twenty-four tin pots, forty-eight tin pans, fifty boxes blacking, and ninety-six bottles pepper. Sometimes a mission to gather stores returned nonregulation items. The *Somerset*'s log records that one sailor smuggled on board "a quantity of champaign cider in a barrel, the bottles being concealed by him by filling the top of the barrel with oysters."[31]

Although Lewis made no regular mention of drinking on board, he noted on one occasion that "all hands got quite drunk." After almost a year on the blockade at Apalachicola he also noted, "I drank more tonight than I ever drank in my life." In doing so, he had broken a pledge given to a girl named Mary as he left to enter the navy. To his physical pain and efforts to "throw up" was added the pain of loss: "She has given up all interest in me and I can no longer stand by my promise to one who is not longer dear to me."[32] While intemperance was a major problem with Confederate land forces at Apalachicola[33] and while the problem was a constant concern in the Union Navy as well, the Apalachicola station was evidently so isolated that supplies of spirits could not create an ongoing problem.

With the isolation, inactivity, and boredom along the blockade, tempers sometimes flared among the officers. Just who was to patrol where and who outranked whom on the Apalachicola station created controversy. Addressing such issues at length on one occasion, George Welch wrote his fellow officer E. Y. McCauley on the *Fort Henry:* "I will come down to the Pass and black your boots if you will show me the slightest order from Admiral Lardner for doing so."[34] The composition of the crews—many of them mustered from the merchant marine and not schooled and disciplined in regular navy practice—gave rise to a certain raggedness in the fleet. In some ways, however, the navy was well served by such men in the unconventional warfare along the west Florida coast.[35]

Relationships with the civilians ashore had generally settled into a routine by mid-1863. The numbers of refugees and contrabands that came out to the ships were such that not all of them could be transported to Key West, as had been the case early in the war; or housed in various shelters on the barrier islands; or kept on board the blockaders themselves, as was attempted at one point. The small complement of ships off Apalachicola simply was not organized in such a way that the officers could coordinate relief services for noncombatants, especially when civilians fled with goats and crates of chickens in their baggage. The naval mission was to maintain a blockade, keep watch on possible Confederate operations in Apalachicola, and apply increasing economic pressure by destroying saltworks.

Most often, the refugees were not cabin passengers but impoverished women from Apalachicola. For men confined at close quarters on the blockading vessels, the presence of women nearby was a distraction. In fact, on the day that the boat expedition pulled away from the *Port Royal* to capture the *Fashion*—and perhaps attack the CS *Chattahoochee*— Lewis gives only a few words to that possibility of action with the enemy; instead, the day's entry is given over to this paragraph: "Spent the morning on the deck looking at a beautiful young lady from the town the first one I have seen yet in this quarter of the globe. She was lovely and attracted considerable appreciation. I was on deck all the time she was there."[36]

Other references in Lewis's diary indicate that women who came from Apalachicola to visit friends housed on St. George's and St. Vincent's islands included the Union ships in their round of calls. Among them were Mary Reynolds and Helen Rearden, who visited Becky Constantine on St. George's. "Not very good looking," Lewis noted about two such visitors, "but voluptuous in the extreme suggesting bad thoughts in the desires of the male beholders."[37] To celebrate July 4, the *Port Royal* had a theatrical presentation to which they invited two Apalachicola ladies, who also accepted an invitation to remain on board overnight.[38]

A circumstance that was "quite interesting" to a young sailor like Lewis created discipline problems for a commander like Welch. His men were not allowed near the St. George's lighthouse except on business.[39] When the lighthouse burned in January 1863, his choice was to leave the women and children in the bitter cold in "sand whirling in clouds on the desolate island" or to house them on the *Amanda*. Stationing a guard over the women and placing covers on the hatches to segregate them from his men created discontent among crew members. They sent a delegation to demand that the guard and the hatches be removed. When the commander refused, the men rolled cold shot across the deck above his cabin for more than an hour that night. He responded by putting the troublemakers in irons.[40]

Confederate deserters like Lee and Cook often came aboard to join the Union crews, a practice encouraged because of a critical shortage of seamen in the blockaders' ranks. In turn, the blockaders also had problems with men deserting to go ashore. Once when a woman known to the blockaders approached in a boat carrying a flag of truce, they welcomed an opportunity to gather information about a force of Confederate guerrillas. After being aboard for a time, she appealed as a woman alone for someone to accompany her back to her boat. Two recruits from Apalachicola who knew the area were dispatched on the chivalrous mission. The next day, however, they were identified as deserters in their commander's report to Admiral Bailey.[41]

To the blockaders in their struggles with navigating Apalachicola waters, refugees were much prized as pilots. The arrangement was not

without problems, however. Sailing over to St. Mark's with coal for the
Young Rover, the *Amanda* returned with her to Dog Island where both
ships were to take on water. "But," Welch reported, "the pilot forgetting
his bearings or his loyalty ran both ships on the Bar."[42]

Such continued tensions caused relationships between the blockading
personnel and civilians to wear thin. Welch gave way to the strain in this
letter to Apalachicola:

Mr. Mimms   Jan. 1st 1863

In reply to your message asking my opinions in regard to your
slaves escaped to this ship previous to Jan 1st and your enquiry if
they will be confiscated in the event of your proving yourself a good
Union man I hereby give it for what it is worth always bearing in
mind that it is but an opinion carrying with it but little weight or
responsibility. If you can prove to the satisfaction of the government
that you are and have been a Union man from the inception of this
rebellion I have no doubt that your claim may be considered but if
you are and have been as represented to me a renegade Yankee and
persistent Rebel who went forth with a sword in your hand and a lie
in your mouth to battle against the flag which next to God you were
bound to reverence and love in that case I opine you will whistle
Yankee Doodle to but little purpose.

The condition of your contrabands when they reached the ship
would lead me to look upon you as the embodiment of cruelty the
incarnation of the Devil himself.

I have never been what is termed an Abolitionist or am I as well
versed in Bible lore as I should be but I cannot refrain from saying
to you in the words of St. Paul thou persuadest even me to be one.

A poor Southern white who has accustomed himself to eat dirt,
cut, gouge and throw himself at the feet of Jesus in regular rotation
I can find some apology for in the force of the example set by those
who should know better, but for a Northerner who has enjoyed the
advantage of a Christian education acting as a conscript officer for
the Rebel government and seeking to lure a loyal man from his duty
by the offer of a bribe I cannot muster the ghost of a regret that his
property is confiscated. Neither would I if I saw him dangling between the precious soil and the God he has offended.

I have no power to confer favors on rebel renegades and if I had I
would not exercise it in your case as I now understand it. It is no

concern of mine if you have lost twenty negroe's the proceeds of years of toil and suffering.

In common with most Northern men [I] am clothed in sackcloth and ashes mourning for our relatives sacrificed to this accursed rebellion.

You will please discontinue your flag of truce on this subject.

> With due respect
> I remain your servant
> Geo. E. Welch[43]

In another letter Welch defended himself to the admiral against his crew's charge about his quick temper. He cited conditions on the blockade as reason enough to cause trouble:

These fellows were wont to style themselves "Regulation" and imagined that a small vessel with a large portion of her crew almost constantly absent on boat service could carry on all her duties with the regularity and precision of a frigate lying in Key West harbor. . . .

Dog Island is a desolate sand heap we have no visiting places. . . . The ship has been in commission 18 months, she is sadly in need of repairs, her caboose is entirely burned and the mens food but indifferently cooked and twice the ship has been on fire. Her berth deck leaks like a sieve and I find great difficulty keeping my wounded men dry and comfortable her bottom encrusted with barnacles is like a half log.[44]

Both letters reflect that the blockading commanders had a more difficult political role and management role than their strictly naval function. Little wonder the Union was finding it a huge drain upon resources to station more than six hundred blockaders along the Southern coast. That meant that thousands of men were confined to close quarters with little to do beyond routine duties. Thus the minutiae of daily management created a greater hardship upon the Union blockaders than waging war.

Weather was, of course, of constant concern to the men, both for their ships and for the comfort and safety of the crews. Not only did the ships have difficulty—and expend needed fuel—to remain on station, but a pitching ship armed with cannon could create a deadly problem. Although a ship's guns weighing nine thousand pounds were secured to the bulwarks with tackle and ring bolts, the roll of the decks in a storm could tear loose a gun and make it a destructive projectile. The gun might tear out a bulwark at the next roll or, worse still, go down a hatch and out the bottom of the ship.[45]

Because the larger vessels were hampered in the shallow waters off Apalachicola, the amount of work the crews did from very small boats created a particular hazard. If a boat capsized or was caught in a squall, sometimes the crew escaped safely and sometimes not. On one occasion Crossman reported that three men were lost when their boat foundered in heavy weather and that their bodies washed ashore days later. The lieutenant then had the sad duty of writing to the families of the men as well as reporting to his commander.[46]

Weather conditions, combined with poor ventilation systems on the blockaders created constant problems with creature comforts. During very cold weather the crew might heat a round shot in the ship's furnace and insulate it in a box of sand. Then a group of men could read while sitting around the box with blankets wrapped around their knees. Or the shot was a good source of heat for two or three hours while two men played chess or backgammon with the box positioned beneath the game board between them.[47] Even in the cozy warmth of the cabin, however, a crew usually had the pitch of rough winter seas to endure.

Summer heat was of particular concern to commanders, in part because of the station in Florida waters and in part because of regulations the U.S. government traditionally maintained. Work was normally cut back in the summer as a measure to protect health.[48] On his ship, Welch gave specific orders to work parties about erecting an awning to supply shade.[49] On shore, fleas were likely to be "knee deep and three fleas to a sand" or sand flies "most enterprising and tireless in their efforts to cheer us up and make things brisk for us."[50]

In summer, crew members were able to move about ship more freely and to sleep on deck. When the wind was seaward, however, the cooling breeze bore clouds of mosquitoes. This presented each sailor with the choice between sweltering below decks with the hatches closed or risking serious insect bites on deck. The men sought escape from the mosquitoes in the smoke from their pipes or risked smothering in their jackets.[51]

On one hot August night, Lewis found it "too warm to sleep in the steerage and too wet to sleep on deck, for it had commenced to rain about 11 P.M. and we were obliged to take up our beds and walk all for the good of our country." "But still it was rather rough," he added. He finally settled down near the ship's chicken coop where he found "the effluvia rather strong." He had no sooner fallen into a restful sleep when the morning watch disturbed all the sleepers on deck and sent them once more down to steerage. The next day found Lewis stiff and sore and generally out of sorts.[52] On successive days, he described the heat as "warm," "uncommonly warm," and, no doubt running out of adjectives, finally settled for "intolerable."

Yellow fever was, of course, a peril; often it would put most of a crew on sick call, and deaths were frequent. The major remedy was to pull a ship off station, send it to Key West where the crew could enjoy shore leave, and thoroughly fumigate the ship. The only known remedy during the Civil War was to fumigate the ships with tar smoke. Every few days, the hatches would be closed and hot iron fire pokers immersed in buckets of tar. The black smoke that permeated the ship was thought to purge it of yellow fever.[53]

John F. Van Nest, acting master's mate aboard the *J. S. Chambers*, wrote his parents about his suffering in 1864. Officers and men ill on board multiplied the strain upon those well enough to work. On July 8 he complained that the "millions of mosquitoes . . . almost eat me up and I can scarcely sleep at night for them." On August 7 he reported that between twenty-five and thirty men were "down sick with some kind of fever" and that the *Chambers* "hardly had enough able bodied men to man one gun." By August 13, he reported himself still well after the death of an officer and twelve crew members with twelve men "still sick and the Captain and 3 other officers also sick." By August 24, Acting Ens. William J. Eldredge reported that he and Van Nest had been the only officers to escape the fever. On August 15, the ship's surgeon had suffered a nervous collapse from his exertions of tending the sick. The report ends with an account of Van Nest's fate: "At 6 p.m. on the 18th instant, Acting Master J. F. Van Nest in, it is supposed, a fit of derangement jumped overboard and was drowned in spite of every effort made to save him."[54]

Even without widespread sickness aboard, officers expressed concern about the general health of their crews. Lieutenant Crossman of the *Somerset* gave his men exercise liberty along the beach on St. George's Island, but he noted in a report to Admiral Bailey "that the slightest cuts or bruises turn to most malignant sores" after thirteen months without shore leave.[55]

As squadron commanders were kept informed of such conditions, they forwarded a steady series of reports to the Navy Department. Through the spring and summer of 1863, Admiral Bailey wrote almost monthly to Gideon Welles. His squadron was in need of seamen, a band to lift morale, and means to repair or replace vessels unfit for service.[56]

When Capt. Theodore Greene replaced Bailey, his reports of 1864 were even more insistent in their warnings that vessels were poorly maintained. Of nineteen vessels in the East Gulf Blockading Squadron in August 1864, he considered only three fit for service.[57]

For the duration of the Civil War, however, the Union Navy had little choice except to keep ships on station. Thus the blockaders settled in as best they could. On Sand Island, a narrow spit of land between Dog Island and the mainland, they piled stores of coal from the tenders. Wood cut on St. Vincent's, or shipped in, supplied lengths of firewood to keep the ship's fires banked and ready to raise steam with coal in case a blockade runner was sighted. On Dog Island they found springs of water for replenishing ship's stores, for supply vessels remained erratic in their visits to remote stations.

On their routine patrols into Apalachicola, the sailors found an almost deserted town vastly changed from the place where the blockade had been proclaimed in the summer of 1861. Initially, Apalachicola was one of the most important points on the blockade of the Gulf coast. By mid-1863, it was one of the least important. The barrier islands and the town had been deserted first by the prosperous cotton traders, then by the Florida militia and Confederate Army, and finally by the citizens themselves. The Confederate Navy planned to open the port, but the way was blocked first by army obstructions sunk in the river, then by the *Chattahoochee*'s heavy draft, and finally by her own crew's ineptitude. The Union Navy might have captured the port, but their heavy ships made Apalachicola inaccessible beyond the shallow bay. Swift blockade runners sought other ports of entry through the blockade, leaving the blockaders at Apalachicola to stand guard over a ghost town.

At a court-martial following Lieutenant Welch's May 27 decision to scuttle the *Amanda,* he claimed that Confederate forces in the area were threatening to capture the ship. His fellow officers testified to his negligence.[58] Given conditions on the blockade, Welch might well have claimed that boredom and frustration drove him to scuttle his ship and have done with the matter. Whatever issues arose in the aftermath of the storm, news of the *Chattahoochee*'s destruction settled the issue of the "phantom ram which comes—and does not come."

We Can Laugh at the Blockade for a While

Life Under the Blockade, 1862–1864

Apalachicola, Florida, in 1837
Edward A. Mueller Collection, Jacksonville, Fla.

By the summer of 1863, the wreck of the gunboat *Chattahoochee* lying partially submerged at Blountstown Bar was the only remaining semblance of important Confederate plans in the area. And it was not until mid-August 1863 that the Confederate Navy made attempts to raise the wreck and return it to Columbus for repairs. As the derelict ship was towed northward to Columbus, it passed through an area as much changed by the war as Apalachicola had been.

The effect of the blockade was setting in as a kind of creeping paralysis. Stage by stage, Confederate influence in the area was withering. The barrier islands off Apalachicola were hardly fortified in the summer of 1861 before forces were withdrawn; by December 1861, Apalachicola was abandoned; by the spring of 1862, actions to the north drew all except a skeleton force away from Florida.

Confederate hopes at that time became fixed on Saffold where the *Chattahoochee* was then under construction. The advance of the ship downriver to Chattahoochee and then to the obstructions below advanced hopes of raising the blockade. With the loss of the gunboat—and, with it, loss of hope for freeing the river system from the blockade—the effects of the blockade began to pervade every aspect of a life that had flourished along the rivers before the war.

I Am Now a Guerrilla in Every Sense of the Word

By 1863, the thriving port had ceased to be the chief economic outlet for the Chattahoochee and Flint rivers, nor was the port any longer an economic gateway. It had become instead a kind of no man's land, not really Union because the blockaders did not come ashore to occupy the town, and yet not Confederate because there were no resources to reclaim the town and defend it. Steamers made regular trips southward until 1862. Engineers Boggs and Moreno moved unchallenged into and out of the town, and civilians continued to ply the river from Apalachicola northward with relative ease. The town, however, had lost the great majority of its population.

Blockading officers noted its difficult position. Confederates stigmatized the inhabitants for being Unionists; the Union suspected them loyal to the Confederacy. Conscript officers had combed the area for men to serve in the Confederate armies and so male inhabitants were not much in evidence in the town. Except for a small population of immigrant fishermen, Apalachicola was inhabited mainly by women and children. With the collapse of the economy, they were in a near-starving condition. In fact, a part of Lt. A. F. Crossman's reasons for proposing to occupy the town was to alleviate the suffering of a populace caught in a political crossfire. The Union Navy could supply necessities for survival, military protection, and in turn, an increased measure of civil stability.[1]

Confederate officials were even more concerned about conditions in Apalachicola. Governor Milton informed General Beauregard that loss of regular Confederate contact with Apalachicola would "expose to famine nearly 500 loyal citizens who are suffering for bread." In a time of critically short supplies for everyone, however, the 500 in need there were negligible compared to 11,673 Floridians in need of state support.[2] Such widespread deprivation among a free population of 78,699 meant that for every Florida soldier in the field a civilian required aid at home.[3]

Conditions became so severe that a growing Unionist sentiment began to appear in some quarters. The Confederate conscript laws were also unpopular; when men were sent northward, their homes were left unprotected. Thus Florida was a politically unstable area at the midpoint of the war. Milton wrote to Beauregard in the fall of 1863 to describe the extent of unrest and disloyalty among the populace and to speculate on how easily the Union might "subjugate and occupy all of Florida west of the Apalachicola River."[4]

The condition Milton described was especially reflected in the number of deserters who took refuge along the rivers and inlets that cut into the mainland in the Florida panhandle. A traveler north along the Apalachicola and Chattahoochee rivers would have been made aware of the large numbers of "lay-outs." Unlike the civilian refugees whom Confederate engineer Boggs had found in the interior, these groups were fugitives sought by Confederate authorities. As the war progressed, they grew in numbers; they also increased their contacts with the Union forces on the Gulf. Finally they became guerrilla forces, no longer committed to the Confederacy, not quite committed to the Union that supplied them arms and supplies, but fully committed to survival. As one reported: "I am now a guerrilla in every sense of the word; we neither tell where we stay nor where we are going, nor when we shall return; [we] assemble the Company at the sound of a cow's horn. We have made some arrests of both white and black, and hung one negro last week."[5]

The deserters lived a desperate life along the coastal rivers and creeks and, according to a letter from Lieutenant Welch of the *Amanda* to Adm. Theodorus Bailey of the East Gulf Blockading Squadron, they made a daring attempt to escape the hardships and isolation of living as deserters. They chose John Harvey as their representative, for they knew that he traveled from time to time from his home seventy miles upriver from Apalachicola to have dealings with Welch on the *Amanda*.

A bond of trust had developed between the Union officer and the man who displayed such emotion upon seeing "the old flag" that Welch respected his sincerity.

Harvey went aboard the *Amanda* on February 15, 1863, with a message from a troop of five hundred deserters who were armed with shotguns. They had had skirmishes with the conscript officers in the triangle formed by southwest Georgia, southeast Alabama, and west Florida near the confluence of the Chattahoochee, Flint, and Apalachicola rivers. Now running low on ammunition and food, they sent word to Welch "that they would follow me or any other leader to any peril they are ordered to rather than leave their families and go north." Thus they proposed to surrender themselves as a group, either as prisoners or as refugees to be taken under the protective custody of Welch at his station off Dog Island. Welch's dilemma, as he described it to his commander, was how to gain safe conduct to the coast for such a large group from a very remote place far in the interior of enemy-occupied territory.[6] Had Welch's scheme proved successful, Confederate strength along the Apalachicola might not have been sufficient to halt the operation.

Judging from contemporary accounts, operations of the Confederate regulars in west Florida were hardly better organized or more effective than the guerrillas'. Not only the port of Apalachicola, but the area inland along the Apalachicola River had become a no man's land, too. The wooded lands near the coast, in what is now the Chattahoochee National Forest, had been largely uninhabited long before the war. James M. Dancy's reminiscences of being a young soldier on the Apalachicola draw a picture of general disorganization. He frequently transferred from one unit or another, at times accompanied by his father, a former U.S. surveyor general and a Confederate Florida official. He was assigned at other times to guard saltworks and fishing operations at St. Mark's.

What Dancy characterized as "the most disagreeable service I was called upon to render" was tracking down deserters near Ricko's Bluff, an area roughly halfway between Apalachicola and Chattahoochee, Florida. Parties of men with bloodhounds would go in search of a deserter who was rumored to be at or near his home. They would either lie in wait to surround the man's home or take a scent and track him with dogs through the swamps and marshes along the river and its numerous tributaries. Such were the hardships deserters had sought to escape when they appealed to Welch on the blockade.

Sometimes the Confederates were tracked in turn by Union search parties up the Apalachicola River. On the whole, Dancy's account reads more like modern accounts of jungle warfare and counterinsurgency than the more traditional depictions of the Civil War.[7]

Camp life in the area was quite informal even by Civil War standards. At one post in Lake City, Florida, the Confederate troops were engaged by day in unloading provisions into a warehouse and, by night, loading provisions out the back door for their own use. By this means, Dancy's body servant kept their private larder well stocked and generally attended his master's needs. After a day's march, Dancy wrote, "As it was past the dinner hour, and I had eaten nothing, I got my body servant to hunt up a colored cook in town to bake us a pone of corn bread (we had plenty of meal). He did so and we ate heartily." On another occasion, Dancy violated some minor regulation and was penalized with the assignment to clean all the small arms in the unit: "This my body servant did while I looked on—not very heavy punishment for me."[8]

Confederate guard duty on remote posts along the river was more difficult. A force of about one hundred conscripts was guarding the obstructions at the Narrows on the marshy, mosquito-ridden riverbanks. The obstructions had themselves greatly reduced the amount of traffic along the river, though there was a bypass to the port through various creeks and cutoffs in the area.

As far north as Ricko's Bluff, there was a small garrison—the same ragtag, poorly armed force viewed so contemptuously by the *Chattahoochee*'s officers. As with conditions in Apalachicola itself, civilian inhabitants along the way were mainly women and children, who were suffering from great deprivation because of the war. The only semblance of the economic activity the area had enjoyed before the war was the presence of a few fishermen.[9]

In other parts of the Confederacy, like northern Virginia or Vicksburg, it seemed that the war had laid waste the economy, but it had redefined a given area in important strategic terms. In Apalachicola and along the river northward, the conditions of war seemed only to have destroyed economic life without producing gains in military importance.

Chattahoochee, Florida, where the gunboat *Chattahoochee* had once been an awesome weapon, remained an important transfer point in river traffic. A force, reported to the blockade to be "a regiment of troops," was stationed there; but these troops had no more than a nominal capacity to defend the area should it have been attacked. Plans to utilize the

Chattahoochee Arsenal facilities for a military school had been made but never fulfilled.[10]

Thus as the major military action in the border states of the Confederacy drew resources away from Florida's coastal areas, they were left with forces that very probably could not have held against a Union offensive—even if the Union had considered the area significant enough to attack.

Traffic as it flowed southward from Columbus along the Chattahoochee no longer continued to Apalachicola. After traffic to Apalachicola was suspended in 1862,[11] the only reliable means of transportation from Chattahoochee and Ricko's Bluff was a dinghy from the wrecked *Chattahoochee* left at the disposal of the Roman Catholic priest from Apalachicola.[12] Steamers and small boats made a U turn at Chattahoochee to travel up the Flint River to Bainbridge and as far as Albany.

What Is The Blockade to Us?

In the triangle drained by the lower Chattahoochee and by the Flint River, and also in the Alabama counties bordering the Chattahoochee, news from the northern sections of the Confederacy was among the riverboats' most interesting cargo. If the effect of the blockade was a slow attrition, casualty reports from Tennessee and northern Virginia made a swift impact.

At first brash and hopeful, messages in the summer of 1861 predicted "I believe peace will be made soon, for they will see that they cannot fight the South." Or "I think they will make peace and have no doubt but we will all be home sometime next fall by the 1st of November anyway."[13] The letter writer was severely wounded at the battle of Seven Pines the next year and died at home of the effects of those wounds by the second autumn of the war. Messages took on a different tone after more than two years of war.

By 1863, the casualty lists telegraphed or carried by mail along the river contained a roll call of the major battles of the war: Bull Run, Malvern Hill, Seven Pines, Mechanicsville, Cold Harbor. Other men were killed or wounded at lesser-known sites: White-Oak Swamp, Chantilly, Boonesboro. Some were killed outright; others died of wounds.

Diseases like smallpox took others, and some casualties were listed as "died of exertion" on the battlefield.[14] The overseer Andrews, who had looked with such pride on the farmlands of Early County, happened upon a neighbor, Anthony Hutchins, "on the classic soil of the Old Dominion . . . both following the plume of our immortal chieftain, General Robert E. Lee."[15] Anthony's brother James was to die in Virginia; two other brothers were simply lost and never heard of again.

Some who had boarded river steamers to join the Confederacy at the Fort Gaines or Columbia landings were returned as dead or wounded.[16] Near the Navy Yard Landing at Saffold, the Shackelfords received news that their brother William had been killed; within a few weeks, a riverboat returned his body in a metal casket.[17] Two women at Columbia, both named Soloman, were in the post office awaiting word from the local unit, the Columbia Blues; because the casualty list that reported a "Soloman" killed did not specify a first name, neither knew which was the widow.[18]

In the wartime communications link, the attention of the populace focused northward to the areas where their men were serving. As the crippled gunboat *Chattahoochee* was towed north past each landing, the Chattahoochee River was no longer a link southward to Apalachicola; it had become but the last short leg of a long journey north to Tennessee and Virginia, a distance traversed by railroad.

By 1863, then, the life of the river had diminished in both economic and strategic importance. Certainly the steamers to Apalachicola no longer shipped out cotton by the tens and hundreds of thousands of bales. Wartime production in the area was more centered upon food production shipped north by rail. Nor did the river steamers bring upriver from Apalachicola the coffee, Havana cigars, brandy, and bolts of rich fabric for equally rich dresses.

A single major crop had flowed down the river in 1860; by 1863, salt was the single major product that flowed up the river. Salt, by ox cart over narrow trails or by smaller boats, had become the chief commercial link with the Gulf Coast in 1863. Whether there was sufficient salt to preserve meat and whether it was available in sufficient quantities during the meat-curing season had a direct effect upon whether individuals had meat for the coming year—and whether the Confederate armies had a meat ration as well.

The self-contained and self-sufficient plantation system had always had the means to provide basic necessities for itself, even before a blockade had been dreamed of. But shaping those individual entities into a massive, coordinated logistics system to feed an army at war became quite another matter along the Chattahoochee.

As one measure to coordinate production and supply, by the third year of the war people living along the rivers were, like other citizens of the Confederacy, asked to devote a tithe of their production to the war effort. Adding a 10-percent levy to an already badly taxed system of labor, supplies, and animals for slaughter became a significant hardship.[19] Away with his cavalry unit in middle Florida and worried about the condition of his farm, Maj. George W. Scott wrote his wife instructions about how to deliver the 450 pounds of pork due the government and how to divide out the sugar and syrup the farm produced. Like the entire economy, Scott struggled with how to satisfy his obligation to the Confederacy and also provide for his family and farm laborers.[20]

In addition to giving a tithe, farmers also sold meat to the government, as reflected in a letter of John Cobb to his mother. As Gen. Howell Cobb attended to the defense of the Military District of Florida, the son was concerned with the family's agribusiness enterprise:

Dear Mother,
I arrived here [Macon] from Sumter [County]. I spent several days with father in Florida and left all well. I have delivered the meat to the government at 35 [cents]. I have not been paid yet. I could have got the money this morning, but as there is a prospect of getting the 50 [cents] I concluded to let the acct. stand open for a week, as the Agt. told me by that time he would be authorized to pay the 50 [cents] per pound. I delivered 23870 lbs. Father was perfectly satisfied with the price and did not think the Government ought to pay more.[21]

Men like Howell Cobb's brother-in-law, John B. Lamar, had prudently laid in supplies of salt, bagging, rope, and shoes and clothing for farm workers at the beginning of the war, saying, "we can laugh at the blockade for a while if salt is $12 a sack." As he wrote Cobb in November 1861: "But how it will be another year if the blockade is not raised it makes me hold my breath when I think of it."[22]

Agents of the Confederate government occupied themselves with purchasing from sources abroad, from private sources, and wherever goods were available. Naval agent Howell in Augusta reported that he had been unable to buy cured meat and so bought a herd of two hundred hogs, which he then had to tend and feed while he awaited favorable weather for hog killing. Such individual efforts, large-scale operations like the Cobbs conducted, and government supply efforts all contributed food for the war. The persistent Union raids upon saltworks along the Gulf during the fall and winter months could devastate production. Even when salt was plentiful, the nature of the task did not lend itself to mass production for a distant army of consumers; even under optimum conditions in peacetime, slaughtering and curing meat was a demanding task.

On a plantation, large groups of workers might slaughter twenty or more hogs in a day. On a smaller farm, four or five hogs was a task to keep a dozen people hard at work for a twelve- or fourteen-hour day. Representative figures exist in the careful records maintained at the time. Richard B. Hill's farm journals for the winter of 1862–63 show six hog killings: nine hogs at the first killing, and on successive killings, twenty-two, seven, eight, thirty, and ten. His year's total was 13,300 pounds.[23] By comparison, John Horry Dent slaughtered fifty-two hogs during the second winter of the war, or about 7,000 pounds.[24]

Slaughtering operations on such a scale required huge volumes of salt. A plantation where the meat ration was about three pounds per person per week also consumed a large volume of cured meat. Dent's rate of production was sufficient, for instance, to feed about forty-five people for a year; in Early County, where D. S. Johnston employed a force of ninety slaves, three pounds of meat per week was the usual ration.[25] It follows that plantations with a work force of seventy-five to a hundred slaves required a significant and sustained production rate simply to meet the needs of a private economic entity.

John Horry Dent was fortunate in having Horry, Jr., acting as a kind of agent for the family at his duty stations in the navy. This meant boxes with bolts of cloth, shoes for Sallie, six bottles of whiskey, and from the *Chattahoochee*'s station at Saffold, barrels of molasses and two fine brood sows to improve his father's stock. Horry also spent weeks dealing with the Saffold shoemaker. On November 12, 1862, the shoes were due "as soon as possible"; November 29, the shoemaker had "promised me faithfully he would have them done by Tuesday week." By December 7 Horry was reminding his father "how unreliable shoe makers are when pressed with demands," and he commented still later, "He is such a liar."[26]

Because the Union blockaders could not attack from the Gulf, the rich productivity of south Georgia and Alabama kept the area economically vital. In the "grainery of the Confederacy," as Gen. Howell Cobb called it, resources eventually began to play out. Even if the Union Navy did not attack, the effects of the blockade grew more severe. At the small settlements and plantation landings along the Chattahoochee, the resourcefulness bred of prewar isolation was being taxed to the limit.

Riverboats and carriages no longer transported people to and fro. The ritual of the visit, which had bound large plantation families before the war, had given way to the working party. At "The Refuge" near Bainbridge, at "The Pines" at Saffold, and northward in Barbour County, the plantation ladies had to exercise their sense of style in new ways. Hats and bonnets were woven from the bullrushes that grew in marsh land or even from pine straw. Much prized was a gift of leghorn that Catesby Jones sent Mrs. McLaughlin; as Augustus McLaughlin wrote Jones about naval matters, he noted that his wife was weaving a hat.[27]

Ladies became skilled in the weaving of cloth and especially in sewing when, one by one, the lack of spare parts shut down sewing machines in the Confederacy. A trip for thread from the Wellborn plantation in Barbour County was a three days' journey; even then, it was no longer the much-prized "Coats" thread shipped in from the North.[28]

Sewing had to be done not only for the family on a plantation but also for the slave laborers. Planters formerly shipped several hundred yards of Lindsey and homespun from the North in a single year.[29] Under wartime conditions, such cloth had to be produced in the South and sewing had to be done on a large scale. The war increased that burden even further; family members serving in Confederate forces, as well as general military needs, were served by volunteer production of clothing.

The ladies of Albany, Georgia, distinguished themselves with their sewing, especially for the wounded soldiers hospitalized there. Work displaced education as schools discontinued class in Albany on Friday afternoons so that children could knit socks. The ladies devoted their Saturdays to relief work among the prisoners at nearby Andersonville.[30] The fabled antebellum leisure class had become endlessly occupied with war work.

The same kind of contribution was repeated again and again along the Chattahoochee. In Eufaula, Mrs. G. H. Rhodes and a group of Eufaula ladies determined to form the Soldiers' Aid Society.[31] In Columbus, George Woodruff donated a building, which the ladies of the town supported as the Soldiers' Home. When the injured from the *Chattahoochee* explosion were transported there, the Columbus volunteers were ready to spend long hours nursing them. One Columbus merchant complained that every time he looked for a clean shirt his wife had used it to shroud a casualty.[32] Columbus ladies worked so indefatigably that two, Mrs. Robert S. Hardaway and her sister, were reported to have made nearly all the bandages used at First Bull Run.[33]

Such women worked with the patriotic zeal that has been well chronicled in Civil War histories. Writing to a captain of the Albany Guards in Virginia, the president of the Ladies' Soldiers Relief Association expressed that fervor: "There are many willing hands stretched out, begging to be permitted to sew for our soldiers. If you could see with how much cheerfulness the ladies do this work for the soldiers, you would believe me when I write, that to them it is a labor of love."[34]

Just as so much else had changed during the war, the Albany ladies recalled how one of their association had been aboard a train on which the first Confederate flag was sewn in Georgia. A party of officers and ladies en route from LaGrange to Atlanta in 1861 had commented that they had no flag. Someone got off at the next stop, bought the material, and the group continued its journey in high good humor as the men drew off the pattern for the stars and the ladies created a flag. A captain left the train at another stop to telegraph Atlanta that a flag would be aboard; in the early enthusiasm for the war, the train was greeted by a cheering crowd.[35] After two years of war, however, women all over the South plied their needles in a more serious mood. As one war widow wrote: "We knit a great deal, and worked, oh, so hard! and I thank God that it was so, for had it been otherwise, had I had time to sit and ponder over all the sad details that the daily news brought me, I should have failed."[36]

The necessity for such labor as it was required throughout the South created "an industry born of patriotism and necessity." The war entailed, in fact, "a temporary industrial revolution."[37] John Horry Dent also noted the good effects of war's necessities upon an increasingly self-reliant people: "With this great evil, a large amount of good must also come from this war. Even Annie and Sallie have knit their own stockings for their winter use."[38]

At the Wellborn plantation near Dent's Barbour County home, governess Antoinette Hague was using her rudimentary knowledge of chemistry to devise substitutes for common household products. Her account of the resourcefulness in the self-contained plantations describes a domestic chemical industry as one feature of the "temporary industrial revolution." Dyes for cloth had to be concocted with whatever ability the ladies had at hand. So also with such common household chemicals as bicarbonate of soda. A woman who learned to cobble herself a pair of shoes also had to know something about the process of tanning leather. In these efforts, the ingenuity of those who lived along the rivers was more than a combination of hard work and an eye for color and design. There were many rustic chemists at work along the rivers.

To dye the wool produced on a plantation, the ladies would use poke berries to produce red, hickory tree bark for green, and walnut hulls for a deep brown. Although indigo was plentiful for blues, black dye presented a problem, solved only by walking for miles to search for a weed called "the queen's delight."[39]

As the blockade retained its hold on the Confederate coast, supplies of medicine ran out, dishes broke, and there was no steamer to bring barrels of china from England any longer. Shoes wore out, and leather was needed for an army. The quartermaster at Columbus was receiving one authorization after another—first to impress all the hides in Columbus, then all the hides in the states south of North Carolina and Tennessee.[40] Leather was also needed for harnesses and for belting to run the machines at the Columbus Naval Iron Works, not for the neat foot of a lady.

"Lesser planters" had tanned hides at home in the years before the war. Now that the blockade moved that necessity several levels up the socioeconomic scale, the Wellborns' Barbour County plantation soon had its home tannery.

When the tanning process was complete, the ladies themselves could use a cobbler's awl for preparing a sole and vamp to stitch their own shoes. Pigskin was a pliable leather—though even dog hides were used in some tanning processes—and seamstresses-turned-cobblers took great pride in their work. Miss Hague wrote:

> I remember, how we used to hold our self-made shoes at arm's length and say, as they were inspected: "What is the blockade to us so far as shoes are concerned, when we can not only knit the uppers, but cut the soles and stitch them on? Each woman and girl her own shoemaker; away with bought shoes; we want none of them!" But alas, we really knew not how fickle a few months would prove that we were.[41]

As for medicine, Miss Hague called the woods "our drug stores." For the fever that so plagued those who lived along the rivers, dogwood berries were found to have the same alkaloid properties of cinchona in Peruvian bark, the source of quinine. For coughs they made their own syrup from the mullein plant, globe flower, and wild-cherry bark. In an era when purgatives were thought an infallible cure for many disorders, the castor bean was cultivated as a source of castor oil. A few rows of poppies in the garden were "at times very needful." The home chemist took the bulb of a ripe poppy, pierced it with a large needle, and allowed the gum from several bulbs "to exude and to become inspissated by evaporation." The governess concludes this discourse on drugs with: "The soporific influence of this drug was not excelled by that of the imported article."[42]

Other common household chemicals had to be concocted from whatever ability the ladies had at hand. Lye could be derived from oak ashes; combining ashes with lard produced a chemical reaction that created soap. Leaven for the hot breads so characteristic of Southern tables was derived from corn cobs, which yielded bicarbonate of soda when reduced to ash. Flour produced starch for cotton clothes or, made into a paste, an adhesive to repair china. Rose leaves left in the sun in pure lard for a week or more produced a fragrant hair oil. Lard oil, cottonseed oil, or the oil of groundpeas (peanuts) served for lamps; and molding candles resumed its former place in the regular round of household chores.[43]

A comment of J. J. Guthrie to Catesby ap R. Jones illustrates how people felt such shortages yet bore them cheerfully: "I wish you could also add two boxes of old fashioned Navy Candles [to supplies for the *Chattahoochee*] for I cannot see either to read or write by the dim glimmering of a lard oil lamp, and for a young Lieut. like myself to put on spectacles would be a sad commentary on my prospects for advancement."[44]

Not only men at war, but women like Miss Hague, who pursued the genteel work of governess, gave themselves over to ceaseless work for the Confederate Cause. Miss Hague and many others did so with a self-reliance bred on isolated plantations along the river and nurtured in a fierce determination to survive the blockade: "While hemmed in on all sides by the blockade, we used to think that if no war were raging, and a wall as thick and high as the great Chinese Wall were to entirely surround our Confederacy, we should not suffer intolerable inconvenience, but live as happily as Adam and Eve in the garden before they tasted the forbidden fruit."[45]

In Miss Hague's reflections at a later time about how the plantation people were able to fare so well, the politics of their sacrifice entered her meditation: "But be it remembered that the Southerners who were so reduced and so compelled to rely entirely upon their own resources belonged to the Anglo-Saxon race, a race which, despite all prating about 'race equality,' has civilized America."[46]

The war and the politics of the era that followed would mount a severe challenge to that mindset. In 1863, on a much larger scale than simply meeting the needs of a self-contained farm or large plantation, all agricultural operations in the Confederacy had to adapt to new demands and conditions. Cotton was no longer the single money crop. The mills in Columbus used many thousands of bales in its war production, but the blockade had closed off the outlet for the mills of England and other foreign markets. The voracious demand of the Southern armies for foodstuffs created a corresponding demand to diversify and step up agricultural production.

The first change required was a movement away from cotton; that required, in turn, a change of belief as much as the decision to plant different crops. Many in the South approached this necessity with an assured sense of the South's agricultural prowess. A writer in *DeBow's Review* commented upon the "Commercial Importance and Future of the South," answering Northern claims about the effects of the blockade with, "All those who have been expecting the South to be 'starved out,' will observe with some surprise that it supplies one-third of all bread stuffs exported from the Union. Hence, if they cannot 'eat cotton' they will not starve."[47] Individual planters like John Horry Dent were mindful of the changes portended by war. He noted in his diary: "Heretofore, we have planted Cotton to purchase all our necessaries and supplies. Hence in the way of clothing, meats, comforts and luxuries, our dependence has been on the North and Northwest. The War has now put an end to all such."[48] Certainly Dent's records indicate his change of practice in farming; his cotton acreage—which had run 470 in 1859, 480 in 1860, and 440 in 1861—dropped to 70 in 1862, 110 in 1863, and only 60 in 1864.[49]

Florida was so intent upon changing the economic reliance upon cotton that the legislature passed a law in 1863 to limit production; under penalty of a fine of $3,000, no more than one acre of cotton per laborer employed could be planted, and no more than one-quarter acre of to-bacco.[50] Georgia passed similar, though not so stringent, legislation to limit production to three acres per hand with a fine of $500 for non-compliance.[51]

Dent recorded a growing sentiment that worked to replace the blind faith in cotton: "As our Country is at War, we must plant more for provisions than for Cotton. As such, I am going to X more cottons and put in Corn."[52] In a wartime economy, the 3,000 to 4,000 bushels he produced in two plantings per year left a salable commodity after his household and stock consumed about 2,800 bushels.[53]

Not only the armies in the field, but all types of war industries made huge demands upon corn production. In the most basic terms, corn meal was a staple of diet in an agricultural system that produced many times more corn than wheat. The concentration of large numbers of workers at the Columbus Naval Iron Works and Confederate Navy Yard upriver from Dent's plantation required a steady supply of all manner of foodstuffs. Even an industry like the salt-making operations on the Gulf placed a considerable drain upon corn supplies—in an era when trans-portation and much of industry were, quite literally, driven by horse power.

Most men of the Chattahoochee country were not at home to jour-nalize and speculate about the effects of the war upon planting; their concerns were more immediate. Letters of the time are full of instruc-tions about farming, like this passage from Maj. George Scott's letter to his wife: "Tell Harry he must push up and get plenty of corn planted. . . . Tell him to select the best land to plant in field back of old quarters. I want all the corn planted that he can manage tell him now is the time to push early and late if he wants to make a crop."[54]

Among the myriad concerns of corn for food versus corn for feed was the additional need for corn to supply whiskey. Under very primitive conditions of medical practice, civilians, as well as *Chattahoochee* crew members and Johnston's work crew, needed whiskey as a stimulant in a fever-ridden climate. To mediate the conflicting demands upon the corn supply, the Georgia General Assembly passed legislation to regulate distillation of spirituous liquors.[55] As the war progressed and corn sup-plies became even more severely taxed, the competition between distill-eries and food production became increasingly severe.

With the shortage of corn, farmers sought ways to supply other feed products for their stock. Dent experimented with feeding cottonseed meal, a by-product of the ginning process, to his hogs. Farmers also began to realize a greater usefulness from ground crops like peanuts, sweet potatoes, and chufa. These could be planted in the rows between stalks of corn and thus extend land use.

Wheat had not been widely grown in the Chattahoochee country before the war, and one farmer's experiment with a twelve-acre planting in Glennville, Alabama, created widespread interest among his neighbors. They discussed the field at dinner, watched its progress closely, and Antoinette Hague rode from the Wellborn plantation with her students to see "wave on wave of long amber wheat gently rolling in the wind." The party dismounted and stood on tiptoe to gaze over the field at eye level. On an impulse they took off their broad straw hats and "gave them a sail on the already ripening grain . . . and there they lay without perceptibly bending the stalks of wheat."[56]

This curiosity of a new crop was also, more and more, a grim necessity among wartime shortages. As Miss Hague took a longer view of the struggle to survive the blockade, she wrote:

> Yet with the nicest economy, and the most studied husbandry,— however generously the earth might yield of grain, fruits, and vegetables—the South was awakening to the painful reality that the produce grown on our narrowing space of Confederate soil was inadequate for the sustenance of those at home, our soldiers, and the Northern soldiers whom we held as prisoners.[57]

Miss Hague was citing the inadequacy of the South's greatest strength in antebellum times—agriculture. As the agricultural system worked overtime to supply wartime needs, industry in the area gained a sudden, critical importance.

Even the "temporary industrial revolution" on the plantations and smaller farms had proved insufficient by 1863 to supply local needs and contribute to supplying an army at war. The small factories and mills in northwest Florida and south Georgia and Alabama had supplied some few items and laborers for building the gunboat *Chattahoochee* to defend them; but, inevitably, they were even more severely taxed than the agricultural system.

In Florida, the only antebellum cloth factory was a small operation at Montecello. With a shoe factory and a wool card factory, this small complex was the single industrial installation for the state. The government purchased 60 percent or more of its output, but that did not supply all that the armies needed; it did, however, plunge the civilian population into deeper shortages.[58]

Along the Chattahoochee in Early County near Johnston's Navy Yard, there was a small thread factory that had been in operation since 1855. Such a small water-powered mill turning out one hundred bunches of thread each day could not make a measurable difference for the Confederacy.[59] So also with many local factories designed to meet limited local demand in a Southern economy that had operated on an international market. There was a small woolen mill near Columbia, a nail factory, and saw mills and turpentine operations located here and there in the Chattahoochee country, but these did not and could not approach the scale of production demanded by war.[60] There were no resources to expand such works; yet the war demanded increased production to the greatest possible extent.

In Albany, the Tift brothers, Nelson and Asa, were able to expand their thriving antebellum business. They had already proved their entrepreneurship by building a floating sawmill; the bargelike craft could be anchored in the river while the flow of water powered a saw. In an area where few roads cut through the dense growth of timber, that had been a creative bit of technical problem solving.

Within three months' time, the Tifts constructed a three-story steam-operated corn and flour mill with a contract to grind exclusively for the Confederate Navy. This facility was soon followed by a bakery, a kiln to dry meal for use at sea, later a slaughterhouse to provide meat, and, as a logical outgrowth of the slaughterhouse, a tannery at nearby Palmyra.[61]

As Columbus naval facilities expanded to tap into resources along the Chattahoochee, J. W. Young's prewar machine shop in Clayton, Alabama, became a major supplier to the Columbus Naval Iron Works. Wood, charcoal, scrap iron, and a long list of other supplies flowed through him as a middle man to the Confederate government. His far-sighted investment in the advanced technology of the day paid large dividends for him and the Columbus Naval Iron Works in parts for steam machinery.[62]

Whatever gains occurred in stepped-up production in places along the rivers like Albany, Saffold, Columbia, and Eufaula, there was the corresponding loss of economic activity among the people. When stores sold out of items that could not be replaced, they closed. When people could not subsist where they were, they moved on to become refugees.

Travel—Refugee-style

The ritual of the visit that had carried travelers about the area before the war became the often-desperate search for safety and bare subsistence. Families that had once lived in affluence now crowded into two or three rooms, "refugee-style" as nurse Kate Cumming termed their life style.[63] Major Scott, who had written his wife instructions for planting, also wrote her directions about how to seek safety. With a husband's anxiety that left no detail to chance, he told her to take the parlor carpet to cover their possessions on the wagon and also to serve as a tent.[64] Guthrie of the gunboat *Chattahoochee* moved his family from their home on the coast of North Carolina to Eufaula.[65] Columbus newspapers advertised safe havens. F. R. Starr and William Bawn offered in Talbotton "A safe and pleasant retreat; house, garden, No. 1 cook, washer, ironer."[66] In time, more notable Confederates than Guthrie sought out the Columbus area. Archsecessionist Edmund Ruffin fled South Carolina to spend the last days of the war at Eufaula. Navy Secretary Mallory sent his family to refuge with Benjamin Harvey Hill's family in LaGrange, just forty miles north of the major naval facility in Columbus.

The sea, which had once offered Southern travelers ready access to the world beyond their plantations and river landings, was closed by the blockade. The banker McNabb of Eufaula no longer enjoyed his yearly trips abroad but, in anxiety about his cotton receipts, he was able to arrange one trip disguised as a steerage passenger. In London he conducted his business and returned with a fortune concealed within his disguise.[67] John Horry Dent, Sr., remained at home—worried about Horry, Jr., absent from home in the navy.[68]

The riverboats—including the *Jackson*, the *Indian*, the *Munnerlyn*, and a new boat constructed in Columbus, the *Shamrock*—continued to ply the Chattahoochee as far as the landing at Chattahoochee, Florida. Most of the vessels had been taken into the control of the government in 1861: the *Indian*, the *Mary A. Moore*, the *Music*, the *River Bride*, the *Uchee*, the *Wave*, the *William H. Young*. The *Chewala* gave up her engines for the ironclad *Tuscaloosa;* the *Times's* machinery was used in the original design of the ironclad *Jackson* at Columbus.[69]

Loads of cotton for the coast had been replaced with supplies slipped in through the blockade or supplies shipped northward from the plantation landings. Antebellum excursions in a well-appointed cabin had been replaced by troops of soldiers who "made themselves free and easy in all parts of the boat."[70]

Because of the blockade, river traffic was locally confined to one system. The railroads, not coastal packets or ocean steamers, became the link to other parts of the Confederate States. Inadequate before the war, they became further overcrowded and overtaxed as the war progressed. In the first war in which railroads were widely used for strategic troop movements, soldiers became accustomed to long trips in box cars where they slept and stood by turns in crowded conditions.[71]

Civilian diaries of the period portray frequent travel—and make it seem to the modern reader an interminable series of delays, breakdowns, missed connections, and high prices along the way. Business travelers and excursionists were replaced by the officer en route to an assignment, the wounded man returning home, a widow with her children trying to relocate among family at some distant point, a courier accompanying a load of machinery on a boxcar, machinists assigned to another project site—and women traveling unescorted, a condition of life undreamt of before the war changed the conditions of everyone's life.

Nurse Kate Cumming recorded in her diary a journey from Atlanta to Columbus. The famous "Beulah" of George Gift's acquaintance, Augusta Evans Wilson, was one of a party en route to see a badly wounded brother in Columbus. The group's progress was interrupted by a derailment near Opelika. After a crew had struggled for hours to right the train, an officer took the party of ladies in hand; they found a deserted schoolhouse, spent the day, enjoyed a rare cup of coffee, and later made their way to Columbus in an open rail car shaded by tree branches they had broken to use as parasols.[72]

Augustus McLaughlin, like Kate Cumming, traveled throughout the Confederacy without mishap. His wife was not so lucky. On a return trip from Richmond to Columbus in late 1863, her car derailed and tumbled down a fourteen-foot embankment, coming to rest upside down. Henrietta was so badly injured that a month passed before she could continue her journey back to McLaughlin's station at the Confederate Navy Yard.[73]

Yet accounts of such hardships are either offhanded or are replete with notes about meeting friends from elsewhere who were caught in the same circumstance. In a network of chance meetings that would rival an eighteenth-century picaresque novel, a lady might happen upon an officer known to her family who could steer her through the rail depot and see that she made her connection in Macon. Or a mother and daughters might encounter a similar group from Montgomery, distant cousins to a neighbor at home or connected in some way in the social matrix that bound the affluent and mobile planter class before the war. The ritual of the visit was replaced under such conditions by the ritual of the chance meeting and falling into step together for a perilous journey.

Coming upon such scenes with an outsider's viewpoint, a Union prisoner en route to Andersonville observed of the crowd gathered at the Columbus depot: "The people here seemed determined to prolong the war to the last, confident of ultimate success."[74]

However cheerfully the civilian travelers bore up under their hardships, and however confident they might have been that the South would ultimately triumph, they were living and traveling in a system operating under an ultimate strain of logistics and supply. In their private moments—in confiding to a family member, as John Lamar wrote to Howell Cobb, or musing over handwork like the war widow Antoinette Hague described—the realization crept in quite early that the blockade had placed the South in very deep trouble indeed. As Nelson Tift witnessed the destruction of his gunboat *Mississippi* in New Orleans—and experienced the realization that it would not break the blockade—he was, in the words of a contemporary account, "unmanned" and wept openly.[75]

No Other City in the Confederacy Has Been So Fortunate as Columbus

Private citizens and officials in their private lives did not hear negative views from their leaders or read such news in the press. Even as the gunboat *Chattahoochee* lay wrecked in the Apalachicola River in the summer of 1863, the editor of the *Columbus Daily Sun* was writing: "No other city in the Confederacy has been so fortunate as Columbus."[76] Many external appearances bore out his statement: at 17,000, the population of the city had swelled to almost twice its antebellum population. Banking upon a geographic location that lent it safety, the Confederate government had moved in to make the small river city an increasingly important supply depot. The cloth production of the Eagle Mills and the tailoring establishment of S. Rothschild and Brother became subject to rapid mobilization for supplying uniforms for the Army Quartermaster Department. F. W. Dillard was commissioned as a quartermaster officer so that he could use his experience in Columbus business for the government. In what was to become a pattern of operation, when the production capacities of a civilian contractor lagged, he established a government clothing factory. The same held true with shoe manufacture, which began with S. M. Sappington's shoe shop on Broadway and later expanded to a government factory.[77]

Such efforts in Columbus early in the war brought praise from *De-Bow's Review.* An article—"Commercial Importance and Future of the South"—in the spring of 1862 was continued in a later number under the title "How Our Industry Profits From the War." In this catalog of the South's industrial strength and potential, the greatest praise was reserved for Columbus:

Louis Haiman's factory was producing 100 swords per week—but "can increase to 200"; on January 1, 1862, he had begun manufacturing rifles—five per day, but he "can increase to 30."

Brands and Kerner were manufacturing 1,200 yards of India Rubber cloth per week—and "can make 2,500"; they had, by 1862, made 1,000 bass and kettledrums—and "can make 100 per week." The writer added: "They also make fifes."

S. Rothschild had made 4,000 uniforms for the quartermaster and 1,500 for military companies.

Sappington and Company had sold to Quartermaster Dillard 1,000 pairs of shoes—and "can make 8,000 per year."

A. D. Brown's shuttles and supplies for cotton mills "over the whole Confederacy" were added to his domestic production of spinning wheels.

S. D. Thom was making caps and buttons.

Cadmon manufactured military buttons.

W. S. Loyal manufactured military caps.

Barringer and Morton manufactured gun carriages.

The Eagle Mills had increased production from 2,000 yards of cloth per week—and "can produce 12,000"; it had adapted some machinery to produce mariner's stripes for soldiers' shirts, turning out 7,000 yards weekly. All this was in addition to 8,000 yards of tent cloth per week, osnaburgs, sheetings, kerseys, yarns, ropes of various sizes, thread and twine, and 500 yards per week of India Rubber cloth for overcoats, capes, cloaks, knapsacks—and "can increase" that production to 1,000 yards per week.

After a year of war, however, Eagle Mills was no longer Columbus's flagship company. The Columbus Iron Works had supplanted the cotton industry with its capacity for building ships and casting cannon. In a group of buildings along the Chattahoochee on the present site of the Columbus Iron Works Convention and Trade Center, W. R. Brown had a collection of shops and sheds where workmen operated twelve or fifteen large and small lathes, a foundry 300 x 40 feet, a new blacksmith shop 100 feet long, and a 60-foot-square foundry with an air furnace capable of melting twenty tons of pig iron. Brown had cast field pieces for the defense of Florida, and Confederate Ordnance Chief Josiah Gorgas had made a proposition with Brown for 1,000 pounds of shot and shell.[78] Then in September 1862, Warner took over Brown's works and bought his stores of iron, castings, and machinery. Warner went about transforming a small steamboat works into a major facility for the Confederate Navy.

The *DeBow's* article concluded on a boastful note designed to refute any Yankee or Southern questions about the South's capacity: "The demand for many articles required by our mills for manufacture of our goods has been met by mechanics in our midst." Columbus inventiveness had already produced a machine to make shuttles, another to make bobbins and spools, and others to manufacture loom harness and pickers—all for the cotton industry. "In fact, nearly all the articles wanted by our mills, are now or soon will be supplied by our own people."[79]

"Or soon will be." That prediction was not entirely fulfilled in Columbus. The daily records kept at the Columbus Naval Iron Works and the Confederate Navy Yard more nearly tell a story of chronic shortages and constant searches for the labor and material that *DeBow's Review* so confidently described.

Augustus McLaughlin was among those to experience such difficulties most acutely. As the gunboat *Chattahoochee* arrived at the Columbus wharf, McLaughlin wrote Catesby ap R. Jones in Selma about his former command and crew. He was hopeful about the gunboat's repair and early return to service. He reported news of the crew— Guthrie blockade running out of Wilmington but in Eufaula with his refugee family at times; others of the crew scattered on furlough from the navy.

The worst damage the *Chattahoochee* suffered was not from the explosion but from the plundering of D. S. Johnston's workers. Furthermore, Johnston had contracted with Moreno to build a barge to obstruct the river—news that must have recalled to Jones his former arguments with the two. Thus, he must have relished McLaughlin's report from Florida that "Old Milton says he will blow them all to the devil and open the river."

The best news in McLaughlin's letter to Jones, however, was a progress report on the ironclad—still referred to at this point by a "yard name" but later to be officially named *Jackson*: "The *Muscogee* is all ready for launching. I am only waiting for the river, which, from present appearances, will not keep me waiting long."[80]

Of all the issues cataloged in McLaughlin's letter—the conditions of the ship and its machinery, the whereabouts of officers and crew, Johnston's work, the obstruction of the river (and the politics of that policy)—his success and Warner's turned upon the ability of Columbus and the Chattahoochee country to function under conditions of the blockade. To the degree that officers like Warner and McLaughlin were able to make good the *DeBow's* predictions, and their own, they wrought a miracle, not of military strategy or naval design, but of management.

PART FOUR

Last Stronghold of the Confederacy

CHAPTER 6

Conducting the Business of War

Chief Engineer James H. Warner, C.S.N.
James W. Woodruff, Jr., Confederate Naval Museum, Columbus, Ga.

By the time the gunboat *Chattahoochee* was towed to Columbus for repairs in December 1863, the small river city of the 1850s had become a major facility for the Confederate Navy. In 1862, Lt. Augustus McLaughlin had begun operations in Columbus at the Confederate Navy Yard, which supplied labor, materials, and management for the completion of the *Chattahoochee* downriver at Saffold. Chief Engr.

James H. Warner had transformed the Columbus Naval Iron Works into an operation that supplied ships' machinery, ordnance, and engineering expertise throughout the Confederacy.

An ironclad ready for launching in December 1863 was further evidence of their hard work and resourcefulness. In less than two years, McLaughlin and Warner had created with the ability they had at hand a facility for constructing and repairing the wooden hulls of ships, a machine shop for constructing and repairing large marine engines, and a rolling mill to provide armor plate for a state-of-the-art ironclad vessel.

Situated far inland at a river port, the facility was—and would be to the last battle of the Civil War—so far removed from centers of military and naval action that it was safe from attack. What Warner and McLaughlin accomplished had progressed along a line that closely paralleled the development of Confederate naval policy from the beginning of the war.

In formulating a policy and plans to execute policy, Secretary of the Navy Stephen R. Mallory first concentrated on coastal defense of ports like Apalachicola, where McLaughlin first served.[1] Once the war began, Mallory began exploring options for a fighting navy: to purchase ships in the United States and Canada that might be converted, to look to England and Europe either to buy ships or commission their construction, and also to undertake a large-scale construction effort in the Confederate states. In time, he would exercise all these options.

As the war progressed, and as delays and financial problems hampered the construction projects in England, Mallory's plans were cast back more and more upon construction in the South itself. In time, that expedient would make Columbus increasingly important to the war effort.

The first, most logical sites for naval construction in the Confederacy were along the coast, where facilities already existed: Norfolk, Pensacola, New Orleans. Charleston and Jacksonville were also favorable sites for construction works. Such sites enjoyed early success. At the time McLaughlin and Warner were negotiating a contract with D. S. Johnston in October 1861, at Norfolk the burned-out hulk of the *Merrimac* was being armored and rechristened the *Virginia*. In New Orleans, Asa and Nelson Tift from Albany, Georgia, had agreed to construct one large ironclad at a cost of $800,000 and two smaller ironclads at $150,000 each. Hughs and Company in New Orleans had also negotiated a $1 million contract with the navy for an ironclad. By the end of the year, an ironclad was under construction at Norfolk and three more were planned. There were construction plans for Savannah and Charleston and further plans for work at New Orleans. Farther north on the Mississippi, two ironclads were being built at Memphis.[2]

Although the gunboat *Chattahoochee* fully reflected one component of Confederate policy—to construct smaller, well-armed wooden steamers—Mallory had determined early in the war that his navy's best hope lay with the ironclad. By May 1861, he was reporting to the chairman of the House Naval Affairs Committee that the "possession of ironclad ships [is] a matter of first necessity." In leading up to that conclusion, Mallory researched various construction efforts in the United States, France, and England in the 1840s and 1850s, along with test results on machinery, armament, and ordnance. Technical feasibility dictated his decision: "thus not only does economy but naval success dictate the wisdom and expediency of fighting with iron against wood, without regard to first cost." While he recognized the need for ships like the *Chattahoochee*, Mallory could also see their historical position: "Naval engagements between wooden frigates, as they are now built and armed, will prove to be the forlorn hopes of the sea, simply contests in which the question, not of victory, but who shall go to the bottom first, is to be solved."[3]

Having committed the navy to a construction program, Mallory found that success in construction was followed by a measure of success in battle: the engagement of the *Virginia* with the *Monitor* in March 1862, the success of the *Arkansas* on the Mississippi River in July and August, the launching of the *Savannah* in May, the commissioning of the *Baltic* at Mobile in May, the launching of the *Chicora* at Charleston in August, and the launching of the *Palmetto State* in October. If Chief Engineer Warner was caught up in an active effort at Columbus through the summer and early fall of 1862, the entire Confederate Navy was constructing ironclads along the shortest path possible to defending its ports, breaking the blockade, and opening the South once more to ocean and river commerce.

From the initial plans in Mallory's early reports in 1861, his report of February 27, 1862—one year and one week after the Navy Department was organized—showed that a fleet had sprung fully armed from the rivers and ports of the South. There was a Confederate ship on both the Potomac and the Rappahannock rivers, seven ships on the James, ten along the Georgia and Carolina coast, three ships and two armed barges at Mobile, and a fleet of sixteen ships and six barges at New Orleans. Aware of the odds against this small navy, Mallory noted: "The United States have a constructed Navy; we have a Navy to construct." And at that stage of development, the Navy Department's report contained only a sentence about Columbus: construction of "one gunboat . . . and two others under contract for completion."[4]

Mallory's policy also proved to be a political success, for the Confederacy was caught up in the romance of the ironclad. Ladies' gunboat associations sprang up all over the South; gunboat fairs were held to raise money for their construction, gunboat quilts were auctioned, and Confederate ladies became the chief champions of this new weapon of war. Within that context, George Gift wrote Ellen Shackelford from Columbus after seeing the *Jackson* under construction: "She will be formidable; will mount five heavy guns, each capable of whipping a fleet of Yankees. I shall rest perfectly secure in knowing that 'The Pines' will never be molested by the enemy."[5] Many in the South did believe that the ironclad would assure Confederate victory.

Early successes in construction and naval combat were soon balanced out with defeat. By mid-August 1862, Mallory was reporting the destruction of much that the navy had been able to accomplish initially. In April New Orleans fell, with the loss of the ironclads *Louisiana* and *Mississippi*. Memphis was abandoned in the 1862 spring offensive that drew troops away from the fortifications at Apalachicola; the abandonment also meant that work stopped on the first ironclad *Tennessee*. After her engagement with the *Monitor*, the *Virginia* was lost, and her executive officer, Lt. Catesby ap R. Jones, and many of her crew were transferred first to Drewrys Bluff and then to the *Chattahoochee*. In July, the *Arkansas*'s brief career ended, sending one of its lieutenants, George Gift, to Saffold, Georgia. Norfolk, with a greater capacity for naval construction than any other site in the Confederacy, was lost.

In one incident after another, officers elected to destroy a vessel rather than have it fall into enemy hands. Of the ironclads laid down in 1861, only five remained. Public support for the ironclads began to erode; in time, the Confederate Congress would investigate the conduct of the war. More importantly, Confederate construction efforts were driven back from the coast to smaller facilities in the interior.[6] Columbus figured prominently in these new plans.

If Columbus became the beneficiary of a government policy to foster the growth of its naval construction industry, the Naval Iron Works also fell heir to problems that had plagued the navy from the beginning of the war: developing facilities, recruiting skilled labor, acquiring machinery and tools, and procuring materials for naval construction. Mallory had taken into account all these factors in laying plans for a navy.

In May 1861, only ninety days after his department was organized, Mallory dispatched Capt. Duncan N. Ingraham to various sites in the Confederate states where iron plates might be produced for gunboats. His reports from Kentucky, Tennessee, and Atlanta were not encouraging.[7]

In August 1862, just before his report of the disasters that had befallen the navy, Mallory asked William P. Williamson, the acting engineer in chief, to report on building machinery for gunboats. More than a year of war had given him the perspective to list three major problems: a shortage of skilled laborers in "the mechanical branches"; the shortage of metals and equipment, "which have heretofore been obtained from the North"; and the "want of proper machinery, tools, and facilities for heavy work." The one encouraging note in his report was that a steam hammer had been saved from the Pensacola Navy Yard and would soon be operational in Charlotte, North Carolina.[8]

Mallory drew upon these data from his subordinates to lobby for government support for the navy, which struggled to match the more spectacularly successful armies of the Confederacy.[9]

As Mallory and other administrators in the Navy Department were investigating, reporting, and lobbying about the problems of construction, Warner and McLaughlin lived out those problems on a daily basis. Resources that the two officers had at hand in 1863 were already taxed to the limits of their industrial system. Each disaster or unfavorable condition elsewhere in the navy's overall construction system worked to create more and more pressure on Columbus. If the war put a coastal construction facility out of action, then an interior facility like Columbus had to make up the deficit. If military action in Tennessee cut the Confederacy off from copper deposits or if transporting coal from north Alabama was a perilous business, those shortages and difficulties registered upon productivity in Columbus. If the approach of Sherman's army upon transportation lines and the South's agricultural heartland called skilled workers into the Confederate Army, that pressure also had a severe impact upon the Confederate Navy in Columbus. The basic disadvantages of a scattered, underdeveloped system of naval facilities, materials, and labor bore with increasing severity upon the work Warner and McLaughlin had to accomplish.

The chart that follows illustrates the multiple tasks the two officers had to manage along several different tracks. The ironclad *Jackson* and the transport steamer *Shamrock* were two major construction projects. As these projects were underway, completing them depended on the simultaneous activities of building facilities to construct the vessels and procuring equipment and necessary supplies for the work. Construction, fitting out, and repairs on vessels elsewhere sent crews to other points in the Confederacy; there were also subsidiary facilities in Eufaula and Prattville to manage.

The picture that emerges is a piling up of projects, one upon another, in a logjam of work. As new projects entered the system, material or labor shortages or transportation delays impeded the flow. Repairs to machinery in operation created constant, unscheduled pressures of ad-

1863 CNIW/CNY	J	F	M	A	M	J	J	A	S	O	N	D
Construction	*Jackson*									. . . *Shamrock*			
Facilities				Rolling Mill							
		Equipment Procurement, Maintenance									
		Supplies Procurement, Allocation									
OTHER SITES													
Machinery	*Chattahoochee* Repairs										
	Columbia									
	Tuscaloosa							. . . . . Repairs		
							Milledgeville					
	Savannah		Repairs							
	Huntsville							. . . . . Repairs		
									Tombigbee Boat			
									Tombigbee Boat			
									Savannah Repairs			
CNIW Crews on Roll	Savannah									
												Charleston	
	Selma							
									Mobile			
			Eufaula							
	Prattville									

ditional work. Few projects followed a horizontal flow through the system toward timely completion.

As the war progressed, that picture of work in Columbus was to become even more complex. As Mallory had quite rightly observed, in modern warfare a steam engine had become as essential to a fighting ship as a battery. Toward the latter days of the war, the Columbus Naval Iron Works was to become virtually the power plant of the Confederate Navy. What the navy could accomplish along the coast at Charleston, Savannah, and Mobile often hinged upon the status of Warner's work in Columbus.

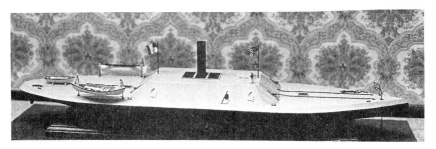

C.S.S. Jackson *model on display at the James W. Woodruff, Jr., Confederate Naval Museum. This model shows the sloping casemate familiar to Confederate ironclad design.*
James W. Woodruff, Jr., Confederate Naval Museum, Columbus, Ga.

She Will Be Formidable: Design of the Ironclad *Jackson*

The *Jackson* was to be the showcase for combined CNY-CNIW capabilities, for the design of the ironclad was state of the art for 1862. A prototype was already under construction at New Orleans that, in principle at least, exactly suited Confederate needs. Like the *Louisiana*, the *Jackson* would be formidable, more than two hundred feet long and nearly fifty feet wide. Iron would make her invulnerable, a kind of floating fortress. She was to be flat-bottomed like a river steamer and was to be propelled by a conventional paddle wheel; Chief Constructor John L. Porter favored the paddle wheel as a standard design feature because the propulsion system amidship was safe from enemy fire. Such features were also known quantities to experienced river men like Warner, Sam Whiteside, Charles Blain, and Harry Hall.

Most practical for navigating the local rivers and Apalachicola Bay, the *Jackson* was a flat-bottomed "diamond class" gunboat. Replacing the graceful curves of seasoned, select woods familiar to conventional marine construction was the more angular design adapted for green pine and unseasoned shipwrights. Mechanical practicality also figured into the paddle-wheel design. An existing high-pressure engine need generate no more than 20 RPMs, while ship's screws required at least 40 RPMs from low-pressure engines. Using a familiar and readily available power plant did not require the risks involved in gearing up a high-pressure engine and shortening the cylinder stroke to drive propellers.[10]

Thus the highest and best engineering knowledge of 1862 combined new weaponry, older tested and tried riverboat technology, and a practical and economical adaptation to the ability Confederates had at hand. As the Civil War raged elsewhere, the battle in Columbus was against time and limited resources. Despite the variety of projects Warner and McLaughlin had to manage in Columbus and other sites, the *Jackson* was certainly a major priority; yet in their records and correspondence to distant locations, the *Jackson* occupies a relatively minor place. Details of its construction and progress toward completion tend to surface from time to time as only one project in the general onrush of activity needed to clear multiple projects through the Columbus system.

To McLaughlin was left the task of applying design principles in constructing the *Jackson*'s hull; Warner would complete the project with machinery and iron plating. An account of their work during 1863 describes the path toward McLaughlin's December 26 letter to Catesby ap R. Jones: "The *Muscogee* is all ready for launching. I am only waiting for the river, which, from present appearances, will not keep me waiting long."

Through January 1863, McLaughlin marshaled wagons, teams of four and six mules and horses, and teamsters for transporting materials. By February he was ordering lumber by hundreds of thousands of board feet, ordering 201 pounds of 6# nails, 100 1-pound hammers, and wheelbarrows, along with large lots of bacon, fifty-one bushels of corn, 4,000 pounds of fodder, and 94 pounds of salt to provide for the men and horses he had at work.

Warner's work on the *Jackson* would have to wait for two or three months until the hull was ready to receive machinery, and wait still further until the casemate was ready to receive armor. The *Columbia* was laid down in Charleston in January and the need for marine engines there increased the need for expanded facilities in Columbus. Negotiations continued for a 1,000-pound steam hammer in Mobile, setting up a planing machine made available when Mobile facilities had been moved to the Charlotte station, and locating suppliers all over the Confederacy for increasingly large orders of scrap iron. He was occupied with the work he had subcontracted to William Penny in Prattville, Alabama.[11]

Sam Whiteside was at work on the gunboats at Selma with a crew of five other machinists. Warner had to express such items as a pair of bellows; he also carefully noted the $3.50 cost when he issued a twelve-inch file. In a regular pattern of meeting the Savannah payroll on the 6th and 20th of each month, payment was mailed to P. J. Ryan, who continued work on the ironclad *Savannah*. As the year progressed, other sites would be added to the regular rolls of the CNIW, and similar payments would mark the progress of Warner's work.[12]

Warner's successful appeal to have J. W. Young sent home from the army to Eufaula began to pay dividends. From February 15 through March, Warner kept the steamer *Indian* occupied with regular trips to deliver and return machinery and supplies. Cargoes of steam pumps and fifteen tons of castings going downriver indicate that Warner had contracted with Young to manufacture parts. The shipment of alloys like white and red lead fill in details of Young's work. Cargoes of machinery hauled to the wharf at Eufaula and shipped back to Columbus indicate that the Eufaula operation became quite important to CNIW operations.[13]

As he attended to large matters, Warner also arranged to have the Columbus Gas Light Company install lighting for his office.[14] And February brought one of his periodic requests to J. W. Young in Eufaula that bills be itemized "saying how much wood & oil & the price with all materials."

Warner continued shipments of "sundry articles of machinery" for the *Savannah*, and by March both Warner and McLaughlin were making major scrap iron purchases. In the flow the CNIW was designed to keep in motion, Warner made a major order from Goldsmith and Sons in Charleston and was also able to ship back to Duncan Ingraham at the Charleston naval station a lot of 1¼-inch iron bars on March 1. On March 18, he made a shipment of machinery for the *Huntsville* in Selma.

Expanding his production capabilities, he located a steam engine in Columbus to run the forge attached to the steam hammer. Expanding his list of suppliers, he bought another set of boilers from M. Russell and Brother in Dalton on March 12.

A major indicator of Warner's progress on one project was his sending the *Huntsville*'s machinery to Mobile. But the feat is recorded in a letter only two lines long. Warner had to hasten on to other matters, among them clarifying the contract with Russell and Brother in Dalton that they, and not the CNIW, were obligated to pay a delivery charge of $55 on the boilers.[15]

In his preparation for constructing the *Jackson*'s hull, McLaughlin located a regular supplier of lumber in Brooks's mill on the river near the navy yard. Good progress can be measured by his increasingly specialized orders for lumber: 72,055 short, 39,000 long, 3,713 "extra long," and 20 pieces cut 18 inches by 13 inches by 56 feet. These massive timbers cut by B. A. Thornton were for the well of the *Jackson*'s center wheel. McLaughlin laid in 391 pounds of putty on March 17—another sign of his progress on the Columbus project. The same day, Warner dispatched the *Huntsville*'s machinery to Mobile as he coordinated his various tasks. Machinery for the sister ship *Tuscaloosa* came next. A month later, former CIW owner W. R. Brown sold the CNIW boilers from the river steamer *Chewala* for $2,000.[16]

Warner also spent a great deal of time in April on plans to expand CNIW facilities. To replace the rolling mill that had burned in October 1862, he began several months of construction work with an order for eight carloads of rock and sand. By the end of the year he would also have a coke oven under construction. He continued to develop the capacities of his machine shop with the addition of a drill press from the South Carolina Railroad. There were more specialized orders for casting and tubing from Charleston. Louis P. Henop was dispatched to Charleston for iron and brass castings and thirty-six boxes of machinery, a mission that required seven days of travel each way via Savannah and Macon.[17]

Increasing the productivity of Warner's operation called for a corresponding adjustment in management and record keeping for the CNIW subsidiaries. When he sent end-of-the-month payrolls to Savannah, he sent a letter by the *Indian* to Young at Eufaula to notify him of changes in procedure. Workers there were to become part of the CNIW force and were to be paid twice a month from its payroll. In an additional effort to bring Young's accounting procedures into line, there was the request to

*Samuel Judd Whiteside. Along with such men as Charles Blain and Harry
Hall, Whiteside made a transition from peacetime work in river transport
and construction to wartime work for the Confederate Navy. After the war
he was successful first in ice production in Apalachicola and later in
railroads. Work to be accomplished and new technologies to work with
seemed more important to these men than the politics of the Civil War.
Whiteside family*

"omit the ½ cent, instead 4.12½ make it 4.12 or 4.13." In a struggle with his own accounting procedures, he wrote Penny in Prattville that the balance on the month's vouchers would be sent when "the Pay Master will be over here the latter part of this month with funds."[18]

McLaughlin continued his specialized orders for lumber and added orders for saws and a grist stone to keep them in good repair for the work that pushed forward. And by the last of April, both Lt. George Gift and would-be deserter William Martin wrote letters noting the *Jackson*'s progress. Gift wrote to Ellen Shackelford, "[The vessel] is progressing much faster than I expected." With the practiced eye of an ironclad man who had helped to fit out the *Arkansas*, he judged that "she will be ready to launch in about two months. Say the first of July and will be completed and ready for service by the first high water in the coming fall or winter."[19]

When the deserter Martin reached the Union blockade at Apalachicola, he gave a more detailed report, which Lt. George Morris passed on to Admiral Bailey: "her frame is all up, and [men] were at work planking her outside and ceiling her; boilers are in. She is to be a propeller; her engines are from the old steamer *Times*. The mill for rolling out iron is in progress of construction; they have but little iron on hand to use. She cannot be ready before November next. She is built of green pine timber; frame timber 1 foot square."[20] These specs were not entirely accurate, for the ship had at that stage of construction a center paddle wheel. In other respects, however, the report was reliable.

In May, McLaughlin continued the constant orders for lumber, and Warner drove toward the completion of the rolling mill. Mason B. F. Coleman supplied months of man-days and huge orders of brick, sand, and lime to the effort. Horace King, the noted bridge builder, supplied as many man-days and corresponding orders of lumber to add to the structure. At the Charleston site, work was far enough advanced to send Chief Engr. Virginius Freeman to work on the *Columbia*.[21]

But such results were bought at a price as supplies dwindled. A call went out in the Confederacy for private citizens to contribute to the war effort their church bells, plantation bells, and whatever other metal they could find; Warner added many more local names to his list of suppliers of scrap iron and various other metals. And he also had to pause in his labors to make a large order for drawing paper and office supplies to replenish his stores.

As work on the *Jackson* continued, Union officers at Apalachicola continued to receive reports from refugees. In June Lt. A. F. Crossman reported to Admiral Bailey that the Confederates had abandoned the sunken *Chattahoochee* at Blountstown "to devote all their means toward the ironclad. . . . Various reports are current about this ironclad, and the prevalent idea now is that she draws seven or eight feet water. If so, she cannot cross the bar off the town."[22] The Union skippers were already too well schooled in the perils of negotiating their own vessels in the shallow waters of the area to think the ship could clear the harbor and create further perils for them.

Heedless of the Union's skepticism about the Confederate Navy, in June Warner increased the crew at work on the *Savannah* from the usual six to ten. The work of assuming the obligations of the CIW also continued when Warner paid A. N. Miller $5,500 for boilers for the *Savannah*. Repairs to put the boilers in working condition required eight laborers and a foreman thirty-five days, five days' work of two boilermakers and a foreman, nine days' pay for two helpers, twenty days' hire of a flatboat, and drayage on hoisting tackle, or $1,500 for that part of the CNIW's work in July.[23] Warner transferred Chief Engineer Tynan, one of his most experienced men, as construction on the wooden gunboat *Milledgeville* created more work at Savannah.

Just as the Savannah operation seemed to be running smoothly, disaster struck: the *Savannah* broke a cylinder on an August 3 trial run. Called to account for the malfunction, Tynan headed a team of three engineers who submitted a report the next day. They did not know the term "human error," but they concluded that workers in Columbus had left a ⅝-by-2½-inch rivet in the steam passage. Steam pressure wedged it into the ¼- to ⅜-inch clearance between the piston and the cylinder head. They recommended a new cylinder, new piston with a follower and rings, a new cylinder head, and straightening the piston rod.

Receiving this report on August 7, Warner estimated twenty days were needed to "restore the machinery to good working condition." Promising Flag Officer W. W. Hunter that he would spare no effort "to accomplish the repairs in the shortest time possible," Warner redeemed the CNIW with a Saturday, August 22, telegram: "Machinery for the Sav'h will arrive Monday morning."[24]

Still engaged in a constant search for materials, Warner sent his agent, W. W. Ansell, on a two-week trip to Quincy, Lake City, Madison, and Gainesville, Florida. The five days Ansell spent in Lake City and the telegraph bill to Columbus are sure indications that railroad iron from

Lake City contractors would soon follow for the plating of the *Jackson*.[25]

McLaughlin's order for 5,000 oak wedges, eight barrels of tar, and 436 pounds of oakum were indicators that caulking the *Jackson*'s hull had begun. Such signs of progress are borne out in his June 15 letter to Catesby ap R. Jones at Selma: "Caulkers have commenced today and I am laying the spar deck. The engines are about being placed in position." His note that the 6.4-inch rifle from the *Chattahoochee* had been sent to Charleston for double banding indicated that the battery would not follow too far behind in the rush toward the project's completion.[26]

Warner's work through August, September, and October was diverted from the *Jackson* to Mobile. Fitting and repairs on boilers for the *Huntsville*, *Tuscaloosa*, and the "Bigbee Boats," at Oven Bluff on the Tombigbee River, also placed demands on the CNIW system. He maintained constant communications with Chief Engr. William Frick, Jr., who was working with Graham and Warren and with Hughs. As he searched out supplies for this project, rivets—which had cost Warner 35¢ per pound at the time he bought the stores of the Columbus Iron Works—were $2.00 and $2.50 per pound. Blacksmiths' wages had risen from $6.00 to $12.50 per day.

Finally, Warner brought the Mobile project under his direct control. This move added another payroll to his office system, and Frick was apprised of standard billing procedure.[27]

While crews, money, machinery, and correspondence continually flowed out of the CNIW, large shipments of machinery flowed in during September. William Anderson made a twenty-day trip to Charlotte, hiring nine hands in Augusta to transfer the cargo from one railroad line to another. James T. Code of Mobile had an even more tortuous journey from August 29 to September 16, transporting machinery by wagon from Prattville to Columbus. Meanwhile, the steamer *Indian* kept up a steady flow of machinery and materials to and from Eufaula. Efforts to manage that flow required periodic reminders to all stations about billing procedures.[28]

On October 20, Warner made a shipment to Charleston that points to the progress of the *Columbia:* four loads of machinery under the care of A. Ravenscroft on a six-day trip with time in Macon to transfer the cargo from one depot to another.[29] Warner's efforts to move the logjam of projects on his schedule sent other subordinates on similar missions: James T. Code to Montgomery October 12–17; H. E. Holmes to Jacksonville November 8–December 8; A. Ravenscroft to Selma November 3–10

Horace King. Born a slave and later freed by a special act of the Alabama legislature, King was a highly respected craftsman. Before the war, King and his former master and friend, James Godwin, constructed several bridges over the Chattahoochee. During the war he supplied special cuts of lumber for constructing the ironclad Jackson *and built a stable and other buildings for the Columbus Naval Iron Works. After the war he gained enduring fame as a designer and builder of covered bridges.*
Thomas L. French and Edward L. French, Covered Bridges of Georgia.
© *Frenco Co.*

and November 29–December 19; T. H. Abrams to Charleston December 8–26.

Reallocating his labor force, Warner reduced his Savannah crew to Chief Engineer Tynan and three others; by December 22, payrolls for Ryan's crew were being sent to Charleston where they were at work on the *Columbia*. From time to time, P. J. Ryan, James Riley, John Globe, and others of that group would be paid at Columbus or reimbursed for travel to the CNIW. As an added increment of difficulty and delay in the system, they had to perform a part of their work on valves and cylinders at the home facilities.[30]

Interwoven with the projects at other sites, with facilities development in Columbus, and with the ceaseless concerns of materials, supplies, and labor were continuing signs that the system was moving more rapidly toward the *Jackson*'s completion. A sheet-iron chimney shipped from Park and Lyons in Mobile on August 8 meant that the ironclad was moving that much closer to launching.[31] Payment to Horace King for two thousand shingles in October meant finishing work was added to the rolling mill. Shipments of railroad iron that began coming in from Lake City, Florida, in September and October meant there was iron to roll for the *Jackson*'s armor.[32]

Through the same period in the late summer and early fall, McLaughlin was ordering planed lumber; finishing nails, copper nails, and tacks for finishing work on the *Jackson;* and small hardware like a lock and box handles. An order for sixty pounds of chromate green from Mobile meant priming and interior finishing. An order for 63½ gallons of linseed oil meant painting was underway by mid-September, though Warner finally had to order all the way to St. Mark's, Florida, for paintbrushes at an exorbitant price.[33]

Launching the *Jackson* could not be too far away from McLaughlin's October order for 2 pine logs for shears and 124 pine logs for pilings, followed by an early December order for 74 more logs. Orders for spikes by the keg bespeak the fitting of armor plate. Warner received 404 pounds of smoke pipe rings from Columbus supplier M. McHale on November 18, and on November 21 he paid a Mobile supplier $12 per yard for a lot of old carpet to wrap steam pipes.[34] His Columbus crews were using huge stores of files, sand paper, and emery paper for finishing and fitting machinery—and Warner was paying huge prices for such supplies.

As the CNIW system ran at full steam day and night to have the boat ready for launching during the winter season of high water, two renegade soldiers were making their way along the Chattahoochee southward toward Apalachicola. Losing their boat in the rapids above Columbus, they traveled three days and nights on foot, so weary that they would "stagger and reel about as a man who is stupefied with liquor, and at times seem to be almost blind." Finally they saw the spires and smokestacks of Columbus and, "like beasts of prey, betook [themselves] to a safe hiding-place." Two backwoods foot soldiers, they were puzzled by the "constant clattering sound" they heard from the vicinity of the town "as of a hundred workmen with hammers. This noise came from near the river, where they appeared also to be a great light."

At dawn the deserters saw that the sound of the hammers came from workmen "engaged on a vessel, which they were covering with iron." That night, before stealing a workman's boat tied up at the dock nearby, they were able to inspect the vessel more closely: "she was a powerfully-built gunboat, which they were evidently in great haste to complete, as the hammers of the workmen never ceased on her, night or day, nor for a single moment."[35]

A year of such unremitting labor finally brought the *Jackson* project to the point where McLaughlin could write Catesby ap R. Jones that he was only waiting for the river to have the *Jackson* launched to steam down the river toward the blockade at Apalachicola. He and Warner had steered this project through a system that was overburdened at every point along the ironclad's path to completion.

With what anticipation, then, McLaughlin must have written Jones on December 26, "I am only waiting for the river, which, from present appearances, will not keep me waiting long."

Others in Columbus were watching the river level and anticipating the *Jackson*'s launching. Much of the town's system of labor and supply had been involved with this government project for more than a year; and their safety was bound to the vessel. Columbus was fully invested in the ironclad's success.

I Am Only Waiting for the River

On New Year's Eve, the *Columbus Enquirer* announced: "The Gunboat, we hear, is to be launched this evening, but have not heard the horn." The editor expressed his best wishes for the enterprise, adding "may she have better luck than her consort the *Chattahoochee* which is now lying at our wharf a perfect wreck of her former self." On New Year's Day, the *Daily Sun* reported that the river had taken a sudden rise of ten feet overnight, causing concern for the dams and suspending operation at the cotton mills. The optimism of the *Enquirer*'s New Year's edition overrode such fears with: "This noted craft, which reports said was to have been launched yesterday, will probably be lifted from its timbers by the rising waters without the labor to the launching of so heavy a boat. The water has already pretty well surrounded her, and it will take but a slight additional rise to . . . lift her . . . , and a little more labor will complete her."[36]

In more technical terms, the river had risen so rapidly that McLaughlin's crew had no time to remove the blocking; thus they were left dependent upon the rising current to lift the ship off the ways.[37] When the river steamer *Marianna* arrived at Columbus on January 1, she was immediately engaged to tow the *Jackson* off the blocks. Even with the bow partially afloat, and the *Marianna* towing in sixteen feet of water, the *Jackson* could not be moved.[38] By McLaughlin's estimate, had the river level increased by only a few inches more, the launch would have been successful.[39]

Instead, the river kept McLaughlin waiting still longer. On January 2, he noted in his daily log: "River falling slowly." On Sunday, January 3, he made another one-line note: "River falling—still over blocking." Monday left no time for even a line in his log, for he summoned all hands to the work of wedging up the vessel, removing the blocks, and cleaning the ways of mud and trash. As they worked, McLaughlin kept observations on the river level as it fell about one foot per hour.[40] By the time the prelaunch work was completed late that night, the river had receded too much to permit the launch.

McLaughlin continued to observe the weather and the river for the remainder of the week; it rained each day, but the river continued its steady fall. Saturday, Sunday, and Monday the river was "at a stand." Monday night brought more rain, and on Tuesday and Wednesday the river rose about one-half inch per hour. By Thursday, January 14, water covered the lower ways. As McLaughlin waited and watched, the river began to fall again Friday, Saturday, and Sunday. Monday, January 18, the river was again at a stand, but at 7 A.M. there was a "smart shower" and the wind was westerly at eight miles per hour. Later in the day the wind shifted northwest; the weather turned "cold and clear." And so it remained. As the week passed, McLaughlin simply wrote "ditto" in columns beneath the phrases "weather clear and mild," "wind changeable," "river falling slowly."[41]

As he waited for the river, McLaughlin still had business at the navy yard to occupy him. He received word on Tuesday that Lindsman, a crew member of the *Chattahoochee* on furlough at Apalachicola, had died. The next day he dispatched Third Asst. Engr. Armand DeBlanc to Chattahoochee, Florida, and on Saturday he set about reporting an inventory of the *Chattahoochee*'s ordnance stores to John Mercer Brooke at the Bureau of Ordnance and Hydrography. The twelve tanks of powder and thirty-one cases of cartridges were waterlogged, the copper tanks "in fair order," but the precious zinc "badly damaged and inserviceable."[42] Ever frugal, he suggested that Brooke return the tanks and boxes from his department's ordnance supplies because they had been specially constructed to fit the *Chattahoochee*'s magazine.

On Tuesday, McLaughlin made his monthly report of officers and men on the *Chattahoochee* and at the navy yard to John K. Mitchell at the Office of Orders and Detail. Guthrie had furloughed them after the explosion and Blanc had been sent south to reassemble the crew along the river and coast. The same day, he wrote Maj. J. C. Dennis, conscription bursar at Montgomery, that one Hiram Renfew had been absent since January 1 from his detail at Brooks's sawmill in Russell County and was therefore eligible for conscription. On Thursday, two weeks after his first launch attempt, he telegraphed David P. McCorkle at the Naval Ordnance Works in Atlanta for dimensions on the seven-inch rifle from the center of the trunnions to the face of the muzzle so that he could continue his work of planning the *Jackson*'s armament.[43] Busying himself further as he waited for the river, he notified the Office of Orders and Detail about discharging Hiram Renfew.

Warner was engaged in similar administrative duties as the wait continued: his monthly requests that J. L. Coppedge and James Clemm be continued on furlough from the army to work at the CNIW, payment of bills to Savannah and Mobile, and a request to J. W. Young that he send two leather rolling machines from Eufaula by the steamer *Uchee* on her stop there the following Wednesday.[44]

Thinking ahead to replacing the equipment of the *Chattahoochee*, McLaughlin wrote on Monday, January 18, to the Office of Orders and Detail that he had heard about material that might be available from a wreck in east Florida. Certainly he was in no mood to receive the news on Wednesday that major lumber supplier William Brooks had been furnishing lumber to civilians instead of meeting his contract to the navy yard. McLaughlin responded swiftly to the situation: "I now beg to inform you that unless you at once discontinue this I shall turn over to the conscript officer all the men whom I have had detailed to work at your mill. You will please call to see me at this Yard at once."[45]

On Friday, now three weeks since the unsuccessful launch attempt, McLaughlin wrote to Jones about the battery for the *Jackson* and the work of cleaning out the *Chattahoochee* and replacing her boilers—"as filthy a mess as I have ever seen." He continued at length about the difficulties with D. S. Johnston and the goings on among others of the crew: Gift, Guthrie, Midshipman Craig, and others among their acquaintances. Of the *Jackson* project he wrote: "I have not yet had an opportunity of launching—Strange to say the rivers elsewhere have been full to overflowing. I am ready as soon as the river rises to saw away the blocks. A rise of six feet is all that is required."[46]

On Saturday, January 23, Chief Constructor Porter arrived in Columbus. Presumably on a routine visit, he had been at Charleston and, being so nearby, thought he might visit the navy yard to check progress there.[47]

In similarly routine fashion, McLaughlin made an accounting to Secretary Mallory: "I regret having to report her still on the ways tho in all other respects nearly complete, with the exception of the iron on the Shield." He went on to describe in some detail water conditions that had prevented the launch. Three days later, McLaughlin sent Mallory a formal request that he be given command of the *Jackson*. He had supervised her construction; now he wanted to take the ironclad into action. He even proposed a name for the craft: *Muscogee*, for the county of which Columbus is county seat.[48]

Within a few days, McLaughlin received a reply from Mallory that revealed Porter's visit as by no means routine. He had traveled to Columbus from Charleston under orders from the Navy Department to investigate the situation and substantiate reports of the rise in the river's water level. Porter's account to Mallory was that no such rise had taken place, doubtless leaving a question about the launch failure. Although the secretary reported himself to be well satisfied with Porter's report, McLaughlin was not to launch the vessel at all if, in his opinion, it would draw more than six feet when armed, manned, coaled, and equipped for sea.[49]

With this news, McLaughlin determined to confer with Mallory personally and set out from Columbus on February 6. He arrived in Richmond by February 11 and joined George Gift in paying a call on the secretary. Together they proposed that the ship's draft be decreased by arming only the shield portion back along the casemate just past the gunport on the bow. Iron on the knuckle would protect against shot that might strike at the waterline. According to that plan, the ship would be well armed enough to engage the Union blockaders at Apalachicola, yet sufficiently lightened to negotiate the rivers and bay. The port could be opened, the cotton presses put back into operation, and cotton shipped out to Havana.[50] In some ways, this plan was like another of Gift's surefire schemes for victory; but in this instance, the far more conservative McLaughlin joined forces with him.

Nevertheless, Mallory resisted their arguments until they raised the issue of time: significant design changes to increase the *Jackson*'s bouyancy would keep her on the stocks for twelve months or more. As Gift wrote to Ellen Shackelford later on February 11, "the old fellow began to come to terms." Although he agreed that their plan was feasible, Mallory withheld a decision from McLaughlin and Gift until the following day.[51]

The two had already retired to their hotel for the night when it occurred to McLaughlin that their naval strategy might benefit from political support. Losing no time, he drove Gift to Col. Charles Munnerlyn's headquarters, where they laid their strategy for the next day. Munnerlyn was to gather the Florida congressional delegation for a meeting with Gift at 11 A.M. From there they would proceed in a body to Mallory with a plea that he send the *Jackson* to reopen Apalachicola.[52]

Moving to implement the plan, McLaughlin saw Mallory on February 13 to repeat his previous request for command of the *Jackson*. Mallory refused, citing his value to the navy yard. As McLaughlin left the secretary's office, Gift entered with his request for assignment as executive officer. To his great surprise, and McLaughlin's, he was assigned the command and given "carte blanche to procure stores from all directions." Assigned to continue as construction officer, McLaughlin immediately sent orders to begin removing part of the armor from the vessel.[53] By February 15, Gift had his orders to transfer from Charleston to Columbus for command of "the new steamer built at that place."[54]

Guns were the most critical items of supply for the *Jackson*. Knowing that he would be in competition with Admiral Buchanan's force at Mobile for rifled cannon cast at Selma, Gift immediately wrote to Catesby ap R. Jones. That John Mercer Brooke had assigned first priority to Mobile was already well established,[55] but Gift's letter to Jones employed a full range of persuasive techniques. He began by describing the technical advantage to be gained from the plan to put the *Jackson* in Apalachicola within six weeks. Next he asked Jones's advice about tactics: "Do you think I will be safe in undertaking the Port Royal with a VII in. rifle and IX gun with my hull, boilers, and end protected as I described?" Continuing to discuss the plan, he wrote, "I would very much like to have the old crew of the 'Chattahoochee' in the same condition they were the day you left her." Moving from Jones's past success to his future prospects, Gift continued, "I have long since hoped to hear of brilliant successes achieved by you in the 'Tennessee' and I am lost in wonder to know why you have not long since been ordered to Command her. The Country has lost much by the delay." Moving from Jones's virtues to those of his comrades, Gift went on to give an account of John Taylor Wood and Benjamin P. Loyall in action on the Neuse River, illustrated with a small map of the operation. "I am all admiration for Wood," he concluded, "he is modesty personified, conceives boldly & executes with skill & courage."

From the technical, the tactical, and the professional in the letter, Gift proceeded to the social. He confided his hope that his marriage to Ellen Shackelford would soon take place. "Nothing would give me more pleasure than to see You upon the occasion," he wrote. Then in a postscript, Gift dropped the name of his brother-in-law-to-be, Colonel Munnerlyn, a "very pleasant and intelligent gentleman" with whom he had become "quite intimate" in Richmond.

In this letter of almost a thousand words, the operative sentence was, "Therefore, Sir, I hope you will send the VII in. as soon as possible."[56]

Within two weeks, Gift had a very courteous reply from Jones giving the asked-for advice. While he reiterated the necessity to send to Mobile the one gun per week Selma produced, he added, "Please write me immediately of the condition of your vessel, and if necessary I will send you a VII in a fortnight, or as soon as you will need it."[57]

Jones was evidently excited by the plans for taking Apalachicola. His concept of the mission extended to include the capture of a Union cruiser for a "roving commission" like the *Alabama*'s. In that area, he and Gift were in similar circumstances. Gift had cast about for a post with more

Chief Constructor John L. Porter, C.S.N. Porter designed most of the
warships built within the Confederacy, including the C.S.S. Jackson *and the*
C.S.S. Chattahoochee. *His change order calling for redesign of the* Jackson
taxed the resources of Columbus construction facilities—and the patience
of Augustus McLaughlin.
Mariner's Museum, Newport News, Va.

action after the short career of the *Arkansas* ended; Jones was now at a desk job after his historic service on the *Virginia*. Certainly he was in a position to understand Gift's desire to do high deeds.

To Make Himself Useful in Carrying Out His Orders

As Jones was communicating with Gift in strategic and tactical terms, Constructor Porter arrived in Columbus to conduct a construction review of the *Jackson*.

In immediate practical terms, the vessel would draw too much in the shallow river waters and needed redesign for bouyancy. There was also a more basic design flaw. By the spring of 1864, more than ample time had elapsed for testing the paddle-wheeler at New Orleans. The design had not proved out. Instead, turbulence from the wheel's wake amidship made the vessel ride high in the water; thus the wheel could not bite deeply enough into the water to propel a heavy ironclad. Also, twin screws were needed to enable such a vessel to steer around sharp bends in a river or maneuver and fire in narrow passages near a river's mouth or in a bay.

Porter's change order to McLaughlin amended the flaws in his initial design for Confederate ironclads. By focusing on the narrow scope of his technical concerns, Porter did not account for two additional factors. Redesigning the *Jackson* meant a significant strategic loss because the ship could not move upon the blockade at Apalachicola. Of even greater immediate significance, the work he ordered placed an additional burden upon the Columbus system.

Having won the battle against time and resources, McLaughlin had first lost a battle with the river. Now he had no choice about surrendering in this engagement with the system. He was to lengthen the vessel twenty-seven feet to the center stern post, shorten the shield fifty-four feet, remove the center wheel, close the well, place the engines in the hold, and install two eight-foot propellers. Porter had exercised his power to change plans more than he had exercised his responsibility to set a consistent, workable course for his subordinates. If the situation was unfair and Porter's plan inefficient, McLaughlin was by no means the only middle manager ever caught in such a situation.

In specific operational terms, McLaughlin understood factors that his superiors probably did not: completion of the *Jackson* would have cleared an entire track in the navy yard, relieving at least some of the pressures of schedule, labor, materials, budget, and machinery. As the chart below illustrates, the *Chattahoochee* was towed to Columbus in December, to enter the system as the *Jackson* made its exit. The *Shamrock* was still incomplete, and during the first quarter of 1864 the torpedo boat *Viper* would be placed on a fourth major track within the construction system. As added increments, Warner's work of supplying machinery for projects elsewhere continued as he also expanded CNIW facilities. Materials in short supply became critical deficits as the war continued. Shipping delays became periodic shutdowns of rail transportation as Union action struck closer to Columbus. Workmen were dis-

1864 *CNIW/CNY*	J	F	M	A	M	J	J	A	S	O	N		D
Construction	*Jackson*...												
	Shamrock												
				Viper									
Repairs	*Chattahoochee*..												
	.... River Steamers												
Facilities	Rolling Mill												
	.... Coke Oven												
	.... Stables												
	Equipment Procurement, Maintenance												
	Supplies Procurement, Allocation												
OTHER *SITES*													
Machinery	Charleston												
	Wilmington												
	Mobile												
	Tombigbee												
												Black Dwarf	
Crews on Roll	Savannah												
	Charleston												
	Mobile												
	Eufaula												
	Prattville												
NAVAL ACTION	.... Apalachicola												
MILITARY ACTION	Drill............... Atlanta................ Drill............... Savannah												

gruntled on the job, and Warner kept up a constant effort to keep skilled men from conscription in the army. Retaining the *Jackson* in a system operating under such adverse conditions placed an almost intolerable strain upon Columbus resources. Then two additional burdens were added to the system in 1864: a naval assault was planned on Apalachicola and military pressures in Atlanta and Savannah called the Coumbus work force away to do double duty as soldiers.

The chart illustrates the comprehensive understanding McLaughlin had to have of operations in Columbus and how further work on the *Jackson* would impact the system. Porter, with the authority of top management to issue orders, doubtless went on his way to other important matters without having time to listen to a detailed explanation of why his plan was impractical.

McLaughlin relayed Porter's recommendations to Mallory and, in three one-sentence paragraphs, addressed three related matters: alterations would delay launching the *Jackson* for several months, the *Chattahoochee* was less than two months away from completion, the Office of Orders and Detail would have to find assignments for the officers already assigned to the *Jackson*.[58] What modern readers usually consider a quaint ending, "Very respectfully, your humble and obedient Servant," was probably more than a simple convention of the time when McLaughlin signed that letter to Mallory. The highest and best knowledge of an engineer, and McLaughlin's superior, overrode plans for action. He was left to translate an order into man-days, board feet, and x number of nails and spikes as he worked to manage an all but unmanageable system.

News of Porter's change order soon spread to other stations. David McCorkle, Jones's counterpart at the Atlanta Naval Ordnance Works, passed along to Jones word from McLaughlin about delays on the *Jackson*. He also confided to Jones his growing resentment of Gift. He had signed for Gift to become a lieutenant for the war; now with the new command, McCorkle supposed "he will soon [out] rank me." In the meantime, for a man like him or Jones to make "himself useful in carrying out his orders" merely resulted in slowing his career.[59]

McLaughlin confirmed McCorkle's news in a February 28 letter that gave Jones an account of all the delays and frustrations of the preceding eight weeks. In a pattern that had developed in their letters—and as illustrated also in McCorkle's letter—there was more and more open criticism of Gift. He was restless, certainly—always darting from this scheme to that—and he was critical—calling Guthrie to account for his conduct on the *Chattahoochee*. Now Gift was rich besides—because of profits running the blockade—and about to win the prize of a belle of good family and even better fortune.[60]

The more flamboyant Gift had enjoyed greater success than McLaughlin, who had made himself useful—even indispensable—at the navy yard in obeying his orders. First, low water on the Apalachicola frustrated his work at Bloutstown; then high water at Columbus frustrated his work on the *Jackson*. Now work on both vessels was to begin all over again.

McLaughlin's first task in this new phase of operations was to prepare the *Chattahoochee*, which would perhaps carry his rival to further success and recognition. The job was as detailed and tedious as it was thankless. The riggings and sails of the gunboat had disappeared somewhere in the navy's supply system and efforts were made to track them down at the Marion, South Carolina, station. The ship's medicine chest was also lost. A galley returned to the Montgomery Supply Depot in August 1862 was no longer in the department's inventory; a letter to Savannah did not produce it; but it turned up on the *Tennessee* at Mobile. McLaughlin had to pause in his labors to attend to correspondence related to the deaths of two *Chattahoochee* crew members.[61]

Turning back to the work of refitting the *Chattahoochee*, he had to locate a length of hide rope to be strung from the wheel through the steering mechanism to the rudder of the ship. On February 24, his clerk made an entirely routine inquiry to supply officer Samuel Z. Gonzales at Montgomery about whether he had any "good hide rope" McLaughlin might requisition.[62] This one item would keep him occupied from time to time for an entire month.

On March 5 the transfer of Gift and the *Jackson*'s crew to the *Chattahoochee* was effected. Because work on the gunboat was not far enough advanced to plan an assault upon Apalachicola with her, another plan had to be devised: to take an expedition of small boats to capture a blockader and, with that ship, capture the others.[63]

During the same period, the CNIW was of course engaged in similar correspondence and record keeping to maintain the flow of its system. Sheet iron arrived from Wilmington for the *Jackson*.[64] There was the usual steady flow of payments to Selma and Mobile, with St. Mark's,

Florida, added to the sources of supply; and there was word to Savannah that Warner could build a caboose for the *Savannah* if Acting Master Fairfax could supply the #8 or #10 iron for it.[65]

As Warner and McLaughlin managed the details of keeping their system functional for the navy, pressures from the Confederate Army began to weigh heavily upon the system in 1864. Included in the paperwork for February was compliance with a regulation that was to become more and more stringent as military action in north Georgia increased through the spring and summer: providing a roster of employees to the various enrolling officers, assigned by congressional district.[66] The 1860 census had indicated a general flow of population from rural Georgia and Alabama to Columbus industries. The war greatly increased that flow and increased, in turn, the necessity for a strict accounting of able-bodied men.

Already suffering a chronic shortage of skilled labor, both the CNIW and the navy yard were about to enter a period of even more critical labor problems. The pressure was not only general and official, it was situational and personal as well. Instances of absences and outright desertion increased as morale in the South began to suffer. Case-by-case, men had to be sought out and set back to work or turned over to the army. In other cases, special requests were made to keep particularly skilled workers in Columbus. Jonathan R. Ford applied for transfer from the army to the navy as a carpenter. Carpenter Daniel Beverley was cited in a special appeal to Gen. Joseph E. Johnston. Recorded in McLaughlin's own hand is a letter requesting that Mallory assign James Shorter to the navy.[67] As the navy worked to secure its labor force, a March 3 circular letter from Secretary Mallory ordered the submission of a roster of all employees.[68]

As Warner and McLaughlin received some men from the army to meet their demands for laborers, Gift was combing the area around Chattahoochee, Florida, and requesting that soldiers from a Florida regiment be transferred to the *Chattahoochee*.[69] He would have much preferred to go on with plans to assault Apalachicola, for he wrote to Ellen when he was ordered back to Columbus: "I was heartily glad to get rid of Chattahoochee, the place is very dull and odious when one has nothing to do. It was bearable when the gunboat was there, but with only a stray soldier or two to converse with it became intolerable."[70]

Further pressure came to bear on the system when the Columbus labor force became companies of militia—like the present-day reserves who add military drill on Saturday to their weekly labors. Men who were managers also became commanders of ten companies of militia, the Twenty-seventh Battalion of Georgia Seige Artillery, Maj. A. Bonaud commanding.[71]

Supplies to feed the Columbus work force began to run out, despite supplies received from the quartermaster and sent in from such sources as the Shorter plantation in Eufaula. Prices continued to rise. Taking his turn at keeping the navy yard log on March 5, McLaughlin noted a rise in the cost of board at a local hotel to fifty dollars per month—"strong indication of my having to select rooms in the Poor House." As the CNIW began to barter for supplies on a regular basis, Warner responded to a request from Capt. William M. David at Henderson, Georgia, with his regular rates: for a 100-gallon kettle, 60 bushels of corn, 3½ barrels of flour, or 275 pounds of bacon; for a sixteen-inch sugar mill, 110 bushels of corn, 6 barrels of flour, or 475 pounds of bacon.[72]

Under conditions of severe inflation, funds to continue operations were running out. In an effort to consolidate Warner's accounts, Paymaster John W. Nixon ordered accounts of the individual stations closed as of March 26, 1864, and any unexpended balance deposited in his name with the assistant treasurer of the Confederate States.[73]

Weaving through this record of major and minor problems with keeping naval facilities productive in Columbus was McLaughlin's continued search for hide rope. On March 3, he sent a direct appeal to John K. Mitchell, head of the Office of Orders and Detail in Richmond: "Enclosed I beg to hand requisition for Hide Wheel Ropes required for the C. S. Steamer *Chattahoochee* from Naval Store Keeper at Montgomery."[74]

On March 14, he sent another requisition to Gonzales at Montgomery: "Enclosed please find duplicate requisitions for 19 Fathoms Hide Ropes, which please send of the largest size you have and ship as early as possible as I expect to send the vessel down the river very soon." Within the week, he was writing once more to Gonzales: "I am [sorry] to report that the Hide rope is unfit for use—besides being badly cut by rats, it is so tended that we cannot put even a moderate strain upon it. If you have any other even of small size, please let me have it—if not I will thank you to fill the requisition with Manilla rope—I will return the hide rope if you wish it."[75]

As he dealt with the *Chattahoochee*, McLaughlin also had to manage alterations on the *Jackson* and even further demands on the system of labor and supply. From the first day, reconstruction work had been slow and difficult; after McLaughlin's order from Richmond, two gangs began very early on February 13 and by noon had removed only five of the two-inch plates.[76] McLaughlin notified Porter on March 19 that his instructions for redesign were creating major structural problems. Reducing the spar deck by six feet would necessitate new beams, and he asked Porter to reconsider that design requirement. Charles Blain had received instructions on closing the wheel well but no specifications in Porter's further correspondence. While the letter is neutral in tone, McLaughlin used these data to make clear to Porter the difficulties his orders had imposed on the project. Counterbalancing his implied criticism with a positive affirmation of the orders, he asked for an early answer inasmuch as the approaching completion of the *Chattahoochee* would free all hands for work on the *Jackson*.[77]

Added to such technical concerns was the disaffection of the *Enquirer.* Popular disillusionment with the ironclad elsewhere had finally reached Columbus.

> If anyone will but take a stroll on the banks of the Chattahoochee, just below our wharf, they will find that there has been enough money wasted upon an old "slantin dicular" looking craft, propped up on legs, to feed a brigade of soldiers for a considerable period. What could ever have been expected of such a looking craft we cannot imagine—unless a second flood is expected—and we are quite sure that nothing but a general inundation can ever lift the thing from its present position. To say the least, it is decidedly a great failure; and in our opinion the best thing that can be done with the whole concern is to take it to pieces & commence over again.[78]

In a long letter to Jones on March 25, McLaughlin echoed the editor's advice with: "I am tearing the Muscogee to pieces preparatory to carrying out the new plan." To his friend he confided more frankly the problems communicated to Porter in a respectful tone: "To show you how unreliable this man Porter is he has proposed two screws of 8 ft. to be used, when there is not room for one over 7½ ft. and hardly that. In order to place in her an 8 ft. screw it would nearly come through the deck." The letter referred to another episode in the ongoing saga of George Gift. That his marriage to Ellen Shackelford was to take place on March 30 was news; "the report of his having been previously married and that his wife is still living" approached notoriety. McLaughlin hardly need have concluded, "Gift is very unpopular here. The people do not fancy him."[79]

For once, there was no mention of a seven-inch rifle in McLaughlin's letter to Jones. Doubtless he knew all too well the more pressing need for ordnance at Mobile. On March 30, however, McLaughlin wrote once more to John Mercer Brooke, ending his letter with: "It is presumed that one gun may be devoted to [the *Chattahoochee*] without detriment to the Mobile Squadron."[80]

U.S.S. Adela. *Confederate Lt. George W. Gift's plan was for a boarding party to capture the* Adela *and use it to capture the larger blockader U.S.S.* Somerset. *Although Gift advanced many such plans—including a naval attack from Lake Erie upon the northern United States—the Apalachicola expedition was the only scheme he was authorized to carry out.*
U.S. Navy

He Looks for a Grand Affair

McLaughlin had not received his seven-inch rifle—or a suitable lot of hide rope—in March; but the navy yard and CNIW together had advanced a remarkable amount of work through their system during the first quarter of the year. On March 26, the navy yard completed a small launch to be attached to the *Chattahoochee*. This vessel was a relatively minor accomplishment in nautical architecture, but there were major plans to use the craft in the assault on Apalachicola to be commanded by Gift.

At last the Confederate Navy in Columbus was introducing a battle plan into the system. Construction officers could look up from the drawing board, set aside concerns with Navy Department action, and level their sights on the Union Navy. The quartermaster system was activated to send a steady supply of pistols, ammunition, and cutlasses downriver to the gunboat's moorings at Eufaula. On March 28, the steamer *Swan* was chartered at thirty dollars a day to serve as transport and tender for the expedition. And on March 30, 1864, the navy yard and the CNIW brought off an almost incredible feat under conditions of war in the Confederacy: the steamboat *Shamrock* was launched at Columbus.[81] The steamer would serve the navy to transport supplies along the river system, reducing competition with the army for transport. The launch also cleared the system of at least one major construction project.

As Gift made his plans for the Apalachicola expedition, conducting the daily affairs at the CNIW and navy yard continued to immerse Warner and McLaughlin in routine duties: payrolls were sent out to Savannah and Charleston, machines or tools continued to come in ($25 to Savannah for a key wrench), and payment for express travel went out ($125 to Miss Fanny Leaphart for a hotel bill in Columbia, South Carolina). There was the old business of a Daniel's planer, which, like the steam hammer of 1861–62, had been some time in negotiations; once it was safely requisitioned, delays on the railroad held up delivery. J. W. Young in Eufaula was sent a reminder about procedures—directions this time to make a separate, itemized billing for work done by D. S. Johnston for the Eufaula works.[82]

Problems began to arise in the operation that signaled even worse problems to come. Warner's clerk sent John Wythe Parks in Montgomery $775, in itself not unusual; but he sent it in $5 notes with directions that are, in turn, an indicator about the Confederate monetary system at that stage of the war: "If [C. H. Cleveland] will not receive these notes—give $500 to the Captain of the Coal Boat & take his receipt for same & send the balance $275 by Express to these Works with the receipt for the $500."[83] Another negative sign of conditions in the Confederacy was McLaughlin's request to Secretary Mallory that Joseph Hanserd of Columbus be granted a passport to leave for Europe via Wilmington. A British subject, Hanserd had been a supporter and supplier to Columbus industry; claiming ill health, he now wanted to leave the Confederacy.[84] In time, other foreign-born workers initially drawn to Columbus by peacetime industry would want to escape wartime working conditions.

To those administrative duties was added the work of assembling a crew for the *Chattahoochee*. After the explosion of the previous May, there had not been a sufficient number of positions on vessels in service to place the crew; moreover, Confederate armies had more urgent demands for manpower than the navy. When the navy began its search for a crew to man the gunboat and refit her for service, Gen. Joseph Johnston's headquarters at Dalton agreed to transfer seventy men. Surgeon Ford, Mdn. Gale W. Sparks, and a Quartermaster Sheppard were sent to escort them back to Columbus.[85]

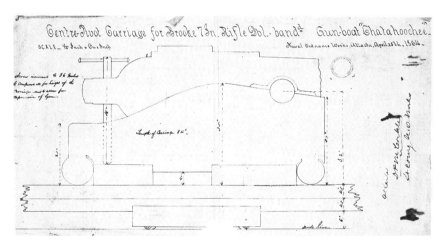

Lt. David McCorkle's design for a C.S.S. Chattahoochee *gun carriage. In a widely dispersed production system, carriages were produced in Atlanta, guns in Selma, sights in Atlanta or Richmond. "There are no two alike," complained McCorkle; yet the Confederacy attempted mass production of such individually designed and fitted weaponry.*
National Archives

In April 1864, such demands on the system were incidental to the priority work on the *Chattahoochee*. By midmonth, McCorkle was sending Jones specs for elevating screws: thirty-six inches for the *Chattahoochee* and thirty-one inches for the *Jackson*. McCorkle's statement of those specifications serves as an excellent indication of how the entire construction system operated. Observing that there were "no two [Confederate vessels] alike" except the two Bigbee Boats, McCorkle inveighed against a system where each gun carriage had to be matched exactly to the specs of the individual cannon and, beyond that, to the specs of its exact placement at a given point on the *Chattahoochee*'s gun deck (or the *Jackson*'s or the *Tennessee*'s or the *Columbia*'s and so on). The heavy muzzle loaders always operated in close quarters; thus Mc-Corkle's letters to Jones and Brooke deal in inches and fractions of inches in discussing carriages shipped from Atlanta to ships in Columbus to be fitted with guns shipped there from Selma.[86] As he wrestled with such details, McCorkle also sent shellac for the *Chattahoochee* from supplies in Atlanta,[87] and a requisition went to Richmond for boatswains' supplies for the gunboat.[88]

Plans to attack Apalachicola competed in the system with the work of reconstructing the *Jackson*, with work on the *Chattahoochee*, and battles with the army over manpower. McLaughlin was able to report to Mallory that, by April 23, most of the floor timbers "of the new work" had been laid and "the new" machinery was being put in place. In such subtle ways, McLaughlin was sending constant reminders to his superiors of the cost in time and naval effectiveness assessed by Porter's engineering decision.

McLaughlin's letter also expressed some cause for exasperation with Gift. Gift had traveled to Drewrys Bluff during the last of March to testify at a court-martial, evidently using the trip to lobby for increased construction and action in the Columbus-Apalachicola corridor. Untroubled by the duties that already overworked McLaughlin and Warner, he wrote to Ellen on March 27 that he had talked with Mallory "and am satisfied that I shall have his support in all I may undertake." A visit to Treasury Secretary C. G. Memminger brought similar success: "he proposes to build a half dozen blockade-runners adapted for Apalachicola, and seemed delighted with the idea of finding a point from which the blockade can be run with so much ease and certainty. He, too, will do everything he can to forward my plans."[89]

When Gift passed through Columbus the first week of April en route to his wedding at Saffold, he evidently gave McLaughlin the news that constructing a torpedo boat would be introduced into the Columbus construction system. Gift's ebullience, processed in McLaughlin's way of thinking, would become x board feet of lumber $+ x$ tons of iron and coal

$+x$ man-hours of labor added to what he and Warner already had on their books to accomplish. Even so, it was a project McLaughlin was eager to undertake. He addressed the matter to Mallory: "Having been informed by Lieut. Gift that it was your intention to have two Torpedo boats Constructed here, I would respectfully request that the drawings for same may be sent me as early as possible. I have increased my force of carpenters & could now work upon them to great advantage."[90]

In his eagerness to begin an even newer, more radical design than the *Jackson*, McLaughlin was moving ahead of the Navy Department's administrative machinery. The torpedo boat was a new weapons system just being introduced; the secretary's November 30, 1863, report listed only one in commission. His April 30, 1864, report listed eight "torpedoes" being laid down: four at Richmond, two at Wilmington, and two at Charleston.

The Confederates had seen enough success with torpedo warfare to commit to this new construction program. As had proved out along the James River in 1861 and at Charleston in 1863, torpedoes offered a way for a smaller and weaker force to attack by stealth. Used first in a kind of mine warfare, a torpedo was constructed rather like a small powder keg with conical metal ends. The device that made the charge explode on contact with a ship's hull brought into play rudimentary electrical equipment—and created a sudden rise in demand for batteries and sulfuric acid (at twenty-five dollars per pound), sensitive tubes, and insulated wire.

From those early torpedoes set afloat in random fashion, a more sophisticated method evolved whereby units could be connected to a triggering device on shore. As a ship approached the torpedo, the remote control device could detonate an explosive. An even more certain—and considerably more daring—method was to equip a small craft with one or two torpedoes. A *Viper*-class vessel was designed to carry a torpedo attached to a movable spar extended from the bow. Operating off a mother ship like the *Jackson*, a crew of six or eight might carry the *Viper* from the ironclad's mooring near Apalachicola and easily clear the bar to offshore waters where Union blockaders kept watch. Riding very low in the water and protected by armor, the vessel might glide in under the guns of a large ship like the *Somerset* or the *Port Royal* and position the torpedo at a precise point against the hull, well below the waterline. Protected from the explosion, it might withdraw, reload, and attack again; then the *Jackson* might clear the port of Apalachicola at her leisure. This application of torpedo technology left little to chance, except the survival of the crew and the ship.[91]

Constructing the *Viper* for such a mission against the Apalachicola blockade placed McLaughlin and Warner in the very forefront of naval technology. Nevertheless, McLaughlin was rankled by being placed in a position where he learned at second hand about plans for his own work— a project that was, in part, another of George Gift's ideas. Overriding such tactical concerns of rivalry between the two was the great tactical advantage to be gained by having the *Viper* work in tandem with the *Jackson*. The project seemed not only exciting but more possible when completion of the *Chattahoochee* freed McLaughlin's system of a major project.

Finally the *Chattahoochee* was launched on April 20 and was supplied for Gift's Apalachicola expedition. She was without her full complement of machinery—or the seven-inch rifle from Selma. Her draft, four feet one inch forward and five feet five inches aft, was a hopeful note.[92] And she was in the hands of an experienced river pilot, Capt. Hezekiah ("Hez") Wingate. However, the ship negotiated only six miles of the river below Columbus before running aground at Woolford's Landing; a rise in the river would be needed to refloat her.

As his command was being fitted out, Gift traveled on to Saffold to marry Ellen Shackelford on April 6. They arrived in Columbus about April 10 to be received by friends and relatives at a round of parties.[93] Meanwhile, as Gift fulfilled his social duties, McLaughlin attended the business at hand. Supplies continued to come into the navy yard for the gunboat: pistols and ammunition from McCorkle in Atlanta, camp kettles from Quartermaster Dillard, and from the Columbus arsenal eighty cartridge boxes and belts, eighty haversacks, and twenty-five artillery swords. Indeed Gift had received carte blanche while other Confederate operations suffered from shortages.

Rain and a rise in the river freed the gunboat on the afternoon and evening of April 28; by 4 A.M. April 29 the ship was once more underway to Eufaula. Sunday, May 1, the steamer *Swan* was sent downriver to deliver supplies and to tow a yawl borrowed from the steamer *Uchee* for the expedition. On Monday, May 2, more stores were loaded onto the *Marianna*, the steamer and a launch were given into the command of Gift for the expedition, and the party cast off for Eufaula.[94] On board with Gift was his bride, who would accompany him as far as her home landing at Saffold.

At 5 P.M. that day, McLaughlin received a telegram that the *Chattahoochee* was grounded again, this time at Francis's Landing. The next day, the report came that the gunboat had at last reached Eufaula, a trip of eighty-five miles in two weeks.[95]

Hairbreadth Escapes by Land and Sea

Gift's expeditionary force remained at Eufaula to make a final check of their seven boats. Gift was to command one boat, Surgeon Ford another, and each of the others was in charge of Midshipmen Samuel P. Blanc, Henry L. Vaughan, Gale W. Sparks, William S. Hogue, and Carman Frazee. Midshipman Blanc, as second in command, kept records as each man received his equipment issue.

The *Chattahoochee* was to be left behind at Eufaula until a rise in the river could assure a safer passage south; the expedition departed on the steamer *Marianna* for a rendezvous with additional volunteers at Chattahoochee, Florida. At the obstructions on the Apalachicola they were to be set adrift for the remainder of their mission to the Gulf.

With the expedition well underway, McLaughlin had time to write one of his periodic letters to Jones. He related the events leading up to this attempt to recapture Apalachicola, but McLaughlin was not optimistic about Gift's leadership: "he looks for a grand affair, though I am fearful the matter has been too much talked about, he himself being most prominent in giving the affair publicity; every one knows it. He spoke of bringing all his young men back lieutenants, etc, etc. That, I think, is one of Gift's great failings."[96]

At Saffold, Ellen Gift had returned home to "The Pines." She wrote longingly to her husband about the "agreeable surprise" of seeing his uniform in her closet and the Bible and volume of Shakespeare where he had left them on a table in their room. Gift wrote to her from the *Marianna:* "I felt lonely last night, I retired early, and the little room seemed a vast and desolate waste. There was no Ellen to welcome me, as she did on our honeymoon trip, when I came in." In anticipation of his successful venture, he added, "But won't we be blythe and gay when I return? Won't I tell of the hairbreadth escapes by land and sea, won't I build castles in the air?"[97]

On May 10, McLaughlin wrote once again to Jones. He had just received instructions from the Navy Department about building two torpedo boats. Although he had no way of knowing Gift was already in trouble on the Gulf, McLaughlin once more expressed his concern: "I am fearful . . . that he has talked too much about what he intended to do. I was informed by the Comdr. of the Post that the evening before leaving Eufaula there was an entertainment given on board the Chattahoochee and that the expedition was freely discussed, and a W. Baker has heard it at Marianna. I think the information had proceeded the expedition some days."[98]

What happened on Gift's Apalachicola expedition has been told from more than one point of view. Mdn. J. T. Scharf was to write a firsthand account in his *History of the Confederate Navy*.

The party reached Chattahoochee, Florida, at 7 o'clock on the morning of May 4. Sixteen volunteers from the First Georgia Regiment, Fifth Georgia Cavalry, and the First and Second Florida Battalions joined them there. At 10:40 the expedition left Chattahoochee and made its way down the Apalachicola to Ricko's Bluff, nearly halfway to Apalachicola. There they received thirteen additional volunteers. After dark on the same day the boats reached Fort Cobb, a battery at the obstructions. Capt. J. R. Blount, who was in command there, assured Gift of reinforcements from his command if they should be needed.

Upon reaching Apalachicola, the Confederates crossed St. George's Sound at night and landed at East Point near where the *Adela* and *Somerset* lay. There they took cover to await a dark night and a rough sea to cover their move against the *Adela*.

Gift and his men remained on St. George's Island for a week. The rough sea for which they had hoped did not come and Scharf later wrote: "The sea was smooth and the dipping of the oars in the phosphorescent water emitted a luminous light which shone brightly some distance beyond."[99] Delay caused by the weather introduced further problems, for the party ran low on supplies and was forced to obtain more from Apalachicola. The scouts who delivered the supplies told Gift that Unionists in Apalachicola had informed the blockaders of his plan.

This combination of circumstances led Gift to decide to abandon his plan for attack, withdraw from East Point, and attempt an escape up the Apalachicola River. Late on May 12, as a storm was rising on the sound, the boats left St. George's. Gift's boat and another manned by ten soldiers took a course across the sound for Apalachicola while the other boats hugged the shore toward Cat Point.

The next several hours proved that Gift's course across the sound had been an unfortunate choice, for the wind rose rapidly in the north. The boat containing the soldiers was swamped and the survivors swam to grasp the outside of Gift's boat. After several hours, Gift became ill. He then transferred command of the boat to Scharf, who later recorded the experience:

> At this time the boat was half filled with water and seventeen men on the inside, ten men from the swamped boat hanging on the outside and the sea washing over her. The boat was but two miles from the shore and all expected every moment would be the last. Finding that it would be impossible to reach the town in the face of the storm, Midshipman Scharf informed Lieutenant Gift that the only hope was to turn around and go to sea before the wind. The commander instructed Midshipman Scharf to do what he thought best, and immediately Midshipman Scharf informed the men of his determination. There was great fear of swamping in the trough of the sea in turning, but having confidence in his judgement, the crew were ready to obey his commands.

In preparation for turning about, the guns, ammunition, lanterns, baggage, water casks—all the precious supplies issued at Columbus—were jettisoned. Six of the nearly exhausted men were taken from the outside of the boat.

> Finally, as a large wave struck under the quarter, nearly lifting the boat out of the water, it was turned and headed toward St. George's. Soon afterward the remaining four who had been clinging to the outside of the boat were taken into the already over-loaded craft. The "storm driven Confederates" approached St. George's fearfully in the sound of the breakers pounding the beach. Abandoning the boat as they neared the island, they were able to swim to safety. For two days they were cast away on St. George's without provisions, foraging the island for palmetto cabbage, alligators, and oysters.[100]

In the meantime, the other Confederate boats had reached Apalachicola, where they were confronted with further dangers.

The Union account of this expedition picks up on the night of May 12. With the hope of capturing the raiding party, which he knew to be in the vicinity, Lt. William Budd of the *Somerset* made plans to strike the town at dawn on May 13. Budd's combined navy and army force found seventy or eighty of the *Chattahoochee* party on the upper wharves preparing to man their boats. Seeing the Union launches, they abandoned everything except their rifles and retreated through the town on foot, followed by two shells from the *Somerset's* howitzer.

The retreating Confederates took the river road northward, passing within a short distance of the Union landing party. The army lieutenant, thinking that they were a part of his own command, allowed them to pass unchallenged. This mistake allowed the Confederates time to scatter into the swamp before Budd's sailors could land their boats and set out in pursuit. After going two miles up the river through dense undergrowth in search of the Confederates, Budd and his men returned to take possession of the deserted boats and supplies.[101]

Before leaving Apalachicola, the Confederates had arranged to send three citizens of the town in search of Gift and the rest of the crew. The relief party found them on May 14 and ferried them from St. George's to Apalachicola. When they learned that the other members of the crew had been driven from the town, they lost no time in pushing off from Apalachicola. After traveling some distance up the river, Gift ordered their small boat sunk in a bayou. From there he and his party traveled overland to join the remainder of the expeditionary force above the obstructions on the Apalachicola.[102]

Budd's report gave an accounting of the supplies issued to the expedition and so carefully inventoried in Blanc's diary. Left behind as spoils of war to be issued on the blockade were six of the boats, the rifles, cutlasses, a thousand rounds of ammunition, all of the compasses, signal flags, blankets, haversacks, and medical stores. Three of the Confederates from Company F of Bonaud's Florida battalion were taken prisoner: Andrew McCormick, Napoleon Terry, and Louis Gay. Joseph Sire [Sia], captain of the after-guard on the *Chattahoochee*, told his captors that he had intended to desert, deliberately lagging behind his retreating mates to allow his capture.

Three men from Apalachicola—Thomas McLean, Anthony Murray, and James Anderson—had participated as scouts for the expedition and had been captured with Confederates aboard their small boat. They were shipped away to Key West as prisoners. Although they claimed to have been forced into Gift's service, they came under particularly heavy criticism from Budd for having first gained and then violated the trust of the blockading officers. They had enjoyed immunity as noncombatants and now they had participated in an armed raid. The small boat they had been allowed to keep for fishing to save themselves and others in Apalachicola from starvation was used in a plan to attack their benefactors. Budd recommended to Admiral Bailey that they be forbidden to return to Apalachicola.

Budd reserved his greatest contempt for the retreating Confederates of the expedition: "They abandoned everything and ran like sheep, without firing a shot. Had it not been for the unfortunate mistake of the officer in command of our troops, we should have captured or destroyed the entire force."[103] He had settled to his own satisfaction the question of whether the former comrades on the Gulf or on the river were the better men.

While the hairbreadth escapes by land and sea had been going on in Apalachicola, life at the navy yard proceeded uneventfully. The weather was logged in each day as "pleasant"; there was news from Wilmington that the ironclad *Raleigh* had run aground, and a blockade runner had made harbor; the quartermaster sent 30 pounds of bacon and 404 pounds of fodder, and J. W. Pease supplied the navy yard with a ream of paper. On May 15 the mail was cut off from Richmond with news of heavy fighting there. The evacuation of Dalton, Georgia, was noted. May 18 contained the notes: "Began work on the 'Viper' yesterday; News glorious—Lee driving back the Yanks on the Rapidan—Beauregard driving them from Petersburg R road—Communications re-opened with Richmond. Gold at New York $12." And as the last line of the day's entry: "Lt. Gift's grand Expedition a fizzle." Late that night, more details reached the navy yard by the *Marianna*. The paymaster reported all the boats lost except one launch and "a general failure of the whole expedition." The May 14 entry ends with: "Telegraphed Gift to report here without delay."[104]

After "The Late Unfortunate Expedition"

The failure of the Apalachicola expedition had three immediate effects. If the expedition "fizzled," it had also backfired. First came an increase of blockading strength off Apalachicola; the Union report of May 15 shows reinforcements already en route to the station.[105] May 23 brought a letter to McLaughlin from Col. John W. Robertson, the new engineer appointed to superintend defenses and obstruction of the Apalachicola. The times favored renewed plans to improve and extend the obstructions, and by May 27 McLaughlin had forwarded Robertson's report with his own transmittal to Mallory. The third effect occurred in the dynamics of the professional relationship between Gift and McLaughlin.

If Gift's expedition had not been a naval tour de force, McLaughlin's steady, systematic handling of the matter was an administrative tour de force. McLaughlin had not won command of the *Jackson* to fight the Union, but he was a seasoned veteran of the bureaucracy. As Gift had sailed to South Pacific islands in the Old Navy, McLaughlin had seen supply-ship duty. As Gift had moved from one assignment to another as a Confederate officer, McLaughlin had kept a steady, unvarying course. McLaughlin cleared his desk for administrative action, carrying into the battle with Gift an informed sensitivity to strategy, tactics, and most of all, procedure. From his post in Columbus he began to lay down a barrage of messages to Eufaula, where Gift had returned to continue fitting out the *Chattahoochee*. His May 19 telegram asking that Gift report to Columbus was followed by a routine notification that a recruit was being sent to Eufaula aboard the *Munnerlyn*. It contained the added note: "I telegraphed you yesterday directing you to report to me—which you will please do in person without delay." Gift arrived on the *Indian* on Saturday, May 21, and returned downriver with Paymaster Marshall L. Sothoron the next day.

After Gift's return to Eufaula, McLaughlin maintained his steady communications during the next week. He sent Gift two letters dated May 22. The one was a routine transmittal for an invoice of supplies either requisitioned and shipped on the *Munnerlyn* or unavailable. The second communication was a quotation from Naval Regulations Article 7, Chapter 34, on correspondence reports: "Officers are prohibited from commenting in their private correspondence upon the operation of the vessel or squadron to which they may be attached or from giving in time of war any information of their destination or intended operations lest such communications may be published to the injury of the public service." McLaughlin added the comment: "As this order has not been observed I have to call your attention to it & to request that you will impress upon all your officers the necessity of strict obedience to same."[106]

On Monday May 23, McLaughlin forwarded to Mallory Gift's May 19 report of the Apalachicola expedition with his transmittal letter. He began by expressing his "great annoyance" that the expedition had "resulted unsuccessfully." He went on to say: "I am not, however, surprised," adding that he felt "much relieved that no greater disaster was met with."

Just as letters among fellow officers had become openly critical, McLaughlin's statements to Mallory about Gift are very frank: "The officers connected with the expedition, not excepting the Commanding Officer, it would seem used little caution to keep their proposed movements secret, but on the contrary discussed all their plans so freely in public that the Citizens both here and at other places on the River were in possession of all the particulars." At the same time McLaughlin criticizes Gift, he describes a situation that explains the rapid transfer of intelligence. From Colonel Robertson he learned that a gang of deserters had been captured nearby, making authorities aware that regular communication had been going for some time. In fact, men from the gang had gone downriver to Apalachicola just about the time the expedition was preparing to leave—"no doubt for the purpose of notifying the Enemy of the intended attack."

McLaughlin singled out Midshipman Blanc for special criticism. Command had developed upon him "after the separation of Lieut. Gift from the party" and he had remained in Apalachicola for twenty-four hours, his boats at the wharf in full view of the town. The Union search party had surprised Blanc and his men so completely that they had to abandon all their supplies in their effort to escape. McLaughlin also cataloged the loss of boats. The launch Gift had with him, along with the *Swan* chartered for the expedition, were left downriver—"but it is thought by Lt. Gift that they were in no danger." Fortunately there was no loss of life; by Gift's report the only loss was Sia's desertion.

McLaughlin concluded his lengthy transmittal letter with news about the discharge of his own duties: the drawings for the torpedo steamer were in hand at the navy yard and he would report within a few days progress on its construction.

In a series of long letters, McLaughlin continued the systematic discharge of his duties. One of the navy yard clerks transcribed Colonel Robertson's plans for river defense. McLaughlin then forwarded that report to Mallory with a request for favorable consideration. Robertson's conception was not only bolder than Moreno's had been, it also involved the navy. He suggested using the nine-inch Dahlgren and two 32-pounders from the *Chattahoochee* at Fort Gadsden, fifteen miles south of the present obstructions. He proposed having engineering troops in the area construct two torpedo boats at Saffold, to be hand-propelled rather than steam-driven, though fitted out with iron at Columbus.

The *Chattahoochee* would figure prominently in Robertson's plan in that the obstructions would be cleared and the way opened to restore Confederate control of Apalachicola. The transfer of the *Raleigh's* boilers from Wilmington for use on the *Chattahoochee* would speed her completion. McLaughlin took care to let Mallory know that the *Viper* was well underway and a pair of small engines at the CNIW was ready to be installed. To inform himself of the new weapons technology, he asked permission to visit the Charleston construction site so that he could see firsthand how to attach torpedoes to the vessel. Finally, he reported work on the *Jackson* "well advanced."

Before his workday was complete that Friday, McLaughlin fired off a volley of administrative details to Gift about shipping wind sails and blocks; completing requisition blanks for bags, hammocks, and canvas awnings; and storing shells in the Columbus magazine. Gift was asked to "make out at once a full report of all the missing articles furnished from this yard, for the Expedition & also take steps to recover the boat, which was left down the river." Moving along to the next item, "It will not be necessary for you to visit the obstructions at present [or to use that duty as a means to visit Ellen at "The Pines"]." McLaughlin expressed his expectation that boilers for the *Chattahoochee* were to be received from Charleston in a few days and Gift should remain aboard the gunboat "to instruct and discipline the crew." Finally, he noted that the *Swan* had been detached from the *Chattahoochee* and the master would thereafter report to Colonel Robertson for his work in defending and obstructing the rivers.

To reinforce his command about a trip downriver to the obstructions, McLaughlin telegraphed Gift: "Remain with your vessel until you hear from me by mail." When that communication reached him, Gift was already losing patience with McLaughlin's procedures. On May 25, he had retaliated by writing Mallory to request that Chief Constructor Porter make an investigation of progress on the *Chattahoochee*.

Lieutenant Gift was a man who had withstood the heat of battle on the *Arkansas*, the deprivation and exposure of his expedition to Apalachicola, and the bitterness of controversy over his orders to a clerk on the *Chattahoochee* the previous May. However, he was not so constituted that he could long withstand the rigors of bureaucratic procedure. Working up a full head of epistolary steam, he devoted a part of Saturday, May 28, to writing McLaughlin:

> From the tenor of your communications and telegrams I perceive that you consider this vessel as yet remaining under your command. I therefore beg that you will furnish me with the precise authority from the Department at Richmond for such assumption on your part. In the absence of such special authority, I beg to remind you that your proceedings are opposed to all precedents and the expressed will of the Hon Secty of the Navy, as communicated to me by himself: wherein he desired me to perform any and all acts which I considered necessary for the speedy outfitting of the vessel, ratifying and confirming all such acts in advance. He further granted me carte blanche upon all Naval Establishments & stores—I now communicate these facts to you officially that there may be no further misunderstanding concerning my rights, provided you have no later and better authority.

On Monday, May 30, McLaughlin carefully copied Gift's letter into his letter book and then wrote Secretary Mallory a systematic rebuttal:

> I have the honor to hand the enclosed communication from Lieut. G. W. Gift Cmdg C. S. Str. Chattahoochee.
>
> The "Communications & Telegrams" therein referred to are I suppose my letter of 22nd & a telegram of 27th inst copy of which herewith enclosed.
>
> I had previously (on 19th—after the return of the late Expedition) sent him a telegram directing him to report to me—which he promptly did.
>
> The letter of the 22nd you readily understand.
>
> My reason for telegraphing him on the 27th was that learning from Mr. Gift it was his wish to visit the obstructions in which at the time he mentioned it, I concurred but I subsequently on being informed by Chf Eng Warner that there was a prospect of obtaining the boilers for the *Chattahoochee* in a short time, I concluded that it was most important for him to remain with the vessel & attend to drilling and disciplining the crew that his vessel might be ready for

service at an early date, I sent the dispatch to detain him until he could receive my letter (an extract of which I now enclose). This letter had not reached Lieut. Gift at the time his communication was written.

Lieut. Gift replied to my telegram of 27th "I had no intention of leaving my vessel" but he had never before informed me of having changed his intentions.

The officers of the vessel are young men with but little experience and the crew being totally unacquainted with the usage and discipline of the service I considered Mr. Gift's constant attention absolutely necessary—up to the time of the Expedition he and his crew had seen but little of each other.

I have too much at heart the interest of our Country & the good of the service to wish to throw any obstacle in Mr. Gift's way in the performance of his duty—on the contrary, I have on all occasions done my utmost to forward his views, & as I cannot for a moment think that the Department would allow me to be placed in the humiliating position as stated by Mr. Gift I shall, until instructed to the contrary, continue to consider him under my command.

On May 31, McLaughlin settled the issue of his authority with a short letter to Gift: "Your communication of the 28th inst has been received. I consider you under my command and any disobedience of orders will be reported to the Secty of the Navy."

On June 2, it was business as usual, as McLaughlin sent Gift a routine order: "I hand herewith Transportation Invoice for 7 in Rifle Cariage & also for the articles requested in your letters of 26th & 27th ult. which have been shipped by Munnerlyn. Should you need any assistance in laying down the Circle inform me & I will send a carpenter from the yard." On June 10, Gift was sent an order from Richmond to transfer the *Chattahoochee* to Columbus and into McLaughlin's charge because preparing the engines would require an additional four months. The mass of administrative detail continued to increase.

On June 13, McLaughlin forwarded to Gift the official government report on the Apalachicola expedition. The report cited McLaughlin's own statement as evidence "that the failure of the object of the Expedition arose in part if not wholly from public discussion of the character of the enterprise which we communicated to the Enemy." After repeating the importance of reticence, the report went on to quote verbatim

McLaughlin's description of Blanc's leaving his boats at the Apalachicola wharf "(after the separation of Lieut. Gift from the party)."

In a division of responsibility, the department's censure devolves upon Blanc, the junior officer, for abandoning the boats and supplies. Gift, the report stated, "seems to have done his duty after having started on the Expedition"; but he did not entirely escape censure. The report concluded, "consequent failure arose it would appear from a public discussion of its object before its departure."

Continuing the push-pull of policies on one level and duties on another, McLaughlin transmitted that report on larger issues and then renewed his attention to smaller issues with a request for specific details of stores lost: "I call your attention to the letter I addressed you under date of May 27th—& now request you will forward that report asked for without further delay." He also enclosed for Gift's signature invoices for the gun carriages and a receipt for Blanc.

McLaughlin had no sooner forwarded the Apalachicola report to Gift than he received a June 15 directive containing a copy of Gift's orders to return the *Chattahoochee* to Columbus. When he telegraphed Capt. S. S. Lee at the Office of Orders and Detail that he had forwarded the dispatch, he also noted that Gift was absent from his command. Moving quickly to obey orders, McLaughlin telegraphed Gift on Friday, June 17, that he was sending the *Uchee* down to tow the gunboat as soon as possible.

This timely response to Captain Lee necessitated a flurry of activity on McLaughlin's part: paying the master a $1,000 advance on the $5,000 towing fee and then summoning all hands to work overtime to replace the steamer's paddle wheel, which had been pulled for repair. Navy yard workers finished the job by 3 P.M. on Sunday afternoon. Because late June and July were the low-water season on the river, a heavy rain and signs of a rise in the river increased the pressure of time to tow the *Chattahoochee* back to Columbus.[107] After taking on a store of wood, the steamer left at 3 P.M. the following Tuesday, June 28. As this work proceeded in such haste in Columbus, Gift had evidently been away until June 17 on a visit to "The Pines" at Saffold.

In arranging for the *Chattahoochee*'s transfer to Columbus, McLaughlin had assured Captain Lee that he could have her returned by June 25. On June 28 the *Uchee* came upon the *Chattahoochee* eighteen miles below Columbus, aground with a propeller broken. Although such a mishap was all too common, McLaughlin made sure Richmond knew of it; he wired Lee for further instructions. On July 2, the ship finally docked in Columbus—and her crew disembarked to receive orders for Savannah.[108]

On July 4, Gift wrote his wife, "My officers are loyal to me to a man, and I am much gratified that we shall not be separated. Upon the whole it was right. I was absolutely wasting my time where I was."[109]

By July 6 he was writing Ellen that he had reached Savannah and was living in very pleasant circumstances ashore while on duty mining the Savannah harbor with torpedoes. He expressed his expectation to return to Columbus once the ironclad had been launched again. By the end of July he was writing about his prospects for commanding a fleet of torpedo boats "to be constructed independent of the Navy." After a month had passed, he was once more proposing to Secretary Mallory a brilliant and daring solution to strategic problems at Apalachicola. His plan called for constructing a fleet of six torpedo boats at Cardys' foundry in Tallahassee. Five carpenters from the *Chattahoochee* could be employed in the work, and "with a little assistance of boiler tubes" from the CNIW, the work could be dispatched quickly to free the west Florida coast around St. Mark's where the railroad connected the port to the interior. The navy's answer was not a transfer to Tallahassee.

By the end of August, Gift was writing instead from the ship *Tallahassee* in Wilmington, preparing to run the blockade. Whether the wife circulated her letters among the family as she had during Gift's courtship is not certain, but he added, "I am sure that Mr. Shackelford will second me in the view that I am doing the best in endeavoring to secure a competency instead of idling about a Naval station. I must persevere and succeed. The golden opportunity must be grasped."[110] By that time, one fact was certain: Gift had missed whatever golden opportunities there may have been in his service along the Chattahoochee River near "The Pines." Competent as officers like him had been under sail in the Old Navy, Gift had become an anachronism in a system where steady, consistent, even plodding bureaucrats like McLaughlin made themselves successful by doing their duty.

Sherman: A Troublesome Customer

As Gift pursued his affairs, McLaughlin and Warner worked to recoup losses of time from Gift's expedition—settling once more into a morass of grinding administrative detail. The slow wearing away of resources in Vicksburg under siege and the exhaustion of Lee's army at Petersburg are vivid images of the Civil War. In time, that same slow and measured decline would be spelled out in business and technical letters from Columbus. Logistics, supply, production schedules, labor, transportation, budget—one by one, each system staggered under the economic and industrial burden of the war and began to collapse. Not only was the industrial situation critical in Columbus, but military pressure mounted as Union strategy sent Grant to engage Lee in Virginia and sent Sherman's army south into Tennessee and Georgia. As naval plans sought an outlet through Apalachicola, Sherman's army was closing in on north Georgia. As the spring and early summer of 1864 wore on, an increasing degree of tension and uneasiness registered in Columbus.

The wide-ranging work of the CNIW became more restricted; suppliers from distant points in the Confederacy disappear from the records. Except for the few Florida suppliers, the tons of scrap iron and feet of tubing and belting almost ceased to arrive from Charleston, Wilmington, and Mobile. Among 118 vouchers paid by the CNIW between January 11 and June 30, 1864, only 14 were to suppliers out of the immediate Columbus-Girard-Eufaula area.

Warner's agents continued to search out and purchase materials or to accompany shipments of machinery to and from various construction sites. William Anderson, J. C. Morton, A. Ravenscroft, S. H. Hill, William A. Campbell, Henry Jetson, George W. Smith, George Mooney, S. L. Mullins, George Chaffin, W. W. Ansell, and Joseph Troslowski— all of these men crisscrossed the South, often on assignment for a week or for a month or more. Reimbursement for lodging, meals, omnibus and rail fares bespeak a constant battle against travel conditions, even if these agents were not officially combatants.

In addition to travel, there was the necessary maintenance of daily operations at the CNIW. A day's labor at $8 was required to repair a bellows. The foundry sieves had to be replaced. A replacement lock for the till had to be located at Schuessler's store. A teakettle was ordered from Hall and Moses for $20. A barrel of salt was ordered for $112. Not until June 30 did C. E. Dexter of the Columbus Gas Light Company receive payment for service from January 1 to April, and then only after a series of notices in the *Columbus Daily Sun* that service would be cut off if bills were not paid.[111]

As McLaughlin worked through June to conclude matters related to the "late unfortunate Expedition," Warner had similar work to keep on schedule. He continued to search for iron for the torpedo boat. Labor presented an increasingly severe problem; not only was the river a ready avenue of escape, but there was the constant competition with the army for men and the constant paperwork to extend the time individuals were detailed to the Columbus works.

The variety of nationalities that the river and sea had brought to Apalachicola and Columbus before 1850 became an increasing problem to the Confederate government. To avoid further service, various workers began claiming foreign citizenship and immunity from prosecution: Louis Arano walked off the job at the CNIW, saying that Warner could not detain him. McLaughlin spent a good portion of June handling the case of Patrick Reedy, a blacksmith who also claimed foreign citizenship.[112]

To handle the massive amount of paperwork for such transactions, Warner had Thomas A. Gilbert's printing company print 300 requisitions for details, 200 recommendations for details, and 240 applications for details. Because a list of men detailed to the Columbus works had to be supplied each month, he paid Gilbert $30 to print their names. He incurred a further expense of $5 to print an advertisement for the return of an absent worker, Bill Hoten.[113] The enrollment officer at Prattville, Alabama, called for a copy of his contract with William Penny to substantiate claims that workers there were employed by the navy for the duration of the war.[114]

As had been the case since the earliest days of operation, scheduled work at other naval stations continued to create peak demands upon the CNIW. In Charleston, the *Columbia* was at a stage of construction that required a series of actions in Columbus. Warner shipped boilers to the station on June 13. On June 20 he sent Chief Engineer Freeman tracings to show how the smoke pipe was to pass through the upper deck and asked for a reply by telegram whether this design would accord with construction of the hull and deck. There were the usual routine exchanges with Wilmington and Savannah for iron, anvils, and payrolls.[115]

As changing conditions in the Confederacy brought corresponding changes in sources of supply and routes of communication, Warner's operations became even slower than usual. Payment of $510 to W. A. Young in Quincy, Florida, necessitated sending cash by the steamer *Indian* to Messrs. Meachum and Brother in Chattahoochee, Florida, with the note: "If there is any kind of communication between Chattahoochee & Quincy you will confer a favor by sending [the money] through [to Young]."[116]

Warner was also sending instructions to Montgomery so that Capt. J. E. Mayhew of the steamer *Iron King* would keep accounts in order. Mayhew's work was very important to Warner, for transport steamers built by the Confederate government on the Alabama River created a vital link in the flow of supplies and production from Columbus to Selma and Mobile.[117]

Coal for both Columbus and Selma was mined in north Alabama near Ragland on the Coosa River. From there it was carried by rail to Selma, or by river to Montgomery, where it could be diverted to Columbus by rail or continue to Selma. Shipped in barges, a ton of coal would be several days in transit even under the best conditions: three days from Ragland to Montgomery and that many or more to Columbus via Opelika. The 50-by-18-by-2½-foot barges made traffic on the Coosa a kind of white-water rafting on a grand scale and any reliable supply of coal a near impossibility.[118] But this daring operation was beginning to relieve, to some degree at least, the chronic shortage of coal for Columbus and Selma. Mayhew's deficiency in accounting weakened an already weak transportation system, and on July 2 Warner transferred Capt. Charles Brockway to Montgomery to replace him on the *Iron King*.[119]

As Warner and McLaughlin fought their own peculiar battles, the navy yard log recorded how they kept north Georgia anxiously in the periphery of vision. On May 17, the log noted Gen. Joseph E. Johnston's fight at Dalton. The May 20 entry contained a reference to action at Kingston wedged in beside a note on the planing mill. May 23 noted "Gen. Johnston falling back" and May 29 referred to more fighting. June 14 noted the death of Gen. Leonidas K. Polk at Kennesaw as Sherman bore down upon Atlanta.[120] Aside from those brief notations, however, neither Warner nor McLaughlin made other references to Sherman in their correspondence through May and June. The plight of McCorkle's naval ordnance work in Atlanta impacted their work in Columbus, but their overall operations continued to function along a line from Charleston and Columbia, through Augusta and Macon, and past Columbus to Montgomery and Selma. Even the *Columbus Daily Sun* carried little more than brief bulletins on the action around Atlanta. Lengthy dispatches about Lee's battles in Virginia appeared on the front page while news of Sherman most often appeared on page two in a column devoted to brief items about action on all fronts.

Once Sherman's December attack upon Savannah created an immediate impact on the Columbus operation, Warner and McLaughlin expressed their concern. Through the summer of 1864, their records reflect their immediate concerns with the work of the navy.

McLaughlin's long letter to Secretary Mallory on June 25 serves well as a progress report of work at Columbus for the first two quarters of 1864. He reported work progressing well on the torpedo boat *Viper*— and "strictly in accordance with" Constructor William A. Graves's plans. Although there were engines on hand at the CNIW that were suitable for the vessel, there was evidently some problem with authorizing their use if the plans did not specify alternative engine designs. Warner had forwarded drawings to Chief Engineer Williamson in the hope of setting that issue to rest.[121] As well as the work had progressed thus far, however, the frames and planking for the boat still awaited installation because no bolts and spikes were available. McLaughlin had been waiting since May 17 for iron from Selma. Not the least of his troubles was the conduct of the blacksmith Reedy. Despite such difficulties, work on the *Jackson* had progressed "as fast as circumstances would permit."

Again McLaughlin used a simple fact to drive home to Mallory his point about work delays: "Mr. Porter's plans and specifications for the new work reached me 13th Mar. Since which time I can assure you that not a moments time has been lost." Adding another edge to the statement, he continued: "Excepting the time required in making the repairs on the Chattahoochee and the time occupied in building & fitting out boats for the late unfortunate Expedition." He also cited bad weather, which delayed outdoor work, and concluded that portion of his report with: "no delay has occured that could by any possible effort on my part be avoided."

He went on to point out delays caused by the nature of the work itself: removing the after part of the shield and a large part of the forward end, fifty-four feet in all; the solid construction of the original work served only to increase the present labor. Nevertheless, the frames were nearly complete and planking ready to begin by the following week.

Responding more directly to the secretary, McLaughlin acknowledged his anxiety about delays that had done "as you say, no credit to the service." By way of an "if you had only listened to me," he added: "I respectfully submit that it has not been through any fault of mine. The vessel was ready for launching Early in Jany and but for the unfortunate error in her construction would have now been ready for any service the

Deprtmt might have required of her." He concluded with a projected completion date of September 1, "but I can scarcely hope to have a chance of getting her into the water before the winter rains set in." Once again, the river would keep him waiting.[122]

McLaughlin did not mention military conditions or the effect they might have on his work, though he or one of his clerks continued to make brief notes about action in Virginia and the progress of the fighting in north Georgia. The *Chattahoochee*'s 32-pounders and nine-inch Dahlgren had been sent to McCorkle for Atlanta's defenses on May 28.[123] By the time McLaughlin wrote his June 25 letter to Mallory, McCorkle was writing to Jones the same day: "Have all surplus stores packed & ready to move. I hope Joseph [E. Johnston] will give me time to save everything."[124] Even in such circumstances, McCorkle took time to note: "McLaughlin & Gift have had a falling out—they don't agree."

Work on the *Jackson* continued to progress at Columbus as action continued around Atlanta. On July 15, McLaughlin's log cited "work progressing rapidly, began calking" and the next day "finished planking bottom." By July 18, Sherman's Atlanta campaign became a sharper reality to Columbus. As the exhausted and depleted Confederate forces were driven back toward Atlanta, the navy began losing its battle for workmen.

The navy yard log notes that "At early dawn this morning the Bells for an Alarm were sounded all the men excepting Company J sent to the front." The men remained until Friday, July 22, dates of very heavy fighting at the DeGress Battery and along the rail line just east of Atlanta toward Decatur. On Saturday July 23 the log simply notes that the men "resumed work."[125]

The CNY and CNIW men had scarcely returned to work when they received news the following Saturday, July 30, that Macon was threatened by attack from Union units moving southwest from Atlanta. The next week brought more bad news—this time from Mobile. As Columbus's strategic location became less and less a safe haven, the workers continued to spend Saturday afternoons at drill.

Despite such added stresses to the system, Warner maintained a steady flow of correspondence with stations at Charleston, Charlotte, and Wilmington. Atlanta had fallen, Sherman had begun laying down a path of destruction toward Macon, Savannah lay in the path of his advance, and work continued much as usual in Columbus.

Work on the *Jackson* had won Warner and McLaughlin notice far beyond the Confederacy and the blockade off Apalachicola. A detailed account of the ship from a Washington, D.C., reporter appeared in the *New York World*. In mid-1864, the ship was still described as a center wheeler, but other data were accurate—even down to the method used to roll and install iron plating. The *Columbus Daily Sun* reprinted the article without editorial comment on June 29, and a Liverpool newspaper carried the identical article on September 14. The article described the ironclad as "a monster" that would exit the port at Apalachicola and join Admiral Buchanan in the Gulf.[126]

Even in such critical times, the CNIW continued to produce results for other stations and to plan further production. Assistant superintendent Whiteside was directed to make an on-site visit at Charleston to check progress on the *Columbia* and return through Savannah to hasten a promised shipment of coal from the *Water Witch*.[127] Warner sent Ashton Ramsay, commander of the naval works in Charlotte, carefully marked instructions about shafting. George W. Smith was sent to Savannah to receive a steam pump from Asst. Engr. Loudon Campbell for delivery to Ingraham at Charleston. Then he was to meet agent Ansell and Chief Engr. E. W. Manning in Wilmington to take charge of a pair of fine English engines, which the *Coquette* had run in through the blockade.[128]

By late 1864, transportation for such shipments had become even more problematic. A system that had always been overtaxed began to falter because of military action. Warner responded to Sherman's presence to the east when he advised Smith either to route the shipment around Augusta or to use his own judgment about travel conditions. Ashton Ramsay's agent from the Charlotte iron works reached Columbus only to discover that his passage to Mobile was blocked by a Union raid's destruction of track on the West Point and Montgomery Railroad. A detour sent him by rail to Union Springs on the Mobile and Girard and then by wagon thirty miles before he could resume rail connections.

On the Chattahoochee, steamers still made regular runs to Eufaula. Facilities were proving their worth when Warner could write that he was sending down a pattern for slide valves and requesting drawings for a piston head in return. The Montgomery-based steamers kept lines open to Selma, but the break in the rail line created a critical delay. Often Warner resorted to horses and wagons for shipping, but care of stock in such a transportation system was a particular concern. Warner had forage but no means to transport it to the teams, and feed could seldom be obtained along the wagon routes; William A. Campbell in Lochapoka and S. L. Mullins at Opelika had to be sent money to buy whatever they could find.

The general shortage of fuel and the inability to haul it made Warner's new coke oven of little use to meet military or civilian needs. He replied to John Mathews at a landing downriver: "We have no Sugar Kettles on hand & for want of Coke are not Casting any. Have now orders that we cannot fill."[129]

As they struggled to keep their facilities in full production, the CNIW and the navy yard found more and more areas of critical shortage. On Monday, September 20, a clerk noted in the log: "Pay day—no money in Pymstrs hands." Continually plagued by labor problems, Warner paused from other concerns to dispatch agents in search of two black workers and to publish a reward of $1,000 for each man.[130] It seemed that Warner and McLaughlin increasingly had to immerse themselves in the most tedious details of management to keep the system moving at all.

With links to the east cut off, Columbus and Selma facilities began to exchange supplies from their limited stores. McLaughlin was able to send Jones a list of items in August: ammonia (at $12.50 for 1¼ pounds), a promise that leather belting would be sent, but "with the exception of what I fear you most need, the shoes." He had tried in vain to get 50 pairs from the local quartermaster in a faltering system slowed almost to a halt. A circular order from the quartermaster general left the sergeant without discretion to act unless he had approval from his commander. The quartermaster advised McLaughlin to advise Jones to apply directly to Gen. A. R. Lawton for an issue of shoes; two cases at the time (120 pairs) could be had, but not 50 pairs, unless Jones had the proper authorization from the quartermaster general himself.[131]

McLaughlin's comment to Jones in an August 30 letter showed their supply and production systems operating within an ever narrower perimeter of safety: "It is thought by some that Sherman is retreating but I am afraid not. I look upon him as a troublesome Customer."[132] In writing Jones, McLaughlin reported the *Chattahoochee* ready except for her boilers, which were en route from the *Raleigh* at Charleston. "I should like to report her ready," he wrote, inasmuch as the Navy Department's scheduled report was coming up in November, "and if you can possibly spare the gun I will be much obliged."[133]

On September 14 he sent Campbell as messenger to Selma with sup-

U.S.S. Isonomia *was one of many Union blockaders off Apalachicola,
where men served hardship duty and fought more battles with weather,
disease, and generally harsh conditions than with Confederate vessels.*
Mariner's Museum, Newport News, Va.

plies for Jones and with a further note about shoes: "I see no Chance
unless you obtain an order from Genl Lawton. If the order comes I will
see that Major Dillard acts promptly in the matter." Even such critical
times left a sentence or two at the end of McLaughlin's letter to mention
Gift. If Jones were planning a trip to Columbus, "I want to show you a
correspondence between Gift & myself."[134]

Amid the delays, the reporting schedule for the *Chattahoochee*
passed McLaughlin by; Mallory's November 5 report on Navy Department operations noted only the expectation that she would "soon be put
in commission again." Overall, Columbus showed well in the report: the
Jackson "on the stocks and ready for launching as soon as the river rises"
and a torpedo boat "in a state of great forwardness." And for all the
difficulties and delays that McLaughlin and Warner were battling in
Columbus, the CNIW showed to excellent advantage throughout the
report of vessels in progress elsewhere. While the work force at Richmond had been called to the field, Columbus was turning out machinery
for Wilmington, Charleston, Savannah, and Mobile.[135]

Although the report went on to cite the shortage of iron (which would
prevent fully plating the *Jackson*), the shortage of coal (which would
slow the iron work necessary for completing machinery), and the difficulties of transporting coal (which, with other transportation delays,
would delay CNIW work), a department report could not adequately
convey the daily pressures of work in Columbus.

Union blockading officers on the Gulf were receiving their own reports from refugees and deserters. They were highly aware of the industrial capabilities of Columbus. First on a list submitted to Adm. Cornelius K. Stribling from Lt. Cdr. Edward Simpson of the *Isonomia* was the CNIW, "employing 400 white men." Next were the 175 workers employed at Haiman's manufacturing pistols, swords, and bayonets. Major Humphries was named as head of the ordnance works and supervisor of 150 white men and 150 white women who turned out saddles, bridles, harness, equipment for the artillery, shot, shell, and work in an ordnance laboratory. Major Dillard was named as quartermaster in charge of a tannery and shoe factory employing 225 white men and 25 men engaged in tailoring uniforms for the army.

Simpson continued with war-related industries: Grant's cotton factory employing 75 men, Brown's factory employing about 200 white men, and Fountain's factory with 60 white male workers. Winters's paper mill employed 25 white men. Simpson gave only a line to the fact that all these work forces were nearly doubled by the slave population of the area, some employed at regular wages and others impressed and working by contract with their owners. His figures address the Union's need to know the amount of armed resistance the Confederates might mount to an attack on the area; even more important, the economic war against the ability to wage war—as the blockaders carried out that strategy against saltworks—also figured prominently in the emphases of his report.

Absent from Simpson's report was the concern so often expressed from blockading officers earlier in the war. One person after another had come aboard the Union vessels to tell appreciably the same story: construction was delayed, be it on the *Chattahoochee* or the *Jackson;* machinery was inoperable or unavailable; batteries were incomplete; and, in any case, drafts were probably so heavy that the warships would fall victim to navigational conditions before they could break out into Apalachicola Bay to victimize the blockading fleet.

The only possible cause for concern lay in reports that Confederate Army Capt. J. L. Dunham had a company of about 140 men and four guns near Iola Landing and Ricko's Bluff on the Apalachicola below Chattahoochee, Florida. The steamer *W. H. Young* served as his headquarters while his men camped without tents and their families lived in the Chattahoochee Arsenal. Other river steamers also kept up regular commerce along the rivers: the *Jackson, Munnerlyn, Mist, Uchee,* and *Marianna.*[136]

The Union Army was also compiling a series of reports on the area. M. D. McAlester of the Office of Chief Engineer in New Orleans filed an October report from Apalachicolan Harrison Lewis about soundings and channels in the Apalachicola area. Lewis cited Elias Roderick on St. George's Island as a pilot "who knows every inch of the bay and adjacent waters."[137]

Capt. E. H. Newton, engineer in charge at Barrancas, filed an October 17 report from three members of the First Florida Cavalry; each man could pilot boats to the head of navigation at Columbus on the Chattahoochee or to Albany on the Flint. They reported the channel depths at Chattahoochee, Fort Gaines, Georgetown, Barber's Shoals, and Bainbridge as well—reading into the Union's strategic inventory the familiar names of landings and navigational landmarks in the river system. They reported the obstructions partially washed away and a schooner, doubtless the *Kate L. Bruce*, at anchor and ready to sink in the Apalachicola River.[138]

That Union engineers and planners, and not just officers or men of war, entered the reporting process is a telling sign for late 1864. There is in the army reports and inventories a recognition that forces were present to resist a Union attack; problems of navigation they had always with them. But there is also a certain assured objectivity that no such obstacle would be insuperable.[139]

I Am Inclined to the Opinion that Savannah Is Lost

Daily notations and correspondence at the CNIW and CNY create a taut chronology through November and December of 1864 as there were more immediate pressures than the blockaders on the Gulf. Chronic shortages of supplies and labor had become acute and were fast terminating some functions of the production system. Atlanta and Mobile fell and Sherman moved toward Savannah. Columbus's communications flow continued a shift toward Selma as one of the few installations still untouched by military action. Just as war had forced the affluent travelers of the plantations along the rivers to constrict their world from the easy passage by steamer and rail, Warner and McLaughlin had begun to function like the Dents, Shorters, McNabbs, Shackelfords, and Munnerlyns: borrowing, bartering, and keeping in close touch with their nearest neighbor, Catesby ap R. Jones at Selma. Keeping naval facilities productive was becoming a more and more desperate battle.

On November 1, Warner wrote Jones a letter that is also a record of the pressures of work, shortages, and delays. A small railroad engine, "The Black Dwarf," had been located for hauling coal. Upon inspection, Warner found it "a pretty 'hard case'" but promised to try to have it up and running by the middle of the month. There was also pressure to complete work for Flag Officer Ebenezer Farrand at Mobile. And there was the endless inventory of supplies to be searched out: ammonia (perhaps more could be located at Mobile), shellac (not enough, but Warner would divide with Jones), and the list of nails with the required sizes (misplaced, would Jones send another? And could he, in turn, supply Warner with belting?).

From such concerns, Warner went on to McLaughlin's project, the "Muscogee" (or *Jackson*), which he reported "about ready for launching." With the launch plans were "prospects" for opening Apalachicola and *"blockade running."*[140]

McLaughlin supplied his own account in a November 15 letter to Jones. The ship lacked only the iron on her shield; and echoing his words of the previous year, "she is all ready for the next rise in the river." The boilers for the *Chattahoochee* had arrived and required only the steam drums. The *Viper* was only three weeks shy of completion. He now needed guns for the ironclad from Selma and had left a place forward to receive them; but his tone changed from previous requests for the *Chattahoochee*'s rifle: "I have not asked for them sooner as I thought there were other points which needed them more." Echoing many previous hopes, he wrote: "I . . . am in hopes the Government will turn their attention toward this point. Now that the enemy is making such strenuous efforts to clear the port of Wilmington I think the advantages that would present themselves upon opening the port of Apalachicola would be a strong enducement to use extraordinary efforts to complete this vessel."

McLaughlin's letter concluded with a graceful touch that delays, shortages, the rigors of travel, and the imminent clash with ignorant armies had not erased: "Mrs. McL wishes to be kindly remembered."[141]

Three days later, Sherman's advance on Savannah called a halt to work at the CNY and CNIW, leaving "only the negro force with sufficient white men to keep them employed—and guard these works."[142] Warner also set about securing supplies against the possibility of an attack. Copper, sheet iron, and other stores were loaded on the *Swan* and shipped to Eufaula, with orders to J. W. Young to secure them in scattered caches.[143]

A November 28 letter from McLaughlin to Jones about the seven-inch rifle strings together reports of the destruction of the railroad at Macon by 1,000 cavalry, disrupted communication, and a matter-of-fact determination to work within the limitations imposed by bad news. He concluded with a series of rapid-fire sentences: The "Muscogee which I am now waiting to launch has been named the Jackson after the Capital of Mississippi. The Naval Battalion has been ordered to the front; I leave tomorrow to take command." And as a parting word, "When am I to look for the Jackson's guns?"[144]

Warner's response to Sherman's Savannah campaign was reflected in a very strong letter to Mallory. Unlike the July call for men to shore up the defense of Atlanta, the November call for his workers resulted in their being placed in a regular unit under the command of McLaughlin, the essential counterpart of his work in Columbus. Not only was that unwise in terms of continued production, it was unfair; the Macon operatives were sent back to their jobs once danger to their city had passed. Yet Warner's force from Columbus was unaccountably hastened to Savannah. Moreover, the local newspaper on that very morning had pointed out such inequities in the clipping that Warner enclosed for Mallory's perusal.[145]

The need for Confederate forces near Savannah overrode Warner's need to resume full operations. Rivalry between navy and army for manpower now tipped the balance toward the army. Warner was cast back upon such ability as he had at hand.

With his clerks absent in Savannah, the "pr. Stockton" and "pr McGehee" of Warner's letter book were replaced by Warner's writing. The steady, persistent tone of Warner's letters to Jones also began to give way to comments on the disasters at hand. Just more than a month after Mallory's official and generally optimistic report on the status of the department and vessels under construction, these field notes stand in sharp contrast to the official word from Richmond:

I am inclined to the opinion that Savannah is lost—had a letter from there on the 7th in which I was informed that they were preparing to throw overboard the Machinery from the Iron Clad

"Milledgeville" (recently launched) and that they were prepared to capsize and burn the large Iron Clad up on the stocks. The opinion was expressed that Savannah could not hold out, and in any event would soon be starved out. Sherman has all three R. Roads—the Albany & Gulf, the Central and the Charleston & Savannah. He will therefore have Savannah a most eligible base from which to operate in future.

With the fall of Savannah the Navy will lose heavily—the Iron Clad "Savannah," the Battery "Georgia" (not much acct. except for the iron on her), the Milledgeville recently launched having her engines on board & partially Cld.—the Iron Clad building by Messrs Kinston & Hawks—all complete except the plating—and several wooden Gun Boats—among them the "Water Witch." We shall lose severely in Men. I have reason to believe that all of our men will either be Killed or Captured. The position they occupy is such that they are entirely surrounded by the Yankees—with no possible chance of escape. We have been most shamefully treated in this matter by the Military Authorities. We were regularly swindled out of these men. I am thoroughly disgusted—I have been rendering assistance to the Army, but now I would not let them have a six penny Nail.[146]

Having let fly those statements, Warner returned perforce to short business communications. Interwoven in them, however, is his underlying bitterness and frustration. To Capt. J. F. Jaiman at Selma: "I may not be able to find a valve that will send. We cannot make one as our men have been all taken and sent to Savannah—which is probably the last of them. I have an anchor down the river which I will send you as soon as it arrives—I had one at Savannah which I intended for you but I presume it is in the hands of the Yankees."

To Jones at Selma: "Our work being stopped, and our men captured by the Yankees, relieve our necessities very much on the matter of Coal."[147]

Launched at Last

Despite Warner's gloomy mood, there was significant success to report in Columbus in the Friday, December 23, edition of the *Enquirer.* Finally, the *Jackson* had been launched:

C.S.S. Jackson, *in a photograph apparently taken soon after her launching on December 22, 1864. The large opening in the forward end of the casemate was left for installing the vessel's armament and steam machinery. The indistinct shape behind the* Jackson's *stern is the C.S.S.* Chattahoochee *with awnings rigged over exposed machinery spaces.*
Louisiana Historical Association Collection, Tulane

This splendid ram was successfully launched yesterday at about 11 o'clock and now sits as calmly upon the Chattahoochee as a duck upon a pond. Mr. Chas. Blain, her builder, superintended the launching, while Capt. S. H. Hill, the indefatigable superintendent at this place of the Southern Express Company, commanded on board during the launching. Too much praise cannot be bestowed upon the manner in which the whole affair was conducted. An eyewitness says that she glided into the water so smoothly and easily that there was not motion sufficient to have shaken the water in a tumbler. Capt. Hill informs us that after launching he went entirely through her and that she did not leak a parcel. She draws now five feet four inches forward and four feet three inches aft, and it is judged that after all her machinery and armament is aboard she will not draw six feet. Those capable of judging who have examined this craft inform us that she is one of the snuggest and most compact, and securely built craft yet afloat upon our waters. Success to her say we, and may she be manned by able and capable officers who will neither get scared and blow her up or stick her in the mud the first time a booger says booh at her.[148]

The *Daily Sun* also reported the event:

LAUNCHED AT LAST

The gunboat *Muscogee*, we believe that's the name, was launched yesterday about twelve o'clock and a beautiful launch it was—she glided so gently into the river that the water in a glass would hardly have been spilled. At first her motion down the "way" was scarcely perceptible, but soon she moved quickly to take her place amid the waters, and now she sits there like a thing of life and beauty.

This boat has been building here over two years, and has cost enough to build a number of "Alabamas." Her first model, about a year ago, was rejected, and the present one adopted. It was built under the superintendence of Lieut. McLaughlin, of the Confederate States Navy. Capt. Charles Blain, one of the most superb of boat builders, was master mechanic, and he has done this work perfectly. She does not leak a particle. Capt. Blain personally superintended the successful launch. He never yet at Columbus has failed in one.[149]

After the editorial criticism of the *Jackson*, the Columbus papers were full of pride for the feat—less patriotic pride for the Confederate Navy than civic pride because the Columbus area had contributed so much. The navy had scored a double victory over two fickle adversaries: the river and public opinion.

An Early County writer signing himself "Farmer" chose the launch date to fire off a barrage of criticism at Columbus and the entire naval operation there. After an attack upon the rapacious speculators who sought only to profit from the war, "Farmer" took his text upon the *Jackson:*

She is much larger and looks a good deal stronger than *our* gunboat, the *Chattahoochee*. She has sloping sides which are to be covered with iron to keep out cannon balls, and generally, I am of the opinion, that she would do very well if *completed!* You naturally enquire, when will she be done? I did the same of a person who seemed to know something of such matters,—and received for answer an ominous shake of the head, accompanied with the words, "After the war is over." The whole affair appears to be in a hopeless state of incompletion.

Not content with his critique of the ship itself, the writer went on to level charges against McLaughlin: "The person having charge of this work is one McLaughlin, who I understand is in the navy, however, I have never noticed such a name in any of the papers connected with a naval engagement, consequently I incline to doubt the information, and take him to be one of the many speculators engaged on contracts for *themselves* and the Government."

Near the close of his letter, however, the writer's partisanship for Early County began to emerge:

The job of building was taken away from our enterprising fellow citizen, Col. David S. Johnston, and transferred to Columbus and its present inefficient contractor. We all know what Col. J. did in the building of the *Chattahoochee;* we know that he commenced without improvement, and no other material than was growing in the woods, and in a few months produced a gunboat; and further know that had he been given the contract on the present unfinishable folly, it would long since have proved a terror to the enemy and the pride of our country. At present it is nothing, a mere drain to pour money into, an excuse to keep a speculator and a crowd of skulkers out of the ranks.

"Farmer" ended with a plea that the citizenry speak up so that the government might know the falseness of its agents and remove them before it was too late.[150]

Conditions in the Confederacy as a whole, and in the river system that had been so prosperous four years before, were desperate enough to explain the venting of such anger. The songs and fireworks and fiery oratory of the secession parties of Christmas 1860 had died away. The men who had built the *Jackson* were called away to defend Savannah, which, as people in Columbus had no way of knowing, would become Sherman's Christmas present to Mr. Lincoln.

With so many men absent, and in a town crowded with displaced persons, Columbus was not preparing for a festive holiday. The front page of the *Daily Sun* carried a list of unclaimed letters sent to refugees via general delivery at the Columbus post office; the list increased to one and then two columns as a barometer of homelessness. A local military hospital was advertising its need for 1,000 turkeys, 1,000 pounds of butter, 1,000 pounds of sweet potatoes, eggs, onions, red pepper, pickles, and soft soap. For farmers there was a "recipe" on how to use corn stalks for feed. In Auburn, Alabama, William F. Samford was advertising his 720-acre plantation for sale.

For Christmas shoppers, Sanford and Company advertised "BLOCKADE GOODS! NOW'S THE TIME TO INVEST." The list included 100 pairs of ladies' shoes, five gross of silk shoestrings, five dozen French felt hats, fifty reams of English note paper, 20,000 envelopes, 100 dozen spools of "Coates thread," and 200 dozen spools of Clark thread.

Cultural pursuits were not neglected in the news. The theater season was beginning at Temperance Hall with a performance of *Lady of the Lake*. Readers were no doubt interested in the page-one filler from London: two Shakespeare autographs had been discovered in a 1496 Book of Common Prayer purchased in a lot of waste paper. Page two of the November 20 *Sun* contained a list of the British royal family— including the birth and wedding dates of each of Queen Victoria's nine children—and a list of members of the House of Lords.[151]

Only scraps of news came back from the Navy Battalion. The *Sun* printed a notice November 25 that [Militia] Capt. L. H. Golder would take messages and some small packages to Savannah if they could be left at the iron works office. News of tragedy returned soon after the men were underway: Joseph B. Hill fell to his death between two rail cars at Butler. There was a report in the December 21 *Sun* that a part of the men had been captured though others had made a hairbreadth escape down the Altamaha and Ogechee rivers. On Christmas Eve, the *Sun* reported that a black who had accompanied the Navy Battalion had reached Columbus with a letter; the men were camped six miles from Savannah.[152] Such concerns overrode the pride and relief that the *Jackson* was launched at last.

It was a bitter Christmastide all along the rivers. The churches were in constant use for prayer and days of special services.[153] Casualty lists left many families in mourning. In Barbour County, John Horry Dent heard of Horry's death from yellow fever the previous July.[154] At "The Refuge" young Charles Munnerlyn, the homesick schoolboy of a few years before, left for the army, "swallowing his tears and sobbing in spite of himself" in bidding his family good-bye.[155] George Gift was at home at "The Pines" for Christmas, furloughed from the *Olustee* to recuperate from ill health.[156] Ellen, now pregnant with their first child, had feared for his safety. But he did return, bringing with him three bottles of champagne and some fine old sherry for Mrs. Shackelford and guitar strings smuggled through the blockade for Ellen. He also brought with him accounts of family friends in Savannah and of tea tables very scantily supplied.

Farther south along the river at the Chattahoochee Arsenal, Confederate troops camped without tents while the splendid buildings served as barracks for their families. Below Chattahoochee, at the remote posts along the river, at least the winter season was fever free. Even if news of the *Jackson*'s launch had reached the blockade, an attack from the Union Navy did not pose the immediate threat to west Florida that bands of deserters presented. Both a threat and an embarrassment to state officials, the force had swelled to 2,219; and in real terms, they held undisputed military control of most of west Florida. When a force of 80 Confederates were sent out to hunt deserters at one point in 1864, 57 of them deserted to the Union.[157]

Off Apalachicola on the almost derelict ferryboat *Fort Henry*, Acting Volunteer Lt. I. B. Baxter anxiously reported to Acting Rear Adm. Cornelius K. Stribling of the East Gulf Blockading Squadron. The *Jackson* was ready to launch in Columbus, the *Chattahoochee* was undergoing thorough repair, and a torpedo boat was nearly complete. The *Jackson* was said to be "more formidable than the Tennessee," and the Confederates "are making every preparation to make a raid on the blockade at this place." More than one squadron commander received more than one such report. The blockade force off Apalachicola had not been increased by December 31 or by January 16, 1865, and probably would not be.[158] Stripes and epaulets were being won elsewhere in the Union Navy. All remained quiet on the Apalachicola blockade; the town itself remained a ghost town.

Even in the absence of fighting action, the war had worked a frightful destruction along the rivers. At Bleak House in Barbour County, the grieving John Horry Dent reflected in his diary: "Christmas sad & gloomy. Our once merry and prosperous days have past. War! with all its heroes, troubles, and sorrows has overtaken our land, and left its traces broad cast."[159]

CHAPTER 7

Concluding the Business of War

Columbus Navy Yard in April 1865
Leslie's Illustrated

In Richmond, Secretary Mallory used the first week of 1865 to write a status report for President Davis. Conditions in the navy were, to some extent, hopeful. Citing the work at Selma, Charlotte, Richmond, Atlanta, and Columbus, Mallory also noted the lack of skilled laborers, the shortage of iron, the difficulty with transportation, and the shortage of supplies—most of the difficulties, in fact, that the very earliest reports to the Navy Department had included. Now, however, there was an additional burden on an already overtaxed system—skilled workers being called away from navy projects to fight the last desperate battles of the war as soldiers.[1]

Reports on that administrative level could hardly have concerned the weary men who returned from Savannah to Columbus. En route home they saw sights the official reports did not catalog: thousands of refugees, most of them women and children, housed in huts and abandoned railroad cars along a hundred-mile stretch between Columbus and Fort Valley, subsisting on a government ration of corn meal.[2]

Official logistics could not adequately picture the trains crowded with the staff and patients of entire hospitals on the move, or towns like Americus, Albany, Smithville, LaGrange, Opelika, Eufaula, and Columbus housing wounded in every available shelter. The Navy Battalion who saw such sights knew that there would be no more crews making the trips to and from the CNIW and the Savannah Squadron. The machinery they had installed and repaired had, when put to the test, failed to save Savannah. The *Savannah* had been operational, but the Confederates' own torpedoes blocked her passage to sea; then her heavy draft prevented an escape upriver. The smaller wooden gunboat *Macon* turned and fled, powered upriver to Augusta by CNIW engines. By Christmas 1864, Sherman had closed the books on the CNIW's Savannah operation, and neither their labor in Columbus nor their military duty in Savannah worked to prevent that.

Members of the Navy Battalion stacked their arms and took up their tools again on January 6, exactly four years after a beleaguered ordnance sergeant had opened the Chattahoochee Arsenal to Florida forces and, with it, opened the rivers to war. They still had much work to accomplish if the rivers were to be open again and the blockade lifted. High water in the river, which had finally launched the *Jackson*, cut with a double edge; through January and February, rain and cold impeded their work. At times, economic and military conditions almost stopped their work altogether.

By the last week of January, McLaughlin and Warner were once again fully engaged in their technical work of readying the *Jackson*, the *Chattahoochee*, and the *Viper* in expectation of action. To that point toward the end of the war, they had first adapted to conditions of the blockade; then they had learned to accomplish their work within an inefficient system for distributing insufficient supplies. By late 1864, steady Union encroachments upon their supply sources and upon distribution points at naval construction sites forced their work into the narrow compass of

Columbus and whatever communications they were able to maintain with naval facilities in Selma. The conditions combined to place Columbus facilities in a state of siege; yet, with a concentration upon technical matters amounting almost to tunnel vision, the two continued to work at their projects until Union forces began to move upon their works.

Work had scarcely resumed in Columbus before the Union navy at Apalachicola made plans to act upon reports of military activity by the steamer *W. H. Young* around Ricko's Bluff and Chattahoochee, Florida.

On January 16, the Union bark *Midnight* dispatched a boat expedition from its blockading station at St. Andrew's west of Apalachicola. The mission was to capture the *Young*, said to be transporting supplies from Columbus to the Confederate garrison at Ricko's Bluff. The Union strategy was to travel overland to the Chipola River, enter the Apalachicola above the obstructions, and ambush the steamer as it tied up at Ricko's.

On the afternoon of January 16, a party of thirty men under the command of Acting Master Charles Cadieu left the *Midnight* in two boats armed with a howitzer. Ascending a creek as far as possible from St. Andrew's, the group concealed the launch in a lagoon near Wetapo Creek. Working their way inland, the party held a prearranged meeting with three Confederate deserters at noon the next day. One of them led Cadieu and several others to his home, where he gave the Union party a yoke of oxen and a wagon for transporting their second boat overland to the Chipola River.

Cadieu's party remained in the vicinity of Ricko's Bluff for a week, exploring the nearby tributaries to the Apalachicola and keeping a close watch upon the movements of the Confederate garrison there. They received reports that the steamer was expected daily, but an incident on the evening of January 24 caused them to abandon the plan of waiting to capture the *Young*.

At seven o'clock that night a small slave girl stumbled upon the picket guard that Cadieu had posted near his camp. Ignoring their orders to halt, she escaped—carrying, Cadieu was certain, news of the Union's presence to the garrison at Ricko's. A council of war among the group led to the decision to move immediately while they could still do so with an element of surprise.

The Union party first accosted five Confederates at a nearby camp and took their horses and arms without firing a shot. Moving on the guard post at Ricko's Bluff, they captured the picket guard of four men and burned a storehouse containing a large quantity of corn.

During the Union soldiers' absence from their camp, a group of about thirty contrabands gathered there. When they asked that they be taken to the Gulf, Cadieu agreed to let them travel with his party. Setting out on the morning of January 25, they returned overland and reached the *Midnight* four days later.[3]

Confederates who had escaped capture were aware of the Union's presence around Ricko's Bluff and were particularly intent upon recapturing some horses that Cadieu had left behind. James M. Dancy described his company's search for the horses on a "bitter cold night." The Confederate troop had to ford a creek and somehow find a match and dry wood for a fire to save themselves from freezing. Once they reached Ricko's Bluff, they approached carefully because of signs they had learned to read in the wild: they heard swarms of bees among broken gum trees left by the Union incursion.

They sought out and questioned an old woman standing in the door of her cabin. Asked whether she had the missing horses, she replied that she "did not expect to give them to any rebel." When the officer said he was duty-bound to take the horses to headquarters, she said he "would do so over her dead body." That expedient did not become necessary, but the Confederates arrested the old woman and accomplished their mission by tearing down her lot fence to free the horses.[4]

Cadieu's force, in the meantime, remained in the area instead of returning to the *Midnight* with the main body of Union men. Eleven men under the command of Acting Ensign Gruff took a small boat through the Chipola cutoff and Gum Swamp and into the Apalachicola below the obstructions. Their objective was Fort Gadsden, which they reached on the night of January 26. After capturing a sergeant and a private there, they searched along the river for three other guards who were residents of the area nearby.

The net gain of the two expeditions was one lieutenant, three sergeants, twelve privates, and nineteen stands of arms, along with forty-three contrabands returned to the Union. The most significant accomplishment of the expedition was the destruction of the warehouse containing an estimated 150 bushels of corn.

Even though the force from the *Midnight* had seen little that could pose any threat to the blockade, strength was increased during February and March. On February 1, the *Matthew Vasser*, a mortar schooner with a battery of three guns, joined the *Beauregard, Fort Henry, Somerset*, and *Sunflower*, all of which had held the blockade for several months. On February 15 the *Mahaska* with ten guns and a crew of 145 joined this group at Apalachicola.

Two weeks later the *Fort Henry* and the *Mahaska* were sent east to St. Mark's to join a large group of vessels, no doubt to support the Union Army's movement to Tallahassee in March. This force of seven steamers and three schooners placed strength of forty-nine guns and 722 men within easy striking distance of Apalachicola.

Even though the raid struck relatively close to Columbus, reports of such action were quite minor in comparison to events elsewhere in the Confederacy. Fort Fisher on the North Carolina coast fell in a final assault begun January 13. Conclusive action at other ports along the Atlantic coast freed a sufficient number of Union vessels to close off Wilmington by early February. Sherman had begun his move upon Charleston. With this gloomy news of the war came a report that another CNIW project had come to naught. The ironclad *Columbia*—only recently completed and one of Warner's finest accomplishments—ran aground in Charleston harbor and sustained irreparable damage.

Striking even closer home than either the Apalachicola River raid or news from the Atlantic coast was a second attack from "Farmer" in the January 11 edition of the *Early County News*. An accompanying editorial took up "Farmer's" charges. The writer defended D. S. Johnston as a contractor who could have completed an ironclad by August 1863, and charged McLaughlin with delays, corruption, and incompetence: "At the end of the year it was confidently hoped that we would hear favorable things. But we were to be disappointed. The contrivance was a failure, and had to be altered; and now another year has nearly passed, and still it is not finished!"

Not content with criticism of McLaughlin, the writer played upon the fears of the people, called upon analogies to military service, and reached a fever pitch by invoking the actions of Napoleon who "purged his army of incompetent, neglectful and dishonest persons by shooting a few Quartermasters and Commissaries; and it is to be deplored that the same power is not lodged in some party in the Confederacy."

Overlooking the necessity for routine industrial transport as well as warships, the writer launched a particularly vitriolic attack upon the *Shamrock:*

It can be shown that he has permitted skilled labor to be diverted from the public work, to be employed upon that of a private nature. . . . This is almost too preposterous to believe—yet it is so—a steamboat complete and perfect, built, as we have already described, is now navigating the Chattahoochee River, and the gunboat is, as our correspondent remarks, "in a helpless state of incompletion!"

The attack ended with a resounding call that McLaughlin be removed and "brought to trial and punishment by a Military Court."[5]

These attacks set off a chain reaction of speculation among McLaughlin, Jones, and Warner. As news of one disaster after another reached them and as their own work was jeopardized by each new bulletin, they took time—and precious paper—in letters about this latest episode in the Gift affair. In a long letter dated January 24, McLaughlin wrote Jones that not only did he suspect Gift to be the author but that D. S. Johnston had implicated Gift "during a state of intoxication." McLaughlin's strongest evidence, however, was his feeling that "attacking people thru the public prints seems to be a favorite method of Mr. Gift to carry out his vindictive spirit."

In some sense, McLaughlin had already satisfied his honor in the matter of Gift. Before the letter's publication on January 11, McLaughlin had met with Mallory during his trip to Richmond. He confided to Jones that he had "spoken plainly" to the secretary and also mentioned to John Mercer Brooke "Mr. Gift's unfitness to command." Perhaps more politic than affirming, Mallory had "seemed" to agree but had "remarked that he did not see how we could dispense with his services." McLaughlin ends his long letter by asking Jones's advice.

Neither personal battles at home nor reports of naval action elsewhere deterred naval activities in Columbus. Pleased to find the *Jackson* afloat when he returned from Richmond, McLaughlin set about making alterations to place her on a more even keel. He described to Jones how he had moved the coal bunkers aft thirty-five feet and also located the magazine and shell room aft, confident all the while that the addition of stores, the battery, and her crew would not increase the draft over six feet. He also reported that he would dispatch Golder to Selma to discuss delivery of iron plating.[6]

Jones continued his interest in the *Jackson*'s progress and his response about Gift was immediate and pragmatic: "Tis not worth notice as long as it is confined to that paper. Where Johnston is praised I would prefer being abused." In writing Jones about the matter, Warner took a similarly practical view: "He [Gift] has over reached himself and by his bitterness and venom has no doubt rendered the attack comparatively harmless."[7]

That personal comment in Warner's letter to Jones shows a stronger bond developing between the two men. McLaughlin's letters of course maintain a warm and friendly tone, especially in his January 24 note: "Rumor says you are about to commit Matrimony. I have heard it from so many different people that I am half inclined to believe it. Do let me know in time to order a new suit of Confederate grey." And once again, "Mrs. McL wishes to be Kindly remembered." Such departures from the business at hand were rare, however, for these men were under severe pressures of work in two of the last operational industrial sites in the Confederacy.

One after another, however, outlets for their production closed. Their general concerns for the Confederacy increased, and their letters ranged further from technical subjects. Warner continued to pass along to Jones news of progress at Columbus. On January 28, he estimated that the *Jackson* would be ready for action in six weeks to two months. He projected a similar completion date for having steam on the *Chattahoochee* and *Viper* as well—"to give a chance for some of the evacuated officers from lost ports." To aid Jones's work, Warner was shipping iron—returned from Eufaula once the Sherman scare had passed—and promising more "as soon as I can get it through from Charleston, where I have plenty." Noting conditions elsewhere in the Confederacy, Warner wrote, "Savannah gone, Wilmington going, is encroaching upon the naval sphere of operations. We will soon be restricted to river navigation. I understand that Mobile will, in all possibility 'go up' if an attempt is made by the Yankees to take it."[8]

In that inventory, Warner must surely have assessed the effectiveness of his own contribution at each point of conflict: the *Savannah* blown up by her own crew to avoid capture; the *Wilmington* to be destroyed on the ways at Wilmington; the Bigbee Boats never launched to defend Mobile; the *Tuscaloosa* and *Huntsville* launched but used as floating batteries; the *Gaines* grounded to escape capture the previous August; and by early 1865, only the *Morgan* at Mobile to stand for the CNIW's heroic labor.

In the same letter—and with singular optimism—Warner shared with Jones his plan for a *Monitor*-class vessel: 175 feet long, 45-foot beam, 9-foot depth of hold with a 6-foot draft. The design would be topped by a tower: 21 feet in diameter within and plated with 11½ inches of iron over 14 inches of wood. Guns with an 11-inch bore would make the vessel quite formidable, but Warner needed specs for the 11-inch guns from Jones so that he could incorporate them in the tower design. Estimated completion date for such a vessel from start-up in the spring of 1865: early 1866.

Jones replied on February 2 with a tracing of the eleven-inch gun and with encouragement about the design and effectiveness of such a vessel. A revolving turret would offer great advantages to a ship confined to navigation in a river, but particular care should be taken to avoid the initial Union mistake of not providing sufficient strength to protect the turning mechanism at the turret's base. He added that McLaughlin had sent him a picture of the *Jackson*, "a very fine looking vessel." "Her battery ought to be heavier," he noted; certainly the Selma works were already hard at work to remedy that.[9]

Before Warner had time to receive Jones's reply about his new ironclad, he submitted a lengthy design proposal to Mallory dated February 3.[10] Within the context of the recorded history of the moment, such plans seem almost incredibly optimistic. Whatever the long-range plans, however, there was also the short term to consider: shipping and rolling the iron for the *Jackson*'s guns[11] and facilitating the process with a bit of bureaucratic politics. "I think if you had come here yourself," Jones wrote, "you would have got your iron much sooner. Colonel Hunt is very susceptible to personal influence."[12]

Such messages continued to pass back and forth every few days until, on February 17, Jones wrote that he would ship two seven-inch guns the following week. That hopeful news came at the same time that the news from Charleston was disastrous, for the city was being evacuated the day Jones wrote. Adjusting to that news, he wrote alerting McLaughlin to intercept a ten-inch gun and an eleven-inch gun being shipped to Charleston and reverse their direction to Mobile. One disaster followed another until, by late February, communications with Richmond were cut off.

As they could not know in Columbus or Selma, Mallory was trying to communicate orders that would have concentrated Confederate naval action in Columbus. He addressed a February 24 letter to John Newland Maffitt in Nassau, outlining a plan whereby Maffitt might employ the shallow-draft blockade runners *Owl* and *Chameleon* to enter shallow coastal waters. He authorized Maffitt to exercise more than one option.

He might send either ship into a southern port that would permit drafts no deeper than six feet. He might sell the *Chameleon* at Nassau, purchase a smaller vessel, and buy arms to run through the blockade. Or he might deliver the ships to their owners in Liverpool.

While allowing Maffitt latitude to take what he considered the best course, Mallory described one option in detail: "You can enter Apalachicola Bay [with a 5½- to 6-foot draft] and pass the 'Bulk Head,' a mound built near the city, and go up the river to Columbus, Georgia." Maffitt chose to make sail for Liverpool, but he saved Mallory's letter and, in later years, noted that it had been the last order issued by the Confederate Navy Department.[13]

Lacking department orders of any sort, Warner expressed doubt that he could receive approval to begin constructing his turreted ironclad. On March 1, he wrote Jones of more routine matters. Of the continued bad weather he said, "But I suppose it will be unfavorable for the Yankees, should they desire to give us a call," and he noted the "considerable dread of a Yankee raid in this direction." As had become his custom, he commented on overall conditions in the Confederacy:

> I suppose the Department would be somewhat discouraged from the attempt at building ironclads or other vessels, as so many have been lost, three at Savannah and six at Charleston (four in commission and two unfinished). I believe they have also abandoned the completion of the one at Wilmington. If they evacuate Richmond, which is not improbable, there will be but very little of the Navy left. There is not much now, but because we lose vessels, we should not cease to build them.[14]

As the Confederacy crumbled elsewhere, he and McLaughlin and Jones had no plans to cease building ships and guns. On March 3, news about the *Jackson*'s battery was good. Many months of personal assurances about delivery became official written notice when Jones ordered his agent in Montgomery to ship McLaughlin a 6.4-inch rifle, hardware for mounting, and shells.[15] March 8 brought more encouraging news in a message to McLaughlin included in a letter to Warner: "Tell McLaughlin I have sent him three VII inch guns and that the other three are ready, and will leave as soon as the quartermaster can take them."[16] That word, however, was to be the last good news Warner or McLaughlin would receive from Selma. A Union attack was feared to the west, and Jones was soon advised to ship to Georgia any machinery for which he had no immediate use. To reduce any disruption of production, Jones sent boxes carefully marked so that their contents could be easily matched and quickly put to use.[17]

Jones's March letters illustrate a combination of concerns as his Selma operation all but shut down and as reports spread about an impending attack. He wrote of Warner's new ironclad design, continued production at Selma, his efforts to ship machinery to a safe place, and shipping guns to McLaughlin. Even in such perilous times, he often added personal comments at the end of a letter, as he did on March 8: "I have been very much interested in 'La Navale.' Will return it in a few days by express." Then recalled to the gravity of his situation, he added a postscript: "I have advised Gonzales [in Montgomery] to remove his stores."

Communications were breaking down, however. Jones wrote John Mercer Brooke in Richmond on March 21: "In the absence of instructions, I shall continue to act heretofore, as I think will advance the general interests."[18] Cut off from regular mail and telegraph service, the Selma and Columbus facilities had become isolated enclaves, not components in a functional system.

Jones had little choice but to continue his work as Gen. James H. Wilson's Raiders moved closer and closer to Selma.[19] And Warner and McLaughlin had little choice but to continue their race to complete the three vessels that might break the blockade after all. As the Confederacy was collapsing, McLaughlin's log recorded daily events of the navy in Columbus in the most routine way:

Thursday 16	Heavy rains this morning. wind blowing Bar 29.70
Friday 17	Weather fine—Mr. H. L. Vaughan arrived this afternoon
Saturday 18	Weather splendid—Issued to Lt Comdg Lewis St. Spray (St. Marks) 2 coils 6 in Rope 4 Coils 3 in 2 lanterns (one ex Macon) 1 ball spun yarn
Sunday 19	Weather fine
Monday 20	Ditto River falling
Tuesday 21	Heavy rain during the forenoon—afternoon clear. Asst Engr Haley reported March 6th 1865, Asst Engr McDonald reported March 18th 1865
Wednesday 22	Clear & pleasant

Thursday 23	Weather pleasant. Got box under "Jackson" Recd from Selma 400 Bolts & Shells
Friday 24	Weather very pleasant. Shipped starboard Propeller in "Jackson" Recd from Selma 1 Box Lights & Locks for 7 in & 6.4 Guns from naval Storekeeper at Albany 3 bunk Matresses
Saturday 25	Weather continues very fine. Shipped Port Propeller & took off the box Wm Austen Pvt. Co A 2 Fla. Cav: reported as Pilot for Jackson. detailed by Genl. Imes for 30 ds @ 14th inst.
Sunday 26	Weather pleasant. Slight white frost—forwarded letters to Secty & office O&D
Monday 27	Cloudy—Jos. Silva reported this a.m. for duty on Jackson—pr order Brig Genl. Miler Comdg Reserve Fla Disct. Tolar & Clayton, Carpenters, and Pilot Munn retd from leave. 1st Asst Engr. Foster reported for duty on "Chatta"
Tuesday 28	Cloudy—some rain early—Hauled the third 7 in Gun down. broke foreleg of one of Mr. Brooks Mules
Wednesday 29	Cloudy. Loaned Ord: Depmt for blockade business Launch Mast Sail. oxen-1 brace 1 compass & Brass Lantern & John Chase.
Thursday 30	Cloudy. Strong Wind. S.W. Lieut. [William Watts] Carnes reported for dty. [as commander of the *Jackson*]
Friday 31	Blowy & cool. Launched Torpedo Boat this P. M. Recd from Macon 200 sensitive fuses.[20]

The record would have been good progress in conducting the business of war if, during that two-week period, the final assault upon Mobile had not begun; if Lincoln had not begun making an almost routine inventory of movements on the James River; if Grant had not redoubled his efforts against Lee at Petersburg; if the Confederacy had not been in its death agony.

The March 31 *Columbus Daily Sun* made no mention of the *Viper* launch. The issue did, however, carry a story of Mr. St. Ledger of Eufaula. A supplier during initial construction on the *Chattahoochee*, he spent much of 1864 as a Union prisoner. Returning home via Savannah, he brought a report of a city once more bustling with activity. Supplies were in abundance after three months of Union occupation. Across the state, he found Columbus still in a state of war. Warner was still in search of supplies, advertising in the March 31 *Sun* for lightwood to be delivered at any accessible point along the railroad or river.[21]

The navy yard log continued into April, with "April 1, 1865" elaborately inscribed:

Saturday 1   Weather Pleasant. Recd. from Asst. Paym Tift
              Boxes Bread Bbl Beef 50 Bags Peas 16 Bbl Flour
              stored at Barnard Comer Got steam up on Torpedo
Sunday 2   Warm & pleasant. Nothing to note. [In Richmond,
              Jefferson Davis was summoned from church to
              receive the news that the city had to be evacuated,
              and Lee withdrew from Petersburg that night;
              Wilson's Raiders entered Selma.]
Monday 3   Pleasant. 3rd asst Engr Conway reported for duty
              Got from Eagle Mill 2 pcs [illegible] 5 pcs
              Domestic [Secretary Mallory was ordering the
              destruction of the James River Squadron; Wilson's
              Raiders were destroying the Naval Iron Works in
              Selma].
Tuesday 4   Pleasant. Issued [supplies to] Haley, Foster,
              McDonald; loaned Marshall Collins Pistol #1261;
              loaned McKomer Pistol #1267

The *Daily Sun* reported that there was no news of action to the west, "Owing to the absence of Montgomery papers by last night's mail." Col. Leon Von Zinkern printed a notice to local militia that, in case of an emergency, six guns would be fired on Broad Street. At that signal, militiamen were to rendezvous fully armed and equipped, supplied with twenty-four hours' rations, and ready to take the field. "Local Intelligence" for the day included the notice that the steamer *Mist* would leave for Chattahoochee and Bainbridge Friday morning at eight A.M.[22]

The navy yard log continued:

Wednesday 5   Weather continuing pleasant
Thursday 6   Weather continuing pleasant
Friday 7   Rainy Act. Mst. Cragg reported for Jackson

The *Daily Sun*, without the usual bulletins and reprints from papers elsewhere in the Confederacy, had less and less news to print. Advertising also diminished from six columns, or half of the twelve-column edition, to two. The editor was having to resort to fillers; on April 7, page one featured a lengthy report on the evils of life in San Francisco: gambling, prostitution, and general rapacity.[23]

The weekend was logged:

Saturday 8   Pleasant
Sunday 9   Pleasant Lt. Golder left for Albany.

Warner began advertising in the *Daily Sun* for provisions: "The following articles will be exchanged for provisions of all kinds, Corn, Forage and for Cash: assorted bar iron, plantation iron, sugar mills, nails, horse shoe iron, nail rods, spike rods, mill gearing." The ad continued by offering CNIW services to the public: "Castings of all kinds either brass or iron; Engine, machine, and mill work executed with dispatch, upon reasonable terms Orders for the exchange of provisions will be made by Mr. J. Ennis, No. 95 Broad Street. Applications for work required should be made to Superintendent S. J. Whiteside, at the works."[24]

Since Golder usually kept the log, the dates Monday 10, Tuesday 11, Wednesday 12, and Thursday 13 are enclosed with a large brace and the single entry: "Mr. Golder absent at Albany." Beneath that fact is another: "The enemy occupied Montgomery last Sunday."

The *Sun* reported on Wednesday, April 12, that Montgomery had been evacuated the previous night, but the brief note was signed, "RUMOR." A full column on page one was given over to a piece describing Paris fashions.[25] And the following day, *Sun* readers were no doubt edified by another lengthy filler, an account of an Egyptian king translated from Herodotus. In the meantime, refugees from Montgomery brought firsthand news of the city's capture.

Outside Montgomery on April 11 a contingent of the Seventy-second Indiana Volunteer Infantry were bringing up the rear of General Wilson's column. Traveling with little sleep and fighting their way through swamps and across creeks in the flatlands south of Montgomery, they were subsisting mainly on sweet potatoes. Making twenty-five to thirty miles a day, they received word about noon on April 12 that Montgomery had surrendered without resistance to the units forward of their position. Instead of rushing into battle, the troopers pitched camp and awoke in a rain-flooded camp outside Montgomery on April 13.

That same day the *Sun* published its last issue until the following August 31. There is no hint of that prospect. Columbus continued to conduct much of its business as usual while Wilson's troopers approached. Advertised on page one were "a few large sheets of parchment suitable for kettle drums or banjo heads." There was to be a benefit concert with the Confederate Nightingales as the featured performers. J. H. Moshell offered a dapple gray stallion for sale, the Rock Island Paper Mill had eleven barrels of sugar for sale, and O. F. Fogarty ran an ad headed "Corsets, Corsets." Looking to the future, city clerk G. W. Roberts published a call for sealed bids for the construction of two bridges.[26]

At the CNIW, Warner issued a directive about relocating his operations to a safer place. It was to be his last order as officer in charge of that facility:

> Navy Department
> Office C.S. Naval Iron Works
> Columbus, Georgia
> April 13th, 1865

Capt. A. O. Blackmar
Sir:

You will proceed down the river to the point of Bainbridge, Georgia, or any other point, for the purpose of selecting a suitable location for our Bar Mill. Capt. Tally will accompany you, and will judge as to the fitness of the place.

You will make the best arrangements you can as to terms, etc. A place must be found, and if parties are not disposed to act for the interest of the Government, you are authorized to inform the parties, that the Government must have the ground, if with consent of the owner, so much the better, but it must, and will be obtained, with, or without their consent.

I have no doubt you will be able to arrange the matter satisfactorily. You have the full power to act as may be necessary for the interest of the Government.

Entitled to transportation.

J. H. Warner

> Very respectfully,
> J. H. Warner
> Chief Eng. C.S.N.
> In charge.[27]

The following day at the navy yard, the log noted Lt. L. H. Golder's return and added, "Enemy advancing on this place."

Wilson's advance column was moving toward Confederate fortifications erected on the west bank of the Chattahoochee in Girard; those in the rear were making slow progress at the heavy work of burning bridges and destroying rail and telegraph lines along the route east of Montgomery.

The navy yard log recorded:

> Saturday 15   The enemy reported 12 miles from here—the troops ordered out to the trenches.

Under a direct threat of military attack, Warner systematically went about the business of securing stores. In addition to ordering Blackmar down the river, he sent the *Young* with a load of stores to Rock Bluff. Warner dispatched the *Marianna* to Chattahoochee with a cargo of the most valuable articles, while McLaughlin ordered Lt. William Watts Carnes to use the torpedo boat *Viper* to tow the *Chattahoochee* down-river.[28] The Seventy-second Indiana was pressing on toward Tuskegee, where their foraging turned up flour, meat, and "10 dozen eggs for Easter." The weary troopers pitched camp at Crawford, Alabama, about 9 P.M. on Easter Sunday. It was at about that time that the main body of Wilson's troops broke the Confederate line on the Alabama side of the river and stormed into Columbus.

As the day was described in the navy yard log:

> Sunday 16   Easter Sunday—weather pleasant—The excitement in town intence—Began early this morning loading stores & on Chattahoochee & Jackson—about noon sent the Chattahoochee off in tow of the "Young" in charge of Master Vaughan—About 2 P.M. a smart skirmish occurred at lower bridge which was burned by our forces. Firing also at upper bridge which continued an hour or two. About 8 P.M.—Heavy firing at upper bridge which lasted until between 9 & 10. When the enemy broke thru our lines & obtained possession of the bridge & City. Our forces leaving as rapidly as possible.
>
> About 9½ Lieut McL ordered all the officers at the Yard on board the Torpedo to proceed down the

River—Excepting himself, clerk, & Dr. Stoakley who retreated by the land route & were captured by the Enemy.

Carefully inscribed below that account is the word FINIS.[29]

The labor force, which had defended Atlanta and Savannah in 1864, were deployed to fend off an attack on their own city. In the melee lit by exploding shells, the Confederates first made a stand on the Alabama side and then fled pell-mell across the bridges into Columbus. Navy yard clerk C. C. McGehee, functioning as a militia captain, set fire to the bridge to forestall the Union attack. Some naval personnel like Carnes were on standby on the *Jackson* during the battle, judging whether to flee or stand and fight and trying to judge the battle's progress in the darkness.

When Carnes heard the Union troops thundering across the bridges, he and a CNIW engineer named Oliver decided to make their escape. Steam was upon the *Viper*, so they raised anchor and dropped downriver to the *Chattahoochee*'s mooring. The distant glow of fires and the sounds of explosions told them that Wilson's Raiders were laying waste the naval facilities in Columbus. When others escaping the battle brought confirmation of their fears, the decision was made to destroy the *Chattahoochee* rather than allow it to fall into Union hands.

The crew doused the vessel with ten barrels of kerosene and, lighting slow fuses, fled overland. They had not traveled far when light from the burning vessel was so intense that they might have seen a pin on the ground. The gunboat was left adrift to run aground at Race Pass, twelve miles below Columbus.[30]

Carnes decided that "there seemed little use for Navy officers" and notified the navy that he had left to search for the last remnants of Gen. Bedford Forrest's troops.[31] Thus the *Viper*, like the *Jackson*, was left to fall captive to Union cavalry.

As the battle and destruction continued in Columbus, Wilson's rear column approached the city on the morning of April 17. They feared the worst as they came within earshot of heavy artillery barrages. Soon they came within sight of "vast columns of smoke, black and sulphurous, rising a thousand feet into the air." They were certain that a terrible raging battle awaited them. At about 10 A.M., when they reached the bluffs overlooking Columbus, they could see the city's factories, domes, churches being laid waste by their own forces. The sounds and sights that had so alarmed them were from the burning city, "forts, arsenals, machine shops, steamboats, locomotives, cars, cotton, commissary stores." There was "so much war material taken that no complete inventory was ever taken of it."[32]

Despite the trooper's statement, Gen. E. F. Winslow wrote a lengthy inventory on April 18 of all that could be accounted for in the previous day's destruction.[33] Included were many items that had been a point of pride to the *DeBow's Review* writer of 1862. There was the Eagle Factory, Haiman's Pistol Factory, the Howard Oilcloth Factory, the Grant Oilcloth Factory, the Rock Island Paper Mill. The list continued with the Columbus Iron Works, McElhaney and Porter's foundry, the Muscogee Iron Works, Hughes, Daniel, and Company's warehouse, the Fountain warehouse, the Alabama warehouse. The presses and type of local newspapers also fell victim to the destruction: *Daily Sun, Enquirer, Times*, along with the *Memphis Appeal*, which had taken refuge in Columbus.

In Girard the troops destroyed a rope factory, two Confederate blacksmith shops, and much of the works and the rolling stock of the Mobile and Girard Railroad. The same systematic destruction was carried out at the Central of Georgia railroad, which linked Columbus to Macon. The remaining bridges across the Chattahoochee were burned, breaking another transportation link. Thus, most of the peacetime industries that had been such a source of pride to Columbus and such a source of strength to the Confederacy found their way onto a Union inventory of destroyed property.

The chief items of interest on the inventory, of course, were the Confederate naval facilities in Columbus. General Wilson's first task had been to overcome resistance from Confederate fortifications to capture both the ironclad *Jackson* and the facilities that had constructed the ship. His second, and equally important, task was to inventory and then destroy those capabilities. As long as the *Jackson* was afloat and armed, she was like a fortress that might be turned to Confederate advantage. As long as there was a foundry, machine shops, and a rolling mill, the Confederates might continue wartime production.

The naval armory contained a small rolling mill with a blast engine, two sets of rollers, and three furnaces capable of turning out four thousand pounds of iron per day. There was a large new rolling mill—"nearly complete" after the months of construction work invested by B. F. Coleman, Horace King, and their crews. Included with the 150-horsepower engine and the three large furnaces was the engine Warner had managed to find for operating the much coveted steam hammer from Mobile.

In the machine shop was other equipment Warner had painstakingly assembled through endless paperwork: three small and two large planers; sixteen iron lathes; one large lathe; three drill presses; fifteen thousand pounds of brass, assembled in small lots from one person and another; and thirty vises that had been brought in along with anvils, one, two, and three at the time. The Union inventory noted that all the lathes and planers "had full sets of tools." Without noting, of course, how dearly bought each item had been, the inventory continued: ten forges in the blacksmith shop, a pattern shop, three wood lathes and a wood planer, a foundry, a boiler shop, and a copper shop with tools and other contents.

At the navy yard, the inventory included a brass foundry, a boat-building house, a machine shop with a hot-air furnace, a large planer, a rip saw and drill press, a blacksmith shop with tools, and five thousand rounds of large ammunition. Most of those items, too, had come into the yard in small lots or piece by piece. Also burned were "several offices and drawing rooms, with their contents," where Warner and McLaughlin had managed the procurement and utilization of all that was now captured and destroyed.

Winslow made a separate report of the *Jackson*, noting that he assessed this prize with the eye of a cavalryman, not a naval officer. The basic dimensions Winslow used to begin his report were: length 250 feet, beam 45 feet, draft 6½ to 7 feet with a solid oak ram extending 15 feet from the bow. The power plant in the hold consisted of two engines with thirty-six-inch cylinders and thirty-six-inch stroke fed by four boilers. Had he been a navy man, he would have noted that each of the 7½-foot propellers was powered by one of the engines. In adopting that design feature, the Confederate Navy had learned to avoid the difficulty of having a single unified system that could be entirely shut down if one part malfunctioned. Winslow could not have noted that McLaughlin had at least prevailed over Porter in fitting the ship with 7½-foot rather than 8-foot propellers.

Winslow also gave the dimensions of the gunroom, twenty by forty feet with nine feet of headroom, and the arrangement of guns, two fore and aft and two broadside, with ten gun ports along the bulkheads. Once again, if Winslow had had an educated eye for naval construction, he would have noted that the gunroom had more space for muzzle loading and accommodating recoil than the cramped quarters aboard other ironclads. Ten ports would allow smoke in the gunroom to be more easily dispersed than on earlier vessels. In particular, an arrangement that allowed the fore and aft guns to fire broadside overcame an earlier design problem, ports so snug that guns could not be trained more than five degrees. The pilothouse elevated two feet above the gunroom, but opened directly into it, would permit coordinating the ship's course with the battery's direction of fire.

Finally, Winslow noted the armor curved over the knuckle and extended below the waterline. This practical design feature meant that the ship rode low in the water with decks partially awash, a design protecting her near the waterline where naval cannon traditionally directed the most damaging fire. The use of plate curving over the knuckle was a distinguishing feature of Confederate ironclad construction and one of those design innovations for which two men, Porter and Brooke, each claimed credit.[34]

General Winslow did not note, and had no need to understand and appreciate, all those characteristics of the *Jackson* as he filed his report. He was, besides, an officer who had just put in three weeks of hard riding and hard reporting of countless items of captured Confederate property. Even if Confederate naval design had benefited from trial and error and had reached a stage of perfection in the *Jackson*, that technical success came too late. The order to destroy the *Jackson* inscribed a FINIS upon the Confederate Navy on the Chattahoochee.

With the navy accounted for, the Confederate Army in Columbus had to be dispatched: Major Humphries's arsenal with a magazine, machine shops, a foundry, and a sixteen-forge blacksmith shop; Major Dillard's quartermaster stores: 8,820 pairs of shoes (an ample store for the small lot Catesby Jones had needed at Selma), 4,500 Confederate uniforms (from which McLaughlin might have bought a new suit, as his letter offered, for Jones's wedding), jeans, socks, osnaburgs, caps, gray jackets, pants, shirts, cotton drawers, tin cups, tin plates, tin pans, wooden buckets, telegraphic instruments, carpenter's tools, wall tents and flies, axes and helves, picks and helves, spades and shovels. For all the wealth of stores, they were a pittance in comparison to what the Confederacy needed in April 1865, and they were cut off as well from transportation lines.

Rather than burn the Columbus stores, Winslow ordered that they be distributed to his men and to the column of blacks that was traveling with the Union forces. At the sight of the food and stores, the people of

Columbus also mobbed the site. More than five thousand laborers had been put out of work by the destruction of Columbus's industry. They were described by General Winslow as "thousands of almost pauper citizens and negroes, whose rapacity under the circumstances of our occupation, and in consequence of such extensive destruction of property, was seemingly insatiable. The citizens and negroes formed one vast mob, which seized upon and carried off almost everything moveable, whether useful or not."[35] There were also descriptions of women snatching smoldering ears of corn from piles of burning stores, and well-dressed ladies jostling with laborers and blacks for whatever they could lay hand on.

There were throngs of prisoners to deal with in more orderly fashion. McLaughlin, who had been captured the day of the battle, was paroled on April 17. Golder was taken to Macon and paroled there on April 27.[36] In Columbus, 3,700 were paroled, and 225 were paroled at Eufaula.[37] These paroles did not represent a spirit of clemency so much as Wilson's inability to guard and provide for the great numbers of Confederates captured during his raid, 59,878 total in April and May 1865.

As his men moved swiftly to carry out a military operation, General Wilson also had immediate business problems to address. Because Columbus had been more an industrial complex than a center of direct military action, citizens who had fought as militiamen two days before now set upon Wilson as civilian claimants. The industrial facilities he had put to the torch included a Confederate government installation, to be sure, but most of the buildings and much of the machinery were privately owned before 1862. The ashes had not cooled before Wilson was beset with civilian claims at a time when he had to get on with the business of war and push forward toward Macon.

As an officer and a gentleman, he gave Columbus businessmen verbal permission to set about the reconstruction of local industries. An agent would be dispatched to Washington to affirm that permission with an official request to the secretary of the treasury. Issues of what was private property and what was Confederate naval property in the ruins and among captured stores—these Wilson left for someone else to determine as he left Columbus to do his military duty.[38]

Wilson's troops moved out of Columbus singing "Hail Columbia" and boasting that they had given Columbus "hail." The unit history concluded the account of the battle for Columbus: "In less than 24 hours from the time our men had appeared in front of the place, our whole army, trains, niggers and all, like a besom of destruction, had swept through one of the fairest cities of the South, and left but little of it, and nothing in it, that would be of any benefit to the rebel cause."[39]

Just as the Union troops left, Alfred O. Blackmar returned from his mission downriver. With what perplexity he must have rounded the river bend to see Columbus destroyed. In such a case, there was little left to do except write a report:

> Capt. Tally left Columbus, Georgia with me April 13th, 1865, on Steamer Mist: he fell overboard on the night of April 14th, about half mile above Columbia, Alabama and was drowned, his body recovered and sent to this city: his drowning necessitated my return to the city for another engineer—on my arrival found the entire naval plant destroyed, including all other industrial works and the enemy under General Wilson, enroute for Macon, his rear column just going over Wynn's Hill, east of the city.
> A. O. Blackmar.[40]

The war had ended—in Columbus, and for the Confederacy.

CHAPTER 8

Concluding the Business of Peace

Columbus, Georgia, in 1868
Harper's Weekly, *Sept. 19, 1868*

The calvary troop Alfred Blackmar saw departing over Wynn's Hill on Easter Tuesday 1865 had concluded its work of destroying Columbus industry. The city was left to conduct a massive rebuilding effort. Coming from Barbour County in search of her family, governess Antoinette Hague came upon the same scene of destruction that had startled Blackmar. Turning to biblical and literary allusions to give voice to her feelings, she recollected the scene:

> As the train slowed up on the Alabama side of the Chattahoochee River, I looked eagerly over to the opposite bank, where the home of my father was situated. For a few seconds my pulse must have ceased to throb, as I beheld the ruins of the city of Columbus. With others I took my seat in an omnibus and was driven to the river's edge, there to await the coming of the ferry-boat which had been built since all the bridges on the river had been burned by the hostile army. . . . Had I not had my coin in my hand to pay the ferryman, I should have imagined we were all shades, flitting about on the shore of the Styx![1]

She was overjoyed to find her family home intact, with only a few provisions lost in the Union raid. She was even happier to find her two brothers returned safely from the war. Thus reunited, they joined other families in trying to sort out the wreckage of their lives and to repair the destruction of the land around them.

As civilian pursuits resumed, the business of peace also began. The official work of sorting out the affairs of the Columbus Naval Iron Works proved to be a task that would drag on for months.

In their dealings with D. S. Johnston, Warner and McLaughlin found that the Confederate policy on private contractors later came back to haunt them. That weakness of the system well outlived the war as the Union spent months trying to substantiate claims and make settlements with Columbus civilians. Without waiting for further official word after Wilson's departure, Warner returned the ruins of the iron works to the original owners on April 23. In this, Warner scarcely paused in the transition from manager for the Confederates to manager for the Union captors. He had to proceed without his navy yard counterpart, however, for McLaughlin and his wife left for their Baltimore home on May 5. Whiteside and Golder remained, and U.S. quartermaster's agent L. P. Dodge was soon sent to Columbus to untangle issues of ownership.

Warner was eager to have matters settled. He wrote to Col. J. H. Alexander, a U.S. Treasury agent at Pensacola, to express his anxiety about the property "being constantly stolen and destroyed" and his wish to "be relieved from any further responsibility."[2] The Treasury Department did not respond to Warner's request and he was left to manage the remains of the iron works with whatever ability he had at hand. The Union was moving so slowly, in fact, that the blockaders were still off Apalachicola and the army did not trouble to occupy the city until May 31.

The navy also moved slowly in decommissioning the blockade it had mounted along the Gulf coast; thus Warner simply transferred his work from the delays and frustrations of one naval bureaucracy to another. Matters at New Orleans and Mobile were higher on the Union Navy's list of priorities than the ruins of the Columbus Naval Iron Works.

A very practical reason for delays at Apalachicola was the need to restore navigational aids to Apalachicola waters and resume lighthouse operations. The buoys, lighthouse mirrors, and other such items stripped from the barrier islands in December 1861 had to be retrieved from as far north as Eufaula. Only then could any except a very small force be landed at Apalachicola.

Blockading officers were also busy making evaluations and deciding

whether to reassign, sell, or scuttle each vessel in a conglomeration of
Union ships in various stages of repair, some few captured Confederate
vessels, and captured river steamers like the *Black Diamond* and the
Iron King.[3] This battle of schedules, reports, and inventories was to
occupy the Union for many months—while Warner's plans were kept
waiting.

As civilians concerned themselves with surviving the peace, Union
decision making moved to dispose of the *Viper*. She was to be towed to
Apalachicola, taken in command by the navy as a captured property, and
then sent northward to Norfolk. As the last vessel in the Confederate
Navy on the Chattahoochee was towed southward, she passed through
an area vastly changed from the prosperous life of antebellum times.

The torpedo boat must have been a strange picture, a warship towed
past wharves that were beginning to come alive again for shipping out
cotton and shipping in all those necessities and luxuries that the blockade no longer cut off. She was the very latest in marine architecture and
weaponry yet was suddenly anachronistic as places like Eufaula and
surrounding Barbour County went about the business of peace. And she
may have been a bitter reminder of war to the veterans who disembarked from steamboats. They were a mere remnant of the confident
troops who had set out from Fort Mitchell four years before: of Kolb's
battery, only 60 of 170 returned; the Fifteenth Alabama had surrendered only 172 men at Appomattox after service in forty-eight battles.[4]
Henry County in Alabama and Early, Dougherty, and a roll call of other
Georgia counties told similar losses. The song that sent its men off to
war in 1861 came back to haunt the Chattahoochee country in 1865: "We
Conquer or Die."

Men like John Horry Dent, who had remained at home, were counting
the economic costs of the war as well. Reconstruction introduced trou-
bling and unfamiliar problems of labor and productivity. His slaves
had their freedom, but they were equipped only with the skills they had
learned on the land. They were left few or no options except to take up
the same work they had always done, but in a different economic system;
in many cases they merely exchanged one kind of slavery for another.

Writing in his journal became a way for Dent to evaluate his concerns
over the concept of sharecropping with his former slaves, a system he
found inefficient and difficult to manage fairly. He had developed a large
farming operation on the edge of a frontier; now, however, he confronted
a new kind of poverty. The degree to which the economic and political

changes of Reconstruction preyed on his mind can be measured in this journal entry: "Had an ominous dream last night—[I was] pulling fodder."[5] Such labor to recover from the Civil War would become an ominous reality for many planters along the rivers.

Wartime conditions destroyed many of the improvements that earlier settlers had wrought on the land before the war. Roads were impassable, and bridges either were destroyed by Union forces or had fallen victim to four years of neglect. Once more, people in the Chattahoochee country were thrown back upon the rivers as the primary means of transportation.

Men who returned found houses in bad repair; rugs, furniture, and all such household items had worn out, had been broken beyond repair, or had been sold for Confederate money. Metal tools needed for farming and vessels needed for syrup making and hog killing had worn out or had been donated to the Confederacy. Every small farm that had contributed its bell to the Cause was stripped of an essential means of communication: to summon workers to work in the morning, to announce meals, and to warn neighbors within earshot of fire, sickness, or any other disaster.

While the land had not been fully productive during the war years, it had not been idle either. During the long Southern growing season, and in warm rainy winters when temperatures rarely fell to twenty degrees, men absent at war had not been able to fight the constant battle every farm required: to walk and repair fences, to clear seedling trees and brush from fence lines; to keep woodlots clear of saplings and accumulated leaves that could send a wood cutter knee-deep in wet compost; to oversee and maintain even fields lying fallow so that brush would not overrun them.

Men who were on patrol in northern Virginia could not perform the ancient, almost daily ritual of an agricultural society that even Chaucer's Reeve performed: to walk the land, to spot and secure the loose shingle on the barn or corncrib or smokehouse, to replace the rotting fascia board before a new roof was required, and to send to town for a barrel hoop or wheel spoke before the barrel burst or the wagon collapsed.

Men exhausted and emaciated from war had another long campaign to begin: performing the *omnia opera* of tasks economic recovery required. They might win that battle in time, but in April and May 1865 they could not change the natural course of seasons. Appomattox had come very late in the growing season to plant most crops.

The *Viper* passed by the devastated fields and was towed past the Navy Yard Landing. But the wartime entrepreneur David S. Johnston had long since fallen victim to the economics of the conflict, first struggling with conscription laws that depleted his work force and then selling off his plantation to a Gwinnett County developer in 1863.[6] Wartime loyalist Col. Martin Stamper first sold his Early County land for Confederate bonds; then emancipation took his investment in slaves; finally, Appomattox left his three sons with poverty as the legacy of his politics.

Anthony Hutchins, the only one of four brothers to survive the war, married and began the slow reconstruction of his life in a one-room log cabin. His bridal bed was a frame contrived from fence-post rails covered with plank and nailed at the head to the wall. Writing long afterward, the overseer Andrews commented, "How was that for a bride who had graduated at the Wesleyan Female College and had never soiled her hands in a pan of dough?"[7]

Thus the postwar years reintroduced frontier conditions to life along the rivers; economic gains that the affluent planters had made from the 1830s to 1861 had been largely destroyed. Even the wealthy planters became "land poor" with their thousands of acres to manage and keep current on the tax rolls. They had to begin again on a common footing with the poor who had always lived by the natural law of "root hog or die poor."

Some, of course, survived the war better than others. From Sumter County, John Cobb wrote his father about selling corn and cotton—this time to a Union contractor. Although General Cobb was still involved with military correspondence with General Wilson, his son needed advice: "Write me at once which to sell for gold or greenbacks. I think myself it will be better to take the gold."[8]

The *Viper* passed near "The Pines" on Shackelford's Landing. George Gift had spent the last days of the war there recovering from the rigors of sea duty. He had left the U.S. Navy in the 1840s to grow up with the economy of California; returning to "the land of second chance" now seemed to offer a better future than a devastated South. Such a decision would have to wait, for Ellen was nearly seven months pregnant when the war ended.[9] Like many other couples left in the war's wake, they were young and had much to hope for.

Farther south at the Chattahoochee Arsenal at Chattahoochee, Florida, work would soon begin to inventory and ship naval stores that had been secreted there during the closing days of the war. To the east of the

Apalachicola River at Tallahassee, a detachment of General Wilson's force arrived from Macon on May 10. In an action more symbolic than substantive, Brig. Gen. Edward M. McCook and his five staff officers rode into town to receive the surrender of the last Confederate capital and to preside over radical changes in the governmental, economic, and social life of Florida.

Mary Brown Archer, daughter of a former governor, keenly felt the strictures of postwar poverty. In the same way Miss Hopley, Miss Hague, and the elder Shackelford aunts had tutored affluent children before the war, she said her sister taught the family children. Miss Archer might have established a school, but as she wrote a cousin, "I don't care about placing myself upon the level of these 'Yankee School Marms' who teach darkies."[10] Poverty was equally bitter to a Tallahassee woman who regarded her worn-out shoes and observed that she had never been one of those Southern children who begged to go barefoot.

If poverty was bitter, politics was more so as people throughout the river system experienced massive social change; black men in Union uniform exercised the authority of a government against which the people had rebelled. Ordered to resume the Prayer Book petitions for the president and Congress of the United States, an Episcopal priest in Tallahassee sighed, "This *is* a peace that passeth all understanding."[11]

When the *Viper* completed its passage through the region and reached Apalachicola in late May, the Union blockade was still left to bide its time and await orders to disband. The town and the harbor had not yet revived to the sound of steamboat bells and steam whistles and the sight of wharves piled high with cotton bales.

The *Yucca* was dispatched from its blockading station to Apalachicola to take the *Viper* in tow for the long voyage to Key West and transfer northward. In preparation for the May 25 departure, the Union crew hauled her alongside, tarpaulined and battened the hatches, and put a man aboard to keep watch during the voyage. The *Yucca* was not many hours out of Apalachicola before a storm rose on the Gulf; gale winds and heavy seas, while not as severe as the storm of late May 1863, were enough to threaten the *Viper*. The forces of waves against green pine timbers became too much and she began to leak. At 2:30 P.M. on May 25, the crewman aboard her was removed to the *Yucca*. The next day, efforts to keep her afloat continued; by 4:15 that afternoon, however, she sank—ultimately falling victim to unseasoned timbers, unskilled labor, critical shortages, and a construction schedule that overshot the end of the war. A buoy placed at Latitude 20° 12′N and Longitude 83° 20′W marked the place, leaving the *Viper* to suffer sea changes where she lay ten fathoms deep in the Gulf.[12]

Not until May 31 was a force sent to occupy Apalachicola. Gen. Alexander Asboth was sent from Barrancas with orders to open the port and make it a transfer point for supplies being shipped inland to Wilson's forces and for captured stores being shipped out to sea. Asboth's men found the effects of war and the blockade still very much in evidence. A member of the 161st New York wrote: "Apalachicola contained before the war a population of two thousand, but we found on our arrival only a few hundred. All the places of business except one cotton press was closed, the streets were covered with grass, the houses and sidewalks were falling to decay, all the churches were closed, and an oppressive quietness everywhere prevailed."[13]

Soon the general noted "people returning to Apalachicola from rebeldom as well as from the North, anxious to resume their former vocations." He also found 868 bales of cotton already arrived at the port and another 76 being shipped in. The steamboat *William H. Young* embarked on a new career as a Union transport commanded by Capt. John C. Lamson of the Seventeenth Indiana Volunteers.[14]

Under these changed circumstances, the names and titles of personnel changed. Now the U.S. Navy owned and shipped cotton; kegs of spikes and copper tubing and engines were shipped down the river instead of upriver to Columbus. The established order of things had taken a radical shift of direction, but the port and the river system were back in operation; at least that feature of life was quickly returning to normal. As another measure of renewal, George Washington Gift, Jr., was born at "The Pines" on May 31.

In Columbus, Warner continued his work. He had already delayed nearly three months to begin normalizing life for himself and for Harriet and their seven children. They had made plans to move to New Orleans, to capitalize upon its location for his engineering practice.[15] In a very real sense, Warner continued to protect his handiwork from the Union. A July 17 letter to Alexander argued in a pleading tone for saving a pair of fine English engines sent through the blockade.

Warner also made an inventory of other engines and equipment on hand in Columbus. It can be viewed as a measure of how near he had come to winning his own managerial war. Ready for shipment to

Wilmington when Sherman cut the railroad was a pair of high-pressure engines (twenty-eight-inch cylinder and twenty-four-inch stroke for propelling two screws). A complete set of castings and heavy forging for one of the Charleston ironclads was next, for a pair of engines with forty-five-inch cylinder and twenty-two-inch stroke. Intended for the Bigbee Boats was a pair of engines "in an advanced state" with thirty-six-inch cylinders and twenty-two-inch stroke. And for Wilmington, there was a full set of castings for a pair of engines, twenty-eight-inch cylinder and twenty-four-inch stroke.

The rolling mill that Horace King and B. H. Coleman had spent so many months constructing was another item to which Warner gave careful attention. The machinery had survived the fire: thirty-inch cylinder and forty-two-inch stroke and a twenty-two-foot flywheel weighing twenty-eight tons. He ended the description: "Three setts of rolls for this mill were nearly completed, neither labor or expense was spared to render this machinery as perfect as possible."

Warner's steam hammer also survived the fire and "could soon be refitted." But the planing machine, a smaller planer, and several lathes had been "more or less damaged." From the Selma works there were a lot of gun flasks and other machinery for manufacturing guns.

Warner reported that the *Chattahoochee* had been towed fifteen miles below Columbus and burned. The machinery was "very little injured" and could be raised. The 17,000-pound boilers, which had been shipped from the *Raleigh* at Wilmington, still remained at the CNIW.

The *Jackson* had not survived the fire as well as the *Chattahoochee;* the work of more than two years was "in all probability useless except as old iron." The two hundred tons of plating on board and the plate scattered about the Columbus yard should have some postwar value; again, a low stage of water would permit salvaging the iron. With additional machinery that might be salvaged from the wreckage there was the locomotive "Black Dwarf," the "hard case" Warner had tried to rehabilitate for hauling coal from Montgomery.

Warner concluded his letter with another request about these stores: "I beg leave to renew my suggestion that you should come at once and secure this machinery to the Navy Dept. to which it properly belongs. After it becomes scattered, it will be difficult to collect again."[16]

Enclosed with the letter was an inventory of stores on hand at the CNIW as of April 8, 1865, ten days before Wilson's raid. From "augers, ships carpenters" to "zinc," it is a neat list of 130 items collected from almost that many sources. Anvils from Savannah, ammonia (which had been at such a premium for Jones at Selma), refined English borax, Bath bricks from Augusta, 143 brass and iron cabin door bolts, leather and rubber belting, four reams of emery paper, thirty-two German steel compasses, 3,822 English files and 318 pounds of worn-out and condemned files, nineteen steam gauges, twenty-five auger handles, 3,690 pounds of bell metal brought in in small lots, oil (linseed, peanut, tallow, sperm, and lard brought in for various suppliers), manilla and tarred rope (though no hide rope), 162 pounds of tallow, shellac, and bright varnish, which Warner had traded with Jones and McCorkle. Warner had about three hundred tons of iron on inventory in April 1865 but, by that time, insufficient labor to work it, insufficient transportation to ship what they made, and few places left free in the Confederacy to receive it. Now all Warner's official inventory and reporting duties shifted to the Union side.

By July 26, work at Apalachicola had progressed well enough that a part of Asboth's force could be withdrawn. Upon leaving, John S. Jones of the 161st New York noted the transformation of the place: "The appearance of things at our departure was different from what it was at our arrival; then, hardly a person was to be seen, and a spirit of utter desolation brooded over the place. Now the levee was covered with bales of cotton, the wharf was astir with citizens, and handkerchiefs were waving from many of the windows and sidewalks." This Union soldier's valedictory expressed a feeling shared by his naval counterparts who had served out the war there: "Farewell, sandy, dry, hot Apalachicola, may we never see thee more!"[17]

When the main Union force bid farewell to Apalachicola, there was still no move from authorities to conclude the business of dismantling the Confederate Navy in Columbus. As Warner waited, the city was rebuilding and adjusting to Reconstruction. On August 31, the *Daily Sun* resumed publication. The editor reported most stores open but "empty shelves are the chief commodities." In the aftermath of the war, some parts of the war industry were still on sale. John Egger had seven button machines for sale. Harris Levy in Butler had a tan yard for sale with a house, fifty acres, and a good well.

The *Daily Sun* had some news that remained constant from before the war: "The river is lower than ever; only the *Swan* can run." But flatboats were being built to float cotton either for transshipment to steamers at Eufaula or for the entire distance to Apalachicola. Other cotton was sent by rail to Macon and then by river to Savannah. There was an ad for a New York weekly newspaper to put Columbusites in touch with the larger commercial world.

Familiar names reappeared in the ads: Ellis furniture, Jaques Carriage Repository, W. A. Redd groceries, J. P. Murray gun repair, W. L. Parker dry goods, Kent and Company, and Miss Carrie Birdsong's primary school. There was Porter, McIlheny, and Company's City Foundry offering skillets, lids, pots, and ovens for sale. There was also this large ad:

COLUMBUS IRON WORKS CO.

Having completed their reconstruction of their works at the *Old Stand, Corner of Lower bridge* are now prepared
to furnish all kinds

CASTINGS

IRON OR BRASS

-and-

Machinery for Railroads,
Steamboats, Mills, Cotton Gins
Steam Boilers
of any description

SHEET IRON WORK

Transportation was still hampered by the bridges that had fallen casualty to the war—though two ferries and bateaux, "some with awnings," conducted a thriving business. The *Sun* reported one bridge would be open to foot traffic by the first week of September and fully completed in three weeks.

Railroad schedules were very much in evidence with connections to Macon, Atlanta, and north to Chattanooga and Nashville; to Eufaula, Smithville, Albany, and south to Brunswick and Savannah. Even if the river was low and only the *Swan* could run, a large segment of the population had become familiar with rail travel during the war years.[18]

Naval stores continued to wait for the river's rise and for the U.S. government to take action. Admiral Thatcher had a long list of other administrative tasks to attend. On October 10 he stationed the *Mahaska*, commanded by Lt. Charles H. Cushman, off Apalachicola because the ship was unsuitable for a long cruise north in winter.

On December 6, Cushman arrived in Columbus to take charge of captured naval stores and to write voluminous reports to Admiral

Thatcher. End-of-the-war promotions were coming through (Edward Simpson, late of the *Isonomia*, would serve as fleet captain in 1865) and Cushman tackled his special assignment with unusual energy.

December 8 brought forth his assessment of the situation. Warner had prepared most property for shipping. Local claimants to the iron works could claim the site, but not the equipment, and the Columbus Iron Works owners could submit a separate claim. To facilitate salvage operations, Warner sold the old brick from the CNIW for $400 and the rolling mill should be sold "as it lays" to save salvage costs. Cushman was leaving for Macon to attend matters there and so Thatcher should send any reply in care of Warner.

By December 12, Cushman was back at work in Columbus. He then planned a trip to the wrecked gunboats to make a survey for salvage. On December 15 he sent Acting Ensign Carter to Macon to inventory and ship stores through the port of Savannah. On December 22 and 23, Cushman addressed Thatcher on the complex questions of ownership and disposition of the Columbus Naval Iron Works property.[19]

Pausing in his flurry of activity, Cushman may have scanned the morning newspaper before setting to work, but he could hardly have appreciated the extent of change in Columbus on the anniversary of the *Jackson*'s successful launch. Ads in the *Daily Sun* were announcing "CHRISTMAS WILL BE HERE SOON!" Certainly it would be a happier season than the previous one when Columbus men were camped six miles from Savannah. Advertisers registered strong signs of economic recovery. For the season, Blackmar and Candler had a stock of bourbon whiskey and Havana cigars; the Saratoga restaurant was serving Apalachicola Bay oysters; Blount and Chipley had family or orthodox flour; William H. Phelps had recently bought the Rynehart Bakery; D. B. Thompson had received a shipment of pianos; J. Ennis advertised "FIRE WORKS!" and Balmoral skirts for the height of Victorian fashion; Bedell and Pope had shoes in stock; and at J. W. Pease Company, Christmas shoppers might buy photographs of Confederate generals or books like *Little Red Riding Hood* and *Goody Two Shoes*.

Yet there were some signs of the old order passing. W. L. Williams had thirty thousand old bricks for sale, doubtless for the new houses the *Sun* editor called "mostly iron works." And Urquhart and Chapman was selling out to Dawson and Collier. But signs of a reconstructed Columbus were predominant. Hall and Moses was selling scales, steam sawmills, and "all kinds of mill gearing." Louis Haiman had established the Phoenix Foundry. J. A. Cody had plantation iron for sale, and J. M. Frazer was still selling wood. Both Joseph Kyle and Messrs. Schobler and Eifler had safes to sell for securing Columbus's postwar wealth. As another sign of recovery, D. F. Wilcox had resumed selling Travelers' Insurance of Hartford, Connecticut.

Commerce was reviving with agents' ads placed for New Orleans, Mobile, New York, and Liverpool. Hotels advertised special accommodations for the business traveler in Louisville, Kentucky, and Washington, D.C.; and, as a sign of the times, agents in Macon and Savannah cited the advantages of shipping goods by rail to the Atlantic port; as of December 1865, there was only one ad from an Apalachicola agent. The professions were reviving along with commerce. Dr. V. H. Talaiferro and Dr. A. J. Ford had resumed practice; Drs. Schley and Raines had established offices at Odd Fellows Hall. Attorneys at law were A. W. Persons, V. W. Wynne, E. W. Moise, R. J. Moses, James J. Abercrombie, and the firm of Russell and King.[20]

Cushman could probably have benefited from the services of all those attorneys as he labored over the pages of Warner's letter book and the tangle of issues surrounding ownership of the Columbus Iron Works property. His "very full and necessarily long" report with ten enclosures discussed the iron works in peace and war. The Confederacy had first contracted with, then leased, and later seized the works during a period from early 1861 to August 1862. Having made an exhaustive review, Cushman recommended that the property be released to the claimants.

Cushman reported his task much complicated by hard bargaining from the claimants. They placed a lien upon the ruins of the rolling mill as compensation for their losses to the Confederate government. On the one hand, to yield to their claim would "really be a free gift from the Government for the purpose of encouraging manufacturers in the south." If the Columbus group persisted, however, "their claim will seriously embarrass the sale, in as much as others will be unwilling to purchase under the possibility of loss from their [CIW] action." He considered himself—and indeed the U.S. Navy—fortunate to have negotiated a private sale for $25,000, up to 50 percent more than a public auction would have yielded.[21]

Cushman began 1866 with another lengthy report to Thatcher, not failing to note the difficulty of his position. He caught a severe cold on his trip to examine the wrecked Confederate gunboats. Steamers on the river were charging exorbitant freight rates. Lines of communication from Pensacola were slow and difficult, as much as fifteen days via Apalachicola.

One of Cushman's few positive comments concerned Warner. He had made a bonded contract to have Warner raise both gunboats at low river for 50 percent of the salvage value. "He has been very valuable to me as an assistant," Cushman wrote, "and the pay he receives is scarcely sufficient for his own personal expenses besides which his knowledge of the machinery and build of the vessels will enable him to recover whatever is valuable in the best condition."[22]

As Columbus business began to revive, Warner had business cards printed in anticipation of his move to New Orleans. During the last summer of the war, the navy yard log had recorded on June 29, 1864, "Mr. Warner's child died this afternoon"; now Harriet was expecting their eighth child in March 1866.[23]

Neither Warner nor Cushman could move on with their personal lives, however, until they established ownership for, inventoried, and shipped what remained of the Confederate Navy. To this end, Cushman wrote another of his convoluted discussions of issues, this time to Navy Secretary Gideon Welles. Cushman described himself as "desirous of closing my duty here promptly," and he asked for a reply by telegraph in care of J. H. Warner.[24]

A week later, on January 11, Cushman found a means of transporting stores to Apalachicola on the government transport *Swain*. In two trips the steamer could carry everything to port and his duty would be ended.

As he waited to negotiate final transportation arrangements, Cushman addressed the Freedman's Bureau in Albany about the tannery, gristmill, bakery, and blacksmith shop that Nelson and Asa Tift had developed as a naval supply complex.[25] He dispatched Acting Ensign Carter to deal with such business in Albany, Cuthbert, and Bainbridge.

The work was largely complete except for shipping, though the size of the *Chattahoochee*'s boilers continued to worry him. Warner's work was complete except for a trip to Macon where his knowledge of inventories was needed to settle conflicting claims. Cushman himself was "anxious to get thro'." He had found his temporary duty quite expensive and had been "more or less sick during my entire stay." But all such plans moved slowly: "The tardiness with which work of any kind is done here is lamentable, but there seems to be no way of helping it."[26]

By January 29, Cushman delayed his intended departure to February

7, although his work continued well in most respects. Also by that time, the sheer bulk and variety of inventory items had blunted Cushman's enthusiasm to account for, ship, and report to Thatcher his every decision about every single item. He decided simply to leave the *Chattahoochee* boilers, shaft, and propeller for sale in Columbus rather than to attempt shipping them. Another major task was taken care of when Warner presented a formal proposal for raising the *Chattahoochee* and *Jackson*.

By January 31—after seven weeks of the kind of work that had occupied Warner and McLaughlin for four years—Cushman began negotiating for retirement. He had made a previous request, the admiral had refused, and now "on the nearest approach to official paper I can obtain," he renewed his plea in a sustained sentence:

> I am grateful for such an expression of regret on the part of my commander in chief—but my whole nervous system is so impaired as to make me not only a physical but a mental sufferer constantly at sea and to render me too insolate for useful service so that I am sure that I am doing right not only for myself but for the service and I should be glad if my application could receive your recommendation and endorsement.[27]

The next day, he further detailed his continued efforts to Thatcher. By the following week he hoped to have the CIW sale closed; the company, in fact, had already deposited the first note payment. The Columbus Iron Works owners also offered to buy the *Chattahoochee*'s boilers, shaft, and propeller at $168 per ton. There was a likely buyer for another shaft at $975. One barge was loaded with machinery and Warner might ship the rest, leaving Cushman free to return to Apalachicola.

Cushman's February 7 departure date came and went; on February 8 he was reporting once more to Admiral Thatcher about details and delays of shipping captured stores. Having booked a February 13 departure on the steamer *Hard Times*, Cushman confessed himself "glad to get away and hope soon to be able to report the arrival of the last freight at Apalachicola."[28]

A letter from Macon about naval stores arrived February 10 with news that he was needed there. This duty delayed Cushman by two or three days, but his shipments remained on schedule. He concluded final details of his work in a last letter to Thatcher and left the rest "in Mr. Carter's charge" as he prepared to take his leave.[29]

On February 13, all such plans collapsed. Cushman's duty was not all ended; instead, he had a message of urgent importance for Admiral Thatcher:

> I regret to inform you that a disturbance occurred here yesterday between the Negro troops and the citizens and that Mr. Warner while quietly on his way home was shot from the windows of the Barracks by one of the Negro Soldiers so that his leg had to be amputated above the knee. I shall therefore I suppose be obligated to remain and personally attend to the . . .[30]

Here the worn and fragile paper of the last page of Warner's letter book becomes entirely illegible. Only a word or phrase here and there can be deciphered; the message is very clear, however: the shooting brought an end to any further plans to salvage the *Jackson* and *Chattahoochee* for peacetime use.

Daily news reports pick up where Cushman's letter trails off. In the political conflicts of Reconstruction, trouble erupted between townsmen and black troopers in a Union cavalry unit. One trooper sat in an upstairs window of a barracks boasting that he would shoot the first white man who passed by. That man happened to be Warner. The bullet might have found many hostile targets in Columbus in the bitter aftermath of the war, but Warner was not one of them. Despite his Confederate service, he had also rendered invaluable service to the Union Navy and to the recovering Columbus economy in the transition from war to peace. More than he was a naval officer, he was a competent technical expert fulfilling an important but essentially apolitical function. Thus the cruel illogic of the incident was intensified.

Daily bulletins in the *Sun* and *Enquirer* gave detailed notes on Warner's medical condition. There was also an outpouring of public sympathy, for the incident seemed to elicit a special anguish for Warner and his family. Only through careful negotiation were local officials and the army commander able to avoid a pitched battle among the citizens and the occupation force. Within days, the cavalry unit was transferred elsewhere and the angry mood in Columbus subsided as the town kept a vigil over Warner.

The combined shock of the wound and amputation of his leg proved too much and, after three weeks, Warner died. On February 22, exactly five years after the formation of the Confederate States, the *Enquirer* carried a notice of the funeral from Trinity Episcopal Church. The obituary was laudatory, in the style of that time. More eloquent was a resolution from local merchants to close their businesses that day. Eloquent in its simplicity was a letter from a mechanic who praised Warner, not only as a "courteous gentleman" and "true patriot," but as a "friend to the laboring class."[31]

The Warner family possessions had been packed and ready for a move to New Orleans; instead, Harriet returned to her family home in Portsmouth, Virginia, where in early April she gave birth to their son Charles. During her lifetime she never unsealed the box of mechanical drawings Warner had preserved from his Confederate service. That was left to Charles, who returned to make Columbus his home. He talked with Charles Blain, corresponded with Sam Whiteside, and sought out fragments of his father's story along the rivers.[32]

Warner's death, however, had inscribed a swift and decisive FINIS upon any further plan to salvage the gunboats. The engines and iron plate were his handiwork, he could accurately assess the condition of the wrecks, and he might have salvaged some of his investment of time and labor after the war. The Union Navy was not interested in continuing that enterprise; Cushman already had more equipment and machinery than he could ship or sell. Columbus became in peacetime, as it had been in 1861, an industrial nucleus directing its energies toward the South's economic development. The wrecks of the *Jackson* and *Chattahoochee* became less Civil War relics than two more derelict ships along a river that had always exacted a heavy toll. Stories about them wove in and out of the general lore of navigating the distance between Columbus and Apalachicola. Many more men than Johnston or Saffold, Gift or Guthrie, or McLaughlin and Warner had launched their fortunes on the rivers and lost. Warner's death closed the Confederate Navy's chapter in that story.

EPILOGUE

Chief Engr. James Warner's death brought a swift conclusion to the last remnants of Confederate naval activity in the Columbus-Apalachicola corridor. In one way or another, all Civil War stories conclude with an account of Confederate defeat and an end to hope. Only individual details, like those in Warner's case, differ. Beyond the fact of the South's ultimate failure in war, the story draws writers and readers back to the subject again and again to assess the degree to which each side in the conflict won or lost in all that was attempted.

In conventional terms of warfare, there was no clash of arms to determine a victor off Apalachicola or along the Apalachicola and Chattahoochee rivers. Ships of the Union and Confederate navies never engaged. The only shots fired were aimed at an enemy in full retreat. No significant casualties were inflicted, except self-inflicted damage from accidents. While more dramatic stories of the Civil War were played out elsewhere, the history of the navies here becomes a record of frustrated efforts and potential never fully realized.

Both Union and Confederate officers and men were less men at war than they were men at work. Whether Union or Confederate, each force confronted two systems, a man-made system of naval operations and a natural system of navigational conditions. To the degree that they could work within one system and overcome the other, to that same degree they failed or succeeded. The time happened to have been the years 1861–65. The setting was a small port on the west Florida coast and a small river city at the head of navigation on the Chattahoochee River in Georgia. But every war is played out on a human and individual level and on a daily basis. In that respect this story is no different from any other.

Although the Union won the Civil War—and the blockaders off Apalachicola certainly shared fully in that victory—naval operations to blockade the port were in many ways ineffective. The small flotilla there was ill equipped for navigation in the shallow waters of the coastline. Entering Apalachicola Bay to reach the port was difficult; ascending the rivers to strategic industrial, naval, and agricultural sites was out of the question. Even in peacetime, seagoing ships and river steamers found trips into Apalachicola or north to Columbus and Albany a perilous risk.

Thus the primal enemy of tides, currents, and shifting sandbars became a kind of counterblockade that always frustrated and most often defeated the Union Navy at Apalachicola.

The blockade as an economic strategy also militated against decisive fighting action by the Union Navy. Rather than to square off and engage an identified enemy, the Union sailors spent much of the war dealing with social and political issues. The port of Apalachicola was a potential target, but it was also a place where hungry and defenseless civilians needed aid. Refugees came aboard warships needing medical attention or transportation to safety. Contraband slaves came seeking sanctuary; their owners followed after, demanding their property rights. The Union recruited pilots and sailors from the population along the Florida coast with a wary uncertainty about their true political allegiance. Thus men eager to confront an opposing naval force found, instead, blurred distinctions between friend and foe. Willing to risk all in a naval assault upon the Apalachicola–Chattahoochee river system, they risked, instead, drowning on routine patrols or in storms, death from yellow fever, the almost unendurable heat, and the equally unendurable boredom from inactivity.

Isolated and inactive as the Union blockaders off Apalachicola may have been, they operated under a series of significant advantages when compared to their Confederate counterparts. Although the United States Navy had begun the war in a state of unpreparedness, the Navy Department comprised an existing management system and, on an operational level, the navy was an established organization with a set, identifiable chain of command. Both gave shape and direction to Union efforts toward building a blockading fleet. Defining that overall naval strategy was the political dimension of President Lincoln's blockade proclamation. On an even larger historic and diplomatic scale, the blockade existed within the traditional context of maritime law and precedent.

Those larger policies for the Union Navy as a whole encompassed the individual ship at anchor at a remote station like Apalachicola. Perhaps some officers and men were inept or inefficient, but all had a defined mission. Perhaps the U.S. naval bureaucracy was ponderous and unresponsive at times, but the supply ship arrived eventually and there was a designated dry dock at Key West whether a particular ship was overhauled or the individual sailor enjoyed shore leave there or not. On at least some level of effectiveness, then, the Union Naval system functioned to direct and supply the fleet, and the system was a known quantity to the men who served out the war on the blockade.

Whatever the Union Navy accomplished at Apalachicola, and however individuals performed their duties there, the decisive statement must be that the port of Apalachicola was closed. Even if adverse navigational conditions hampered any Confederate attack on the blockade, and despite the degree to which Confederate failures made the Union's task easier, the Union blockaded Apalachicola.

If the Union Navy began the Civil War with too few ships and sailors, at every level there was a defined law, policy, strategy, or procedure. The Confederate Navy faced the task of imposing such order upon its resources. Navy Secretary Mallory could claim these assets: able and experienced officers, seaports and river landings in an economy tied to shipping, facilities to construct or repair vessels, a skilled labor force, and an area rich in wood, iron, and coal needed for shipbuilding. All the components for a navy existed; the navy's task was to combine those components for productive operation that could, if not win a victory, at least make invasion so costly that the Union would desist and allow the Confederacy to exist as separate states.

Mallory and his staff set out to explore every avenue that might help the South build a navy: to purchase or construct ships in England and Europe or in the South. To foster Southern industry, plans included use of existing facilities and construction of private facilities at the same time that ships were built by civilian contractors. Finally, the navy itself became active in construction. Plans called for converted commercial vessels, conventional wooden gunboats, newer ironclads, and, as the war progressed, even newer torpedo boats and submarines. In time, most of the Confederacy's domestic plans would be attempted along the Chattahoochee River and at Columbus.

The gunboat *Chattahoochee* collected in one project a list of methods used to build a navy. In design she was fitted with sail and steam; she was armed with conventional smoothbores and the more up-to-date rifled cannon; her officers included men like Catesby ap R. Jones, a veteran of the *Virginia-Monitor* fight, and George W. Gift, a veteran of the *Arkansas*. Experienced engineer James H. Warner designed machinery constructed at an existing facility at Columbus, Georgia. Augustus McLaughlin, experienced from U.S. Navy service like the others, oversaw the ship's construction. Private contractor David S.

Johnston, working at an interior site at Saffold, Georgia, utilized nearby stands of timber and his work force of slaves to handle the job. The October 1861 contract called for a completed ship within 120 days; then the *Chattahoochee* could steam down the Chattahoochee River from Saffold, down the Apalachicola River to the bay, raise the blockade, defend the port, and restore a vital avenue of commerce.

During the first year of the war, the Confederate Navy projected similar plans at Mobile, Pensacola, Jacksonville, Savannah, Mars Bluff (South Carolina), and Wilmington and Elizabeth City (North Carolina). Eleven gunboats would fill a critical need.

Execution fell far short of the conception of a gunboat fleet. In time, the *Chattahoochee* became an example of all the ways Confederate planning failed. Like the Union sailors off Apalachicola, those who worked at Saffold had two systems to battle: the natural conditions of river navigation and the management system of the Confederate Navy. Ultimately the project foundered in both systems.

The plan to employ a loosely supervised private contractor did not work, and by late 1862 construction work was moved from Saffold to the Confederate Navy Yard and Columbus Naval Iron Works in Columbus. The *Chattahoochee* was finally commissioned a year past the contracted completion date. Her machinery, while well designed, was poorly constructed and unreliable. She had not traveled many miles downriver before grounding in a narrow bend significantly damaged her hull. Even if the launch and first run had proceeded well, impatient citizens and local officials had already worked with the Confederate Army to obstruct the Apalachicola River and block the gunboat's passage to Apalachicola. Finally, in May 1863, a boiler explosion at Blountstown, Florida, placed the *Chattahoochee* out of action altogether. The end of war found her still not fully restored for service.

The *Chattahoochee* came to reflect the failure of the Confederate construction system instead of a fulfillment of its plans. Other such projects did not fare better. Of the eleven similar ships begun in 1861, the *Pee Dee* was commissioned in April 1864 and destroyed during Sherman's move into South Carolina in February 1865. The *Macon* was commissioned in August 1864 and fled Savannah at Sherman's approach in December. The *Morgan* and *Gaines* were completed in 1862; the *Gaines* was run aground to escape capture in the August 1864 battle of Mobile Bay, and only the *Morgan* served out the war in defense of Mobile before being captured in April 1865.

If plans for a fleet of wooden gunboats failed, by 1862 Confederate planning had shifted, in any case, to building ironclads. For construction facilities, the navy had much narrowed choice; by the fall of 1862, New Orleans, Pensacola, Memphis, Nashville, Jacksonville, New Berne (North Carolina), and Norfolk had been lost. Naval construction was driven back along Southern rivers to sites in the interior.

Such charges registered very powerfully in Columbus. While the *Chattahoochee* had reflected one policy of the Confederate Navy, the Columbus Naval Iron Works became an essential component to the success of another, the ironclad program. As Mallory had stated, a steam engine was as important to a modern warship as a battery of cannon. Supplying machinery for ships and constructing the ironclad *Jackson* placed the work of Warner and McLaughlin in the forefront of the navy's plans. As engineering and construction officers they put forth heroic efforts, not against an enemy navy but against the familiar obstacles of the rivers and the navy system itself.

Like the Confederate Navy as a whole, Columbus operations had the basic components to make a success of the work assigned there. The Columbus Iron Works was an established facility for building and repairing steam engines before the war. As an industrialized city, Columbus had a large, relatively skilled labor force. Like Saffold, Columbus could claim nearby stands of timber and sawmills. Again, the task was to shape those components into a productive system to fulfill the navy's plans for powering ironclad ships.

The naval blockade off Apalachicola existed in a Union system that tended to maximize its efforts; in contrast, Warner and McLaughlin spent their best efforts in a fragmented, inefficient system.

Constructing and equipping facilities to perform their work was a sizable project in itself. Yet this work continued along a parallel track with other duties for the duration of the war. Nor was all work centered in Columbus. Instead, some functions were delegated to satellite facilities in Eufaula and Prattville, Alabama, and among crews at work throughout the war in Selma, Mobile, and Oven Bluff, Alabama, as well as in Savannah, Charleston, and Wilmington. Purchasing agents traveled throughout the Confederacy in search of supplies and parts. Compared to other sites like the Tredager works in Richmond—or sites along the rivers of North and South Carolina, Mississippi, Alabama, and Louisiana—the CNIW had the most widely deployed operation.

Geographically fragmented, CNIW projects had to rely upon a basically inadequate and badly overtaxed rail system, on a small fleet of river steamers, which the iron works kept in repair, or at times on wagons and horses. Always, their needs for transportation had to compete with the army's reliance upon rail transport and the needs of a civilian population uprooted by war and increasingly on the move.

A highly fragmented construction system made the need for transportation even more critical. Instead of being located at a few comprehensive facilities, navy construction sites were scattered throughout the South. Valves, pumps, and boilers were fabricated at Columbus, though many such parts were made at Eufaula and shipped upriver. Shafting could be cast and finished only at Charlotte. Rifled cannon were cast at Selma, gun sights were made in Atlanta, and gun carriages at Atlanta, Charlotte, Charleston, or Richmond. At times, a machinist at work in Savannah had to travel more than twenty-four hours back to the Columbus facilities to complete a task and then return to his work site. In an era when men and horses supplied the force to transport heavy loads to rail cars, to ship equipment weighing many tons was a routine operation in the construction system.

Still another increment of difficulty in the system was an almost total absence of standardization. Except for the two ships laid down on the Tombigbee River at Oven Bluff, and as ordnance officer David McCorkle complained, no two Confederate ships were alike. Any gun carriage had to be designed for a specific position on a specific ship—and designed to the fine tolerances that a more advanced technology required. Even a standard part like the port for a propeller shaft required individual design of size and angle, followed by custom casting, finishing, and installation.

Each project assigned the CNIW increased the magnitude of the task and amplified the basic flaws in the system. Of the twenty-two ironclads commissioned by the Confederate Navy, Warner and his operation supplied machinery for the *Huntsville, Tuscaloosa*, the *Tennessee II*, and the two Bigbee Boats at Oven Bluff, Selma, and Mobile; the *Savannah* at Savannah; the *Columbia* at Charleston; the *Wilmington* at Wilmington; and the *Jackson* at the Columbus facility. But Warner's work was by no means limited to the navy's ironclad plans. The *Chattahoochee* and *Macon* received CNIW machinery; the *Chattahoochee*'s engines were repaired in Columbus; engines were supplied both for the torpedo boat

Viper and for the river transport *Shamrock* constructed in Columbus; and a fleet of river steamers like the *Uchee, Indian,* and *Munnerlyn* were maintained.

Managing so many projects and trying to clear a logjam of work through a construction system required a large, skilled, and well-disciplined work force. Despite some defections—and a growing dissatisfaction among foreign-born laborers later in the war—records give every evidence that Warner and McLaughlin were highly effective in managing their work force. Their major problem occurred in another part of the Confederate system with the army's constant demand for more manpower. This was a paper war fought by the unceasing clerical labor required to list, account for, and justify the exemption of each skilled worker from military service. Sherman's advance upon Atlanta eroded Warner's position on the need for workers; the attack upon Savannah finally swung the advantage to the Confederate Army as the Columbus Navy Battalion was ordered away to fight its Union enemy. By the time Warner's and McLaughlin's crews returned from Savannah in January 1865, time had all but run out.

While the war lasted, Warner was to see only four of the ships for which he supplied machinery become operational: the *Tennessee II*, the *Savannah*, the *Macon*, and the *Columbia*. Of those, only the *Tennessee II* and the *Savannah* were effective fighting ships. The *Columbia* was damaged beyond repair in a grounding; the *Macon* retreated from Sherman's advance upriver to Augusta. The Bigbee Boats were never completed, the *Wilmington* was destroyed on the ways to escape capture, and the *Huntsville* and *Tuscaloosa* were little more than floating batteries. At Columbus, the *Chattahoochee* was burned by her own crew, the *Viper* escaped Wilson's raid only to be captured later, and the formidable ironclad *Jackson* was captured and destroyed in Wilson's raid in the last battle of the war.

Not only the irony and indignity of the *Jackson*'s capture by Union cavalry, but the entire history of the project typifies the inadequacy of the systems in which Warner and McLaughlin worked. The impact of shifting water levels in the Chattahoochee River during the first launch attempt supplies a prime example of how forces beyond human control could ultimately determine the navy's success. Of all the systems to be battled, the river was most unforgiving.

Despite all the disadvantages of multiple projects in progress and massive demands upon their system of labor, supply, and facilities,

Warner and McLaughlin constructed the *Jackson* and had her ready for launch and completion in one year. Then two capricious systems intersected their progress toward timely completion. First, a rapid rise and a rapid fall of the river prevented a launch. Then Chief Constructor Porter appeared on the scene to conduct a construction review. His initial plan for a center paddle wheel had not worked well in the *Louisiana* at New Orleans; redesigning McLaughlin's work offered an opportunity to rectify his mistake. The year required to redesign and reconstruct the *Jackson* in response to Porter's change order produced a better design but, in more practical terms, the delay dashed all hopes of sending an ironclad down the river to raise the blockade at Apalachicola. In April 1865, the Union cavalry found her less than a month away from completion.

Even so, the entire Confederate ironclad program fared little better than the work Warner accomplished or influenced. Only a fraction of ships laid down were ever launched. Of those, few or none became the decisive strategic factor Mallory had hoped for. And of all components of the Confederate fleet, steam machinery was most inadequate. In the final analysis, if the Union blockade failed on a daily basis but ultimately won, work at Columbus succeeded for the most part—in facilities, labor, design, and schedules—and ultimately lost.

Young Horry Dent had written his father from the gunboat *Chattahoochee*, "There is no honor to be attached to such a ship as an Engineer." Certainly Warner and McLaughlin appear rarely in Confederate records, never on the honor rolls. Their Civil War story is told in terms of the unremitting, usually anonymous labor that engineers so often perform.

In assessing their failure, it is important to note that they worked during a transitional time when the technology of naval warfare was just being fully developed. The ironclad had been long established as a concept in weaponry, just as aviation technology was well known at the time of World War I. War greatly accelerated the development of steam propulsion and ironclad ships. But applying new technology effectively in wartime requires, first of all, sound planning and a sophisticated management system. The Confederate Navy lacked both. Confederate armies showed how heroic individual effort can turn the tide of battle; Confederate construction officers learned that a manager's heroic efforts cannot overcome deficiencies in closely interdependent technical systems.

Not only in developing and applying new technology, but especially in naval construction, sufficient time is essential for design, construction, and testing. And the Confederate Navy did not have time. The *Arkansas* steamed into battle with mechanics still at work on her machinery. Not only with the ironclad, but with the torpedo boat and the submarine as well, the navy conducted training and testing maneuvers with live ammunition in actual combat. Thus the Confederate Navy launched a massive technical effort without fully understanding either the technical requirements or the full implications of such an undertaking. Like the introduction of rocket technology in World War II, the ironclad and the torpedo had a measurable psychological impact and no more. Neither achieved the decisive effect the Confederacy so much needed. Full realization of the potential for iron ships, submarines, and torpedoes was left to other engineers and later wars. Ultimately Warner and McLaughlin failed; they were technocrats before their time.

By Civil War standards, the story of their work for the Confederate Navy on the Chattahoochee River is unromantic. Like their Union counterparts who served on the blockade, war was neither heroism nor glory, but work. Unlike the Union blockade crews, neither Warner, McLaughlin, nor their work crews gained the reward of working within a larger national effort that succeeded. Their story ends as all Civil War stories do: the South lost, the North won, the federal Union was preserved.

To measure their success in human and individual terms, however, Warner and McLaughlin were like the majority of men, in peacetime or in war, who work within systems and organizations. They battle the daily problems of budget, labor, materials acquisition and allocation, quality control, production and transportation schedules, and the petty warfare that erupts among people who work together. Like every man in every war, they waited: for the carloads of coal from Montgomery, for the valve from Savannah, for the letter from Richmond, and for the river to rise.

If romance and honor can be found in this Civil War story, it resides in the passion that some men have for machines and for understanding and refining how things work. If Warner and McLaughlin did not triumph and prevail in battle, they compiled an honorable record. They made themselves useful by doing their duty. They believed in, and endured, their work.

A P P E N D I X E S

These records from the collections of the James W. Woodruff, Jr., Confederate Naval Museum, Columbus, Georgia, have been compiled and transcribed under the direction of Robert Holcombe, curator. Variant spellings are preserved.

APPENDIX 1

A. Table of Contents, Chief Engineer James H. Warner's Letter Book, Columbus Naval Iron Works, 1862–1866

Page	Correspondent	Place	Date
1	Janney & Co.	Montgomery	09/04/62
2	Schofield & Br	Macon	09/13/62
3	Janney & Bro	Montgomery	09/13/62
4	L. Haiman & Co.		09/20/62
5	Capt. Edward Croft CSA	Columbus	09/20/62
6	Capt. Edward Croft CSA	Columbus	09/20/62
7	Hon. G. W. Randolph	Richmond	09/23/62
8	Maj. W. G. Swanson CSA	Notasulga, Ala.	09/27/62
9	Mr. Robert Warrick	Savannah	10/02/62
10	Mr. A. N. Miller	Savannah	10/02/62
10–11	Eng. in Chief Wm. P. Williamson CSN	Richmond	10/03/62
12	Eng. in Chief Wm. P. Williamson CSN	Richmond	10/03/62
13	General Mercer	Savannah	10/03/62
14	Schofield & Markham	Atlanta	10/03/62
	Schofield & Markham	Atlanta	10/03/62
15	First Asst. Eng. Wm. Frick, Jr.	Columbus	10/06/62
16	Maj. Dunwoodie CSA—Cmdr. Camp Randolph		10/06/62
17	Benjamin B. Davis, Esq.	Montgomery	10/08/62
18	Schofield & Markham	Atlanta	10/09/62
19	Henry D. Bassett	Selma	n.d.
	Benjamin B. Davis, Esq.	Montgomery	10/11/62
20	Mr. Robert Warrick	Savannah	10/14/62
	Capt. Haynes		10/17/62
21	Mr. George W. Brown		10/18/62
22	Capt. E. Farrand CSN	Selma	
	William P. Williamson CSN	Richmond	
23	William P. Williamson CSN	Richmond	10/18/62
24	Hon. S. R. Mallory	Richmond	10/17/62
25	Hon. S. R. Mallory	Richmond	10/17/62
26	Mr. C. C. McGehee	Columbus	10/20/62
27	Mr. Robert Warrick	Savannah	10/20/62
	LaRoche & Bell	Savannah	10/20/62

Page	Correspondent	Place	Date
28	Mobile Register & Advertiser		10/27/62
	Southern Confederacy	Atlanta	10/27/62
29	Mr. W. R. Brown	Mobile	10/27/62
	Charleston Mercury		10/27/62
30	Montgomery Advertiser		10/27/62
	Richmond Enquirer		10/27/62
31	Savannah Republican		10/27/62
	Richmond Examiner		10/27/62
32	Richmond Dispatch		10/27/62
33	A. N. Miller	Savannah	10/28/62
34	Missing (not indexed)		
35	Skates & Co.	Mobile	10/28/62
	J. M. Peters		11/01/62
36	William P. Williamson	Richmond	11/03/62
37	W. P. Wiley	Savannah	11/04/62
38	Josiah Tattnall CSN	Savannah	11/06/62
39	Eagle Man. Co.	Columbus	11/06/62
40	Capt. R. M. Cuyler	Macon	11/06/62
41	George H. O'Neal	Selma	11/21/62
	Cameron & Co.	Charleston	11/22/62
42	George H. O'Neal	Selma	11/21/62
	Col. M. J. Crawford	Columbus	11/23/62
43	L. E. Brooks	Johnston Ldg.	11/24/62
	W. P. Wiley	Savannah	11/25/62
44	Daniel Pratt	Mobile	11/25/62
	George H. O'Neal	Selma	12/03/62
45	Frank Jarvis	Mobile	12/09/62
46	William Penny & Co.	Prattville	12/16/62
	Cameron & Co.	Charleston	12/16/62
47	Skates & Co.	Mobile	12/17/62
	Schofield & Markham	Atlanta	12/18/62
48	A. N. Miller	Savannah	12/19/62
	W. W. Potter	Evergreen, Ala.	12/19/62
49	William & Co.	Mobile	12/20/62
	P. J. Ryan	Savannah	12/22/62
50	Maj. R. M. Cuyler	Macon	12/22/62
	Savannah Republican		01/12/63
51	Joseph Pierce, Esq.	Selma	12/26/62
52	Mr. D. St. Ledger	Eufaula	12/30/62
	Barney Brothers & Co.	Mobile	01/06/63
53	P. J. Ryan	Savannah	01/06/63
54	Park & Lyons	Mobile	01/06/63
	J. W. Young	Eufaula	01/13/63
55	H. Clark	Jacksonville, Fla.	01/12/63

Page	Correspondent	Place	Date
	Chief Eng. J. H. Warner	Savannah	01/16/63
56	E. Farrand	Selma	01/17/63
	Wm. Anderson & Co.	Mobile	01/19/63
57	P. J. Ryan	Savannah	01/20/63
58	P. J. Ryan	Savannah	02/06/63
59	R. S. Izard	Pocotaligo, S.C.	02/07/63
	P. J. Ryan	Savannah	02/09/63
60	Col. Hardee CSA	Decatur, Ga.	02/12/63
61–62	Maj. F. C. Humphries CSA	Columbus	02/14/63
63	A. N. Miller	Savannah	02/17/63
64	J. W. Young	Eufaula	02/19/63
65	P. J. Ryan	Savannah	02/21/63
66	Claghorn & Cunningham	Savannah	02/23/63
67	Claghorn & Cunningham	Savannah	02/23/63
68	Josiah Tattnall	Savannah	03/03/63
69	W. W. Ansell	Newport, Fla.	03/03/63
70	P. J. Ryan	Savannah	03/05/63
71	John W. Lewis	Cartersville	03/05/63
72	Capt. Samuel J. Whiteside	Mobile	03/09/63
	Capt. Samuel J. Whiteside	Mobile	03/10/63
73	D. N. Ingraham CSN	Charleston	03/10/63
74	M. Russell Bro. & Co.	Dalton	03/12/63
75	J. R. Jourdan		03/17/63
	F. Buchanan CSN	Mobile	03/18/63
76	P. J. Ryan	Savannah	03/21/63
77	J. W. Young	Eufaula	03/24/63
	M. Russell Bro. & Co.	Dalton	03/24/63
78	David C. Heidt	Eufaula	03/26/63
	Benjamin B. Davis	Montgomery	03/26/63
79	Maj. Charles S. Hardee CSA	Decatur, Ga.	03/26/63
80	M. Russell Bro. & Co.	Dalton	04/04/63
81	P. J. Ryan		
82	J. W. Young	Eufaula	04/09/63
	A. N. Miller	Savannah	04/16/63
83	J. W. Young	Eufaula	04/16/63
84	J. W. Young	Eufaula	04/21/63
85	P. J. Ryan	Savannah	04/22/63
86	F. M. Pope	North Carolina RR	04/22/63
	Cameron & Co.	Charleston	04/24/63
87	Wm. Penny & Co.	Prattville	04/27/63
88	J. W. Young	Eufaula	05/06/63
89	P. J. Ryan	Savannah	05/06/63
90	V. Freeman	Charleston	05/11/63
	J. W. Young	Eufaula	05/21/63

Page	Correspondent	Place	Date
91	P. J. Ryan	Savannah	05/21/63
92	Maj. Charles S. Hardee		06/03/63
93	P. J. Ryan	Savannah	06/06/63
94	J. W. Young	Eufaula	06/13/63
	Mobile Register & Advertiser		06/13/63
95	Wilmington Journal		06/13/63
	Richmond Examiner		06/13/63
96	Richmond Enquirer		06/13/63
	Augusta Chronicle & Sentinel		06/13/63
97	Charleston Courier		06/13/63
	Agt. Rail Road	West Point, Ga.	06/19/63
98	H. M. Anderson & Co.	Rome	06/20/63
99	P. J. Ryan	Savannah	06/22/63
100	P. J. Ryan	Savannah	07/07/63
101	Maj. Charles S. Hardee		07/07/63
102	J. W. Young	Eufaula	07/10/63
103	Mr. Nesbitt	Macon	07/15/63
104	P. J. Ryan	Savannah	07/16/63
105	J. W. Young	Eufaula	07/21/63
106	A. N. Miller	Savannah	07/27/63
107	Maj. John Andrews	Decatur	08/07/63
108	J. W. Tynan	Savannah	08/08/63
109	William Frick, Jr.	Mobile	08/31/63
110	Maj. John Andrews	Decatur	09/09/63
111	Chief Eng. J. W. Tynan	Savannah	09/18/63
112	William Frick, Jr. CSN	Mobile	09/18/63
113	Chief Eng. J. W. Tynan	Savannah	09/22/63
114	J. W. Young	Eufaula	09/23/63
115	Benjamin B. Davis	Montgomery	09/24/63
116	Wyman Moses & Co.	Montgomery	09/25/63
117	William Frick, Jr. CSN	Mobile	09/29/63
118	William Frick, Jr. CSN	Mobile	09/29/63
119	V. Freeman CSN	Charlotte	10/03/63
120	William Frick, Jr. CSN	Mobile	10/07/63
121	Capt. Wallace	Columbus	10/08/63
122	Maj. John Andrews		10/08/63
	J. M. Stamford	Eufaula	10/23/63
123	George H. O'Neal	Selma	10/29/63
124	Moses Goldsmith & Sons	Charleston	11/09/63
125	George H. O'Neal	Selma	11/09/63
126	Maj. John Andrews	Camp Randolph	11/09/63
127	John H. Loper CSN	St. Marks	11/25/63
128	J. W. Young	Eufaula	11/26/63
129	Goldsmith & Sons	Charleston	12/02/63

Page	Correspondent	Place	Date
130	Thomas J. Davis	Augusta	12/07/63
131	Maj. John Andrews	Camp Randolph	12/07/63
132	John H. Loper CSN	St. Marks	12/09/63
133	P. J. Ryan	Savannah	12/22/63
134	Hughes Hagan & Co.	Atlanta	12/28/63
135	John H. Loper CSN	St. Marks	12/30/63
136	Maj. John Andrews	Camp Randolph	1/15(12)64
137	L. A. McCarthy	Savannah	01/16/64
138	J. W. Young	Eufaula	01/16/64
139	William Frick, Jr. CSN	Mobile	n.d.
140	George E. Redwood	Alabama	02/01/64
141	William Frick, Jr. CSN	Mobile	02/03/64
142	John H. Loper	St. Marks	02/09/64
143	George H. O'Neal	Selma	02/11/64
144	George H. O'Neal	Selma	02/17/64
145	John H. Loper	St. Marks	02/25/64
146	Graham & Warren	Selma	02/27/64
147	Maj. John Andrews	Camp Randolph	02/29/64
148	M. Clanahan & Dill	Atlanta	03/04/64
149	Moses Goldsmith & Sons	Charleston	03/04/64
150	J. W. Tynan CSN	Savannah	03/04/64
151	Jno. Wythe Parks	Montgomery	03/04/64
152	J. W. Tynan CSN	Savannah	03/05/64
153	J. C. Alexander	Charleston	03/05/64
154	J. C. Alexander	Charleston	03/05/64
155	Maj. Jno. Andrews	Camp Randolph	03/07/64
156	J. C. Alexander	Charleston	03/07/64
157	J. W. Young	Eufaula	03/08/64
158	Wm. Penny & Co.	Prattville	03/08/64
159	Maj. Charles Harris	Macon	03/09/64
160	J. W. Nixon CSN	Selma	03/11/64
161	J. W. Tynan	Savannah	03/11/64
162	J. C. Alexander	Charleston	03/11/64
163	W. A. Young	Quincy, Fla.	03/12/64
164	J. W. Tynan	Savannah	03/12/64
165	W. L. Criglar	Pollard, Ala.	03/15/64
166	John H. Loper	St. Marks	03/16/64
167	Graham & Warren	Selma	03/16/64
168	J. W. Tynan CSN	Savannah	03/19/64
169	O. L. Packard, Esq.	Atlanta	03/22/64
170	George H. O'Neal CSN	Selma	03/22/64
171	William Frick, Jr. CSN	Mobile	03/23/64
172	Capt. William M. David	Henderson, Ga.	03/25/64
173	J. W. Nixon CSN	Covington, Ga.	03/25/64

Page	Correspondent	Place	Date
174	J. W. Nixon CSN	Covington	03/26/64
175	J. W. Nixon CSN	Covington	03/29/64
176	J. W. Nixon CSN	Covington	03/29/64
177	J. W. Nixon CSN	Covington	03/30/64
178	William Frick, Jr. CSN	Mobile	03/30/64
179	J. C. Anderson	Charleston	04/06/64
180	J. W. Tynan CSN	Savannah	04/06/64
181	Missing (not indexed)		
182	John W. Parks	Montgomery	04/18/64
183	J. W. Tynan CSN	Savannah	04/26/64
184	Comndt of Conscripts		04/ /64
185	J. W. Young	Eufaula	04/27/64
186	Jno. Wythe Parks	Montgomery	04/29/64
187	Maj. John Andrews	Decatur	04/30/64
188	William Frick, Jr. CSN	Mobile	05/04/64
189	Missing (not indexed)		
190	A. N. Miller	Savannah	05/18/64
191	Montgomery Advertiser		05/26/64
	Mobile Register & Advertiser		05/26/64
192	Memphis Appeal		05/26/64
	Supt. Alabama & Florida RR		05/30/64
193	W. A. Young	Quincy, Fla.	06/07/64
194	Maj. E. H. Harris	Montgomery	06/08/64
195	W. A. Young	Quincy, Fla.	06/09/64
196	Meachum & Bro.	Chattahoochee	06/09/64
197	J. C. Alexander	Charleston	06/13/64
198	Missing (but indexed)		
	L. H. Cooper		
199	Capt. J. E. Mayhew	Montgomery	06/14/64
200	Maj. Reedy	Notasulga, Ala.	06/14/64
201			
202	Goldsmith & Sons	Charleston	06/15/64
203	Enrolling Officer	Prattville	06/16/64
204	Edward Gotthiel CSA	Savannah	06/25/64
205	V. Freeman CSN	Charleston	06/20/64
206	W. W. J. Kelly CSN	Savannah	06/21/64
207	Capt. W. L. Davis		06/21/64
208	John M. Cooper & Co.	Savannah	06/22/64
209	William L. Lynch CSN	Wilmington	06/23/64
210	John M. Cooper & Co.	Savannah	06/28/64
211	J. W. Tynan CSN	Savannah	06/27/64
212	William Frick, Jr. CSN	Mobile	06/27/?
213	Agt. Navy Cotton Press	Augusta	06/29/64
214	William Anderson	Columbus	06/30/64

Page	Correspondent	Place	Date
215	Capt. Charles Brockway	Columbus	07/02/64
216	Capt. Jno. E. Mayhew	Montgomery	07/02/64
217	Capt. R. A. Talley	Columbus	07/04/64
218	John M. Cooper & Co.	Savannah	07/06/64
219	Charles McVay	Eufaula	07/06/64
220	J. W. Tynan	Savannah	07/06/64
221	(exact duplicate of 222, not indexed)		
222	J. C. Alexander	Charleston	07/07/64
223	J. Thomas Davis	Bath, S.C.	07/08/64
224	A. N. Miller	Savannah	07/04/64
225	J. W. Young	Eufaula	07/13/64
226	Maj. George O. Dawson		07/21/64
227	L. Campbell CSN	Savannah	07/22/64
228	G. W. Smith	Columbus	07/25/64
229	William A. Campbell	Columbus	07/25/64
230	W. W. Ansell	Columbus	07/25/64
231	E. J. Purse	Savannah	07/27/64
232	Capt. Charles Brockway	Montgomery	07/27/64
233	J. C. Alexander	Charleston	07/28/64
234	H. Ashton Ramsay	Charlotte	07/28/64
235	V. Freeman CSN	Charleston	07/29/64
236	J. C. Alexander	Charleston	07/29/64
237	S. L. Mullins	Columbus	07/30/64
238	Philan & McBride & Co.	Selma	08/09/64
239	Capt. Charles Brockway	Montgomery	08/09/64
240	J. W. Young	Eufaula	08/11/64
241	W. A. Young	Quincy, Fla.	08/12/64
242	William A. Campbell	Loachapoka	08/12/64
243	J. A. Marbury (Marburg)	Macon	08/17/64
244	S. J. Whiteside		08/22/64
245	L. P. Henop	Columbus	08/22/64
246	E. J. P. Purse	Savannah	08/09/64
247	E. J. P. Purse	Savannah	08/29/64
248	E. J. P. Purse	Savannah	08/29/64
249	Charles McVay	Eufaula	08/29/64
250	Philan & McBride & Co.	Selma	08/30/64
251	D. C. Herndon	Bibb Co., Ala.	08/30/64
	Jno. Matthews		08/31/64
252	P. G. Corniffe	Charleston	09/13/64
253	W. W. J. Kelly	Savannah	09/16/64
254	A. J. Edwards	Columbus	09/29/64
255	J. W. Churchill	Columbus	09/29/64
256	J. W. Young	Eufaula	10/22/64
257	W. W. J. Kelly	Savannah	10/22/64

Page	Correspondent	Place	Date
258	William Frick CSN	Mobile	11/11/64
259	Missing (not indexed)		
260	E. Farrand CSN	Mobile	11/17/64
261	A. W. Murphy		11/19/64
262	S. L. Mullins		11/19/64
263	William P. Williamson CSN	Richmond	11/19/64
264	M. Spagilburg [Spaleburg]	Charleston	11/19/64
265	S. L. Mullins		11/21/64
266	J. W. Young	Eufaula	11/21/64
267	J. Troskowloski	Columbus	11/28/64
268	Hon. S. R. Mallory	Richmond	11/29/64
269	Capt. J. W. Glenn CSA	Macon	12/15/64
270	J. H. Jackson CSN	Columbia	12/15/64
271	L. P. Henop	Charleston	12/15/64
272	Capt. J. F. Jaiman	Selma	12/16/64
273	Capt. C. ap R. Jones CSN	Selma	12/16/64
274	D. F. Milling		12/20/64
275	J. W. Young	Eufaula	01/14/65
276	William Penny & Co.	Prattville	02/28/65
277–80	Rear Admiral H. K. Thatcher	Pensacola	12/08/65
282–83	Rear Admiral H. K. Thatcher	Pensacola	12/12/65
284–85	Rear Admiral H. K. Thatcher	Pensacola	12/15/65
286–95	Rear Admiral H. K. Thatcher	Pensacola	12/23/65
296	J. A. Alexander	Washington City	10/31/65
297	Memorandum of sale of property		12/22/65
298–99	Rear Admiral H. K. Thatcher	Pensacola	12/26/65
300	M. McEntee USN	Apalachicola	12/30/65
301–06	Rear Admiral H. K. Thatcher	Pensacola	01/02/66
307–08	Hon. Gideon Wells		01/03/66
309	Maj. General Foster USA		01/11/66
310–11	Rear Admiral H. K. Thatcher	Pensacola	01/11/66
312	Supt. Freedman's Dept.		01/16/66
313–17	Rear Admiral H. K. Thatcher	Pensacola	01/16/66
318–19	Rear Admiral H. K. Thatcher	Pensacola	01/19/66
320	Mr. MC		01/25/66
321–23	Rear Admiral H. K. Thatcher	Pensacola	01/25/66
324–25	Rear Admiral H. K. Thatcher	Pensacola	01/29/66
326	Rear Admiral H. K. Thatcher	Pensacola	01/31/66
327–28	Rear Admiral H. K. Thatcher	Pensacola	02/01/66
329–30	Rear Admiral H. K. Thatcher	Pensacola	02/05/66
331	Act. Ensign Carter USN	Macon	02/05/66
332	Rear Admiral H. K. Thatcher	Pensacola	02/08/66
333–34	Rear Admiral H. K. Thatcher	Pensacola	02/10/66
335–36	Rear Admiral H. K. Thatcher	Pensacola	02/12/66

B. Table of Contents, Confederate Navy Yard Log, Columbus, Georgia, 1864, Lieutenant Commanding Augustus McLaughlin

LETTERS

Page	Correspondent	Place	Date
	Capt. H. D. Cothran		
425	Actg. Mst. Julian Fairfax	Savannah	02/13/64
	Brig. Gen. A. R. Lawton	Richmond	02/15/64
426	Hon. S. R. Mallory	Hand Delivered	n.d.
	C. W. Mills	Rome	02/24/64
427	John K. Mitchell	Richmond	02/23/64
	Maj. Samuel Z. Gonzales, Naval Store Keeper	Montgomery	
	Capt. H. D. Cothran		02/26/64
428	J. K. Mitchell	Richmond	02/26/64
	Hon. S. R. Mallory	Richmond	02/26/64
429	Capt. H. D. Cothran		02/27/64
430	Cdr. J. M. Brooke	Richmond	02/29/64
	Furlough Request, Daniel Beverly		
	Capt. H. D. Cothran		03/02/64
431	Lt. Cdr. George W. Gift	Chattahoochee, Fla.	03/02/64
	Quarter Master	Rome	03/03/64
	Capt. Cothran		03/03/64
432	Cdr. J. K. Mitchell	Richmond	03/03/64
	Cdr. J. K. Mitchell	Richmond	03/04/64
	Hon. S. R. Mallory	Richmond	03/12/64
433	Lt. D. P. McCorkle	Atlanta	03/12/64
	Maj. S. Z. Gonzales	Montgomery	03/14/64
	Cdr. J. K. Mitchell	Richmond	03/19/64
434	Gen. Jos. E. Johnston		03/17/64
	Cdr. J. K. Mitchell	Richmond	03/18/64
435	Mr. Jonathan R. Ford		03/20/64
	Mr. John L. Porter, Chief Naval Constructor	Richmond	03/19/64
436	Maj. S. Z. Gonzales	Montgomery	03/23/64
	Capt. H. D. Cothran		03/23/64
437	Paymaster J. W. Nixon	Atlanta	03/23/64
	Passd. Mdn. G. Sparks		04/04/64
438	H. D. Cothran		04/04/64
	Hon. S. R. Mallory		04/14/64
439	Lt. Cdg. Hays	St. Mark's, Fla.	04/15/64
	J. K. Mitchell	Richmond	04/23/64
440	Hon. S. R. Mallory	Richmond	04/23/64
441	B. Parker, Esq., Treasury Department Auditor	Richmond	04/23/64
	Capt. J. R. Blount	Tallahassee	04/22/64
	Miss Fanny Leaphart, Congaree Hotel	Columbia, S.C.	04/25/64
442	Messrs. J. R. Anderson & Co.	Richmond	04/25/64

Page	Correspondent	Place	Date
	Cdr. J. K. Mitchell	Richmond	04/25/64
	Capt. D. P. McCorkle	Atlanta	04/26/64
443	Hon. S. R. Mallory	Richmond	04/29/64
	Hon. S. R. Mallory	Richmond	04/30/64
	Hon. S. R. Mallory	Richmond	05/02/64
444	Lt. Cmdg. D. P. McCorkle	Atlanta	05/03/64
	from G. W. Chayett [Telegram]	Mobile	05/03/64
	Capt. H. D. Cothran		05/07/64
	Constructor Graves [Telegram]		05/07/64
445	W. H. McMain	Macon	05/07/64
	M.S.K.		
	Cdr. C. ap R. Jones	Selma	05/07/64
	Dr. H. M. Anderson	Rome	
446	Cdr. J. K. Mitchell	Richmond	05/14/64
	Lt. Cmdg. D. P. McCorkle	Atlanta	05/17/64
	Major Hunt,	Selma	05/17/64
	Iron Works		
447	Lt. D. P. McCorkle	Atlanta	05/18/64
	Mr. W. H. Peters	Charlotte	05/18/64
	C.S.N.S.K		
	Capt. Cothran		05/20/64
	Lt. Cmdg. G. W. Gift	*Munnerlyn*	05/20/64
448	Lt. Cmdg. G. W. Gift	*Chattahoochee*	05/22/64
	Lt. Cmdg. G. W. Gift		05/22/64
449	Hon. S. R. Mallory	Richmond	05/23/64
450	Lieut. G. W. Gift [Telegram]	received	05/27/64
451	from Col. J. W. Robertson,		
	Tallahassee		05/27/64
452			
453	Hon. S. R. Mallory	Richmond	05/27/64
454	Mr. John F. Hughes	Mariana, Fla.	05/27/64
	Lt. Cmdg. G. W. Gift	*Chattahoochee*	05/27/64
455	Lt. G. W. Gift	Eufaula	05/28/64
	Lt. D. P. McCorkle	Atlanta	05/28/64
456	from G. W. Gift, Eufaula		05/28/64
	Hon. S. R. Mallory	Richmond	05/30/64
458	Asst. Paymst. M. L. Sothoron,	*Chattahoochee*	05/30/64
459	Cdr. J. M. Brooke	Richmond	05/30/64
	Maj. S. R. Hunt	Selma	05/31/65
	Capt. William Davis		06/01/64
	Enrolling Officer		
460	Lt. G. W. Gift	Eufaula	05/31/64
	Capt. Davis		06/02/64
	Lt. Cmdg. G. W. Gift	*Chattahoochee*	06/02/64

Page	Correspondent	Place	Date
461	Maj. J. C. Dennis,	Montgomery	06/03/64
	Bureau of Conscription		
	Asst. Paymst. M. L. Sothoron		06/06/64
	Quarter Master	Macon	06/09/64
	Maj. Hunt	Selma	06/10/64
462	Capt. William Davis		06/10/64
	Lt. Cmdg. G. W. Gift	*Chattahoochee*	06/11/64
463	from Capt. S. S. Lee, Richmond		06/03/64
464	Lt. Cmdg. G. W. Gift	*Chattahoochee*	06/13/64
	Capt. William Davis		06/13/64
465	Capt. S. S. Lee [Telegram]	Richmond	06/15/64
	Office of Orders and Detail,		
	from Capt. S. S. Lee, Richmond		06/15/64
	Lieut. Gift [Telegram]		06/17/64
466	Capt. W. S. Davis		06/18/64
	Capt. W. S. Davis		
467	Capt. S. S. Lee	Richmond	06/19/64
468	W. F. Howell,	Augusta	06/19/64
	Naval Agent		
	Capt. W. S. Davis		06/22/64
469	Hon. S. R. Mallory	Richmond	06/25/64
470			
471	Capt. S. A. Lee [Telegram]		06/28/64

MISCELLANEOUS RECORDS

472	Agency Union Bank, August 5–October 22, 1864
473–80	Cash Account, July–November 1864
481	Small Arms Inventory
482	Ration Account, June 30–July 31, 1864
483	Cordage and Naval Stores, May–September 1864
484	Assistant Paymaster, Southoran, Cash Account
485	Agency Union Bank of Augusta, May 9–July 26, 1864
486–91	Cash Account, May 9–July 26, 1864
492	Navy List [of 46 C.S. Ships]
493	Ration Account, April 21–June 15, 1864
494	Cash Account, April 22–May 7, 1864
495	Mess Fund, April 21–October 31, 1864
496	T. E. Hambleton, February–March 1864
497	Cash Account, February 13–March 12, 1864
498	Pay Roll C.S. Str. Chattahoochee, February 1–July 1, 1864
499	Applicants for Transfer to the Navy, February 6–22, 1864

A P P E N D I X 2

A. Columbus Naval Iron Works Vouchers

1862

Voucher Date	To	Amount
09/17/62	Columbus Iron Works C.S. Navy Department	$12,432.14
12/01/62	Columbus Iron Works C.S. Navy Department	24,000.00
11/14/62	Naval Iron Works	3,293.05

1863

Voucher Date	To	Amount
01/23/63	David S. Johnston	$ 225.25
01/31/63	J. Ennis Co.	271.90
02/03/63	B. F. Coleman	453.11
02/06/63	Goetchius Hodges & Co.	1,567.79
02/07/63	G. H. Peabody & Co.	103.00
02/07/63	John Ligon	158.50
02/09/63	S. H. Hill	810.00
02/12/63	A. Alexander	280.00
02/17/63	Folsom Cody	223.00
02/18/63	Chas. P. Levy	190.00
02/23/63	Claghorn & Cunningham	301.00
03/02/63	Bullock & Radcliff	204.50
03/03/63	Sam Wolff	9,948.95
03/06/63	W. R. Brown	402.00
03/10/63	Spencer & Abbott	1,571.00
03/11/63	Mobile & Girard Railroad (J. N. Dillon, agent)	120.00
03/12/63	A. Alexander	159.00
03/09/63	Brown & Co.	1,065.62
03/20/63	Gene Wolff	890.00
03/26/63	Stan Moses & Co.	4,000.00
03/28/63	Stanford & Golden	817.75
03/31/63	Muscogee Railroad (J. M. Bivins, agent)	485.00

Voucher Date	To	Amount
04/08/63	Patrick Duane	598.50
04/08/63	A. M. Brannon & Co.	625.00
04/09/63	Thomas Gilbert & Co.	211.00
04/14/63	Bullock & Radcliff	119.50
04/16/63	Spencer & Abbott	1,232.25
04/17/63	J. W. Churchill	361.60
04/18/63	Estes & Brother	120.75
04/18/63	Greenwood & Gray	3,894.25
04/21/63	Rock I. Paper Mills (F. J. Stanford)	324.85
04/25/63	Gas Light Co. (Thos. McElhenny, supt.)	727.10
04/25/63	Edw. Bull	500.00
04/28/63	John T. Walker	192.00
04/30/63	S. H. Hill	387.50
05/09/63	Horace King (Florence King)	1,444.50
05/14/63	C. Drew	231.40
05/14/63	J. Ennis & Co.	298.99
05/15/63	J. W. Churchill	131.49
05/16/63	Rosette Lawhorn & Co.	325.00
05/18/63	J. C. Wiley	300.00
05/24/63	A. Alexander	87.00
05/26/63	J. P. Hanserd	600.00
05/26/63	David H. Fowler	126.00
05/28/63	Rock Island Paper Mills & Co.	460.20
05/29/63	Bullock & Radcliff	94.20
05/30/63	Horace King (Florence King)	777.25
05/30/63	Muscogee Railroad Co. (J. M. Bivins)	570.00
06/02/63	A. Alexander	250.00
06/04/63	John B. Dozier	498.00
06/08/63	J. H. Marshall	2,652.00
06/11/63	C. Breyvogel	80.00
06/13/63	Schofield & Brother	2,696.85
06/16/63	H. R. Linthicum	65.00
06/18/63	J. C. Wiley	549.78
06/24/64	A. D. Butt	77.50
06/24/63	G. W. Haynes	111.50
06/25/63	Samuel J. Whiteside	622.55
06/27/63	S. H. Hill	185.00
06/30/63	Horace King	1,197.96
07/01/63	Thomas Gilbert & Co.	126.50
07/06/63	H. A. Cornsod	2,021.15
07/07/63	Radcliff & Bullock	282.25
07/09/63	B. F. Coleman	1,335.40
07/09/63	Hall Moses & Co.	283.10

Voucher Date	To	Amount
07/11/63	Gas Light Co. (Tom McElhenny, supt.)	811.60
07/14/63	J. C. Wiley	1,000.00
07/20/63	R. H. Briggs	75.00
07/20/63	Horace King	493.00
07/20/63	T. C. Nisbet	1,496.55
07/24/63	A. Alexander	495.00
07/20/63	W. H. May	2,700.41
07/28/63	A. Gammell	100.00
07/30/63	Horace King	300.00
07/31/63	J. W. Young	125.15
07/31/63	Stanford & Golden	1,740.23
08/03/63	Bullock & Radcliff	161.00
09/22/63	Horace King	640.50
10/10/63	Rock Island Paper Mills Co. (T. J. Stanford, sect.)	260.00
10/16/63	M. Kofman	217.50
10/17/63	E. Williams	3,332.00
10/20/63	A. Ravenscroft	46.50
10/21/63	L. G. Schuessler	61.65
10/21/63	Goetchius Hodges & Co.	51.19
10/23/63	B. F. Coleman	568.05
10/24/63	Simeon Ashley	124.44
10/26/63	Gas Light Co. (Tom McElhenny, supt.)	1,318.00
10/26/63	Harris & Howell	9,653.50
10/28/63	Horace King	926.44
10/29/63	J. H. Moshell	1,537.50
10/29/63	Wm. Child	187.50
10/29/63	Bullock & Radcliff	259.50
10/30/63	Stanford & Golden	1,769.10
11/07/63	A. F. Moreland	242.17
11/07/63	James T. Code	50.25
11/25/63	O. L. Pease	247.00
11/25/63	A. Ravenscroft	222.20
11/30/63	Bullock & Radcliff	489.00
11/30/63	E. J. Leonard	360.00
12/01/63	Horace King	1,050.00
12/07/63	Bath Fire Brick Works (Th. J. Davis, supt.)	1,100.00
12/08/63	W. R. Brown	1,362.50
12/08/63	Muscogee Rail Road	75.00
12/09/63	A. Alexander	9,601.49
12/09/63	Annie Chapman	600.00
12/11/63	B. F. Coleman	2,204.75
12/16/63	Stanford & Golden	1,900.78
12/18/63	S. & E. Holms	102.00

Voucher Date	To	Amount
12/18/63	A. Alexander	2,407.50
12/19/63	M. P. Ellis & Co.	1,188.50
12/19/63	Folsom & Cody	105.00
12/21/63	A. D. Brown & Co.	315.00
12/22/63	Thomas Moorefield	258.45
12/23/63	A. Ravenscroft	572.75
12/24/63	Horace King	1,750.00
12/28/63	E. Williams	10,102.15
12/30/63	Bullock & Radcliff	233.00
12/31/63	R. H. Abraham	179.50

1864

Date	To	Amount
01/12/64	Gas Light Co. (Tom McElhenny, supt.)	$1,793.80
01/15/64	B. F. Coleman	1,313.50
01/18/64	W. W. Ansell	2,033.00
01/18/64	W. R. Brown	387.15
01/20/64	J. H. Moshell	1,507.50
01/22/64	Horace King	999.00
01/22/64	A. Ravenscroft	125.00
01/26/64	J. B. Roper	240.00
01/29/64	A. Alexander	125.00
01/30/64	Louis P. Henop	1,500.00
02/04/64	Thomas Moorefield	124.96
02/06/64	Rosette Lawhorn	112.00
02/06/64	J. Ennis & Co.	104.90
02/06/64	J. Trosklowski	421.50
02/10/64	Stanford & Golden	2,183.41
02/16/64	J. B. Oliver	618.97
02/25/64	Wm. Anderson	281.45
02/25/64	Mobile & Girard Rail Road	180.00
02/29/64	Bullock & Radcliff	98.50
03/02/64	J. H. Moshell	1,256.00
03/02/64	W. L. Clark	1,120.00
03/03/64	G. W. Haynes	686.62
03/04/64	Dr. N. D. Spotswood	275.00
03/07/64	Horace King	1,333.00
03/07/64	Lewis Wimberly	1,265.90
03/08/64	Wm. Anderson	108.50

Voucher Date	To	Amount
03/09/64	J. W. Pease	440.50
03/09/64	Stanford & Golden	1,652.08
03/10/64	Geo. Chaffin	55.00
03/11/64	Wells & Curtis	71.50
03/11/64	Montgomery & West Point Rail Road	185.55
03/11/64	Chas. McVay	159.00
03/15/64	S. L. Mullin	307.25
03/15/64	E. J. Moses	1,215.00
03/15/64	John D. Gray & Co.	939.00
03/21/64	B. F. Coleman	2,262.10
03/22/64	Hall Moses & Co.	322.00
03/22/64	Geo. D. Chaffin	100.00
03/24/64	Capt. H. D. Cothran AQM	3,302.10
05/10/64	Horace King	1,740.00
06/30/64	John M. Cooper & Co.	416.00

B. Confederate Navy Yard Vouchers

1863

Voucher Date	To	Amount
01/26/63	J. Rhodes Browne	$ 18.00
01/26/63	James Abercrombie	13.00
01/30/63	J. Ennis & Co.	366.70
01/30/63	Estes & Bro.	72.80
01/30/63	Jefferson & Hamilton	18.25
01/31/63	Abraham Gamill	534.00
02/01/63	John W. Bevill	44.00
02/01/63	Goetchius, Hodges & Co.	487.15
02/04/63	J. C. Morton	338.02
02/11/63	Asa Lynch	80.00
02/14/63	E. A. Faber	97.50
02/17/63	A. B. Redding	76.50
02/20/63	Thomas Tuggle	600.00

Voucher Date	To	Amount
02/24/63	J. C. Morton	535.50
02/26/63	J. A. McCarty	7.50
02/26/63	James M. Bugg	237.50
02/27/63	Wm. Brooks	6,245.23
03/03/63	J. H. Moshell	39.50
03/07/63	Henry Godwin	592.00
03/09/63	Hull & Buck	104.55
03/10/63	J. W. Bevill	43.25
03/10/63	Bullock & Radcliff	183.60
03/13/63	Vernoy & Mahaffey	343.00
03/13/63	Ellis, Livingston & Co.	166.43
03/13/63	J. Ennis & Co.	703.30
03/17/63	Long Marshall & Pollard	863.46
03/23/63	Hall, Moses & Co.	442.35
03/24/63	James M. Hughes	190.50
03/25/63	B. A. Thornton	900.00
03/31/63	Estes & Brother	20.25
04/03/63	Thos. W. Stanford	20.00
04/03/63	Thomas Kenny	50.26
04/06/63	Estes & Bro.	40.00
04/08/63	J. H. Chase—Columbus	243.00
04/09/63	Atkins & Dunham—Columbus	138.00
05/08/63	B. A. Thornton	715.00
05/08/63	William Brooks	3,142.40
05/09/63	E. A. Faber—Columbus	50.00
05/19/63	Telegraph Co.	150.80
05/29/63	Rosette, Lawhorn & Co.	78.00
05/29/63	J. R. Ivey Co.	61.27
05/29/63	D. St. Leger	195.15
05/29/63	N. S. Morse & Co.	31.50
05/30/63	Moses Goldsmith & Sons Charleston	7,024.50
05/30/63	Horace King—Columbus	743.00
05/30/63	J. Gammel	376.00
06/03/63	W. H. Hughes	376.00
06/11/63	Wm. Brooks—Columbus	3,412.45
06/12/63	Long, Marshall & Pollard	1,032.29
06/17/63	J. Ennis & Co.	209.60
06/22/63	Goetchius, Hodges & Co.	253.50
06/22/63	Dan B. Dorsey	74.50
06/22/63	Bullock & Radcliff	652.00
06/22/63	Wm. Brooks	1,798.88
06/24/63	J. H. Butts & Co.	1,516.20
07/01/63	W. H. May—Savannah	1,929.50

Voucher Date	To	Amount
07/07/63	Horace King	684.00
07/08/63	Wm. Brooks	1,398.75
07/20/63	Alex J. Robinson—Columbus	210.00
07/22/63	Geo. F. Drew—Columbus	7,051.25
07/28/63	John Scealy—Columbus	93.26
07/28/63	J. C. Blain	120.00
07/28/63	J. C. Morton	315.90
07/31/63	W. R. Brown	78.25
08/08/63	L. G. Schuessler—Columbus	128.50
08/12/63	Goetchius Hodges & Co.	808.55
08/13/63	James M. Peters—Columbus	1,367.37
08/15/63	Wm. Brooks	1,693.80
08/27/63	Hall Moses & Co.	29.50
09/02/63	David S. Johnston	143.25
09/09/63	B. F. Coleman—Columbus	1,796,69
09/12/63	Henry Godwin—Columbus	405.00
09/15/63	J. C. Morton—Columbus	219.95
09/16/63	Wm. Brooks	4,498.65
09/18/63	J. C. Blain—Columbus	39.00
09/18/63	J. C. Blain—Columbus	161.00
09/18/63	J. C. Blain—Columbus	25.25
09/18/63	Horace King	585.00
09/21/63	Wm. Brands & Co.—Columbus	1,045.75
10/10/63	James M. Bugg—Columbus	266.67
10/15/63	P. Champion	94.80
10/23/63	Wm. Brooks	2,947.35
10/23/63	B. F. Coleman	757.50
10/29/63	J. C. Morton	459.70
10/30/63	Horace King	440.00
10/30/63	Goetchius Hodges & Co.—Columbus	166.48
10/31/63	B. Beasly—Columbus	957.60
10/31/63	J. C. Blain	82.50
11/16/63	L. H. Golder—Columbus	2,400.00
11/24/63	J. Ennis & Co.	593.35
11/24/63	Henry Godwin	755.00
12/02/63	Wm. Brooks	848.30
12/07/63	J. C. Morton	355.75
12/08/63	B. F. Coleman	327.50
12/08/63	J. M. Bugg—Columbus	918.81
12/14/63	Henry Godwin—Columbus	425.62
12/19/63	Eagle Manuf. Co.	2,048.92
12/23/63	J. C. Morton	3,482.75
12/24/63	John Williams	1,135.00

Voucher Date	To	Amount
12/28/63	J. C. Morton	2,664.12
12/28/63	Wm. Brooks	6,765.10

1864

Voucher Date	To	Amount
01/08/64	Horace King	$ 835.00
01/08/64	Henry Godwin	67.50
01/14/64	Leslie E. Brooks—Columbus	83.00
01/15/64	J. C. Morton	104.61
01/18/64	J. C. Morton	205.00
02/25/64	Hull & Buck	583.00
02/25/64	Hall Moses & Co.—Columbus	186.00
02/26/64	Columbus Planning Mill	83.55
03/07/64	J. C. Morton	444.00
03/08/64	Mobile & Girard RR—Columbus	23,527.55
03/09/64	Wm. Brooks	5,292.34
03/15/64	B. F. Coleman	398.60
03/18/64	Nathan Bayne	122.50
03/18/64	L. H. Golder	122.50
03/18/64	J. C. Morton	109.75
03/23/64	Hall, Moses & Co. ·	344.00
03/25/64	J. C. Morton—Columbus	202.50
04/01/64	Eagle Mfg. Co.—Columbus	933.75
04/27/64	Geo. D. Chaffin—Columbus	215.00
05/05/64	J. C. Morton—Columbus	248.50
05/19/64	Wm. Brooks	11,071.80
05/31/64	L. H. Golder—Columbus	845.50
06/11/64	George F. Drew—Columbus	7,051.25
06/13/64	J. C. Morton	307.00
06/30/64	Thomas Berry & Co.	1,860.00
06/30/64	Stanford & Golden—Columbus	774.00
06/30/64	Wm. Brooks	7,001.60
06/30/64	Wm. Brooks	1,803.00

C. Confederate Navy Yard Financial Statements During the Construction of the C.S. Gunboat Chattahoochee

1862

Voucher Date	To	Amount
01/01/62	J. W. Pease	$ 1.75
01/25/62	Steamer River Bride	9.00
02/12/62	Southern Telegraph Co.	30.45
02/11/62	Southern Express Co.	49.50
03/25/62	Wiley Williams	5.00
03/25/62	David S. Johnston	21,333.33
03/31/62	Cash on hand and credited 2nd quarter	26,070.97
		$47,500.00
1861		
12/30	By draft on S. R. Mallory Secty Navy Richmond	17,812.50
1862		
03/03	By draft on Jno. Boston (Collector) Savannah	29,687.50
		$47,500.00

Columbus, Georgia   March 31st, 1862
Lieut. Augustus McLaughlin
C.S. Navy

05/17/62	Thomas Berry	$ 1,700.00
05/20/62	David S. Johnston	10,333.33
05/26/62	Columbus Times	3.50
05/27/62	J. Ennis & Co.	529.69
06/04/62	S. H. Hill	98.00
06/30/62	Cash on hand and credited 3rd Quarter	13,406.45
		$26,070.97
1862		
04/01	By amount cash on hand from first quarter	26,070.97
		$26,070.97

Columbus, Georgia   June 30th, 1862
Lieut. Augustus McLaughlin
C.S. Navy

Voucher Date	To	Amount
07/02/62	J. C. Morton	$ 54.60
07/07/62	S. H. Hill	79.50
07/07/62	W. L. Clark	200.85
02/11/62	May & Benizette	261.25
02/14/62	Southern Express Co.	14.60
02/16/62	Jas. H. Warner	337.87
08/01/62	Southern Express Co.	9.50
08/12/62	David S. Johnston	6,333.33
08/13/62	Edward Williams	156.66
08/14/62	J. Rhodes Browne	55.00
08/15/62	Jas. Johnson	5.00
09/08/62	John Kingsley	24.00
09/08/62	J. W. Pease	19.35
09/10/62	Colquitt & Warren	30.00
09/19/62	James Dempsey	440.00
09/20/62	S. R. Hoopes	162.70
09/26/62	David S. Johnston	4,860.15
09/29/62	Richard Robb	45.00
09/29/62	Mr. Thomas Morrill	34.25
	To amount cash credited 4th Quarter 1862	19,283.74
		$32,406.35
1862		
07/01	By amount credited from 2nd quarter statement	13,406.35
07/08	Draft on John Boston Collector Savannah	19,000.00
		$32,406.35

E&C Excepted   Columbus, Georgia   September 30, 1862
   Lieutenant Augustus McLaughlin
   Confederate Navy

08/12/62	Urquhart & Chapman	25.00
08/30/62	Sammis & Roone	158.00
10/04/62	David S. Johnston	14.00
10/04/62	John Rose	53.55
10/24/62	Southern Express	18.00
10/25/62	B. Beasley	136.14
11/13/62	Colquitt & Warren	16.00
12/02/62	D. St. Ledger	194.00
12/03/62	David S. Johnston	1,359.00
12/03/62	Southern Express	11.00
12/05/62	Sammis & Rooney	46.50
12/11/62	J. W. Pease	9.00
12/16/62	Mobile & Girard R. Road	102.20

12/26/62	Steamer Indian	69.00
12/26/62	Steamer Jackson	159.00
12/29/62	Louis Myers	120.00
12/31/62	S. H. Hill	600.00

1863

Voucher Date	To	Amount
01/05/63	Charles W. Godwin	$ 195.50
01/08/63	Steamer Uchee	7.00
01/19/63	David S. Johnston	1,139.85
01/21/63	Jefferson & Hamilton	25.50
01/23/63	C. G. Holmes	12,000.00
01/28/63	S. H. Hill	900.00
01/31/63	Cash on hand to bal. a/c	25,924.50
		$43,282.74

1862

10/01	By cash on hand at end of 3rd Quarter	19,282.74
10/25	By cash of Genl. G. Langford	
	Deposit Montgomery	24,000.00
		$43,282.74

E&C Excepted   Columbus, Georgia   January 31st, 1863
          Lt. A. McLaughlin
          C.S. Navy

1862

Voucher Date	To	Amount
09/05/62	J. H. Sikes	$ 146.00
10/13/62	J. Ennis & Co.	46.25
10/13/62	Southern Express Co.	18.50
12/31/62	A. Harris	35.00

1863

| 01/01/63 | Francis Allender | 63.75 |
| 01/03/63 | John Stokes | 115.00 |

Voucher Date	To	Amount
01/03/63	Henry Grady	115.00
01/03/63	J. B. Hogue	175.00
01/09/63	W. O. Saffold	6.10
01/13/63	O. S. Haynes	95.00
01/22/63	John Stokes	80.00
02/07/63	J. B. Hogue	150.00
02/24/63	Henry Grady	220.00
02/26/63	J. A. McCarty	7.50
04/01/63	To Cash on hand	24,651.40
		$25,924.50

1863		
01/01	By Amt. Cash on hand	25,924.50
	Columbus, April 12, 1863	$25,924.50

Naval Station
Columbus, Ga.
June 30th, 1863

Bolling Baker Esqr.
1st Auditor Treasury Dept.
Richmond, Va.
Sir:
Enclosed please find vouchers and statement for money expended at this station to April 1st 1863.
Vouchers No. 7, 8, 10, 11, 12, 13, are for labor on the steamer "Chattahoochee" after she had been taken from the hands of the Contractor.
Voucher No. 14, work done after working hours. With the exception of one or two small bills I have no further use for the balance remaining in my hands. I have therefore made application to the Hon. Sect. of the Navy for permission to turn it over to Pay-Master J. W. Nixon.

I am very Respectfully,
Your Obed't Servant
Lt. A. McLaughlin
C.S. Navy

A P P E N D I X 3

A. Payrolls of Workmen Employed at Columbus Naval Ironworks Facilities

COLUMBUS, GEORGIA, MAY 1–15, 1863

1	Sam. J. Whiteside	Machinist	$	8.50 per day
2	Chas McVay			7.00
3	R. Hutchinson			7.00
4	E. A. Horton			7.00
5	John McAnenng			7.00
6	James T. Code			7.00
7	P. J. Rayan			5.75
8	John Globe			5.00
9	R. Huffanaggle			5.00
10	Wm Johnson			5.00
11	James Haley			5.00
12	James Milton			4.75
13	D. Bradford			4.75
14	James Durham			4.75
15	Wm Scott			4.12
16	James Lewis			4.12
1	John Powell	Labourer	$	2.50 per day
2	Lewis			2.50
3	Lazarus			2.00
4	James Burns			2.50
5	Frank Ormsby			2.50
6	Henry Gorie			2.50
7	Wm Shields			1.50
8	Bill Young			1.25
9	Bob Fern			1.25
1	R. F. Reedy	Blacksmith	$	6.00
1	Geo. J. Golden	Machinist	$	6.25 per day
2	J. B. White			5.25
3	M. L. Bergin			5.75
4	R. B. Moore			5.00
5	M. Campbell			5.00
6	F. C. Stewart			5.00

7	S. W. Allen		5.00
8	James McGuire		5.00
9	S. J. Smith		5.00
10	U. S. Logan		5.00
11	Thomas Campbell		5.00
12	C. J. Cronin		5.00
13	John D. Clark		5.00
14	Wm P. Sewall		5.00
15	John Colvin		5.00
16	T. E. Murphy		5.00
17	J. G. Burrus		5.00
18	J. Crowley		5.00
19	W. Johnson		5.00
20	O. L. Pease		5.00
21	E. C. Morgan		5.00
22	Isaiah Willett		5.00
23	Wm McBryde		5.00
24	Edwin Johnson		5.00
25	John Madden		5.00
26	P. McGuire		5.00
27	Wm Shobers		5.00
28	Jno. J. Mooney		5.00
29	L. F. O'Brian		5.00
30	Thad. Freeman		5.00
31	J. W. McGrath		5.00
32	W. G. Roper		5.00
33	J. A. Burke		5.00
34	James McCarty		5.00
35	G. S. Cox		5.00
36	J. W. Yeargin		5.00
37	Wm McFarland		5.00
38	James Riley		5.00
39	B. C. Webb		5.00
40	J. C. Wolf		5.00
41	Henry Brown		5.00
42	Phillip Eifler		5.00
43	Walter Tobin		4.75
44	James McFee		4.75
45	Peter Shammer		4.50
46	R. L. Dutton		4.50
47	Chas. Alexander		4.50
48	L. S. Smith		4.50
49	F. T. Murray		4.50
50	Phil Sullivan		4.25
1	J. W. Churchill	Rolling Mill	$ 6.25 per day

2	T. Fitzgibbon		6.00
3	Frank Coppedge		5.50
4	S. R. Reynolds		4.75
5	Alonzo Turner		4.50
6	John Mahoney		4.00
7	J. L. Coppedge		3.50
8	J. E. Brewer		3.50
9	M. Lanahan		3.00
10	H. L. Thomas		3.00
11	M. Haley		3.00
12	J. L. Ragsdale		3.00
13	Martin West		3.00
14	James Clem		3.00
15	Wm Anderson		4.00
16	John Jones		1.75
17	Mingo Jones		1.75
18	Griffen Odom		1.50
19	Chas. Conch		1.25
20	Henry Moore		1.25
21	George Groover		1.25
22	George Lapham		3.00

1	G. W. Haynes	Watchman	$ 4.25 per day
2	John Donnelly		3.00
3	John McGoff		3.00
4	John Hackett		3.00
5	John Candder		3.00
6	Thos. Hannon		3.00
7	Mike Anderson		3.00

1	Dick Odum	Drayman	$ 1.50 per day
2	Rab Wacaser		1.50
3	Matt. Ellis		1.50
4	A. Mitchell		1.50
5	Andy Moffett		1.50
6	Henry Moffett		1.50

1	R. E. Stockton	Book Keeper	$ 6.00 per day
2	C. C. McGehee	Clerk	$ 4.25

1	George Mooney	Principal Foreman	$ 6.50 per day

1	H. E. Holmes	Machinist	$ 4.25 per day
2	James Lachlison		4.25
3	A. D. Short		4.25

4	H. R. Sedberry			4.25
5	W. T. Webb			4.25
6	S. T. Roper			4.25
7	Thomas Burton			4.00
8	A. C. Morton			3.50
9	Geo. A. Huckebee			3.50
1	T. W. Stanford	Blacksmith	$	6.25 per day
2	Judson Warlick			6.00
3	F. S. Golden			5.20
4	Wm Staunton			5.20
5	L. P. Henop			4.50
6	J. W. Brown			4.40
7	Q. F. Carey			3.50
8	J. C. Alexander			3.75
9	Joseph Fair			3.00
10	Booker Allen			2.50
11	Tom Clark			2.50
1	A. T. Finney	Boiler Maker	$	5.75 per day
2	M. McHale			5.00
3	Jas. Tillman			5.00
4	John Crogan			5.00
5	J. H. Stanford			5.00
6	Jas. McAndrews			4.50
7	G. McDonald			4.50
8	J. M. Alexander			4.25
9	Henry Paar			4.00
10	George Phelps			2.50
11	James Gifford			2.50
1	F. A. Pomeroy	Pattern Maker	$	6.00 per day
2	N. B. Love			5.50
3	J. W. Pierce			5.00
4	J. E. Warren			5.00
5	J. E. Johnson			5.00
6	J. H. Conway			4.50
7	John Gibbs			4.50
8	B. F. Gifford			4.25
9	F. M. Thomas			4.25
10	J. W. Jourdan			4.25
11	Wm Link			3.75
12	L. S. Skinner			3.75
13	Wm H. Perrine			3.75
14	Duncan Smith			3.50

| 1 | Chas. Chapman | Draftsman | $ | 6.85 per day |

1	John Atkins	Labourer	$	1.50 per day
2	Ed. Rankin			1.50
3	Jas Corcoran			1.50
4	Geo Salisbury			1.50
5	Sam Salisbury			1.50
6	Felix Frazier			1.50
7	Henry Wittlesy			1.50
8	James J. Wall			2.00

1	D. McFarland	Moulder	$	6.25 per day
2	M. D. Fisher			5.75
3	H. S. Duffee			5.00
4	B. Edmonds			5.00
5	Chas. Rodgers			5.00
6	Evans Sneed			5.00
7	Joseph Tracey			5.00
8	Wm Newcombe			4.50
9	C. J. Gayle			4.50
10	Hugh Smith			4.50
11	J. B. Roper			4.50
12	G. W. Brown			4.25
13	John Hilburn			3.00

1	J. A. Portervine	Carpenter	$	3.75 per day
2	Jeff Spencer			2.10
3	Aaron Spencer			2.10
4	Ed. Spencer			2.10
5	Theo Turner			2.00
6	Henry Clark			2.00
7	John Sheffield			2.00

1	A. Buchanan	Labourer, Boys	$	1.50 per day
2	Kirt Roper			1.40
3	James Powell			1.40
4	Jesse Millious			1.40
5	Wm A. Martin			1.25
6	Chas. Warlick			1.25
7	John Warlick			1.25
8	B. Bochert			1.25
9	Toby Clark			1.25
10	D. Barber			1.25
11	John Madden			1.00
12	Alfonzo Davis			1.00
13	Pat Casey			.70

1	Richmond Massey	Copper Smith	$ 5.75 per day
2	William Fee		4.75
1	D. W. Champayne	Mill Wright	$ 4.50 per day
2	J. R. Wynne		4.25
1	Peter	Labourer	$ 2.25 per day
2	Charles Bass		1.50
3	Harkless		1.50
4	Seab Fleming		1.50
5	Frank Markham		1.50
6	George Stapler		1.75
7	Wash Harris		1.75
8	Wash Peabody		1.75
9	J. M. Coffield		2.50
10	R. Klink		1.75
11	Henry Warlick		1.50
12	N. Hatcher		1.75
13	Bob Hatcher		1.75
14	J. Hatcher		1.75
15	R. Hatcher		1.75
16	F. Hatcher		1.75
17	Alex Spencer		1.40
18	Bill Whitus		1.50
19	N. Sanchez		1.50
20	R. Russell		2.00
21	O. Cody		1.50
22	Travis Stewart		1.50
23	Wm Grover		2.50
24	July Sanchez		1.50
25	Pat Kelly		2.50
26	Moses Kelly		2.50
27	Bob Berry		1.50
28	John McCarty		1.50
29	Jeff Tyler		1.50
30	Hansy Wacaser		1.50
31	Willis Loncus		2.25
32	Anderson Rucker		1.50
33	Tom Rucker		1.50
34	Julius Spencer		1.40
35	Dock Riley		1.50
36	Robt. Whiteside		1.25
37	Squire Amos		1.50
38	Cash Mitchell		1.50
39	Bob McDougald		1.50
40	Sam'l Moore		1.50

41	Andrew Jones	1.50
42	Giles Jones	1.50
43	Abe Colbern	1.50
44	Dennis McNeill	1.50
45	Ed. Markham	1.50
46	Sandy Markham	1.50
47	John Connor	2.50
48	Chas. Brady	2.50
49	Jno. Therlkeld	1.50
50	Casey Lewis	1.50

IRONWORKS PERSONNEL ASSIGNED TO SAVANNAH
[Warner Letters, June 6, 1863]

P. J. Ryan	$138.00
John Globe	110.00
R. Huffanaggle	120.00
James Riley	62.50
James Burns	56.25
Frank Ormsby	60.00
Henry Gorrie	60.00

IRONWORKS PERSONNEL ASSIGNED TO EUFAULA
[John Horry Dent Letters]

Geo. Young	Prop & Sup.	Age 31
Chas. McVay	Fireman	31
Jas. Milton	Machinist	37
Jas. Dunham	Machinist	33
Wm. Scott	Machinist	19
James Lewis	Machinist	19
John Powell	Machinist	38
Wm. Shields	Machinist	20
A. M. Pernell	Machinist	17
W. S. Willis	Blacksmith	29
Victor Bonifay	Blacksmith	47

B. Crew of the C.S. Chattahoochee

1863

1	Catsby ap R. Jones	Lieutenant, commanding
2	William C. Whittle	Lieutenant
3	George W. Gift	Lieutenant
4	H. W. M. Washington	Surgeon
5	Marcellus Ford	Surgeon
6	Leslie E. Brooks	Assistant Paymaster
9	H. H. Marmaduke	Master
10	W. J. Craig	Midshipman
11	W. R. Mayo	Midshipman
12	J. W. Tynan	First Assistant Engineer
13	Henry Fagan	Second Assistant Engineer
14	J. H. Dent	Third Assistant Engineer
15	Joseph Elliott	Third Assistant Engineer
16	John A. Lovett	Gunner
17	Hamilton Golder	Master's Mate
18	Daniel Trigg	Passed Midshipman
19	C. K. Mallory	Midshipman
20	Eugene Henderson	Paymasters Clerk
21	William Young	Boatswains Mate
22	James Cronin	Boatswains Mate
23	George May	Gunners Mate
24	John Allison	Quartermaster
25	Charles H. Berry	Quartermaster
26	Thomas Burns	Ordinary Seaman
27	Joseph Blanca	Seaman
28	Charles Bazzel	Ships Carpenter
29	James Bessant	Landsman
30	Joseph Burnham	Landsman
31	Enoch Lampher	Coal Heaver
32	Samuel E. V. Branch	Landsman
33	Charles Cook	Seaman
34	Jules Chabert	Coxswain
35	Joseph E. Coles	Second Gunner
36	Charles E. Collins	Second Class Fireman
37	George H. Caigh	Landsman
38	John H. Cooke	Ships Cook
40	Thomas Costa	Seaman
41	G. M. Collins	Landsman
42	L. D. Comsod	Landsman

43	Newton Carter	Landsman
44	John W. Cottell	Landsman
47	Nicholas Demond	Captain Top
48	Cornelius Duffey	Second Class Fireman
49	F. J. Egbert	Landsman
50	G. W. Irvine	Landsman
51	Patrick Friel	Coal Heaver
52	L. W. Faulk	Landsman
53	Manassa Faircloth	Landsman
54	J. W. Freeman	Landsman
55	James Hamilton	Ordinary Seaman
56	Joseph Hicks	Coal Heaver
57	Edward Hausahan	Assistant Heaver
58	T. H. Haman	Landsman
59	J. B. Holder	Landsman
60	M. M. N. Hardy	Landsman
61	Joseph Howell	Landsman
62	John Holliff	Seaman
63	Isaac Johnson	Landsman
64	J. H. Jones	Landsman
65	Augustus Lumbles	Captain Forecastle
66	Jacob Lind	Landsman
68	Elias Lee	Master
69	E. F. Labatut	Ordinary Seaman
70	Charles Miller	Quarter Gunner
71	Samuel Morgan	Sail Maker, Master
72	Patrick Martin	Captain Top
73	William Moore	Captains Steward
74	Antone Massena	Officers Cook
75	John P. Moore	Landsman
76	C. V. McKenney	Landsman
77	G. D. Miller	Landsman
78	A. H. Olds	Landsman
79	John Penny	Master of Arms
80	Joseph Pagan	Captain Hold
81	Francis Palinquest	Coxswain
82	Elisha Powell	Ordinary Seaman
83	Mare Provensana	Seaman
84	Ira Payne	Landsman
85	C. P. Prevat	Landsman
86	John Rapler	Coxswain
87	J. Richards	Landsman
88	Thomas Saunders	Second Gunner
89	John D. Sands	Ordinary Seaman
90	Amos R. Shamtt	Ordinary Seaman
91	George Smith	Captain Top

92	Edward Shamtt	Ordinary Seaman
93	Joseph Sia	Seaman
94	John H. Smith	Seaman
95	J. W. Smith	Seaman
96	F. M. E. Syphert	Landsman
97	W. Sheppard	Landsman
98	John S. Spear	Landsman
99	James Thomas	Landsman
100	Henry Thomas	First Class Boy
101	S. E. Timmons	Landsman
102	W. J. Tucker	Landsman
103	G. T. Taylor	Landsman
104	Libe Taylor	Landsman
105	Wilson Tharp	Landsman
107	Arad. Williams	Seaman
108	Antone Williams	Seaman
109	William Whitman	Landsman
110	William Walker	Landsman
111	Thomas H. Wilds	Landsman
112	L. C. Wilds	Landsman
113	Nathan Wilds	Landsman
114	John Haggarty	Coal Heaver
115	James Kennedy	Landsman
116	James Wilson	First Class Fireman
117	Charles Douglas	Coal Heaver
118	William Scaley	Seaman
119	John A. Lucas	Landsman
120	Joseph Cardy	First Class Fireman
121	S. B. Ashby	Assistant Boatswain
122	George W. Sheppard	Second Master
123	Jacob Paulson	Seaman
124	Frederick Meniker	Seaman
125	Thomas Horton	Second Gunner
126	Thomas Muller	Seaman
127	Charles Bush	Captain Master
129	Augustus Schultz	Seaman
130	Edward Cope	Landsman
131	Edward Conn	Coal Heaver
	E. P. Hodges	Third Assistant Engineer
	P. Hamilton Gibbs	Acting Midshipman

1864

1	George W. Gift	Lieutenant, commanding
2	Samuel P. Blanc	Passed Midshipman

3	Henry L. Vaughan	Midshipman
4	Gale W. Sparks	Midshipman
5	Marcellus Ford	Surgeon
6	John T. Scharf	Midshipman
7	Wm S. Hogen	Midshipman
8	Armand DeBlanc	Engineer
9	Carman Frazee	Masters Mate
10	William A. Collier	Masters Mate
11	M. L. Sothoron	Pay Master
12	L. Livingston	Pay Clerk

1	Joseph Blanca	Quarter Gunner
2	C. E. Bazzell	Ships Cook
3	Thomas Costa	Seaman
4	J. B. Holder	Landsman
5	M. M. N. Hardy	Landsman
6	E. F. Labatut	Ordinary Seaman
7	Joseph Sia	Seaman
8	W. A. Tucker	Landsman
9	T. H. Wilder	Landsman
10	W. S. Sealey	Quarter Gunner
11	Frank Klein	Seaman
12	H. F. Oliver	Seaman
13	Thomas Conforth	Seaman
14	Thomas Jefferson	Seaman
15	Lawrence Thompson	Seaman
16	Lewis Bell	Seaman
17	John Peters	Seaman
18	Senature Ady	Seaman
19	R. W. Condell	Seaman
20	J. W. Bradley	Ordinary Seaman
21	Samuel Cooley	Seaman
22	William Brown	Ordinary Seaman
23	M. Downey	Ordinary Seaman
24	Peter Williams	Seaman
25	Joseph C. Daymon	Seaman
26	Edward Millingan	Seaman
27	Benjamin Sharth	Ordinary Seaman
28	Julius Schmittze	Seaman
29	M. Matkin	Landsman
30	R. L. Hill	Seaman
31	B. T. Cowart	Ordinary Seaman
32	Frank Phillips	Seaman
33	William Banker	Seaman
34	George Taylor	Seaman
35	Julius Black	Seaman

36	S. G. Curry	Seaman
37	J. S. Briggs	Seaman
38	Cain Mahoney	Ordinary Seaman
39	L. W. Risley	Ordinary Seaman
40	C. J. Peterson	Ordinary Seaman
41	John McLaughlin	Ordinary Seaman
42	Thomas Bartlett	Ordinary Seaman
43	J. H. Purvey	Ordinary Seaman
44	William Lamshaw	Ordinary Seaman
45	H. Cowart	Ordinary Seaman
46	E. Hoencke	Ordinary Seaman
47	James O'Donnell	Ordinary Seaman
48	James White	Ordinary Seaman
49	George Moody	Ordinary Seaman
50	M. Kearney	Landsman
51	P. H. Cain	Landsman
52	James Taylor	Landsman
53	James Calhoun	Ordinary Seaman
54	Lawrence Oats	Landsman
55	John Flynn	Landsman
56	James Murphy	Landsman
57	William Kain	Landsman
58	James Crawford	Landsman
59	Edward Maline	Landsman
60	George Stewart	Landsman
61	H. D. Elliott	Landsman
62	Richard May	Landsman
63	W. H. Pond	Landsman
64	C. C. Johns	Landsman
65	P. McCann	Landsman
66	G. P. Shipp	Landsman
67	M. H. Steele	Landsman
68	S. A. G. Horne	Landsman
69	Thomas Monk	Landsman
70	T. R. Whitcomb	Landsman
71	F. Bauldree	Landsman
72	Frank Medans	Landsman
73	Thomas Ormand	Landsman
74	G. Hollingsworth	Landsman
75	William McKenny	Landsman
76	W. H. Aldridge	Landsman
77	John Thomas	Seaman
78	Augustus L. Bradley	Landsman
79	William Liverman	Landsman
80	Thomas Joiner	Landsman

C. Register of Officers, C.S. Chattahoochee and Columbus Service

Source: John M. Carroll, ed. *Register of Officers of the Confederate States Navy, 1861–1865.* Mattituck, N.Y.: J. M. Carroll and Company, 1983. Material cited here verbatim from source.

Arents, Fred W. Born in _____. Appointed from _____. Third assistant engineer, _____. Killed May 27, 1863, in boiler explosion. Served on C.S.S. *Chattahoochee*, 1863.

Baker, James McC. Born in Florida. Appointed from Florida. Acting master, March 23, 1862. Lieutenant for the war, February 26, 1863. First lieutenant Provisional Navy, June 2, 1864, to rank from January 6, 1864. Served in C.S. Army, 1861–62. C.S.S. *Louisiana;* escaped at surrender of Forts Jackson and St. Philip, April 28, 1862. Jackson station, 1862. Savannah station, 1862. Naval works, Columbus, Ga., 1862–63. C.S.S. *Chattahoochee*, 1863. C.S.S. *Huntsville*, Mobile Squadron, 1863–1865. Surrender May 4, 1865; paroled May 10, 1865.

Bilbro, William B. Born in _____. Appointed from _____. Pilot. Killed in boiler explosion May 27, 1863. Served on C.S.S. *Chattahoochee*, 1863.

Blanc, Samuel P. Born in Louisiana. Appointed from Louisiana. Acting midshipman, August 29, 1861. Passed midshipman, January 8, 1864. Master in line of promotion Provisional Navy, June 2, 1864. Served on C.S.S. *McRae*, New Orleans station, 1861–62. Jackson station, 1862. Fort Polk, Mississippi River, 1862. C.S.S. *Baltic*, Mobile Squadron, 1862–63. C.S.S. *Savannah*, Savannah Squadron, 1863. C.S.S. *Patrick Henry*, 1863. Mobile Squadron, 1863–64. C.S.S. *Chattahoochee*, 1864. C.S.S. *Nashville*, 1864. C.S.S. *Sampson*, Savannah Squadron, 1864. C.S. torpedo boat *Hornet*, 1865. C.S. ram *W. H. Webb*, Red River defenses, when destroyed April 24, 1865; captured. Released on oath June 13, 1865, Fort Warren.

Bondurant, Walter E. Born in _____. Appointed from _____. Assistant surgeon for the war, May 10, 1863. Assistant surgeon Provisional Navy, June 2, 1864. Served at Columbus, Ga., 1864. C.S.S. *Palmetto State*, Charleston station, 1864.

Bremond, Dennis. Born in _____. Appointed from _____. Acting master, September 24, 1861. Served on C.S.S. *Florida (Selma)*, 1861–62. Richmond station, 1862. On C.S.S. *Louisiana* when destroyed, April 28, 1862. C.S.S. *Patrick Henry*, 1862. C.S.S. *Chattahoochee*, 1862. Charleston station, 1862–63. Captured from the boats of the C.S. steamer *Huntress (Tropic)* when destroyed January 18, 1863; paroled April 25, 1863, Fort Delaware.

Brooks, Leslie E. Born in Alabama. Appointed from Alabama. Assistant paymaster, March 18, 1862. Assistant paymaster Provisional Navy, June 2, 1864. Serving on C.S.S. *Louisiana* when destroyed April 28, 1862; prisoner at Fort Warren; exchanged at Aikens Landing August 5, 1862; C.S.S. *Chattahoochee*, 1862–1864. Mobile station, 1864. C.S.S. *Tallahassee*, 1864. C.S.S. *Columbia*, Charleston station, 1864–65; paroled at Greensboro, N.C., April 28, 1865.

Cardy, Joseph D. Born in Florida. Appointed in Florida. Third assistant engineer, March 14, 1863. Second assistant engineer, June 15, 1863. Second assistant engineer Provisional Navy, June 2, 1864. Served on C.S.S. *Chattahoochee*, 1863. C.S.S. *Savannah*, Savannah Squadron, 1863–64. Surrendered May 10, 1865, and paroled May 27, at Tallahassee, Fla.

Carnes, William Watts. Born in Tennessee. Appointed from Tennessee. Resigned as acting midshipman U.S. Navy, February 13, 1861. Second lieutenant, January 6, 1864, to rank from October 2, 1862. First lieutenant Provisional Navy, June 2, 1864, to rank from January 6, 1864. Served in C.S. Army. Savannah Squadron, 1863–65; in charge of prize steamer *Water Witch*, 1864. C.S.S. *Savannah*, 1864; commanding C.S.S. *Sampson*, 1864–65. Paroled at Macon, Ga., May 10, 1865.

City, George W. Born in District of Columbia. Appointed from Virginia. Formerly first assistant engineer, U.S. Navy. First assistant engineer, August 29, 1861. First assistant engineer Provisional Navy, June 2, 1864. Acting chief engineer, May 31, 1864. Served on C.S.S. *Richmond (George Page)*, Richmond station, 1861. C.S.S. *Virginia (Merrimack)*, 1861–62. Gosport Navy Yard, 1862. C.S.S *Arkansas*, 1862. Jackson station, 1862. Savannah station, 1862–63. Charleston station, 1863. C.S. steamers *Isondiga*, *Savannah*, and *Macon*, Savannah Squadron, 1863–64. C.S.S. *Chattahoochee*, 1864. Paroled May 3, 1865, Augusta, Ga.

Collier, William A. Born in _____. Appointed from Virginia. Acting master's mate, April 12, 1864. Acting master's mate Provisional Navy, June 2, 1864. Acting midshipman, November 30, 1864. Served on C.S.S. *Chattahoochee*, 1864. Savannah Squadron, 1864. C.S.S. *Roanoke*, James River Squadron, 1864. C.S.S. *Patrick Henry*, 1864. Ordered to Washington, Ga., April 27, 1865. Surrendered Augusta, Ga., May 2, 1865; paroled May 3.

Colyer, Charles Miles. [Cowles Miles Collier]. Born in Georgia. Appointed from _____. Lieutenant Marine, Virginia Navy.

Craig, William J. Born in Kentucky. Appointed from Kentucky. Resigned as acting midshipman, U.S. Navy, August 12, 1861. Acting midshipman, August 28, 1861. Passed midshipman, January 3, 1864, to rank from December 5, 1863. Master in line of promotion Provisional Navy, June 2, 1864. Served on C.S.R.S. *United States*, 1861–62. C.S.S. *Virginia (Merrimack)*, 1862. C.S.S. *Huntress*, Charleston station, 1862. C.S.S. *Chattahoochee*, 1862–63; injured in boiler explosion. C.S.S. *Patrick Henry*, 1863. C.S. steamers *Georgia* and *Sampson*, Savannah Squadron, 1863–64. C.S.S. *Virginia* (No. 2), James River Squadron, 1864. C.S.S.

Tallahassee, 1864. Mobile Squadron, 1864–65; surrendered May 4, 1865; paroled May 10, 1865.

Cronin, James C. Born in _____. Appointed from Georgia. Boatswain, July 11, 1863–64. Boatswain Provisional Navy, June 2, 1864. Served as boatswain's mate on C.S. steamers *Sea Bird, United States, Virginia (Merrimack)*, Richmond station, 1861–62. C.S.S. *Chattahoochee*, 1862–63; on board at time of boiler explosion. C.S.S. *Savannah (Oconee)*, Savannah station, 1863. Charleston station, 1863. C.S.S. *Savannah (Oconee)*, 1864.

Dalton, Hamilton Henderson. Born in North Carolina. Appointed from Mississippi. Formerly Lieutenant, U.S. Navy. Lieutenant, December 30, 1861. First lieutenant, October 23, 1862. First lieutenant Provisional Navy, June 2, 1864, to rank from January 6, 1864. Prisoner at Fort Warren, 1861: exchanged in January, 1862. C.S.S. *Livingston*, Mississippi River defenses, 1862. Jackson station, 1862. C.S.S. *Georgia*, Savannah Squadron, 1862–63. C.S. steamers *Tuscaloosa* and *Baltic*, Mobile Squadron, 1863. C.S.S. *Chattahoochee*, 1863. On C.S. steamers *Georgia, Savannah*, and *Sampson*, and commanding C.S.S. *Isondiga*, Savannah Squadron, 1863–64. C.S.S. *Richmond*, James River Squadron, 1865; detached and ordered to Mobile, but failed to reach there before surrendering.

DeBlanc, Armand. Born in Louisiana. Appointed from Louisiana. Third assistant engineer, April 11, 1863. Third assistant engineer Provisional Navy, June 2, 1864. Served on *Chattahoochee*, 1863–64. Savannah Squadron, 1864.

Dent, John H. Born in Alabama. Appointed from Alabama. Acting third assistant engineer, May 11, 1861. Second assistant engineer, May 21, 1863. Second assistant engineer Provisional Navy, June 2, 1864. Served on C.S.S. *McRae*, New Orleans station, 1861–62, C.S.S. *Louisiana*, 1862; captured at surrender of Forts Jackson and St. Philip, April 28, 1862; confined at Fort Warren; exchanged August 5, 1862, at Aikens Landing, Va. C.S.S. *Chattahoochee*, 1862–63. C.S.S. *Hampton*, James River Squadron, 1863. C.S.S. *Charleston*, Charleston station, 1863–64. Steamer *Coquette*, 1864.

Fagan, Henry. Born in Florida. Appointed from District of Columbia. Formerly third assistant engineer, U.S. Navy. Original entry into C.S. Navy, July 23, 1861. Acting second assistant engineer, November 25, 1861. Died May 30, 1863, from the effects of boiler explosion on C.S.S. *Chattahoochee*. Served on C.S.S. *McRae*, New Orleans station, 1861–62. C.S.S. *Louisiana;* taken prisoner at surrender of Forts Jackson and St. Philip, April 28, 1862. Released at Fort Warren, July 31, 1862, to be exchanged. C.S.S. *Chattahoochee*, 1862–63.

Ford, Marcellus. Born in Virginia. Appointed from Virginia. Assistant surgeon for the war, March 11, 1862. Assistant surgeon, May 1, 1863. Assistant surgeon Provisional Navy, June 2, 1864. Served on C.S.S. *Louisiana*, 1862. Richmond station, 1862. C.S.S. *Chattahoochee*, 1862–63. C.S.S. *North Carolina*, Wilmington station, 1863–64. C.S.S.

Chattahoochee, 1864. C.S. steamers *Macon* and *Water Witch,* Savannah
Squadron, 1864. Charleston station, 1864. Paroled at Greensboro, N.C.,
April 28, 1865.

Frazee, Carman. Born in _____. Appointed from _____. Acting
master's mate, April 21, 1864. Acting master's mate Provisional Navy,
June 2, 1864. Served on C.S.S. *Chattahoochee,* C.S.S. *Water Witch,*
Savannah Squadron, 1864. Paroled May 13, 1865, Montgomery, Ala.

Gibbes, Paul Hamilton. Born in South Carolina. Appointed from South
Carolina. Midshipman, January 27, 1863. Midshipman Provisional Navy,
June 2, 1864. Served on C.S.S. *Chattahoochee,* 1863. C.S.S. *Savannah,*
Savannah Squadron, 1863. Charleston station, 1863. C.S. steamers
Patrick Henry and *Nansemond,* James River Squadron, 1863–64. C.S.
steamers *Roanoke, Virginia* (No. 2) and *Beaufort,* James River Squadron,
1864–65. Semmes naval brigade, 1865; paroled at Greensboro, N.C., April
28, 1865.

Gift, George Washington. Born in Tennessee. Appointed from Tennessee.
Resigned as midshipman, U.S. Navy, January 10, 1851. Acting master,
December 27, 1861. Resigned, March 22, 1862. Lieutenant for the war,
March 18, 1862. Acting master, April 7, 1862. First lieutenant Provisional
Navy, June 2, 1864, to rank from January 6, 1864. Served on C.S. floating
battery *New Orleans* and C.S.S. *McRea,* New Orleans station, 1862.
C.S.S. *Louisiana;* surrender of Forts Jackson and St. Philip, April 28,
1862. C.S.S. *Arkansas,* 1862. C.S.S. *Chattahoochee,* 1862–63. C.S.
steamers *Baltic* and *Gaines,* Mobile Squadron, 1863. Johnsons Island
expedition, 1863. Took command of merchant steamer *Ranger* from
Bermuda to Wilmington, N.C., January, 1864. Participated in the capture
of U.S.S. *Underwriter,* February 2, 1864. Commanding C.S.S.
Chattahoochee, 1864. C.S.S. *Savannah,* 1864. C.S.S. *Tallahassee
(Olustee),* 1864. Paroled May 22, 1864, Albany, Ga.

Golder, Hamilton. Born in _____. Appointed from _____. Acting
master's mate, _____. Served on C.S.S. *Chattahoochee,* 1862–63;
slightly wounded in boiler explosion, May 27, 1863. Aide to flag officer,
Savannah Squadron, 1863. C.S.S. *Savannah,* 1863. Participated in
expedition to capture C.S.S. *Water Witch,* June 3, 1864. Paroled May 2,
1865, Augusta, Ga.

Grady, Charles J. Born in _____. Appointed from _____. Paymaster's
clerk, _____. Served on C.S.S. *Chattahoochee,* 1863.

Guthrie, John Julius. Born in North Carolina. Appointed from North
Carolina. Formerly lieutenant, U.S. Navy. First lieutenant, July 13, 1861.
First lieutenant, October 23, 1862, to rank from October 2, 1862. Served
on Rappahannock River defenses, 1861. Commanding C.S.S. *Red Rover*
and C.S. floating battery *New Orleans,* New Orleans station, 1861–62.
Richmond station, 1862. C.S.S. *Artic,* Wilmington station, 1862–63.
Commanding C.S.S. *Chattahoochee* at time of boiler explosion, May 27,
1863. Richmond station, 1863. C.S.S. *Albemarle,* 1863–64. Special
service, 1864; commanding North Carolina steamer *A.D. Vance.*

Appointed voluntary aide on personal staff of Governor Z. B. Vance, March 23, 1865.

Hall, Elias Guy. Born in _____. Appointed from _____. Acting third assistant engineer, July 13, 1861. Second assistant engineer, September 27, 1862. Second assistant engineer, Provisional Navy, June 2, 1864. First assistant engineer, _____. Served on C.S.S. *Patrick Henry*, 1861–62, C.S.S. *Harriet Lane*, 1863. C.S.S. *Missouri*, Red River defenses, 1863. C.S.S. *Patrick Henry*, 1863–64. C.S.S. *Chattahoochee*, 1864. C.S.S. *Tallahassee (Olustee)*, 1864.

Henderson, Eugene. Born in _____. Appointed from _____. Paymaster's clerk _____. Killed in boiler explosion, May 27, 1863. Served on C.S.S. *Chattahoochee*, 1863.

Hodges, Euclid P. Born in _____. Appointed from Maryland. Third assistant engineer, January, 1863. Died May 30, 1863, from effects of a boiler explosion on C.S.S. *Chattahoochee*. Served on C.S.S. *Chattahoochee*, 1863.

Hogue, William S. Born in Florida. Appointed from Florida. Midshipman, November 24, 1862. Midshipman Provisional Navy, June 2, 1864. Served at St. Marks, Fla., 1863–63. Drewrys Bluff, Va., 1863. C.S.S. *North Carolina*, Wilmington Station, 1863. C.S.S. *Patrick Henry*, 1863. C.S. steamers *Isondiga*, *Savannah* and *Resolute*, Savannah Squadron, 1864. C.S.S. *Chattahoochee*, 1864. C.S.S. *Spray*, St. Marks, Fla., 1865. Paroled May 12, 1865, St. Marks, Fla.

Jones, Catesby ap R. Born in Virginia. Appointed from Virginia. Resigned as lieutenant, U.S. Navy, April 17, 1861. Lieutenant, Virginia Navy, May 2, 1861, to rank from April 23, 1861. Lieutenant, C.S. Navy, June 11, 1861. First lieutenant, October 23, 1862 to rank from October 2, 1862. Commander, April 29, 1863. "Promoted for gallant and meritorious conduct as executive and ordnance officer of steamer *Virginia* in the action in Hampton Roads on 8th March, 1862, and in the action at Drewrys Bluff, 15th May, 1862." Commander Provisional Navy (nominated to rank from May 13, 1864). Jamestown Island defenses, 1862. C.S.S. *Virginia (Merrimack)*, 1861–62; commanded her in fight with C.S.S. *Monitor*, March 9, 1862. Participated in engagement with Federal vessels at Drewrys Bluff, Va., May 15, 1862. Commanding C.S.S. *Chattahoochee*, 1862–63. Naval ordnance works, Charlotte, N.C., 1863. Naval ordnance works, Selma, Ala., 1863–64. Mobile squadron, 1865. Paroled May 9, 1865, off Mobile, Ala., on board C.S.S. *Stockdale*.

Littlepage, Hardin Beverly. Born in Virginia. Appointed from Virginia. Resigned as acting midshipman, U.S. Navy, April 25, 1861. Acting midshipman, June 11, 1861. Master in line of promotion, October 4, 1862. Second lieutenant, August 5, 1863. First lieutenant, Provisional Navy, June 2, 1864, to rank from January 6, 1864. Served on C.S.R.S. *United States*, 1861. C.S.S. *Virginia (Merrimack)*, 1861–62; participated in Battle of Hampton Roads, Va., March 8–9, 1862, and in engagement at Drewrys Bluff, Va., May 15, 1862. C.S.S. *Chattahoochee*, 1862. C.S.S.

Atlanta, 1862–63. Service abroad, 1863–64. Passenger on steamer *Margaret and Jessie* when chased ashore by U.S.S. *Rhode Island*, May 30, 1863. C.S.S. *Virginia* (No. 2), James River Squadron, 1864–65. Semmes naval brigade, 1865.

Livingston, L. Born in _____. Appointed from _____. Paymaster's clerk, _____. Served on C.S.S. *Chattahoochee*, 1864.

Lovett, John A. Born in Massachusetts. Appointed from Virginia. Formerly gunner, U.S. Navy. Gunner, June 20, 1861. Gunner, Provisional Navy, June 2, 1864. Served on C.S.S. *Patrick Henry*, 1861–62. Drewrys Bluff, Va., 1862. C.S.S. *Chattahoochee*, 1862–63. C.S.S. *North Carolina*, Wilmington station, 1863–64. Paroled April 9, 1865, Appomattox C.H., Va.

Mallory, Charles K., Jr. Born in Virginia. Appointed from Virginia. Acting midshipman, June 12, 1861. Died June 1, 1863, from the effect of boiler explosion. Served on C.S.R.S. *United States*, 1861. C.S.S. *Beaufort*, 1861–62; participated in Battle of Roanoke Island, February 7–8, 1862, and Battle of Hampton Roads, Va., March 8–9, 1862; commended for gallant conduct, C.S.S. *Chattahoochee*, 1862–63.

Marmaduke, Henry H. Born in Missouri. Appointed from Missouri. Resigned as acting midshipman, U.S. Navy, March 18, 1861. Midshipman, May 8, 1861. Master in line of promotion, October 4, 1862. Second lieutenant, January 7, 1864, to rank from August 24, 1863. First lieutenant Provisional Navy, June 2, 1864, to rank from January 6, 1864. Served on C.S.S. *McRae*, New Orleans station, 1861; participated in attack on Federal blockading fleet at Head of the Passes, Mississippi River, October 12, 1861, C.S.S. *Virginia (Merrimack)*, 1861–62; ordered to Elizabeth City, N.C. in charge of ordnance stores, February 10, 1862; participated in battle of Hampton Roads, Va., March 8–9, 1862; wounded. C.S.S. *Chattahoochee*, 1862–63. Service abroad, 1863–64. C.S. steamers *Sampson* and *Savannah*, Savannah Squadron, 1864. C.S. steamers *Columbia* and *Chicora*, Charleston station, 1865. Captured at battle of Sailors Creek, Va., April 6, 1865; confined in Old Capitol Prison and later at Johnsons Island; released on oath, June 20, 1865.

Mayo, Wyndam R. Born in Virginia. Appointed from Virginia. Resigned as acting midshipman, U.S. Navy, April 25, 1861. Acting midshipman, July 8, 1861. Passed midshipman, January 8, 1864. Master in line of promotion Provisional Navy, June 2, 1864. Served at Barretts Point battery, Va., 1861. C.S.R.S. *United States* and Gosport Navy Yard, 1861–62. Charlotte, N.C., 1862. Drewrys Bluff, Va., 1862. C.S.S. *Chattahoochee*, 1862–63. C.S.S. *Savannah (Oconee)*, Savannah Squadron, 1863. C.S.S. *Patrick Henry*, 1863. C.S. steamers *North Carolina* and *Yadkin*, Wilmington station, 1863–64. Battle of Sailors Creek, Va., April 6, 1865; captured; confined at Johnsons Island; released on oath June 20, 1865.

Merrifield, G. H. Born in _____. Appointed from _____. Acting gunner, October 25, 1861. Served on New Orleans station, 1861–62. C.S.S. *Pontchartrain*, 1862–63. Columbus and Atlanta, Ga., 1863.

Nixon, John W. Born in Louisiana. Appointed from Louisiana. Resigned as paymaster, U.S. Navy, April 15, 1861. Paymaster, April 15, 1861. Paymaster, October 23, 1862 to rank from March 26, 1861. Served on New Orleans station, 1861–62. Jackson station, 1862–63. Atlanta, Ga., 1863–64.

Perry, John. Born in _____. Appointed from _____. Acting boatswain, 1864. Boatswain, _____. Served as seaman on C.S.S. *Virginia (Merrimack);* participated in the battle of Hampton Roads, Va., March 8–9, 1862. C.S.S. *Chattahoochee*, 1862–63. C.S.S. *Savannah*, Savannah Squadron, 1863–64; participated as boatswain's mate in expedition for the capture of U.S.S. *Water Witch*, June 3, 1864. Acting boatswain on C.S.S. *Macon*, Savannah Squadron, 1864. Commanding Shell Bluff Battery, Savannah station, 1865.

Scharf, John Thomas. Born in Maryland. Appointed from Maryland. Midshipman. June 20, 1863. Midshipman Provisional Navy, June 2, 1864. Served on C.S.S. *Patrick Henry*, 1863, C.S.S. *Chicora*, Charleston station, 1863–64. C.S.S. *Chattahoochee*, 1864. Participated in capture of the C.S.S. *Underwriter*, February 2, 1864. C.S. steamers *Water Witch* and *Sampson*, Savannah Squadron, 1864. Ordered to Richmond, December 30, 1864, for duty on C.S.S. *Patrick Henry*. Captured March 5, 1865. Prince Georges County, Md. Released on bond, Old Capitol Prison, Washington, D.C., March 25, 1865.

Sothoron, Marshall, L. Born in _____. Appointed from Maryland. Assistant paymaster, January, 1864. Assistant paymaster Provisional Navy, June 2, 1864. Served on C.S.S. *Chattahoochee*, 1864. Savannah station, 1864. Mentioned by Flag Officer Hunter as still in service in January 1865. Paroled May 9, 1865, Augusta, Ga.

Sparks, Gale W. Born in Louisiana. Appointed from Louisiana. Resigned as acting midshipman, U.S. Navy, April 25, 1861. Acting midshipman, July 8, 1861. Passed midshipman, January 8, 1864. Master in line of promotion Provisional Navy, June 2, 1864. Served on C.S.S. *Mobile*, New Orleans station, 1861–62. Jackson station, 1862. C.S.S. *Patrick Henry*, 1863. C.S.S. *Gaines*, Mobile Squadron, 1863–64. C.S.S. *Chattahoochee*, 1864. C.S.S. *Palmetto State*, Charleston station, 1864. Semmes naval brigade, 1865; paroled at Greensboro, N.C., April 28, 1865.

Stockton, Robert E. Born in _____. Appointed from _____. Paymaster's clerk, January 21 and May 6, 1863. Served at Columbus, Ga., 1863–64.

Trigg, Daniel. Born in Virginia. Appointed from Virginia. Resigned as acting midshipman, U.S. Navy, April 20, 1861. Served as midshipman, Virginia navy. Acting midshipman, C.S. Navy, June 11, 1861. Passed midshipman, October 3, 1862. Master in line of promotion, January 7, 1864. Second lieutenant Provisional Navy, June 2, 1864. Served on C.S.R.S. *United States*, 1861–62. C.S.S. *Jamestown*, 1862; participated in Battles of Hampton Roads, March 8–9, and Drewrys Bluff, Va., May 15,

1862. C.S.S. *Chattahoochee*, 1862-63. Service abroad, 1863-64; passenger on steamer *Margaret and Jessie* when chased ashore by the U.S.S. *Rhode Island*, May 30, 1863. C.S.S. *Virginia* (No. 2), James River Squadron, 1864-65. Captured at Sailors Creek, Va., April 6, 1865; confined at Johnsons Island; released on oath June 20, 1865.

Turner, Samuel V. Born in Virginia. Appointed from Virginia. Resigned as Sailmaker, U.S. Navy, April 18, 1861. Sailmaker, June 11, 1861. Sailmaker, Provisional Navy, June 2, 1864. Served on C.S.R.S. *United States*, 1861-62. C.S.S. *Chattahoochee*, 1862. Charlotte, N.C., 1862-1865; paroled April 28, 1865.

Tynan, John W. Born in Virginia. Appointed from Virginia. Formerly second assistant engineer, U.S. Navy. Second assistant engineer, June 15, 1861. Acting first assistant engineer, December 21, 1861. Acting chief engineer, May 22, 1863. Served on steamer *St. Nicholas*, 1861. C.S.S. *Virginia (Merrimack);* participated in battle of Hampton Roads, Va., March 8-9, 1862. C.S.S. *Chattahoochee*, 1862-63. Savannah station, 1863-64. C.S.S. *Tallahassee.*

Vaughan, Henry L. Born in Louisiana. Appointed from Louisiana. Resigned as acting midshipman, April 25, 1861. Acting midshipman, July 8, 1861. Passed midshipman, January 8, 1864. Master in line of promotion, Provisional Navy, June 2, 1864. Served on C.S.R.S. *St. Philip*, New Orleans station, 1861. C.S.S. *Selma (Florida)*, 1861-62. At Mobile, Ala., 1863. C.S.S. *Patrick Henry*, 1863. C.S.S. *Isondiga*, Savannah Squadron, 1863-64. C.S.S. *Chattahoochee*, 1864. Commanding prize steamer *Water Witch*. Savannah Squadron, 1864. C.S. steamers *Columbia* and *Palmetto State*, Charleston station, 1865.

Warner, James H. Born in Ohio. Appointed from Virginia. Formerly chief engineer, U.S. Navy. Original entry into C.S. Navy, July 18, 1861. Chief engineer, October 23, 1862, to rank from October 2, 1862. Served at Gosport Navy Yard, 1861. New Orleans station, 1861. Savannah station, 1861-62. Columbus, Ga., 1862-1865.

Washington, H. W. M. Born in Virginia. Appointed from Virginia. Formerly passed assistant surgeon, U.S. Navy. Assistant surgeon, Virginia navy. Surgeon, C.S. Navy, June 18, 1861. Surgeon, October 23, 1862, to rank from March 26, 1861. Surgeon Provisional Navy, June 2, 1864. Served on Richmond station, 1861-62. C.S.S. *Arkansas*, 1862. Jackson station, 1862. C.S.S. *Chattahoochee*, 1862-63. C.S.S. *Fredericksburg*, James River Squadron, 1864.

Whittle, William Conway, Jr. Born in Virginia. Appointed from Virginia. Resigned as master, U.S. Navy, May 16, 1861. Served as lieutenant in the Virginia navy. Acting master, C.S. Navy, June 16, 1861. Acting lieutenant, September 19, 1861. Lieutenant for the war, February 8, 1862. First lieutenant, February 8, 1862. First lieutenant, October 23, 1862, to rank from October 2, 1862. First lieutenant Provisional Navy, June 2, 1864, to rank from January 6, 1864. Served on York River batteries, 1861.

C.S.S. *Nashville*, 1861–62. Richmond Station, 1862. C.S.S. *Louisiana* at
surrender of Forts Jackson and St. Philip, April 28, 1862; prisoner;
confined at Fort Warren. Exchanged August 5, 1862, Aikens Landing, Va.
C.S.S. *Chattahoochee*, 1862–63. Service abroad, 1863–65; C.S.S.
Shenandoah, 1864–65.

N O T E S

Chapter 1. History and the Rivers:
The Confluence of Currents

Documentation for this chapter is used as a "suggested bibliography" for readers interested in the Apalachicola-Chattahoochee corridor. Local histories, while seldom scholarly tomes, are nevertheless good sources of colorful and personal details about how people lived out this story.

The number of citations in this chapter and throughout this book reflects the highly fragmentary nature of this story—often mentioned in passing, seldom discussed in detail, never a matter of sustained narration in the larger, more dramatic story of the Civil War.

1. *Official Records of the Union and Confederate Navies in the War of the Rebellion* (hereafter cited as *N.O.R.*), 31 vols. (Washington, D.C.: Government Printing Office, 1894–1927), ser. 1, 16:546.

2. *Chattahoochee Trace Historical Markers in Alabama and Georgia* (Eufaula, Ala.: Historic Chattahoochee Commission, 1983).

3. Harold S. Coulter, *A People Courageous, A History of Phenix City, Alabama* (Columbus, Ga.: Howard Printing Co., 1976), p. 107.

4. David W. Chase, "Fort Mitchell, An Archaeological Exploration in Russell County, Alabama, July–December, 1971," Typescript in Bradley Memorial Library, Columbus, Ga., p. 10.

5. James Gadsden, "The Defences of the Floridas," *Florida Historical Quarterly* 15 (1937): 247.

6. Harry P. Owens, "Apalachicola: The Beginning," *Florida Historical Quarterly* 47 (1969): 281.

7. Horatio L. Wait, "The Blockading Service," *Papers Read Before the Illinois Commandery of the Loyal Legion of the United States*, vol. 2 (Chicago: Illinois Commandery, 1885), p. 211.

8. Joseph T. Durkin, S. J., *Stephen R. Mallory, Confederate Navy Chief* (Chapel Hill: University of North Carolina Press, 1954), p. 13.

9. Harriet Gift Castlen, *Hope Bids Me Onward* (Savannah: Chatham Printing Co., 1945), p. 120.

10. Inventory of County Archives of Georgia, No. 106, Muscogee County. Prepared by the Georgia Historical Records Survey, Division of Professional and Service Projects, Works Projects Administration (Atlanta: Georgia Historical Records Survey, 1941), p. 34.

11. Harry P. Owens, "Sail and Steam Vessels Serving the Apalachicola-Chattahoochee Valley," *Alabama Review* 21 (1968): 199.

12. Dorothy Dodd, "Apalachicola: Antebellum Cotton Port," Typescript in Division of Archives, History and Records Management, State of Florida, Tallahassee, p. 2.

13. Stanley L. Itkin, "Operations of the East Gulf Blockading Squadron in the Blockade of Florida 1862–1865" (Master's thesis, Florida State University, 1962), p. 6.

14. U.S. Congress, Eighth U.S. Census, 1860, Population, Franklin County, Fla. (Washington, D.C.: Government Printing Office, 1864).

15. Harry P. Owens, "Apalachicola Before 1861" (Ph.D. diss., Florida State University, 1966), pp. 195–96.

16. Dodd, "Apalachicola," p. 11.

17. T. Conn Bryan, *Confederate Georgia* (Athens: University of Georgia Press, 1953) pp. 102, 104–05.

18. U.S. Congress, Seventh U.S. Census, 1850, Population, Muscogee County, Ga. (Washington, D.C.: Robert Armstrong, 1853).

19. Coulter, *A People Courageous*, pp. 106, 136–37.

20. Mears and Company, comp., *The Columbus Directory for 1859–'60* (Columbus, Ga.: Sun Book and Job Printing Office, 1859).

21. Owens, "Sail and Steam Vessels," pp. 203, 207, 208.

22. *Historical Background of Dougherty County*, comp. under the auspices of the Works Progress Administration (Atlanta: Cherokee Publishing Co., 1981), p. 10.

23. Catherine C. Hopley, *Life in the South*, 2 vols. (London: Chapman and Hall, 1863), 2:334.

24. Ella Lonn, "The Extent and Importance of Federal Naval Raids on Salt-Making in Florida, 1862–1865," *Florida Historical Quarterly* 10 (1931–32): 183–84.

25. Mrs. Marvin Scott, *History of Henry County, Alabama* (Pensacola, Fla.: Frank R. Parkhurst and Son, 1961), p. 81.

26. Anne Kendrick Walker, *Backtracking in Barbour County, A Narrative of the Last Alabama Frontier* (Richmond: Dietz Press, 1941), p. 158.

27. Castlen, *Hope Bids Me Onward*, pp. 88–89. Benjamin McFarland, *Hines and Allied Families* (Ardmore, Pa.: Dorrance and Co., 1981), pp. 500–504. Notes on Collier were supplied from Ralph W. Donnelly's correspondence with A. Robert Holcombe, curator of the James W. Woodruff, Jr., Confederate Naval Museum, Columbus, Georgia.

28. Castlen, *Hope Bids Me Onward*, p. 112. Ezra J. Warner and W. Buck Yearns, *Biographical Register of the Confederate Congress* (Baton Rouge: Louisiana State University Press, 1975), pp. 182–83.

29. Hopley, *Life in the South*, 2:305.

30. Juanita Whiddon, "David Saunders Johnston, The Man and His Times," *Collections of the Early County Historical Society* 2 (1979): 137–39.

31. R. P. Brooke, ed., "Howell Cobb Papers," *Georgia Historical Quarterly* 6 (1922): 358.

32. W. H. Andrews, "Plantation Life Along the River and Spring Creek," *Collections of the Early County Historical Society* 2 (1979): 131.

33. Ray Mathis, *John Horry Dent, South Carolina Aristocrat on the Alabama Frontier* (University, Ala.: University of Alabama Press, 1979), p. 186.

34. Hopley, *Life in the South*, 2:242–43.

35. Hoyt M. Warren, *Henry—The Mother County* (Auburn, Ala.: Warren Enterprises, 1976), p. 96. Davis W. Campbell, ed., *Lest We Forget, Pen Sketches of Columbia, Alabama* (n.p., 1952), p. 5.

36. Mary Grist Whitehead, comp., "Letters," *Collections of the Early County Historical Society* 2 (1979): 363.

37. Mathis, *John Horry Dent*, pp. 182–83.

38. Edwin C. Bearss, "Civil War Operations in and Around Pensacola, Part 2," *Florida Historical Quarterly* 39 (1960–61): 249.

39. Parthenia Antoinette Hague, *A Blockaded Family: Life in Southern Alabama During the Civil War* (Boston: Houghton, Mifflin and Co., 1888), pp. 5–6.

40. *Dougherty County*, pp. 11–14.

41. Mathis, *John Horry Dent*, pp. 195–96.

42. Walker, *Backtracking in Barbour County*, p. 174.

43. Mark F. Boyd, "The Apalachicola or Chattahoochee Arsenal of the United States," *Apalachee* 4 (1956): 38.

44. Ibid., p. 39.

45. William Watson Davis, *The Civil War and Reconstruction in Florida* (New York: Columbia University Press, 1913), p. 72. On p. 71, Davis refers to "a Col. Duryea." In note 4 on p. 72, he cites the confusion of names for the Florida militia officer who is referred to as Colonel Dunn in Sergeant Powell's report.

46. *The War of the Rebellion: A Compilation of the Official Records of the Union and Confederate Armies* (hereafter cited as *A.O.R.*), 130 vols. (Washington, D.C.: Government Printing Office, 1880–1901), ser. 1, 1:332–33.

Chapter 2. Such Ability as You May Have at Hand: Blockade and Defense of Apalachicola, 1861–1862

1. *A.O.R.*, ser. 1, 1:448.
2. Ibid., p. 449.
3. Ibid., p. 450.
4. Ibid., p. 286.
5. Ibid., p. 472.
6. Ibid.
7. Ibid., 6:287.
8. Ibid., p. 291.
9. Ibid., p. 287.
10. John F. Reiger, "Florida After Secession: Abandonment by the Confederacy and its Consequences," *Florida Historical Quarterly* 50 (1971–72): 128.
11. Wait, "Blockading Service," p. 211.
12. Ibid., p. 213.
13. William H. Anderson, "Blockade Life," in *War Papers Read Before the Commandery of the State of Maine, Military Order of the Loyal Legion of the United States*, 3 vols. (Portland, Me.: Thurston, 1898–1908), 2:2.
14. Wait, "Blockading Service," pp. 213–14.

15. Itkin, "Operations of the East Gulf Blockading Squadron," p. 11.

16. *N.O.R.*, ser. 1, 16:546.

17. Ibid., pp. 531–33.

18. Ibid., p. 544.

19. Ibid., p. 546.

20. Wait, "Blockading Service," p. 212.

21. Itkin, "Operations of the East Gulf Blockading Squadron," pp. 26–27.

22. Wait, "Blockading Service," p. 212.

23. *N.O.R.*, ser. 1, 16:547.

24. Wait, "Blockading Service," pp. 215–16.

25. *A.O.R.*, ser. 1, 1:472.

26. Ibid., pp. 471–72.

27. *N.O.R.*, ser. 1, 16:613.

28. Wait, "Blockading Service," p. 235.

29. *Eufaula Spirit of the South*, Sept. 10, 1861.

30. *N.O.R.*, ser. 1, 16:646–47.

31. Ibid.

32. Anderson, "Blockade Life," p. 3.

33. *N.O.R.*, ser. 1, 16:838–39.

34. Ibid., p. 51.

35. *A.O.R.*, ser. 1, 6:342.

36. Mills B. Lane, ed., *"Dear Mother: Don't grieve about me. If I get killed, I'll Only be Dead,"* (Savannah: Beehive Press, 1977), pp. 6–7.

37. John F. Reiger, "Deprivation, Disaffection, and Desertion in Confederate Florida," *Florida Historical Quarterly* 48 (1969–70): 290–91.

38. S. P. Richardson, *Light and Shadows of an Itinerant Life* (Nashville: Methodist Episcopal Publishing Co., 1901), p. 173.

39. *A.O.R.*, ser. 1, 6:286–87.

40. *N.O.R.*, ser. 1, 16:669.

41. Ibid., pp. 855–56.

42. Ibid., pp. 856–57.

43. Marcus W. Price, "Ships that Tested the Blockade of the Gulf Ports 1861–1865," *American Neptune* 11 (1951): 267.

44. Itkin, "Operations of the East Gulf Blockading Squadron," app. 1.

45. Price, "Ships that Tested the Blockade," p. 265.

46. William J. Schellings, ed., "On Blockade Duty in Florida Waters, Excerpts from a Union Naval Officer's Diary," *Tequesta* 15 (1955): 57.

47. Ibid., p. 58.

48. Ibid., p. 61.

49. George E. Welch, October 20, 1862, Letters, US Bark *Amanda*, Nimitz Library, United States Naval Academy, Annapolis, Md.

50. Schellings, "On Blockade Duty," p. 64.

51. Welch Letters, January 8, 1863.

52. *N.O.R.*, ser. 1, 16:54.

53. Ibid., p. 24.

54. Ibid., pp. 120–21.
55. Ibid., pp. 193–94.
56. Ibid.
57. Ibid., p. 204.
58. Ibid., p. 203.
59. Ibid.

3. A *Steam Ship* and *No Boat:* The Gunboat *Chattahoochee*

1. William N. Still, *Confederate Shipbuilding* (Athens: University of Georgia Press, 1969), pp. 6–7.
2. Confederate Customs Records, Apalachicola Customs House, 1861, National Archives, Washington, D.C.
3. *DeBow's Review* 34 (July 1864): 102.
4. Still, *Confederate Shipbuilding*, pp. 75–76.
5. *N.O.R.*, ser. 2, 2:159.
6. Stephen R. Mallory to Augustus McLaughlin, October 2, 1861, Confederate Subject and Area File, Naval Records Collection of the Office of Naval Records and Library, Washington, D.C., Record Group (RG) 45, Area 6, 0077. Representative files in this collection are Construction (AC), Design and General Characteristics (AD), Auxiliary Machinery (EA), Steam Boilers (EB), Administration of Stations (PB), Industrial Activity (PI), Plant (PN), and Personnel (ZB). Naval Records Collections references are hereafter cited either by RG or by one of the file abbreviations listed here.
7. Stephen R. Mallory to James H. Warner, October 21, 1861, RG 45, Area 6, 0111.
8. McLaughlin's service record was compiled December 23, 1943, by naval archivist Capt. D. W. Knox and is in the Confederate Naval Museum files.
9. James H. Warner to William Ballard Preston, October 16, 1849, ZB.
10. Anne Saffold Johnston to Martha Fort Fannin, October 4, 1861, Fannin-Burnett Family Papers, Georgia Department of Archives and History, Atlanta.
11. Burt H. Flanders, "The Confederate Navy Yard at Saffold, Georgia," *Collections of the Early County Historical Society* 1 (1971): 19; *N.O.R.*, ser. 1, 17:864. Early County historians have been quite active in locating the exact area where the navy yard was operated along the river. Dudley H. McDowell's article cited in the bibliography is only one of his invaluable contributions to this area of study.
12. Anne Saffold Johnston to Martha Fort Fannin, December 16, 1861, Fannin-Burnett Papers.
13. *N.O.R.*, ser. 2, 2:53.
14. *Report of Evidence Taken Before a Joint Special Committee of Both Houses of the Confederate Congress to Investigate the Affairs of the Navy Department* (Richmond: G. P. Evans, 1863), pp. 440–41.
15. Owens, "Apalachicola Before 1861," p. 232.

16. George W. Gift to Ellen Shackelford, April 4, 1863, Ellen Shackelford Gift Papers, Southern Historical Collection, University of North Carolina Library, Chapel Hill.

17. John Horry Dent, Jr., to John Horry Dent, Sr., September 7, 1862, John Horry Dent, Jr., Letters, Amelia Gayle Gorgas Library, Special Collections, University of Alabama, University, Ala. In April 1863, William Martin reported to the Union at Apalachicola that the *Chattahoochee* was painted black. Both the Union and the Confederacy experimented with colors until the now familiar "battleship gray" was found to work best as camouflage because black was surprisingly easy to sight in darkness at sea (Wait, "Blockading Service," p. 228). By March 1863, however, the gunboat was assigned duty as a floating battery on obstructions in the Apalachicola River, where black was no doubt a more serviceable color.

18. Dodd, "Apalachicola," p. 7.

19. Still, *Confederate Shipbuilding*, p. 113. Robert Holcombe has applied the classification system from *Civil War Naval Chronology* (Naval History Division, Navy Department, 1971) to data collected at the Confederate Naval Museum. The classification system for wooden gunboats is based on contract specifications (in feet): *Macon* 150 (length) by 25 (beam) by 10 (draft); *Chattahoochee* 130 by 30 by 10; "Saffold" (contracted though never constructed) 106 by 18 by 8; *Maury* 112 by 21 by 8; *Morgan* 196 by 38 by 13 (side-wheeler). The nonstandardized construction system was such, however, that Confederate ships almost defy efforts at classification.

20. Still, *Confederate Shipbuilding*, pp. 12–13.

21. Voucher, Southern Telegraph Company, October 24 and December 3, 1862. Vouchers are identified (here and hereafter) by payee and date as a reference to the compilation of Columbus-related vouchers being made by Robert Holcombe at the Confederate Naval Museum. Appendix 2 lists the museum's collection of documents that are scattered through the 156 subfiles on 61 microfilm rolls in the RG 45 subject file of the Naval Records Collection (see n. 6 above).

22. Stephen R. Mallory to James H. Warner, October 21 and 31, 1861, ZB.

23. Commodore Josiah Tattnall to James H. Warner, March 9, 1862, ZB.

24. Duncan N. Ingraham to James H. Warner, April 5, 1862, ZB; Thomas Brent to James H. Warner, April 10, 1862, ZB; Travel voucher, April 21, 1862, ZB.

25. Travel voucher, May 22, 1862, ZB; Travel voucher, June 7, 1862, ZB; French Forrest to James H. Warner, June 3, 1862.

26. Travel voucher, March 3, 1862, ZB; Stephen R. Mallory to Augustus McLaughlin, March 3, 1862, ZB.

27. Voucher, Augustus McLaughlin to Paymaster John Debree, April 21, 1862; Augustus McLaughlin, RG 45, Area 6, 0096, n.d.

28. Anne Saffold Johnston to Martha Fort Fannin, March 5, 1862, Fannin-Burnett Papers.

29. *Columbus Daily Sun*, March 4, 1862.

30. Report on *Conduct of the War, Second Session Thirty-Eighth Congress*, 3 vols. (Washington, D.C., 1865) 1:450–51.

31. David S. Johnston, March 25, 1862, Voucher 6, first quarter of CSS *Chattahoochee* financial records. Thomas Berry, May 17, 1862, Voucher 1, second quarter. David S. Johnston, May 20, 1862, Voucher 2, second quarter. See Appendix 2 for an index of the Confederate Naval Museum's collection of *Chattahoochee* financial records.

32. C. G. Holmes, January 1, 1863, Voucher 22, first quarter.

33. *N.O.R.*, ser. 1, 17:262.

34. S. H. Hill, June 4, 1862, Voucher 5, second quarter; D. B. Thompson, June 16, 1863; the scuppers were part of a large bill paid April 1, 1863.

35. *N.O.R.*, ser. 2, 2:208–09.

36. Voucher 16, paid to Johnston January 23, 1863, contains an itemized list of much of this work.

37. McLaughlin to Treasury Department Auditor Bolling Baker, June 30, 1863. Quoted in full Appendix 2.

38. Voucher, D. B. Thompson, December 19, 1863, for deliveries August 4–November 14 and December 13, 1863. Columbus hardware merchant J. Ennis & Co. and furniture dealers Sammis and Rooney also filled large orders for the *Chattahoochee*.

39. *N.O.R.*, ser. 1, 17:864.

40. Undated fragment, Lewis N. Whittle Papers, Southern Historical Collection, University of North Carolina, Chapel Hill.

41. James M. Whittle to Lewis N. Whittle, September 9, 1862, Whittle Papers.

42. Horry Dent to J. H. Dent, Sr., September 7 and October 1, 1862, Dent Letters.

43. Flanders, "Confederate Navy Yard," p. 22.

44. Castlen, *Hope Bids Me Onward*, p. 87. While Gift's daughter's book offers interesting and quite valuable passages from her father's letters, the context she creates for them is, for the most part, quite romanticized.

45. William C. Whittle to Robert D. Minor, September 7 and 23, 1862, Minor Family Collections, Miscellaneous Papers, *W*, Virginia Historical Society, Richmond.

46. Horry Dent to J. H. Dent, Sr., September 6, 1862, Dent Letters.

47. Horry Dent to J. H. Dent, Sr., October 1, 1862, Dent Letters.

48. Castlen, *Hope Bids Me Onward*, p. 88.

49. Voucher, J. H. Sikes, September 5, 1862: "For 4 Cushions $140; Wrapping for Cushions $6."

50. Horry Dent to J. H. Dent, Sr., October 1, 1862, Dent Letters. Tom H. Wells (in *The Confederate Navy, A Study in Organization* [University of Alabama Press, 1971], pp. 114–17) describes the duties of shipboard engineers and how they functioned in the chain of command. Horry was one of the "one to three junior officers sometimes . . . embarked for instruction."

51. Castlen, *Hope Bids Me Onward*, pp. 91, 92–93, 114.

52. D. St. Ledger, August 29, 1862 (voucher paid May 29, 1863). St. Ledger's later adventures are recorded in the account of events for December 1864.

53. Horry Dent to J. H. Dent, Sr., September 6, 1862, Dent Letters.

54. River steamers appear regularly in the list of vouchers. McLaughlin's payment of $159 to the *Indian* on December 26, 1862, itemizes freight or passage to Apalachicola and Johnston's Landing for 1861 (November 22 and 29, December 2) and 1862 (March 3, August 30, September 5, and October 4, 9, 25, and 29) and passage for McLaughlin, Golder, and Fee on October 31.

55. Horry Dent to J. H. Dent, Sr., September 7 and 14 and December 7, 1862, Dent Letters.

56. Augustus McLaughlin to Bolling Baker, naval auditor, December 5, 1862, RG 45, AC.

57. Still, *Confederate Shipbuilding*, pp. 47–60; chap. 3 discusses the general problem of procuring materials for construction and the Confederacy's inability to utilize its raw materials.

58. Vouchers, J. Rhodes Browne, August 13, 1862; James Jackson, August 15, 1862.

59. Albert Mauncey, *Artillery Through the Ages* (Washington, D.C.: Government Printing Office, 1949), p. 52.

60. *Report on Conduct of the War*, 1:23.

61. Voucher, Mobile and Girard Railroad, paid December 16, 1862.

62. *N.O.R.*, ser. 2, 2:100.

63. Horry Dent to J. H. Dent, Sr., October 3, 1862, Dent Letters.

64. *N.O.R.*, ser. 1, 17:700. Wells, *Confederate Navy*, pp. 49–57, contains a discussion of the operation of naval ordnance aboard ship.

65. Horry Dent to J. H. Dent, Sr., October 3, 1862, Dent Letters.

66. Catesby ap R. Jones to Robert D. Minor, August 19, 1862, Minor Family Collections.

67. Whittle to Minor, September 23 and 7, and October 13, 1862, Minor Family Collections.

68. Horry Dent to J. H. Dent, Sr., October 7, 1862, Dent Letters.

69. Horry Dent to J. H. Dent, Sr., November 7, 1862, Dent Letters.

70. Horry Dent to J. H. Dent, Sr., November 29, 1862, Dent Letters.

71. Horry Dent to J. H. Dent, Sr., February 11, 1863, Dent Letters.

72. Urquhart and Chapman, August 12, 1862, Voucher 1, third quarter.

73. Whittle to Minor, September 7 and 23, 1862, Minor Family Collections. In *Rebel Brass, The Confederate Command System* (Baton Rouge: Louisiana State University Press, 1956), Frank E. Vandiver describes the workings of requisitions in army quartermaster procedure (pp. 107–12). In his search for whiskey, Jones functions here in the dual role of commander and "storekeeper" because the staff post of supply officer was not well defined in the Confederate system.

74. Horry Dent to J. H. Dent, Sr., September 14 and 7, 1862, Dent Letters. Contract specifications varied from project to project. Whereas specs for the *Macon* at Savannah called for masts and rigging, Johnston's contract did not.

Johnston was no doubt angered to see planed decking with two coats of paint sacrificed to Jones's change orders.

75. Horry Dent to J. H. Dent, Sr., January 9, 1862, Dent Letters.

76. Catesby ap R. Jones to Hardin B. Littlepage, January 2, 1863, RG 45, Area 6, 0233–0236.

77. Horry Dent to J. H. Dent, Sr., November 29 and December 7, 1862, Dent Letters.

78. Jones to Littlepage, January 2, 1863, RG 45, Area 6, 0233–0236.

79. George Gift to Ellen Shackelford, January 27, 1863, Gift Papers.

80. Jones to Littlepage, January 2, 1863, RG 45, Area 6, 0233–0236.

81. *N.O.R.*, ser. 1, 7:62.

82. Minutes, Columbus, Georgia, City Council, April 28, 1862, Office of the Probate Judge, Columbus Consolidated Government, Columbus.

83. *A.O.R.*, ser. 1, 14:493, 498–99.

84. William R. Boggs, *Military Reminiscences of Gen. Wm. R. Boggs, C.S.A.* (Durham: Seeman Printery, 1913), p. 30; James L. Nichols, *Confederate Engineers* (Tuscaloosa: Confederate Publishing Co., 1957), p. 10. Although Wells (*Confederate Navy*) stresses the point that the Confederate Navy was quite deficient in engineers, Nichols notes the great care taken to select experienced army engineers. Boggs stood fourth in his West Point class, meeting the foremost criteria that Confederate engineers be West Pointers who ranked well above average.

85. Welch Letters, October 20, 1862.

86. Boggs, *Military Reminiscences*, pp. 29–31.

87. *A.O.R.*, ser. 1, 14:506–07, 542–48.

88. Ibid., p. 666.

89. Minutes, Columbus, Georgia, City Council, November 3, 1862.

90. James F. Bozeman to Catesby ap R. Jones, November 5, 1862, RG 45, Area 6, 0207–0208.

91. *A.O.R.*, ser. 1, 14:686–87.

92. Nichols, *Confederate Engineers*, pp. 78–80.

93. Howell Cobb to Catesby ap R. Jones, December 1862, RG 45, Area 6, 0238.

94. *A.O.R.*, ser. 1, 14:682.

95. Nichols, *Confederate Engineers*, p. 82.

96. *A.O.R.*, ser. 1, 14:728, 731.

97. Nichols, *Confederate Engineers*, p. 83.

98. *A.O.R.*, ser. 1, 14:729.

99. Horry Dent to J. H. Dent, Sr., November 29, 1862, Dent Letters.

100. Horry Dent to J. H. Dent, Sr., January 11, 1863, Dent Letters.

101. Horry Dent to J. H. Dent, Sr., January 1 and 11, 1863, Dent Letters. "Uniform and Dress of the Navy of the Confederate States," an appendix in Wells, *Confederate Navy* (pp. 153–61), quotes Secretary Mallory's 1861 dress regulations. Scarcities in the Confederacy created problems of enforcement and compliance for all such regulations.

102. Horry Dent to J. H. Dent, Sr., December 7, 1863, Dent Letters.

103. Jones to Littlepage, January 2, 1863, RG 45, Area 6, 0233–0236; George W. Gift to Cowles Miles Collier, January 30, 1863, Gift Papers.

104. Horry Dent to J. H. Dent, Sr., January 9, November 7, and January 11, 1863, Dent Letters.

105. Horry Dent to J. H. Dent, Sr., January 9, 1863, Dent Letters.

106. Gift to Ellen Shackelford, January 25, 1863; Gift to Miles Collier, January 30, 1863, Gift Papers.

107. Horry Dent to J. H. Dent, Sr., February 9, 1863, Dent Letters.

108. Gift to Ellen Shackelford, February 18, 1863, Gift Papers.

109. George W. Gift to John Grimball, January 21, 1863, Grimball Family Papers, South Carolina Historical Society, Charleston.

110. Gift to Ellen Shackelford, February 5, 1863, Gift Papers.

111. Gift to Ellen Shackelford, January 27, 1863, Gift Papers.

112. Gift to Ellen Shackelford, January 30 and 27, 1863, Gift Papers.

113. Castlen, *Hope Bids Me Onward*, pp. 97, 99.

114. Gift to Ellen Shackelford, January 27, 1863, Gift Papers.

115. Castlen, *Hope Bids Me Onward*, p. 108.

116. Gift to Ellen Shackelford, January 21, 1863, Gift Papers.

117. Castlen, *Hope Bids Me Onward*, pp. 97–98.

118. Gift to Ellen Shackelford, January 24, 1863, Gift Papers.

119. Voucher, D. S. Johnston, February 3 and 19, 1863.

120. Gift to Ellen Shackelford, February 18, 1863, Gift Papers.

121. Castlen, *Hope Bids Me Onward*, pp. 99, 104, 96.

122. Gift to Ellen Shackelford, January 24, 1863, Gift Papers.

123. Gift to Ellen Shackelford, February 4, 1863, Gift Papers.

124. Gift to Ellen Shackelford, February 5, 1863, Gift Papers.

125. Gift to Ellen Shackelford, January 30, 1863, Gift Papers.

126. Lila Howard to George W. Gift, quoted in Gift to Ellen Shackelford, February 17, 1863, Gift Papers.

127. Castlen, *Hope Bids Me Onward*, p. 102.

128. Theodore Moreno to Howell Cobb, March 1, 1863, Howell Cobb Papers, University of Georgia Library, Athens.

129. Theodore Moreno Papers, Floyd County File, United Daughters of the Confederacy Collection, Georgia Department of Archives and History, Atlanta.

130. Theodore Moreno to Howell Cobb, March 7, 1863, Cobb Papers.

131. Ralph W. Donnelly's work in progress on Beaufort County, North Carolina, natives who served in the Confederate Navy supplies quite valuable and interesting information about Guthrie. Since this study began in the mid-1950s, Guthrie has suffered perhaps from a preponderance of references taken from Gift's point of view. Donnelly's work does a real service to a good man's memory.

132. Gift to Ellen Shackelford, March 29, 1863, Gift Papers.

133. John Julius Guthrie to Howell Cobb, March 30, 1863, Cobb Papers.

134. Gift to Ellen Shackelford, April 11, 1863, Gift Papers.

135. Guthrie to Jones, April 13, 1863, RG 45, Area 6, 0268.

136. Gift to Ellen Shackelford, April 11, 1863, Gift Papers.

137. Gift to Ellen Shackelford, May 8, 1863, Gift Papers.

138. Theodore Moreno to Howell Cobb, May 7, 1863, Cobb Papers.

139. Charles K. Mallory, Jr., to Charles K. Mallory, Sr., May 9, 1863, Charles King Mallory, Jr., Papers, Virginia Historical Society, Richmond.

140. *N.O.R.*, ser. 1, 17:866. Following this proposal is a second plan (pp. 866–67) to Secretary Mallory for mounting an attack upon the northern shore of Lake Erie. Gift himself characterized the plan as being "as Quixotic as it is audacious." He discussed it at great length with Ellen Shackelford in a May 14 letter (Castlen, *Hope Bids Me Onward*, pp. 118–19) along with a scheme to run the blockade. These plans and proposals are only three among several that Gift made to Mallory.

141. *N.O.R.*, ser. 1, 17:447–48.

142. Ibid., pp. 868–71.

143. *Columbus Daily Sun*, June 7, 1863.

144. Gift to Ellen Shackelford, May 28, 1863, Gift Papers. A printed version of this letter does not adequately convey the whole of its message. As a rule, Gift's penmanship was elaborate, with flourishes and large shaded characters in the address and complementary close. This scribbled note crowded onto a single page reveals the impact of the tragedy upon Gift.

145. *N.O.R.*, ser. 1, 17:868–69.

146. Gift to Ellen Shackelford, June 3, 1863, Gift Papers.

147. *N.O.R.*, ser. 1, 17:868–69.

148. John Horry Dent, Sr., June 25, 1863; John Horry Dent, Sr., to L. E. Brooks, July 18 and 29, 1863, John Horry Dent, Sr., Farm Journals and Account Books, Troy State University Library, Troy, Ala.

149. Voucher, D. S. Johnston, August 10, 1863, paid December 3, 1863.

150. Gift to Ellen Shackelford, May 30, 1863, Gift Papers.

4. The Phantom Ram Which Comes—And Does Not Come: Life on the Blockade Station

1. *N.O.R.*, ser. 1, 17:457.

2. Oscar D. Lewis Diary, May 27, 1863, New York Historical Society, New York.

3. *N.O.R.*, ser. 1, 17:469.

4. Ibid., pp. 452–57.

5. Lewis Diary, June 6 and 8, 1863.

6. *N.O.R.*, ser. 1, 17:474.

7. Ibid., p. 432.

8. Ibid., p. 745.

9. Ibid., pp. 470–71.

10. Lewis Diary, July 20, 1863.

11. *N.O.R.*, ser. 1, 17:468.

12. Lonn, "Extent of Federal Naval Raids," p. 175.

13. Itkin, "Operations of the East Gulf Blockading Squadron," pp. 95–96.

14. Ibid., p. 98.

15. James M. Dancy, "Reminiscences of the Civil War," *Florida Historical Quarterly* 37 (1958–59): 79.

16. *N.O.R.*, ser. 1, 17:600.

17. Itkin, "Operations of the East Gulf Blockading Squadron," pp. 107–08.

18. Lewis Diary, July 27, 1863.

19. Welch Letters, August 28, 1862.

20. *N.O.R.*, ser. 1, 17:357–58, 472–73.

21. Itkin, "Operations of the East Gulf Blockading Squadron," apps. 1, 2. Itkin lists all prizes taken by the East Gulf Blockading Squadron. The prize formula appears on p. 227 of Wait, "Blockading Service." Because of a change in how prizes were apportioned, amounts for the *Fashion* are approximate.

22. Lewis Diary, August 18 and 22, 1863.

23. Lewis Diary, October 28 and 29, 1863.

24. Samuel W. Powell, "Blockading Memories of the Gulf Squadron," *Magazine of History* 8 (1908): 1.

25. Lewis Diary, July 18, 1863.

26. Lewis Diary, December 26, 1862.

27. Powell, "Blockading Memories," p. 9.

28. F. H. Newcombe, "Nights on Blockade Duty," *Tribune Monthly* 3 (1881): 64.

29. Welch Letters, January 17, 1863.

30. Welch Letters, April 7, 1863.

31. Log, USS *Somerset*, December 16, 1862, National Archives, Washington, D.C.

32. Lewis Diary, August 20, 1863.

33. Davis, *Civil War and Reconstruction*, p. 141.

34. Welch Letters, October 24, 1862.

35. Itkin, "Operations of the East Gulf Blockading Squadron," p. 48.

36. Lewis Diary, May 23, 1863.

37. Lewis Diary, July 16, 1863.

38. Lewis Diary, July 5, 1863.

39. Welch Letters, January 8, 1863.

40. Welch Letters, January 19, 1863.

41. *N.O.R.*, ser. 1, 17:424–25.

42. Welch Letters, August 28, 1862.

43. Welch Letters, January 1, 1863.

44. Welch Letters, April 7, 1863.

45. Powell, "Blockading Memories," p. 3.

46. *N.O.R.*, ser. 1, 17:356.

47. Powell, "Blockading Memories," p. 5.

48. Newcombe, "Nights on Blockade Duty," p. 67.

49. Powell, "Blockading Memories," pp. 5–6.

50. Boyd, "Apalachicola or Chattahoochee Arsenal," p. 34.

51. George E. Welch, Orders, August 15, 1862, US Bark *Amanda*, Nimitz Library, U.S. Naval Academy, Annapolis, Md.

52. Lewis Diary, August 16, 1862.

53. Alice Strickland, "Blockade Runners," *Florida Historical Quarterly* 36 (1957–58): 92.

54. John F. Van Nest, "Yellow Fever on the Blockade of Indian River, A Tragedy of 1864," *Florida Historical Quarterly* 21 (1942–43): 352–57.

55. *N.O.R.*, ser. 1, 17:469.

56. Ibid., pp. 428–29, 458, 526, 538.

57. Ibid., pp. 746–47.

58. Ibid., pp. 469–70.

5. We Can Laugh at the Blockade for a While: Life Under the Blockade 1862–1864

1. *N.O.R.*, ser. 1, 17:358, 348.

2. Reiger, "Deprivation, Disaffection, and Desertions," pp. 281–82.

3. Davis, *Civil War and Reconstruction*, p. 189.

4. Reiger, "Florida After Secession," pp. 134, 137.

5. Reiger, "Deprivation, Disaffection, and Desertions," p. 296.

6. Welch Letters, dated only "1862." Harvey's February 15 visit and Welch's reference to a January 8, 1863, report give internal evidence to place this letter in 1863.

7. Dancy, "Reminiscences," pp. 80–81.

8. *N.O.R.*, ser. 1, 17:432.

9. Boyd, "Apalachicola or Chattahoochee Arsenal," p. 40.

10. Dancy, "Reminiscences," pp. 76–77.

11. John H. Martin, *Columbus, Georgia, from its Selection as a "Trading Town" in 1827 to its Partial Destruction by Wilson's Raid in 1865* (Columbus: John Gilbert, 1874), p. 159.

12. *N.O.R.*, ser. 1, 17:872.

13. Warren, *Henry—The Mother County*, pp. 98–99.

14. Warren (ibid.), along with Anne Kendrick Walker in her histories of Barbour and Russell counties and Harold Coulter in his history of Phenix City, gives thorough treatment to the toll in casualties.

15. Andrews, "Plantation Life," p. 126.

16. Campbell, *Lest We Forget*, p. 35.

17. McFarland, *Hines and Allied Families*, p. 503.

18. Campbell, *Lest We Forget*, p. 7.

19. Walker, *Backtracking in Barbour County*, p. 191.

20. Clifton Paisley, ed., "How to Escape the Yankees: Major Scott's Letters to His Wife at Tallahassee, March 1864," *Florida Historical Quarterly* 50 (1971–72): 59.

21. Brooke, "Howell Cobb Papers," p. 364.

22. Ibid., p. 360.

23. Mary Cole, ed., "A Transcript of Pages from the Plantation Account Book of Dr. Richard Bradley Hill, Early County, Georgia," *Collections of the Early County Historical Society* 2 (1979): 112.

24. Mathis, *John Horry Dent*, p. 206.

25. Andrews, "Plantation Life," p. 129.

26. Horry Dent to J. H. Dent, Sr., November 12, 29, and December 7, 1862, Dent Letters.

27. Augustus McLaughlin to Catesby ap R. Jones, RG 45, Area 6.

28. Hague, *A Blockaded Family*, pp. 57, 59.

29. Charlotte Thomas Marshall, ed., "Taylor Family Letters," *Collections of the Early County Historical Society* 2 (1979): 122.

30. Thronateeska Chapter, Daughters of the American Revolution, comp., *History and Reminiscences of Dougherty County Georgia* (Spartanburg, S.C.: Reprint Co., 1978), p. 368.

31. Walker, *Backtracking in Barbour County*, p. 194.

32. "Miss Teeny" Benning, Gen. Henry Benning's daughter, wrote a reminiscence of Civil War Columbus that survives as a 1928 typescript at the Bradley Memorial Library, Columbus, Ga.

33. Diffie Williams Standard, *Columbus, Georgia, in the Confederacy* (New York: William Frederick Press, 1954), p. 70, quoted in the *Columbus Daily Sun*, September 11, 1861, from the popular periodical *Southern Field and Fireside*.

34. Thronateeska, D.A.R., *History and Reminiscences*, p. 370.

35. Ibid., pp. 367–68.

36. Hague, *A Blockaded Family*, p. 109.

37. Davis, *Civil War and Reconstruction*, p. 211.

38. Mathis, *John Horry Dent*, p. 203.

39. Hague, *A Blockaded Family*, p. 51.

40. Standard, *Columbus, Georgia*, pp. 38–39.

41. Hague, *A Blockaded Family*, pp. 53–54. Frank E. Vandiver's comment on such work as it related to total production capabilities in the South appears in *Rebel Brass* (p. 19): "The dream of the Walter Scott South did not die at Appomattox—it died in the furnaces and clothing mills of a maximum war effort. It died when Southern women copied the 'wage slaves' of Lowell and made bullets, arms, and uniforms, as well as bandages."

42. Hague, *A Blockaded Family*, pp. 46–47.

43. Ibid., pp. 100–104.

44. John Julius Guthrie to Catesby ap R. Jones, April 6, 1863, RG 45, Area 6, 0264–0266.

45. Hague, *A Blockaded Family*, pp. 110–11.

46. Ibid., p. 97.

47. *DeBow's Review* 33 (1862): 121.

48. Mathis, *John Horry Dent*, p. 203.

49. John Horry Dent's corn and cotton yields appear in charts facing pp. 140 and 144 in ibid.

50. Davis, *Civil War and Reconstruction*, p. 210.

51. Bryan, *Confederate Georgia*, p. 198.

52. Mathis, *John Horry Dent*, p. 198.

53. Ibid., p. 207.

54. Paisley, "How to Escape the Yankees," p. 61.

55. *Dougherty County*, p. 35.

56. Hague, *A Blockaded Family*, pp. 20, 21.

57. Ibid., p. 129.

58. Davis, *Civil War and Reconstruction*, p. 211.

59. Mary Grist Whitehead, "Old Factory," *Collections of the Early County Historical Society* 1 (1971): 68–69.

60. Scott, *History of Henry County*, p. 81; Campbell, *Lest We Forget*, p. 6.

61. *Dougherty County*, p. 37.

62. Young advertised his machine shop, with emphasis upon the advantages of steam power, in the *Clayton* (Alabama) *News Banner* in 1859–60.

63. Kate Cumming, *A Journal of Hospital Life in the Confederate Army of Tennessee* (Louisville: John P. Morton and Co., 1866), pp. 168–69.

64. Paisley, "How to Escape the Yankees," p. 60.

65. *N.O.R.*, ser. 1, 17:871.

66. *Columbus Daily Sun*, June 29, 1864.

67. Walker, *Backtracking in Barbour County*, p. 159.

68. Mathis, *John Horry Dent*, pp. 199–200.

69. Martin, *Columbus, Georgia*, p. 174. Bert Neville has made an extensive study of steamboats in *Directory of Steamboats with Illustrations and Lists of Landings on the Chattahoochee-Apalachicola-Flint-Chipola Rivers* (Selma: Coffee Printing Co., 1961).

70. Albert Theodore Goodloe, *Confederate Echoes* (Nashville: Smith and Lamar, 1907), p. 161.

71. Ibid., pp. 163–64.

72. Cumming, *Journal of Hospital Life*, pp. 146–47.

73. *N.O.R.*, ser. 1, 17:871. The *N.O.R.* copy of McLaughlin's December 26, 1863, letter to Catesby ap R. Jones ends with an ellipsis; this account of Mrs. McLaughlin's injury was deleted from the official record, though it appears in the RG 45, Area 6, microfilms.

74. J. J. Geer, *Beyond the Lines: A Yankee Prisoner Loose in Dixie* (Philadelphia: J. W. Daughaday, 1863), p. 90.

75. C. H. M. Blair, "Historic Sketch of the Confederate Navy," *United Services*, 3d ser., 4 (1903): 1169.

76. Standard, *Columbus, Georgia*, p. 53.

77. Ibid., pp. 36–38. Charles W. Ramsdell in *Behind the Lines in the Southern Confederacy* (New York: Greenwood Press, 1944), discusses the rapid move from a laissez-faire economy to almost tyrannical government control (pp. 5–6). The agrarian society widely dispersed along the rivers had no need of government systems like transportation systems, public education, and public works. Government protected property and preserved the law and no more. Immediately upon forming a loose confederation of states, however, the government found itself having to fight a war supplied by a loose confederation of agricultural enterprises feeding its army and a loose confederation of private contractors shipping industrial products on a loose confederation of railroads built to serve

local needs. To mobilize for war brought a swift intervention of its own government more repressive than the South would have ever one time tolerated from the United States.

78. *DeBow's Review* 33 (1862): 75–78.

79. Ibid., p. 78.

80. *N.O.R.*, ser. 1, 17:870–71.

6. Conducting the Business of War

1. William N. Still, *Iron Afloat* (Nashville: Vanderbilt University Press, 1971), p. 8.

2. Ibid., p. 17.

3. *N.O.R.*, ser. 2, 2:69.

4. Ibid., pp. 149–50.

5. Castlen, *Hope Bids Me Onward*, p. 117.

6. *N.O.R.*, ser. 2, 2:242–43; Still, *Iron Afloat*, p. 92.

7. *N.O.R.*, ser. 2, 2:72–73.

8. Ibid., p. 241.

9. Ibid., pp. 150–51.

10. A. Robert Holcombe, "Notes on the Classification of Confederate Ironclads," report prepared for the U.S. Army Engineer District, Corps of Engineers, Savannah District, 1980. Ironclads may be classified as "Standard Hull" and "Diamond Hull." Another study of the *Jackson* is S. Ruby Lang, "Research on the Confederate Ironclad Ram *Jackson*," in Gordon P. Watts, Jr., ed., *Underwater Archaeology: The Challenge Before Us*, Proceedings of the Twelfth Conference on Underwater Archaeology (San Marino, Calif.: Fathom Eight Special Publications, 1981). Both Holcombe and Lang surveyed remains of the *Jackson* housed at the Confederate Naval Museum.

11. Voucher, William Penny and Co., March 31, 1863.

12. Vouchers, P. J. Ryan, February 9, 1863; James Riley, February 12, 1863. James H. Warner Letter Book (hereafter cited as Warner Letters), February 2, 1863, Confederate Naval Museum, January 6 and 21, 1863. Warner's letters are bound in a single volume dating from September 1862, when the navy assumed control of the Columbus Naval Iron Works, to February 1866, as the U.S. Navy concluded its work of accounting for captured Confederate stores. Robert Holcombe has made a complete transcription for use at the Confederate Naval Museum; the letter book itself is housed at the Confederate Naval Museum in Columbus. Quite apart from its content, the book is interesting technically; it is a "press book" made up of tissue pages. When a letter was written, the writer dampened the page lightly and then pressed it beneath a blank page in the press book. The result was a rather blurred, but nevertheless readable, copy. The entire book comprises a correspondence file of the Columbus Naval Iron Works.

13. Voucher, J. W. Young, February 28, March 3, 1863.

14. Voucher, Columbus Gas Light Company, Thomas McElhenny, July 11, 1863; Warner Letters, February 19, 1863.

15. Warner Letters, March 17, 16, and 24, 1863.

16. Voucher, W. R. Brown, April 20, 1863.

17. Vouchers, B. F. Coleman, April 17, September 4, and November 30, 1863, and June 30, 1864; Louis P. Henop, April 17, 1863.

18. Warner Letters, April 21 and 27, 1863.

19. George W. Gift to Ellen Shackelford, April 18, 1863, Gift Papers.

20. *N.O.R.*, ser. 1, 17:432.

21. Warner Letters, May 11, 1863.

22. *N.O.R.*, ser. 1, 17:432.

23. Vouchers, A. N. Miller, June 24 and July 30, 1863.

24. The Savannah Squadron Papers at the Emory University Library in Atlanta supply this well-defined example of an engineering project file: Item 133 is R. F. Pinkney's August 3 report to Flag Officer W. W. Hunter; Item 135 is Hunter's August 4 request for a report from engineers J. W. Tynan, George W. City, and L. Campbell; Item 136 is their report of the same date; Item 140 is Warner's August 7 response to Hunter; and Item 154 ends the episode with Warner's telegram about shipment of the reconstructed machinery.

25. Voucher, W. W. Ansell, June 15, 1863.

26. *N.O.R.*, ser. 1, 17:871.

27. Vouchers, Graham and Warren, October 1, 1863; F. Hughs, September 25, 1863; Warner Letters, September 29, 1863.

28. Vouchers, William Anderson, September 25, 1863; James T. Code, September 19, 1863; Warner Letters, July 10, 1863.

29. Voucher, A. Ravenscroft, October 29, 1863. In 1866, Ravenscroft used the *Daily Sun* to advertise his services as an agent and buyer, continuing the same kind of work he had performed for Warner.

30. Warner Letters, December 22, 1863.

31. Voucher, Park and Lyons, August 8, 1863.

32. Vouchers, Cyrus Bisbee, October 28, 1863; R. W. Briggs, October 14, 1863. On November 11, Warner sent payment to his agent John H. Chase for 4,853 pounds of iron in Jacksonville. Bisbee supplied 50,119 pounds and Compinet 111,516 pounds. CNIW records do not show that any of the Florida iron suppliers were associated with railroad companies. There is ample evidence, however, that the idea of using railroad iron not only caught fire in Florida but also set off a fiery controversy between Milton and Yulee. Robert C. Black discusses their exchanges on the issue in *The Railroads of the Confederacy* (Chapel Hill: University of North Carolina Press, 1952), pp. 208–13.

33. Warner Letters, November 25, 1863.

34. Vouchers, Henry Godwin, October 31, 1863; M. McHale, November 18, 1863; Miles Treat, November 21, 1863.

35. John A. Wilson, *Adventures of Alf Wilson* (Toledo: Blade Printing and Paper Co., 1880), pp. 185–86.

36. *Columbus Enquirer*, December 31, 1863, and January 1, 1864; *Columbus Daily Sun*, January 1, 1864.

37. Confederate Navy Yard Log, January 1, 1864. The large ledger that contains Augustus McLaughlin's letters also contains on pp. 503–25 a daily log

from January 1864 to April 16, 1865, the day Union forces captured Columbus. The log shows the writing of McLaughlin, his assistant (and brother-in-law) Golder, and a third unidentified clerk; however, the log is ascribed to McLaughlin because the writing was performed under his authority and by his direction. William W. Golder, a descendant of McLaughlin's wife, Henrietta Golder, sent the original ledger from El Dorado, Arkansas, to the Georgia Historical Commission in October 1972, so that copies could be used at the Georgia Archives.

38. *Columbus Daily Sun*, January 2, 1864.

39. McLaughlin Letter Book (hereafter cited as McLaughlin Letters), January 23, 1864. As noted in n. 37, McLaughlin letters of January 1–June 30, 1864, comprise pp. 415–71 of a ledger that also includes the CNY Log.

40. McLaughlin Letters, January 22, 1864.

41. CNY Log, January 9–23, 1864.

42. McLaughlin Letters, January 9, 1864.

43. McLaughlin Letters, January 12 and 14, 1864.

44. Warner Letters, January 15 and 16, 1864.

45. McLaughlin Letters, January 18 and 20, 1864.

46. Augustus McLaughlin to Catesby ap R. Jones, January 22, 1864, RG 45, Area 6, 0382–0834.

47. McLaughlin to Jones, February 29, 1864, RG 45, Area 6, 0424.

48. McLaughlin Letters, January 23 and 26, 1864.

49. McLaughlin to Jones, January 28, 1864, RG 45, Area 6, 0424.

50. George W. Gift to Catesby ap R. Jones, January 26, 1863, and February 13, 1864, RG 45, Area 6, 0407–0410.

51. Castlen, *Hope Bids Me Onward*, p. 168.

52. McLaughlin to Jones, February 18, 1864, RG 45, Area 6, 0424.

53. CNY Log, February 13, 1864.

54. *N.O.R.*, ser, 1, 17:873.

55. Ibid., p. 876.

56. Gift to Jones, February 13, 1864, RG 45, Area 6, 0407–0410.

57. Jones to Gift, February 25, 1864, RG 45, Catesby ap R. Jones Letters.

58. McLaughlin Letters, February 26, 1864. Chap. 17 of Wells, *Confederate Navy* (pp. 95–106), is a discussion of Chief Constructor John L. Porter's role.

59. David P. McCorkle to Catesby ap R. Jones, February 27, 1864, RG 45, Area 6.

60. McLaughlin to Jones, February 28, 1864, RG 45, Area 6, 0242.

61. McLaughlin Letters, February 11, 4, and 23, 1864.

62. McLaughlin Letters, February 24, 1864.

63. *N.O.R.*, ser. 1, 17:873. With so many Confederate vessels plagued by construction delays or hampered by shallow waters, the small boat expedition was becoming a popular tactic. John Taylor Wood distinguished himself with a February 2, 1864, raid upon the USS *Underwriter* in the Neuse River, North Carolina.

64. Voucher, Warner, RG 45, File B.15.

65. McLaughlin Letters, February 13, 1864. A detailed study of conscription problems and issues appears in Douglas Clare Purcell, "Military Con-

scription in Alabama during the Civil War," *Alabama Review* 34 (1981): 94–106.

66. Warner Letters, February 1, 1864.

67. McLaughlin Letters, March 20, April 14, 1864.

68. Warner Letters, March 8 and 11, 1864; McLaughlin Letters, March 12, 1864.

69. McLaughlin Letters, March 18, 1864.

70. George W. Gift to Ellen Shackelford, March 15, 1864, Gift Papers.

71. A list of companies and officers is contained in J. Harmon Smith, comp., "Organizational Summary of Military Organizations from Georgia in the Confederate States of America," Georgia Department of Archives and History, Atlanta.

72. Warner Letters, March 25, 1864.

73. Warner Letters, March 26, 1864.

74. McLaughlin Letters, March 3, 1864.

75. McLaughlin Letters, March 14 and 23, 1864.

76. CNY Log, February 13, 1864.

77. McLaughlin Letters, March 19, 1864.

78. *Columbus Enquirer,* March 16, 1864.

79. McLaughlin to Jones, March 25, 1864, RG 45, Area 6, 4089–0492.

80. McLaughlin to John Mercer Brooke, March 30, 1864, RG 45, Area 6, 0493.

81. CNY Log, March 20 and 30, 1864.

82. Warner Letters, April 26, 1864; McLaughlin Letters, April 25 and 25, 1864 (two letters); Warner Letters, April 27, 1864.

83. Warner Letters, April 29, 1864. The Engineer Bureau performed duties similar to Warner's in meeting payrolls and purchasing large stores of equipment and supplies. Those officers also suffered the "paper money disease" that plagued the Confederacy (Nichols, *Confederate Engineers*, p. 35).

84. McLaughlin Letters, April 30, 1864.

85. McLaughlin Letters, April 4, 1864.

86. McCorkle to Jones, April 14, 1864, RG 45, Area 6, 0501; April 22, 1864, RG 45, Area 6, 0506.

87. McLaughlin Letters, April 26, 1864.

88. McLaughlin Letters, April 25, 1864.

89. Castlen, *Hope Bids Me Onward*, p. 172.

90. McLaughlin Letters, April 23, 1864.

91. James Shirah, "The C. S. Torpedo Boat *Viper,*" CS *Viper* File, Confederate Naval Museum. Museum files contain a collection of unpublished papers assigned in college courses. Dr. Joseph Mahan began the practice at the Columbus Center of the University of Georgia; Dr. John Lupold continued to make similar assignments in the Columbus College History Department. Many of these papers date from the 1950s; sources were then almost nonexistent. and the papers show the flaws of most students' term projects. Many such term projects, however, contributed to the interest in the Confederate Navy in Columbus. *N.O.R.*, ser. 2, 2:627–28, contains further data on the torpedo boat, although it has not yet been established just how the *Viper* reflected Confederate Navy

standards for such vessels. Early correspondence about the engines and about procuring iron for armor suggests a vessel like those constructed elsewhere. Lt. William Watts Carnes referred to the *Viper* as "a steam launch," suggesting that the ship was put into service in 1865 before the armored casemate could be completed. Such questions can be resolved only if a years'-long search for ship plans is successful—or the *Viper*'s remains can be salvaged from the Gulf of Mexico.

92. McLaughlin Letters, April 23, 1864.

93. Castlen, *Hope Bids Me Onward*, p. 174.

94. CNY Log, April 28–May 1, 1864.

95. CNY Log, May 2–5, 1864.

96. McLaughlin to Jones, May 5, 1864, RG 45, Area 6, 0510.

97. Castlen, *Hope Bids Me Onward*, pp. 174–75.

98. McLaughlin to Jones, May 10, 1864, RG 45, Area 6, 0528–0529.

99. John Thomas Scharf, *History of the Confederate States Navy* (New York: Rogers and Sherwood, 1887) p. 618. Scharf's "luminous light" and "phosphorescent water" passage has found its way into several sources, particularly Castlen, *Hope Bids Me Onward*, and Itkin, "East Gulf Blockading Squadron."

100. Scharf, *History*, p. 620.

101. *N.O.R.*, ser. 1, 17:698.

102. Scharf, *History*, p. 621.

103. *N.O.R.*, ser. 1, 17:698–99.

104. CNY Log, May 12–14 and 18–19, 1864.

105. *N.O.R.*, ser. 1, 17:704.

106. Except for a May 25 letter from Gift to Mallory (ibid., p. 874) requesting a visit from Constructor Porter, all correspondence in this section of the text appears in McLaughlin's letters of May 20 through June 17, 1864. McLaughlin's meticulous record of communications received as well as sent is treated as a single reference source. Most of the details contained in Mdn. Samuel P. Blanc's captured diary of the expedition appear in the Union report.

107. CNY Log, June 18 and 19, 1864.

108. CNY Log, June 25–July 2, 1864.

109. Castlen, *Hope Bids Me Onward*, p. 178.

110. Ibid., pp. 179, 183, 184–86.

111. Voucher, J. W. Young, June 24, 1864; *Columbus Daily Sun*, June 30, 1864.

112. CNY Log, July 3, 1864.

113. Voucher, Thomas Gilbert, June 30, 1864.

114. Warner Letters, June 16, 1864.

115. Warner Letters, June 13, 20, and 30, 1864.

116. Warner Letters, June 9, 1864.

117. Warner Letters, June 14, 1864.

118. W. H. Blake, "Coal Barging in War Time, 1861–1865," *Gulf States Historical Magazine* 1 (1903): 410–11.

119. Warner Letters, July 2, 1864.

120. CNY Log, May 17, 20, 23, and 29, and June 14, 1864.

121. McLaughlin Letters, June 25, 1864.

122. McLaughlin Letters, June 25, 1864.

123. McLaughlin Letters, May 28, 1864.

124. McCorkle to Jones, June 25, 1864, RG 45, Area 6.

125. CNY Log, July 15–18 and 23, 1864.

126. CNY Log, August 13 and 20, 1864, September 17, 1864.

127. Warner Letters, August 22, 1864. Confederates in Savannah scored more than a minor triumph in morale when a boarding party assaulted and captured the US *Water Witch* at 2:30 A.M., June 3. In his postwar inventory of stores, Warner did not fail to note those from the captured Union vessel.

128. Warner Letters, July 25, 1864.

129. Warner Letters, August 31, 1864.

130. CNY Log, July 20, 1864; Warner Letters, September 29, 1864.

131. McLaughlin to Jones, August 19, 1864, RG 45, Area 6, 0639–0640.

132. McLaughlin to Jones, August 30, 1864, RG 45, Area 6, 0650.

133. McLaughlin to Jones, August 19, 1864, RG 45, Area 6, 0639–0640.

134. McLaughlin to Jones, September 14, 1864, RG 45, Area 6, 0677.

135. *N.O.R.*, ser. 2, 2:751–53.

136. Ibid., ser. 1, 17:772–75.

137. Ibid., 21:674.

138. Ibid., p. 688.

139. *A.O.R.*, ser. 1, 41:26.

140. Warner to Jones, November 1, 1864, RG 45, Area 6, 0731–0732.

141. McLaughlin to Jones, November 15, 1864, RG 45, Facilities at Selma Papers.

142. Warner Letters, November 19, 1864.

143. Warner Letters, November 21, 1864.

144. McLaughlin to Jones, November 28, 1864, Jones Letters, RG 45, Area 6.

145. Warner Letters, November 29, 1864.

146. Warner to Jones, December 15, 1864, RG 45, Area 6, 0781–0784.

147. Warner Letters, December 16, 1864.

148. *Columbus Enquirer*, December 23, 1864.

149. *Columbus Daily Sun*, December 23, 1864.

150. *Early County News*, January 11, 1865.

151. *Columbus Daily Sun*, November 20–21, 1864.

152. *Columbus Daily Sun*, November 29 and December 21 and 24, 1864.

153. Harry P. Owens, "History of Eufaula, Alabama" (Master's thesis, Auburn University, 1959), p. 70.

154. Mathis, *John Horry Dent*, p. 199.

155. Castlen, *Hope Bids Me Onward*, p. 183.

156. Ibid., p. 193.

157. Reiger, "Deprivation, Disaffection, and Desertions," p. 298.

158. *N.O.R.*, ser. 1, 17:784, 786.

159. Mathis, *John Horry Dent*, p. 209.

7. Concluding the Business of War

1. Durkin, *Stephen R. Mallory*, pp. 334–35.
2. *N.O.R.*, ser. 1, 17:773.
3. Ibid., pp. 797–800.
4. Dancy, "Reminiscences," pp. 80–81.
5. *Early County News*, January 11, 1865.
6. McLaughlin to Jones, January 24, 1865, RG 45, Area 6.
7. Jones to McLaughlin, January 23, 1865, RG 45, Area 6, 0823.
8. Warner to Jones, January 28, 1865, RG 45, Area 6, 0823–0825.
9. Jones to Warner, February 2, 1865, RG 45, Area 6, 0834.
10. Warner to Mallory, February 3, 1865, RG 45, AD.
11. Jones to McLaughlin, February 11, 1865, RG 45, Area 6, 0836.
12. Jones to McLaughlin, January 23, 1865, RG 45, Area 6, 0823.
13. Francis B. C. Bradlee, *Blockade Running During the Civil War* (Salem, Mass.: Essex Institute, 1925), pp. 130–32; a description of disrupted telegraph services in Georgia is on pp. 304–10.
14. Warner to Jones, March 1, 1865, RG 45, Area 6, 0859–0861.
15. Jones to Montgomery agent P. Murphy, March 3, 1865, RG 45, Area 6, 0866.
16. Jones to Warner, March 8, 1865, RG 45, Jones Letters.
17. Jones to Warner, March 7, 1865, RG 45, Area 6, 0869.
18. Jones to John Mercer Brooke, March 21, 1865, RG 45, Area 6, 0878.
19. Three modern works treat in detail the military aspects of Wilson's March 22–April 20 raid and the land battle for Columbus on April 16. James Pickett Jones, *Yankee Blitzkrieg, Wilson's Raid Through Alabama and Georgia* (Athens: University of Georgia Press, 1976); C. Robert Watkins, "Wilson's Raid Through Alabama and Georgia" (Master's thesis, Auburn University, 1959); and Coulter's, *A People Courageous*. Coulter gives especially thorough treatment to the fortifications erected in Girard, Alabama.
20. CNY Log. Entries for the last month of operation, March 16–April 16, 1865, are verbatim.
21. *Columbus Daily Sun*, March 31, 1865.
22. Ibid., April 4, 1865.
23. Ibid., April 7, 1865.
24. Ibid., April 9, 1865.
25. Ibid., April 12, 1865.
26. Ibid., April 13, 1865.
27. Alfred O. Blackmar File, Confederate Naval Museum.
28. Warner to Alexander, June 16, 1865, RG 56, Captured and Abandoned Property, Case File 285.
29. CNY Log, April 16, 1865.
30. William Watts Carnes Memoirs, typescript donated to the Confederate Naval Museum by Lt. Cdr. Robert S. Carnes, M.D. Undated clipping from *Montgomery Advertiser* from a relative of *Chattahoochee* crewman Andrew

Olds, contributed to this study in 1956 by Peter Brannon, archivist for the state of Alabama.

31. "William Watts Carnes," in *Tennessee Civil War Veterans Questionnaire*, 6 vols. (Easley, S.C.: Southern History Press, 1985), vol. 2.

32. B. F. McGee and William R. Jewell, eds., *History of the 72nd Indiana Volunteer Infantry of the Mounted Lightning Brigade* (Lafayette, Ind.: S. Vater and Co., 1882), p. 581.

33. *A.O.R.*, ser. 1, vol. 49, pt. 1, pp. 485–87. Winslow's report of April 18 is only one of a series written by unit commanders after Wilson's forces reached Macon on May 20 to find that the Civil War had ended.

34. Ibid., p. 485.

35. Ibid., p. 487.

36. CNY Log. This information appears in two or three lines wedged beneath the word FINIS.

37. *A.O.R.*, ser. 1, vol. 49, pt. 1, p. 415. The tables of prisoners, captured stores, and status of Union troops show Wilson's command engaging in the kind of reporting and record keeping that was so characteristic of work at Confederate naval facilities in Columbus.

38. Warner Letters, December 23, 1865. Navy Lieutenant Cushman, commander of the *Mahaska* at the Apalachicola blockade station, was sent to Columbus to aid efforts to inventory and ship captured stores from the CNIW. The last entries in Warner's letters detail that period of December 1865 to February 1866. It is assumed that Cushman, like so many other officers, retained his correspondence records and took the volume home to Buffalo, New York, in 1866. The Buffalo–Erie County Historical Society presented the volume to the Confederate Naval Museum in 1974.

39. McGee and Jewell, *72nd Indiana*, p. 582.

40. Blackmar File.

8. Concluding the Business of Peace

1. Hague, *A Blockaded Family*, pp. 170–71.

2. Warner Letters, June 16, 1865.

3. *N.O.R.*, ser. 1, 17:844.

4. Walker, *Backtracking in Barbour County*, pp. 216–17.

5. Mathis, *John Horry Dent*, pp. 217, 213.

6. Whiddon, "David Saunders Johnston," p. 144. Governor Joseph E. Brown Letter Book, August 5, 1863, Georgia Department of Archives and History, Atlanta.

7. Andrews, "Plantation Life," pp. 127, 126.

8. Brooke, "Howell Cobb Papers," p. 376.

9. Castlen, *Hope Bids Me Onward*, pp. 197–98.

10. Bertram H. Groene, ed., "A Letter from Occupied Tallahassee," *Florida Historical Quarterly* 48 (1969–70): 72.

11. Davis, *Civil War and Reconstruction*, p. 377.

12. Log, USS *Yucca*, May 25–26, 1865, National Archives, Washington, D.C.

13. John S. Jones, *Military History of the One Hundred Sixty-First New York Volunteer Infantry* (Bath: Hall, Barnes Printers, 1865), p. 48.

14. *N.O.R.*, ser. 1, 17:856.

15. Joan Warner, "James H. Warner," typescript in the Confederate Naval Museum. Miss Warner, the daughter of Warner's posthumous son Charles, wrote this brief biography of her grandfather that contains these more personal details.

16. James H. Warner to J. H. Alexander, July 17, 1865, RG 56, Captured and Abandoned Property, File 825.

17. J. S. Jones, *History of the New York Volunteer Infantry*, p. 48.

18. *Columbus Daily Sun*, August 31, 1865. In his dissertation, "Apalachicola Before 1861," Harry Owens presents a strong argument that the shift from river to rail was accomplished by 1861. While the rivers were essential to an interior transportation system during the war, Apalachicola never recaptured its economic significance as a port after the war.

19. Charles H. Cushman, Warner Letters, December 12, 1865, pp. 282–83; December 15, 1865, pp. 284–85; December 23, 1865, pp. 277–80. Warner's press book—which contains his correspondence from September 4, 1862, to the last day of the war—also served Cushman as a correspondence record for December 6, 1865, to February 12, 1866.

20. *Columbus Daily Sun*, December 22–23, 1865.

21. Cushman, Warner Letters, December 23, 1865.

22. Cushman, Warner Letters, January 2, 1866.

23. CNY Log, June 29, 1864; Joan Warner, "James H. Warner."

24. Cushman, Warner Letters, January 3, 1866.

25. Cushman, Warner Letters, January 16, 1866.

26. Cushman, Warner Letters, January 16, 1866.

27. Cushman, Warner Letters, January 31, 1866.

28. Cushman, Warner Letters, February 8, 1866.

29. Cushman, Warner Letters, February 10, 1866.

30. Cushman, Warner Letters, February 14, 1866.

31. *Columbus Enquirer*, February 16 and 22, 1866.

32. Joan Warner, Warner's granddaughter, wrote a short family biography, which is in the James H. Warner file in the Confederate Naval Museum.

B I B L I O G R A P H Y

GOVERNMENT PUBLICATIONS

Civil War Naval Chronology, 1861–1865. Washington, D.C.: Naval History Division, Navy Department, 1971.

Confederate Customs Records, Apalachicola Customs House, 1861. National Archives, Washington, D.C.

Confederate Subject and Area File, Naval Records Collection of the Office of Naval Records and Library. Washington, D.C.

Official Records of the Union and Confederate Navies in the War of the Rebellion, 31 vols. Washington, D.C.: Government Printing Office, 1894–1927.

Report of Evidence Taken Before a Joint Special Committee of Both Houses of the Confederate Congress to Investigate the Affairs of the Navy Department. Richmond: G. P. Evans, 1863.

Report on Conduct of the War, Second Session Thirty-Eighth Congress. 3 vols. Washington, D.C.: Government Printing Office, 1865.

Squadron Papers, East Gulf Blockading Squadron, 1865. National Archives, Washington, D.C.

U.S. Bureau of the Census, *Seventh Census, 1850, Population.* Washington, D.C.: Robert Armstrong, 1853.

————. *Eighth Census, 1860, Population.* Washington, D.C.: Government Printing Office, 1864.

The War of the Rebellion: A Compilation of the Official Records of the Union and Confederate Armies, 130 vols. Washington, D.C.: Government Printing Office, 1880–1901.

MANUSCRIPT SOURCES

Blackmar, Alfred O. Blackmar File. James W. Woodruff, Jr., Confederate Naval Museum, Columbus, Georgia.

Brown, Governor Joseph E. Letter Book. Georgia Department of Archives and History, Atlanta.

Carnes, William Watts. Memoirs. Typescript donated to the James W. Woodruff, Jr., Confederate Naval Museum, Columbus, Georgia, by Lt. Cdr. Robert S. Carnes, M.D., U.S.N.

Cobb, Howell. Papers. University of Georgia Library, Athens.

Columbus, Georgia, City Council Minutes, 1861–65. Office of the Probate Judge. Columbus Consolidated Government, Columbus.

Dent, John Horry, Jr. Letters. Amelia Gayle Gorgas Library Special Collections, University of Alabama, University, Alabama.

Dent, John Horry, Sr. Farm Journals and Account Books. Troy State University Library, Troy, Alabama.

Fannin-Burnett Family. Papers. Georgia Department of Archives and History, Atlanta.

Gift, Ellen Shackelford. Papers. Southern Historical Collection, University of North Carolina Library, Chapel Hill.

Grimball Family. Papers. South Carolina Historical Society, Charleston.

Lewis, Oscar D. Diary. New York Historical Society, New York.

McLaughlin, Augustus. Letter Book and Confederate Navy Yard Log and Accounts. James W. Woodruff, Jr., Confederate Naval Museum, Columbus, Georgia.

Mallory, Charles King, Jr. Letters. Virginia Historical Society, Richmond.

Minor, Robert Dabney. Minor Family Collections. Virginia Historical Society, Richmond.

Moreno, Theodore. Papers. Floyd County File. United Daughters of the Confederacy Collection, Georgia Department of Archives and History, Atlanta.

Savannah Squadron. Papers. Emory University Library, Atlanta.

USS *Somerset*. Log. National Archives, Washington, D.C.

USS *Yucca*. Log. National Archives, Washington, D.C.

Warner, James H. Letter Book. James W. Woodruff, Jr., Confederate Naval Museum, Columbus, Georgia.

Welch, George E. Letters. US Bark *Amanda*. Nimitz Library, United States Naval Academy, Annapolis, Maryland.

————. Orders. US Bark *Amanda*. Nimitz Library, United States Naval Academy, Annapolis, Maryland.

Whittle, Lewis N. Papers. Southern Historical Collection, University of North Carolina Library, Chapel Hill.

NEWSPAPERS

Clayton News Banner, 1860.   *Columbus Weekly Enquirer*, 1856.
Columbus Daily Sun, 1861–65.   *Early County News*, 1865.
Columbus Enquirer, 1861–65.   *Eufaula Spirit of the South*, 1861.
Columbus Tri-Weekly Enquirer, 1856.

UNPUBLISHED DOCUMENTS

Theses and Dissertations

Itkin, Stanley L. "Operations of the East Gulf Blockading Squadron in the Blockade of Florida 1862–1865." Master's thesis, Florida State University, 1962.

Jordan, Mildred. "Georgia's Confederate Hospitals." Master's thesis, Emory University, 1942.

Owens, Harry P. "Apalachicola Before 1861." Ph.D. diss., Florida State University, 1966.

————. "History of Eufaula, Alabama." Master's thesis, Auburn University, 1959.

Turner, Maxine. "Naval Operations on the Apalachicola and Chattahoochee Rivers, 1861–1865." Master's thesis, Auburn University, 1961.

Watkins, C. Robert. "Wilson's Raid Through Alabama and Georgia." Master's thesis, Auburn University, 1959.

Manuscripts

Benning, "Miss Teeny." Typescript, 1928, in W. C. Bradley Memorial Library, Columbus, Georgia.

Chase, David W. "Fort Mitchell, An Archaeological Exploration in Russell County, Alabama, July–December, 1971." Typescript in W. C. Bradley Memorial Library, Columbus, Georgia.

Dodd, Dorothy. "Apalachicola: Antebellum Cotton Port," Typescript in Division of Archives, History and Records Management, State of Florida, Tallahassee.

Donnelly, Ralph W. "Confederate Sailors and Marines of Beaufort County, North Carolina." In progress.

Georgia Historical Records Survey, Division of Professional and Service Projects, Works Projects Administration. "Inventory of County Archives of Georgia, No. 106, Muscogee County." Atlanta: Georgia Historical Records Survey, 1941. Typescript in W. C. Bradley Memorial Library, Columbus, Georgia.

Lamar, John E. "Reminiscences of Columbus." From *Columbus Enquirer-Sun*, September 20, 1891, to November 15, 1891. Compiled by Thomas J. Peddy, 1982. Typescript in W. C. Bradley Memorial Library, Columbus, Georgia.

Shirah, James. "The C. S. Torpedo Boat *Viper.*" CS *Viper* File, James W. Woodruff, Jr., Confederate Naval Museum, Columbus, Georgia.

Smith, J. Harmon, comp. "Organizational Summary of Military Organizations from Georgia in the Confederate States of America." Georgia Department of Archives and History, Atlanta.

Turner, Maxine. "The Gunboat *Chattahoochee.*" Typescript, 1956, in Huntingdon College Library, Montgomery, Alabama.

Warner, Joan. "James H. Warner." Typescript in James W. Woodruff, Jr., Confederate Naval Museum, Columbus, Georgia.

Reports

Holcombe, A. Robert. "Notes on the Classification of Confederate Ironclads." Prepared for U.S. Army Engineer District, Corps of Engineers, Savannah District, 1980.

Lang, S. Ruby. "Research on the Confederate Ironclad Ram *Jackson*." In *Underwater Archaeology: The Challenge Before Us*. Proceedings of the Twelfth Conference on Underwater Archaeology, edited by Gordon P. Watts, Jr. San Marino, Calif: Fathom Eight Special Publications, 1981.

Watts, Gordon P., Jr., William N. Still, Jr., James Lee Cox, Jr., and Wesley K. Hall. "A Reconnaissance Survey of the Chattahoochee River at Columbus, Georgia." Prepared for the James W. Woodruff, Jr., Confederate Naval Museum, 1982.

ARTICLES

Anderson, William H. "Blockade Life." In *War Papers Read Before the Commandery of the State of Maine, Military Order of the Loyal Legion of the United States*, 3 vols. Portland, Me.: Thurston, 1898–1908.

Andrews, W. H. "Plantation Life Along the River and Spring Creek." *Collections of the Early County Historical Society* 2 (1979): 123–31.

Bearss, Edwin C. "Civil War Operations in and Around Pensacola, Part 2." *Florida Historical Quarterly* 39 (1960–61): 231–55.

Blair, C. H. M. "Historic Sketch of the Confederate Navy." *United Services*, 3d ser., 4 (1903): 1115–84.

Blake, W. H. "Coal Barging in War Time, 1861–1865." *Gulf States Historical Magazine* 1 (1903): 409–12.

Boyd, Mark F. "The Apalachicola or Chattahoochee Arsenal of the United States." *Apalachee* 4 (1956): 29–43.

Brooke, R. P., ed. "Howell Cobb Papers." *Georgia Historical Quarterly* 6 (1922): 355–94.

Cole, Mary, ed. "A Transcript of Pages from the Plantation Account Book of Dr. Richard Bradley Hill, Early County, Georgia." *Collections of the Early County Historical Society* 2 (1979): 85–120.

Cushman, Joseph D., Jr. "The Blockade and Fall of Apalachicola." *Florida Historical Quarterly* 41 (1962–63): 38–46.

Dancy, James M. "Reminiscences of the Civil War." *Florida Historical Quarterly* 37 (1958–59): 66–89.

DeBow's Review and Industrial Resources, Statistics, etc. Edited by J. D. B. DeBow. 30 vols. New Orleans.

Flanders, Burt H. "The Confederate Navy Yard at Saffold, Georgia." *Collections of the Early County Historical Society* 1 (1971): 18–24.

Gadsden, James. "The Defences of the Floridas." *Florida Historical Quarterly* 15 (1937–38): 242–48.

Groene, Bertram H., ed. "A Letter from Occupied Tallahassee." *Florida Historical Quarterly* 48 (1969–70): 70–75.

Hopley, Catherine C. [pseud., Sarah L. Jones]. "Governor Milton and His Family." Reprinted in *Florida Historical Quarterly* 1 (1908–09): 42–50.

Lonn, Ella. "The Extent and Importance of Federal Naval Raids on Salt-

Making in Florida, 1862–1865." *Florida Historical Quarterly* 10 (1931–32): 167–84.

McDowell, Dudley H. "How Saffold Acquired its Name." *Collections of the Early County Historical Society* 1 (1971): 33–35.

Marshall, Charlotte Thomas, ed. "Taylor Family Letters." *Collections of the Early County Historical Society* 2 (1979): 121–25.

Martin, John L. "Confederate Torpedo Boats." *Confederate Veteran* 31 (1923): 93–94.

Mervine, Charles K. "Jottings by the Way: A Sailor's Log—1862 to 1864." *Pennsylvania Magazine of History and Biography* 17 (1947): 121–51, 242–82.

Mills, Elizabeth B., comp. "Old Family Letters." *Collections of the Early County Historical Society* 1 (1971): 83–85.

Moses, Armida. "The Confederate Navy." *Confederate Veteran* 28 (1920): 181–82.

Newcombe, F. H. "Nights on Blockade Duty." *Tribune Monthly* 3 (1881): 64–68.

Owens, Harry P. "Apalachicola: The Beginning." *Florida Historical Quarterly* 47 (1968–69): 276–91.

————. "Port of Apalachicola." *Florida Historical Quarterly* 48 (1969–70): 1–24.

————. "Sail and Steam Vessels Serving the Apalachicola-Chattahoochee Valley." *Alabama Review* 21 (1968): 195–237.

Paisley, Clifton, ed. "How to Escape the Yankees: Major Scott's Letters to His Wife at Tallahassee, March 1864." *Florida Historical Quarterly* 50 (1971–72): 53–61.

Powell, Samuel W. "Blockading Memories of the Gulf Squadron." *Magazine of History* 8 (1908): 1–11.

Price, Marcus W. "Ships that Tested the Blockade of the Gulf Ports 1861–1865." *American Neptune* 11 (1951): 262–90; 12 (1952): 52–59, 154–61, 229–38.

Purcell, Douglas Clare. "Military Conscription in Alabama during the Civil War." *Alabama Review* 34 (1981): 94–106.

Reiger, John F. "Deprivation, Dissaffection, and Desertion in Confederate Florida." *Florida Historical Quarterly* 48 (1969–70): 279–98.

————. "Florida After Secession: Abandonment by the Confederacy and its Consequences." *Florida Historical Quarterly* 50 (1971–72): 128–42.

Schellings, William J., ed. "On Blockade Duty in Florida Waters, Excerpts from a Union Naval Officer's Diary." *Tequesta* 15 (1955): 55–72.

Strickland, Alice. "Blockade Runners." *Florida Historical Quarterly* 36 (1957–58): 85–93.

Turner, Maxine. "Naval Operations on the Apalachicola and Chattahoochee Rivers, 1861–1865." *Alabama Historical Quarterly* 26 (1974–75): 189–266.

Van Nest, John F. "Yellow Fever on the Blockade of Indian River, A Tragedy of 1864." *Florida Historical Quarterly* 21 (1942–43): 352–57.

Wait, Horatio L. "The Blockading Service." In *Papers Read Before the
   Illinois Commandery of the Loyal Legion of the United States*, vol. 2.
   Chicago: Illinois Commandery, 1885, pp. 211–52.
Whiddon, Juanita. "David Saunders Johnston, The Man and His Times,"
   Collections of the Early County Historical Society 2 (1979): 136–46.
Whitehead, Mary Grist, comp. "Letters." *Collections of the Early County
   Historical Society* 2 (1979): 359–73.
_____. "Old Factory." *Collections of the Early County Historical Society*
   1 (1971): 68–69.
_____. "The Shackelford Place." *Collections of the Early County
   Historical Society* 1 (1971): 71–72.

                              BOOKS

Albaugh, William A., and Edward N. Simmons. *Confederate Arms.*
   Harrisburg: Stackpole Co., 1957.
Anderson, Bern. *By Sea and By River: The Naval History of the Civil War.*
   New York: Knopf, 1962.
Black, Robert C. *The Railroads of the Confederacy.* Chapel Hill: University
   of North Carolina Press, 1952.
Boggs, William R. *Military Reminiscences of General Wm. R. Boggs,
   C.S.A.* Durham: Seeman Printery, 1913.
Bradlee, Francis B. C. *Blockade Running During the Civil War.* Salem,
   Mass.: Essex Institute, 1925.
Bryan, T. Conn. *Confederate Georgia.* Athens: University of Georgia Press,
   1953.
Campbell, Davis W., ed. *Lest We Forget, Pen Sketches of Columbia,
   Alabama.* N.p., 1952.
Castlen, Harriet Gift. *Hope Bids Me Onward.* Savannah: Chatham Printing
   Co., 1945.
Chattahoochee Trace Historical Markers in Alabama and Georgia. Eufaula,
   Ala.: Historic Chattahoochee Commission, 1983.
Coulter, Harold S. *A People Courageous, A History of Phenix City,
   Alabama.* Columbus, Ga.: Howard Printing Co., 1976.
Cumming, Kate. *A Journal of Hospital Life in the Confederate Army of
   Tennessee.* Louisville: John P. Morton and Co., 1866.
Davis, William Watson. *The Civil War and Reconstruction in Florida.* New
   York: Columbia University Press, 1913.
Dickison, John J. *Military History of Florida.* Vol. 11 of *Confederate
   Military History,* edited by Clement A. Evans. Atlanta: Confederate
   Publishing Co., 1899.
Dickison, Mary Elizabeth. *Dickison and His Men.* Louisville: Journal Job
   Printing Co., 1890.
Dodd, Donald B. *Historical Atlas of Alabama.* University, Ala.: University
   of Alabama Press, 1975.

Durkin, Joseph T., S.J. *Stephen R. Mallory, Confederate Navy Chief.* Chapel Hill: University of North Carolina Press, 1954.

Fretwell, Mark E. *This So Remote Frontier, The Chattahoochee Country of Alabama and Georgia.* Tallahassee: Rose Printing Co., 1980.

Geer, J. J. *Beyond the Lines: A Yankee Prisoner Loose in Dixie.* Philadelphia: J. W. Daughaday, 1863.

Goodloe, Albert Theodore. *Confederate Echoes.* Nashville: Smith and Lamar, 1907.

Hague, Parthenia Antoinette. *A Blockaded Family: Life in Southern Alabama During the Civil War.* Boston: Houghton, Mifflin and Co., 1888.

Historical Background of Dougherty County. Compiled under the auspices of the Works' Progress Administration. Atlanta: Cherokee Publishing Co., 1981.

Hopley, Catherine C. *Life in the South.* 2 vols. London: Chapman and Hall, 1863.

Johns, John E. *Florida During the Civil War.* Gainesville: University of Florida Press, 1964.

Jones, James Pickett. *Yankee Blitzkrieg, Wilson's Raid Through Alabama and Georgia.* Athens: University of Georgia Press, 1976.

Jones, John S. *Military History of the One Hundred Sixty-First New York Volunteer Infantry.* Bath: Hall, Barnes Printers, 1865.

Lane, Mills B., ed. *"Dear Mother: Don't grieve about me. If I get killed, I'll only be dead." Letters from Georgia Soldiers in the Civil War.* Savannah: Beehive Press, 1977.

Lonn, Ella. *Salt as a Factor in the Confederacy.* New York: Walter Neal, 1933.

MacBride, Robert. *Civil War Ironclads, The Dawn of Naval Armor.* Philadelphia: Chilton Books, 1962.

McFarland, Benjamin. *Hines and Allied Families.* Ardmore, Pa.: Dorrance and Co., 1981.

McGee, B. F., and William R. Jewell, eds. *History of the 72nd Indiana Volunteer Infantry of the Mounted Lightning Brigade.* Lafayette, Ind.: S. Vater and Co., 1882.

Martin, John H. *Columbus, Georgia, from its Selection as a "Trading Town" in 1827 to its Partial Destruction by Wilson's Raid in 1865.* Columbus: John Gilbert, 1874.

Mathis, Ray. *John Horry Dent, South Carolina Aristocrat on the Alabama Frontier.* University, Ala.: University of Alabama Press, 1979.

Mears and Company, comp. *The Columbus Directory for 1859–'60.* Columbus, Ga.: Sun Book and Job Printing Office, 1859.

Montgomery, Horace. *Howell Cobb's Confederate Career.* Vol. 10 in *Confederate Centennial Studies,* edited by W. Stanley Hoole. Tuscaloosa: Confederate Publishing Co., 1959.

Nichols, James L. *Confederate Engineers.* Vol. 5 in *Confederate Centennial Studies,* edited by W. Stanley Hoole. Tuscaloosa: Confederate Publishing Co., 1957.

Preble, George H. *Henry Knox Thatcher, Rear Admiral, U.S.N.* Boston: Williams, 1882.

Ramsdell, Charles W. *Behind the Lines in the Southern Confederacy.* New York: Greenwood Press, 1944.

Richardson, S. P. *Light and Shadows of an Itinerant Life.* Nashville: Methodist Episcopal Publishing Co., 1901.

Scharf, John Thomas. *History of the Confederate States Navy.* New York: Rogers and Sherwood, 1887.

Scott, Mrs. Marvin. *History of Henry County, Alabama.* Pensacola, Fla.: Frank R. Parkhurst and Son, 1961.

Standard, Diffie Williams. *Columbus, Georgia, in the Confederacy.* New York: William Fredrick Press, 1954.

Still, William N. *Confederate Shipbuilding.* Athens: University of Georgia Press, 1969.

————. *Iron Afloat.* Nashville: Vanderbilt University Press, 1971.

Telfair, Nancy. *A History of Columbus, Georgia, 1828–1928.* Columbus, Ga.: Historical Publishing Co., 1929.

Tennessee Civil War Veterans Questionnaire. 6 vols. Easley, S.C.: Southern History Press, 1985.

Thronateeska Chapter, Daughters of the American Revolution, comp. *History and Reminiscences of Dougherty County Georgia.* Spartanburg, S.C.: Reprint Co., 1978.

Vandiver, Frank. *Ploughshares into Swords: Josiah Gorgas and Confederate Ordnance.* Austin: University of Texas Press, 1952.

————. *Rebel Brass, The Confederate Command System.* Baton Rouge: Louisiana State University Press, 1956.

Walker, Anne Kendrick. *Backtracking in Barbour County, A Narrative of the Last Alabama Frontier.* Richmond: Dietz Press, 1941.

————. *Russell County in Retrospect, An Epic of the Far Southwest.* Richmond: Dietz Press, 1950.

Warner, Ezra J., and W. Buck Yearns. *Biographical Register of the Confederate Congress.* Baton Rouge: Louisiana State University Press, 1975.

Warren, Hoyt M. *Henry—The Mother County.* Auburn, Ala.: Warren Enterprises, 1976.

Wells, Tom H. *The Confederate Navy, A Study in Organization.* University, Ala.: University of Alabama Press, 1971.

Wilson, John A. *Adventures of Alf Wilson, A Member of Mitchell's Railroad Raiders.* Toledo: Blade Printing and Paper Co., 1880.

Worsley, Etta Blanchard. *Columbus on the Chattahoochee.* Columbus, Ga.: Columbus Office Supply Co., 1951.

INDEX

Abercrombie, James J., 251
Abrams, T. H., 168
Adela, U.S., 190
Agriculture: antebellum, 16–18; effects of war on, 136, 138–39, 141–43, 242–43
Alabama, C.S.S., 174
Albany, Ga.: location, 12, 20; effects of war on, 144, 210, 220, 252
Albany and Gulf Railroad, 213
Albany Guards, 138
Alexander, J. H., U.S.A., 241
Alligator Bay, 113–14
Alum Bluff, 78, 79, 95
Amanda, U.S. Bark: scuttled, 112; supplies for, 119; refugees on, 121; disrepair, 123; operations, 130–31. *See also* Welch, George E.
Americus, Ga.: location, 20; hospital at, 220
Anderson, James, 192
Anderson, William, 166, 201
Andersonville Prison, 147
Andrews, W. H., 16, 134, 244
Ansell, W. W., 165, 201
Apalachicola, Fla.: antebellum port, 8–9; under Union blockade, 11–12, 48–49, 129, 248; defense of, 30, 35–36; U.S. Marine Hospital at, 51; effects of war on, 28, 46–47, 218, 248, 251; plans to reopen, 173, 174, 184, 227; Union occupation of, 246. *See also* St. George Island; St. Vincent's Island; Blockade
Apalachicola-Chattahoochee River System: map, 4; antebellum economic importance, 5–6; strategic importance, 6–7, 13, 41–42, 45, 134, 209–10, 241; navigational features, 12–13, 56, 210, 241, 248, 255–57; Confederate defense of, 75–78. *See also* Obstructions
Archer, Mary Brown, 245
Arents, Fred W., C.S.N., 101
Arkansas, C.S.S., 65, 83, 155, 156
Asboth, Alexander, U.S.A., 246
Atlanta, Ga.: CNIW workers in battle of,

204-05; nine-inch Dahlgren sent to, 205. *See also* McCorkle, David P.
Augusta, Ga.: location, 20, 135, 220
Austen, William, C.S.N., 229

Bailey, Theodorus, U.S.N., 112, 114, 126, 130
Bainbridge, Ga.: location, 12; effects of war on, 133, 210, 230, 232, 252
Baltic, C.S.S., 154
Barbour County, 137, 139. *See also* Eufaula; Dent, John Horry, Sr.; Hague, Antoinette
Barrancas, 210
Barringer and Morton Steam Manufactory, 10, 148
Bawn, William, 145
Baxter, I. B., U.S.N., 218
Bedell and Pope, 250
Benjamin, Judah P., 38
Benson, W. P., 38
Berry, Charles H., C.S.N., 101
Berry, Thomas, 60
Beverley, Daniel, 180
"Bigbee Boats": CNIW work on, 158, 166, 225; engines for, 247. *See also* Oven Bluff; Tombigbee River
Bilbrow, William, 94, 99
Birdsong, Carrie, 249
"Black Dwarf," 177, 211; salvage value, 247
Blackmar, A. O.: receives orders, 232; makes report, 239
Blackmar and Candler, 250
Blain, Charles: arrival in Columbus, 9; work on *Jackson* construction, 160, 182; at *Jackson* launch, 213; and Charles Warner, 255
Blanc, Samuel P., C.S.N., 189, 195, 198, 199
Blockade: Lincoln's proclamation of, 5, 21; extent of, 30–31; 116–17; under international law, 32; presence at Apalachicola, 48–49, 109–21, 129; effects of, 134, 146,

*Maxine Turner is Professor Emerita of
Communication in the School of
Literature, Communication,
andCulture at the
Georgia Institute of Technology.*